ENTROPY OF MIND AND NEGATIVE ENTROPY

ENTROPY OF MIND AND NEGATIVE ENTROPY

A Cognitive and Complex Approach to Schizophrenia and its Therapy

Tullio Scrimali

Preface by
Arthur Freeman

KARNAC

Κτῆμα τε ἐς ἀεί μαλλον
ἤ ἀγώνισμα ἐς το παραχρῆμα
ἀκούειν ξύγκενταν.

Thucydides, *The Peloponnesian War*, 5th century b.C.

This book is dedicated to Giulia and Susanna,
fantastic daughters, the continuation of life.
For them, a particular gift, a
κτῆμα ἐς ἀεί

Giulia and Susanna know what this means.

To the readers who have not read Thucydides,
(or who don't remember it), I leave this little curiosity,
referring them to *The Peloponnesian War*
(Thucydides, 5th century b.C., English edition, 1998).

Published in 2008 by
Karnac Books
118 Finchley Road
London NW3 5HT

British Library Cataloguing in Publication Data

A C.I.P. for this book is available from the British Library

ISBN: 978-1-85575-661-8

Dtp & copyediting by gabrielecrobeddu.com

Printed in Great Britain

www.karnacbooks.com

CONTENTS

ACKNOWLEDGEMENTS

Many people have contributed to the realization of this book.

Over the last 20 years, numerous colleagues and friends have participated in my research on schizophrenia carried out at the Department of Psychiatry of the University of Catania, at the Institute for Cognitive Science in Enna, and at the Aleteia School.

In order of importance for their help, I want to first cite Lorenzo Filippone, Francesco Grasso, Giocomina Cultrera, Massimo Sciuto, and Manuela De Leonardis.

Many students in Medicine, in Psychological Science and Techniques, in Psychiatric Rehabilitation, in Psychiatry, and at the Aleteia School have collaborated in the research projects cited in this book. To them I own many thanks for their hard work and incredible enthusiasm.

The English version of the book has been translated by Nancy Triolo and it was revised by James Claiborn. I have to thank both for their fantastic job!

Two persons are crucial to the conceptual framework behind the development of *Entropy of Mind* and *Negative Entropy*.

They are, however, two persons who cannot read these pages: Vittorio Guidano and Carlo Perris.

Vittorio profoundly influenced the evolution of my epistemological and scientific conceptualizations.

The seminar we conducted together at the Department of Psychiatry of the University of Catania on Constructivism and Motor Theories of the Mind was crucial for comparing and verifying the ideas I eventually presented in my book, *Sulle tracce della mente*, while Vittorio published *The Complexity of the Self*, the Italian edition of which, *La complessità del Sè*, was presented at an unforgettable conference organized here in Catania.

In 1988, during the National Congress of the Italian Society of Behavioural and Cognitive Therapy, which our group organized in Pergusa (Enna), I presented my first systematic conceptualization of the constructivist theory of schizophrenia, after long discussions with Vittorio.

One of my fondest memories of Vittorio is from 1992, during the National Congress of the Italian Society of Behavioural and Cognitive Therapy in Rome. There I organized and coordinated a symposium on the constructivist and complex model of schizophrenia and its therapy, and I will never forget the great trepidation with which I observed Vittorio enter the hall and sit in the first row to attentively follow the various presentations of our group.

I will also never forget the joy I felt at his compliments at the end of the symposium.

Those positive comments and encouragements made me understand that I was on the right road, even if 14 years of hard work were still needed before publication of this book.

I want to say, and this is the right occasion to do so, that my conceptual elaboration, the research on schizophrenia, and my own *forma mentis*, as a researcher and clinician, would not have taken the direction it took, if I had not had the fortune of meeting Vittorio Guidano, point of reference and teacher, who left us all too soon.

Thank you, Vittorio!

The other great friend, also gone, I want to thank is Carlo Perris.

The development of the clinical conceptualizations described in this book would not have been possible without the fundamental contribution of Carlo, who was the first to formulate a systematic model of cognitive therapy for schizophrenia. Besides this, Carlo ventured into the difficult area of therapy for psychosis and lucidly criticized the inadequacy of the cognitive rationalist model, proposing a constructivist and complex logic for cognitive psychotherapy in its place.

Carlo appreciated my work and encouraged me to keep on going. We always talked, traveling together around the world, from Toronto to Copenhagen, from Budapest to London to Catania, the city in which we jointly held a series of workshops and symposiums.

It was particularly moving to read the chapter he sent me a few days before he died. This contribution was included in the book I published together with Liria Grimaldi, *Cognitive Psychotherapy Toward a New Millennium*.

In this work, he recognized, with great generosity and friendship, the important role our group played in the development of the cognitive psychotherapy of schizophrenia.

Thank you, Carlo!

A particular thank you goes to Vincenzo Rapisarda, with whom I have spent my entire scientific career, from when I was a medical student and began to prepare my degree thesis under his supervision.

My experience as a psychotherapist, oriented to the treatment of psychosis, began in his studio, with his support and help.

Every important step in my career has been marked by the presence and influence of Professor Rapisarda, including, of course, this book.

The person to whom I owe the development of my international scientific experience is Arthur Freeman. Thanks to him I have been able to present and discuss the themes of *Entropy of Mind and Negative Entropy* abroad, especially in the USA, beginning with the conference he organized at the University of Illinois, in Chicago, in 1994.

We too have shared fantastic times abroad.

Thanks to Art, I was able to organize an International Congress on Cognitive Psychotherapy in Catania, in 2000.

During the Congress, I had the chance to exchange ideas with some of the most important scholars working on schizophrenia today.

Thanks again, Art!

To conclude, I would like to mention the bonds of recognition and affection that tie me to all the men and women who have guided me along the desolate streets of the *Entropy of Mind*.

It is, in fact, my dear patients who, over the last 25 years, have provided the information which constitutes the conceptual basis of *Entropy of Mind* and *Negative Entropy*.

And it is primarily to them that I want to extend a warm and heart-felt thank you.

TULLIO SCRIMALI
Catania, January 2007

Preface

Professor Arthur Freeman

Dean School of Professional Studies
University of Saint Francis
Fort Wayne, Indiana

Over the years, my work has been guided, stimulated, challenged, motivated, and rewarded from two major sources. The first source has been my students and collaborators. They have asked questions, posed problems, and challenged ideas. They have been, in many cases, collaborators in theory and conceptual developments. The second source of motivation has been from the patients who have sought my help for coping with problems large and small. I owe both groups thanks for propelling me forward. What I have said on many occasions is that we, as a science, are limited only by our lack of ability to think clearly, see new connections, observe closely, or to be open to new formulations and conceptual formulations.

Psychology has renewed and rejuvenated itself over the ages through the ongoing creativity of its practitioners, researchers, and teachers. Often the most brilliant contributions have stemmed from the clarity of vision to see the obvious despite collegial pressure, taking an unpopular position, or challenging the zeitgeist. We see this in the works of such leaders as Wolpe, Beck, Seligman, Bandura, and many others. These individuals saw problems in new ways, and developed conceptual structures for explaining behavioural. They then presented these ideas to their students who questioned, challenged, or disputed the views presented. This then allowed for the sharpening of the framework, and a clarity of the message.

I remember with great affection my early years at the Center for Cognitive Therapy at the University of Pennsylvania. In the late 1970s the clinical staff, Fellows, and interns would meet with Dr. Beck in a very undistinguished room, It had exposed pipes on the ceiling, and a variety of mismatched chairs. All of this went unnoticed by the staff inasmuch as we were engaged in discussion or debate. Dr. Beck would present ideas and then challenge us to challenge him. The only negative part of the discussion was that it ended. The following week it resumed, being fueled by Dr. Beck's thinking, clinical formulations, and clarity of thought. He took the obvious, that cognitive and behavioural components of behaviour had to be explicated and then viewed as targets for change rather than symbols of underlying conflict.

Through the years, the dramatic personae changed as staff left to found their own centers, their own clinical and research programs, or their own practices. It has been my good fortune to have been a part of that experience.

In a similar fashion, my dear friend, esteemed colleague, and valued collaborator, Prof. Tullio Scrimali, has moved our field further along. I have had the good fortune, yet again, to see Scrimali's ideas develop over the last decade. In his work as a teacher, clinician, researcher, theoretician, and leader of his own school, he has seen various parts of the problem. He has raised the questions, discussed them with his collaborators and students, and has had the clarity to put them together into a coherent and cogent model of treatment. It has been my privilege to not only be a collaborator, but close personal friend. Our work has taken us to many countries and many cities in his native Sicily were he is Professor of Cognitive Psychotherapy at the University of Catania.

Scrimali has targeted perhaps one of the most difficult of patients, those with schizophrenia. This group, often misunderstood and over medicated, have ended up at the periphery of functioning. Seen as untreatable except with major pharmacological intervention, these individuals have languished in hospitals, day treatment centers or residences for the psychotic.

In this major volume, Scrimali offers an integrative biopsychosocial perspective. He focuses on the biological markers and the clinical psychopathology and psychophysiology of the disorder. He examines the cognitive and behavioural manifestations of the disorder in a clear and understandable manner. The sections on assessment and treatment deserve special attention. The assessment chapter describes the neuropsychological, psychophysiological, and family issues that are the essence of schizophrenia. Writing as a psychiatrist, neuro-psychologist, and clinical researcher, Scrimali describes the problems and then describes the treatment.

With a goal of helping the patient with schizophrenia toward more effective coping and enhanced function, Scrimali also takes a rehabilitation focus that describes the social, family, and individual work that must be coordinated in the best interest of the patient.

Whatever small contribution I have made to his work through our many years of collaboration are rewarded in this superb volume.

PROLOGUE

The Salt Works, Negentropic Machine

And finally this book is also finished,
I straighten my desk, shelves, and archives that have been cluttered by scientific articles, volumes, papers, CD's ...for years.

Leafing through the manuscript, I relive the story.

The *beginning*, and above all, the *why*.

The *beginning* was marked by my first patient, assigned to me by my Professor, a few days after my degree.

It was a young woman, sitting in his office, suffering from schizophrenia.

Hallucinations, delusions, bizarre behaviour: a really difficult human and clinical case, but also a first encounter with the role (still improbable) of therapist, fascinated by the Entropy of Mind.

With patience I established contact, then I tried to study the case, only to discover, almost immediately, that there wasn't much to learn in the books already written.

Since then I have always worked with schizophrenic patients, accumulating experiences, emotions, and knowledge.

The *why* of this book consists of the desire to make the results of many years of research and clinical activity, carried out at the Institute of Clinical Psychiatry of the University of Catania and at the Institute for the Cognitive Sciences in Enna, available to colleagues and students.

If one loves to study humankind, one cannot help but be fascinated by the condition of schizophrenia which, unique among pathologies, is not shared with any other living creature.

Schizophrenia is the exclusive prerogative of *homo sapiens*, just like the self-conscious mind.

Thus, to study and understand schizophrenia means to study our own personal existence.

I know, this book is very long and weighs too much for the briefcases of colleagues and the backpacks of the students; but I couldn't have made it any shorter.

From *mind, brain, entropy* to *Entropy of Mind*, or from *Phrenentropy* to *Negative Entropy*, there are no shortcuts, and there is still so much to explore.

I will end the story with some thoughts about my home: this wonderful, incredible Sicily, hologram of life, that every day enchants and stuns with visions, emotions, stories, colors, perfumes, flavours…

It is a land that has already seen everything and embodies every possible form of experience and knowledge.

Disturbing, tormenting, shocking; it is impossible to remain untouched by its appeal!

I go out to shop and I see the beach where Ulysses set ashore; I go to the sea and there I see the rocks thrown by the Cyclops; I go to the bank near where Dedalus, fleeing on wings from Crete, landed; I look at Etna and see the forge of Efesto; I travel to Enna and find myself on the shores of lake Pergusa, in the middle of Persephone's abduction by Hades.

Myth, legend, history, culture, everywhere.

It is true, this land teaches you, captures you, and you cannot do anything about it; it is always and forever surprising. There is a precious gift waiting around every corner. In my case it was *the salt works, negentropic machine.*

The last book I wrote, *Sulle tracce della mente*, began happily inspired by the sweet nostalgia of "When I was a child…"

I described the surprise I felt when I found shell fossils in Enna, high in the mountains, far from any sea.

But, once again, I was in search of inspiration that would also be tied to my own life experience on this enchanted Island, in the middle of the Mediterranean.

In the end, the inspiration arrived in a surprisingly unexpected way.

After long weeks of grueling work, Giulia and Susanna made me promise to take a trip. We decided to go to the western part of the Island, an area I wasn't too familiar with.

We finally left, after making a deal. They said—*No talk of entropy, no thinking about patients, just sea, beach, restaurants, relaxation, and tourism.*

Near Trapani, late one afternoon, we visited the salt works.

I was keeping my promise, and I found the Salt Museum interesting; and then it happened, I was again under a spell.

In a corner, I saw a poster with the alluring title: *The salt-works: negentropic machine.* I couldn't resist. I borrowed pen and paper and began to take notes.

Here was the inspiration for the preface of my new book!

My daughters found me, and immediately suspicious, said: *Papà, this is not OK; you're at it again, what are you writing? Do we have to keep an eye on you every minute?*

It's not my fault—I said, trying to defend myself—*This land of ours is too full of things to discover!*

The Salt Works, exactly like the human brain, creating order from disorder, and doing so by using energy coming from the wind and the sun.

The product is salt, for our daily bread, just like knowledge is a product of the mind, for our daily lives.

ment of schizophrenia. An exhaustive meta-analysis by Warner (1985) of all studies on the course of schizophrenia in the USA and Europe found that recovery rates, after the introduction of neuroleptic drugs, have not significantly improved, and that the decreasing hospitalization of schizophrenic patients during the twentieth century was an already well-established trend *before* the introduction of neuroleptic drugs.

The results of other research also confirm these findings; Wing (1987), for instance, writes that the introduction of neuroleptic therapy has not modified the long-term course of the schizophrenic syndromes (Wing, 1987).

Two studies by the World Health Organization entitled *International Pilot Study of Schizophrenia* and *Determinants of Outcome of Severe Mental Disorders* (World Health Organization, 1979; Jablensky, Sartorius, Ernberg, Anker, Korten, Cooper, Fay & Bertelsen, 1992) both note an apparent paradox: the prognosis for schizophrenia today appears more favourable in developing rather than in industrialized countries. This unexpected result suggests that the organization and management of structured (and costly) health services and the wider use of drug therapy are not correlated to a favourable prognosis for the disorder.

It would seem that a less stressful and competitive social climate and the possibility of the patient to maintain an acceptable social role, in part due to the existence of simpler lifestyles and livelihoods, constitute the most important variables for the successful course of the illness.

Studies on the emotional climate of the family have also incontestably demonstrated its fundamental role in determining the clinical evolution of schizophrenia (Leff & Vaughn, 1989). All this leads us to conclude that still today the problem of schizophrenia remains open since unequivocal models for the etiology and the psychopathology of the illness, or even clear evidence regarding therapy, do not yet exist.

Not only does drug therapy seem to simply modify the clinical phenomenology of the illness and not its course, but sufficient proof of the efficacy as well as the cost-benefits of psychotherapeutic work are lacking.

Emblematic of this situation is the state of confusion and contradiction (it might be the case to call it *entropy*) that exists even in recent literature regarding the cure of schizophrenia.

In answering the question—*How useful is psychotherapy in the treatment of schizophrenia?*—the authors Tsuang and Faraone (1997) from the Harvard Medical School have stated unequivocally, citing the conclusions of the American Psychiatric Commission, that psychotherapy cannot be considered an effective treatment for schizophrenia.

The two authors add that according to the American Psychiatric Association (APA), psychotherapy for schizophrenic patients constitutes an additional treatment to drug therapy, which remains the only valid approach, and the principal aim of psychotherapy should be to improve the patients adherence to the drug protocols.

Yet the guidelines for the treatment of schizophrenia, published by the American Psychological Association in 1997, affirm just the opposite, stating that psychotherapeutic and rehabilitative techniques constitute an important component in any treatment plan (American Psychological Association, 1997).

In 1999, the guidelines in *Expert Consensus Guideline Series: Treatment of Schizophrenia* (McEvoy, Scheifler & Frances, 1999) say that though drug treatment is almost always necessary, it is not sufficient by itself. Persons suffering from schizophrenia need, according to the committee of experts who wrote the report, services and psychological support structures to manage and resolve the fear, isolation, disability, and stigma connected to the illness.

The confusion and inconsistency are considerable and have potentially disastrous consequences for patients and their families. The opinions of Tsuang and Faraone (1997) are cited extensively in the volume on schizophrenia in the authoritative series "The Facts", published by Oxford University Press.

These volumes are considered to be the last word on current research in a number of fields and are used as teaching tools for education of experts and non-experts alike.

It's easy to imagine the negative consequences of assertions like those of Tsuang and Faraone on the family of a schizophrenic patient in psychotherapy or on the family physician.

Even if the evidence is increasing regarding the efficacy of integrated therapeutic protocols based on psychotherapeutic and rehabilitative treatment, especially in the European literature, it should be pointed out that satisfactory experimental data still do not exist, in part because of the methodological, organizational, and ethical difficulties inherent to controlled trials.

In this respect, I would like to make the following points on the one-sided nature of the literature dealing with the efficacy of neuroleptic drugs.

The pharmaceutical companies have enormous resources to finance research on the effectiveness of their drugs.

On the contrary, research in psychotherapy is financed exclusively by public money in the universities, and the difference in available funding is immense; the Farmindustria in Italy admits that 90% of research in the area of health care is financed by the pharmaceutical industry (Farmindustria, 2005).

Furthermore, while experimentation concerning neuroleptics almost always covers brief periods and not the actual natural history of the disorder, research in the psychotherapy of schizophrenia considers not only symptoms, but also relational, social and job-related variables.

Considering all this, it is not surprising that in the face of the much touted success of the neuroleptics which, as I will demonstrate, has not been corroborated in clinical practice, cognitive psychiatrists are much more prudent in singing the praises of the psychotherapeutic model.

Wykes, Tarrier and Everitt (2004) for example, claim that even if the role of psychotherapeutic and rehabilitative treatment in schizophrenia is indisputable for the indubitable capacity to improve the course of the disorder and better the functioning of the patient and the family, more clinical analysis is needed to confirm the efficacy of psychologically-based treatments.

Neither proponents of the systemic approach nor therapists working in the cognitive-behavioural field (which represent the two major schools of psychotherapy dedicated to developing treatment programs) have been able to produce literature that demonstrates unequivocally the efficacy of proposed therapeutic protocols (in part, for lack of the mentioned-above funding).

The comprehensive indeterminacy of the therapeutic approach is also traceable to the lack of a satisfying and documented model linked to the etiology of this serious disorder.

Regarding this, I would also point out that the standard cognitive model, based on a rationalistic approach to the psychopathology and psychotherapy of schizophrenia, also appears to be wanting. This conceptualization of the problem of schizophrenia transposes, *sic et simpliciter*, the rationalist orientation from the field of neuroses and depression to that of schizophrenia.

In the traditional cognitive orientation, the schizophrenic patient, like any other neurotic or depressed patient, is described as affected by a series of errors in the elaboration of information that must be corrected in the course of therapy. Missing is any reference to conscious processes and their alteration in relation to the biology of the brain.

In the new, complex, constructivist model of schizophrenia I have elaborated, I propose a very different vision of the patient as carrier of a personal, specific construction of reality, which is dysfunctional in that it does not permit positive social adaptation and elaboration of a coherent narrative. Such a vision of reality interrupts the developmental process that ought to be characterized by a dynamic of consciousness during the life cycle of *homo sapiens*.

The crucial role attributed to the relational and social aspects in this conceptualization of psychotic phenomena is in agreement with the position of Stanghellini (2002), who states that only with difficulty can a psychopathological theory of schizophrenia deny that psychosis is a disorder of inter-subjectivity.

The constructivist approach to schizophrenia which I have developed is closely tied to motor theories of the mind that constitute the basis of our psychophysiological research at the Institute of Clinical Psychiatry at the University of Catania and at the Superior Institute for Cognitive Sciences in Enna (Scrimali, Grimaldi, 1991).

I also refer to research in human ethology which describes the influence of parenting on the construction of the processes that support the patterns of the coordinated dynamics of the self and its becoming.

Biological psychiatry excludes the psychological dimension of the mind from its field of interest, asserting that the study of this dimension is not possible in scientific terms (it would be better to say in terms of positivistic science).

The majority of the schools of thought are uninterested in the brain, as if the mind and its becoming can be ontologically separated from its physical support.

Both these approaches neglect (the first more than the second) the relational and social dynamics of human affairs.

It should also be said that theorists of the social orientation in psychiatry do not worry much about the biological and intra-psychic dimensions either.

This state of things has harmed, and continues to harm, the understanding of psychopathology, the formulation of a convincing set of etiological theories, and the creation an exhaustive clinical approach.

This trend assumes a special relevance in the field of schizophrenia, a pathology particularly unresponsive to all reductionist and one-dimensional attempts at its understanding, management, and treatment.

Still today, most accredited theoretical approaches to the psychopathology of schizophrenia and its treatment are characterized by an early 20th century reductionistic, deterministic conception. Energy, matter, and linear causality still inform the theoretical elaboration of classic psychopathology.

The aim of this book is to delineate a complex, social, psychobiological approach to schizophrenia, originating from the most recent developments in neuroscience with particular attention to information theory, complexity theories, and the theory of complex systems, as well as to the physics of dissipative structures, unstable dynamic systems, the laws of chance and probability, and to human and animal evolutionary ethology (Thelen & Smith, 2000; Roberts & Combs, 1995).

Rather than limiting observations to single patients, the study of populations constitutes an additional perspective that will be constantly under consideration.

The complex approach to schizophrenia developed and described in this monograph and defined as Entropy of Mind or Phrenentropy, is collocated within the contemporary cognitive-constructivist movement that proposes, in the fields of psychology, psychiatry, and the social sciences, a new vision of reality and of the consciousness of the self (Mahoney, 1991; Lyddon & Schreiner, 1998).

The new theoretical and conceptual perspective on schizophrenia that I have developed under the name *Entropy of Mind* or *Phrenentropy* is articulated around the thematic of a science, born and 'raised' in the second part of the 20th century (*like myself*), with particular reference to information theory, cybernetics, systems theory, complexity theories, and the physics of non-linear dynamics.

When I was seven, my favourite toy was not a gun (energy) or blocks (matter), but a fantastic, tiny Japanese *Nagoya* radio with seven transistors: *a window open to the world!*

When I was seven, my greatest passions, like today, were books, magazines, and the cinema.

Information constitutes the script of my life. Information represents the leitmotiv of this monograph.

The first sciences of the mind, psychoanalysis, behaviorism, and biological psychiatry, which developed between the end of the 19th and the beginning of the 20th centuries, are irremediably tied to the physics of energy and matter.

These sciences describe human beings as deterministically subjected to internal motivations (libido) or external conditioning (reinforcement and environmental contingencies) or rigidly subordinated to one's own biological reality (chemical mediators and nervous structures and pathways).

Today psychoanalysis, behaviorism, and biological psychiatry constitute, for people like me who work with complexity theory, an important legacy, but one necessarily tied to the past.

Each of these reductionist orientations represent only one possible level of interpretation of complex human reality and must be integrated with other levels, including the relational and the social, in light of an epistemology of complexity.

Humans, defined as epistemic beings capable of evolving, problem solving, and exploring their world, construct open societies, informed by principles of solidarity and tolerance. They constitute a paradigm that originates from a Popperian epistemology of hypothetical realism and from complexity theories upon which this monograph is based.

The end of certainty (Prigogine, 1997), the advent of multivalent logics, motor theories of the mind, the systemic and ecological dimension, the ethological model, and the sciences of chance and statistics, create the possibility of a *complex science of the mind.*

The first part of this book, *Mind, Brain, Entropy,* is dedicated to the attempt to delineate a provisional, but already coherent, description of actual trends in research in neuroscience and cognitive science, with particular reference to notions relevant for the subsequent theoretical elaboration of *Entropy of Mind.*

In the second part, *Entropy of Mind* or *Phrenentropy,* a cognitive-constructivist, complex model for the psychopathology of schizophrenia is illustrated that originates from the theoretical framework delineated in the first part of the book.

In the final section of the book, called *Negative Entropy,* an original clinical protocol, elaborated over the years and widely tested with encouraging results, is discussed.

I have imagined the reading of this book as a *journey* towards a mysterious destination: *the desolate and terrifying land of the Entropy of Mind* where disorder imposes its dominion through anguishing delusions (*at the center of the conspiracy*), terrifying hallucinations (*obscene voices that tell me what to do*), the loss of identity (*I am no longer me, if I look in the mirror*), and the regression to more primitive forms of thought that annul hundreds of thousands of years of biological and cultural evolution (*I am being controlled from outside*).

This book is a precious gift of those whom I have met, while exploring the agonizing Entropy of Mind

Lost men and women, frightened, diffident, without emotions, in the dead land of disorder, who accepted to share their terrifying experiences and travel a long and difficult road toward the new dimension of Negative Entropy.

PART ONE

Mind, Brain, Entropy

CHAPTER ONE

Cognitive Therapy and Schizophrenia: From Human Information Processing to the Logic of Complex Systems

Reflection on the development of the cognitive orientation in psychotherapy begins with the consideration that interest in psychosis, especially on the part of some Italian authors (Perris, 1996, Scrimali, 1994; Scrimali & Grimaldi, 1996; Scrimali & Grimaldi, 1998; Scrimali, Grimaldi, Rapisarda & Filippone, 1988), has constituted one of the most important moments of crisis (in a Kuhnian sense) in the classic cognitive paradigm, developed by Ellis and Beck, and redefined as *standard* by Clark (1995).

The epistemological and doctrinal framework of *standard cognitive psychotherapy,* already criticized by Guidano and Liotto (1983), has revealed itself to be especially inadequate when dealing with delusions and hallucinations.

Only the adoption of a constructivist, narrative, and hermeneutic perspective permits us to approach delusion in explanatory and not just descriptive terms, just as adhesion to motor theories of the mind permits the development of a new conception of perception able to explain hallucinatory phenomena.

The work of Perris, on schizophrenia and on the difficult patient, has not only extended the scope of the application of cognitive therapy from emotional disorders and anxiety to psychosis, but has, above all, proposed and implemented an epistemological and clinical revolution in complex, constructivist terms (Perris, 1989, 1993).

Followers of Beck, based on criticisms and solicitations coming from constructivist theory, have long looked for a sufficiently coherent model, with a proven epistemological and scientific background, to tie to the considerable evidence accumulated in the 1980s regarding its undeniable clinical effectiveness (Beck, 1952, 1967, 1976, 1979; Beck & Freeman, 1993).

In the second half of the 1990s, a considerable effort of conceptual elaboration and dialectical synthesis aimed at going beyond a simply generic approach to psychotherapy in order to establish the basis for an actual "School" known as "standard cognitive therapy" (Clark, 1995). To achieve this end, the central axioms of the cognitive approach in psychotherapy have been reconsidered, adjusted, and amplified (Clark, Beck & Alford, 1999).

The most important and frequent criticisms of standard cognitive psychotherapy can be summed up as follows (Guidano & Liotti, 1983; Mahoney, 1991; Perris, 1996, 2001; Scrimali & Grimaldi, 1996):

- standard cognitive therapy attributes secondary importance to emotions that are considered a sub-product of cognition according to the well-known aphorism: *As you think so you will feel*;
- standard cognitive therapy does not adequately take into account relational and social factors;
- standard cognitive therapy does not attribute enough importance to the therapeutic relationship;
- standard cognitive therapy places too much emphasis on the conscious processes of information processing, neglecting the unconscious components.

Following the emergence and development of the preceding criticisms in the 1990s, Beck, together with Clark and Alford, have further reconsidered the original position of standard cognitive therapy (Alford & Beck, 1997). Today the basis of standard cognitive psychotherapy can be restated as follows (Alford & Beck, 1997):

- human beings are constantly animated by a primary mental process, consisting of the attempt to elaborate models of reality that are indispensable to increasing chances for survival. In the area of information processing, the mind does not behave like a passive receiver of stimuli but actively constructs patterns of knowledge. Here the partial acceptance of the constructivist model and a progressive distancing of the computational metaphor are clear;
- the information processing take place at different levels and are not always conscious;
- cognitive processes are differentiated in *lower level of information processing*, tied to the intrinsic characteristics of stimuli, and *higher level processes* that are traceable to semantic and digital codification processes. Here the constructivist position emerges, which includes a tacit component to the processes of knowledge;
- information processing, tied to the immediate adaptation to the environment and to survival, are constituted by schema linked to the biological basis of the individual and, therefore, to motivational processes. Higher order processes help, above all, to better social adaptation and the pursuit of increased well-being. Here the conviction that explicit cognitive processes have a more important role than tacit processes is evident, while in the constructive approach tacit knowledge is of primary importance;
- a crucial aspect of psychopathological conditions is constituted by a malfunctioning in second order information processing which could lead the patient to categorize reality in pathological terms;
- second order information processing and heuristic programs, developed to interpret reality, called schemas, are constructed in the course of individual development, while first order processes are primarily biologically determined.
- the fundamental objective of therapy is to correct second order dysfunctional processes.

These last three points are faithful to the classic doctrinaire framework that Guidano (1992) has called the rationalistic approach to standard cognitive therapy.

Regarding schizophrenia, neither Beck nor his students have seriously addressed these issues until the late 1990s. In England, however, a group of authors, Fowler, Garety, Kuipers, Kingdon, Turkington, and Tarrier have developed therapeutic protocols essentially based on the application of Beckian concepts to the area of psychosis (Fowler, Garety & Kuipers, 1995; Kingdon & Turkington, 1994; Tarrier, 1992).

The work of Robert Liberman and Ian Falloon can be traced to the rationalist-cognitive and cognitive-behavioural approaches (Liberman, 1988; Liberman, 1994; Falloon, 1985).

These authors have developed an interesting, rehabilitative and psycho-educational model for schizophrenic patients, characterized by a very pragmatic attitude and oriented, above all, to the clinical management of symptoms (Falloon & Liberman, 1983).

Beginning in the late 1990s, Beck also realized the importance of this topic for schizophrenia and of the need to expand the protocols of cognitive psychotherapy to the clinic (Beck & Rector, 2000).

On the whole, this amounts to a mere transposition of the standard psychotherapeutic model from the field of depression to that of psychosis.

As part of the international cognitive movement, in Italy, beginning in the second half of the 1970s, an original proposal formulated by Vittorio Guidano (who died prematurely in Buenos Aires on 31 August 1999) and Giovanni Liotti, was being developed.

In 1983, the two authors published *Cognitive Processes and Emotional Disorders*, a work which has considerably influenced the development of international clinical cognitive theory (Guidano & Liotti, 1983).

The model proposed by Guidano and Liotti can be traced to the following fundamental aspects:

- an evolutionary perspective regarding the relationship between cognition and reality;
- an active motor paradigm of the mind;
- the central role of the process of self-consciousness;
- the description of a double articulation of the processes of knowledge, divided into tacit and explicit components.

From this base, a new proposal in psychotherapy and psychopathology was elaborated during the following decade by Giordano. Initially defined "systems-processes" (Guidano, 1988), it was subsequently called "post-rationalistic" (Guidano, 1992).

Central to Guidano's theory is the concept of the *cognitive organization of personal meaning*, which is the result of the development of the processes of knowing and of the structuring of the self.

Every psychopathological decompensation is traceable to a *disturbance of self-referential processes*, aimed at the maintenance of internal coherence and constituting an unstable phase, resolvable only through a new and better articulated equilibrium. This equilibrium originates from the integration of the disturbing experiences into the system of personal consciousness. This integration is activated through *evolutionary or regressive processes*. The task of psychotherapy should be to favour the establishment of the former and the hindrance of the latter.

Guidano's constructivist proposal consists of a psychotherapeutic approach that is no longer focused on the correction of errors that the patient commits in the elaboration of information regarding reality, typical of the rationalistic perspective of classic cognitive therapy. Rather, this approach focuses on the reordering of perceptive experience aimed at the restructuring of the patterns of self-coherence.

The role of emotions becomes central and is no longer considered a sub-product of cognition, but a potent and active form of knowledge that uses parallel and analogue computational processes.

Equally important, in this context, is the function of the therapeutic relationship that constitutes a specific emotional situation in which the processes of reordering perceptive experience and changes in the patterns of self-coherence, are possible.

Another important aspect, according to Guidano (1996), is the conception of the self in terms of dynamic inter-subjectivity.

After having pointed out the significant social aptitude of humans, and the importance of language in the structuring and maintenance of human relationships, Guidano remarks on the relevance of social learning processes in the determination of self-organization.

Relations with others and, in particular, with nurturing figures, constitute the prerequisite for the structuring and development of self-consciousness.

Guidano describes the life cycle as an orthogenetic process of development that proceeds through different phases of equilibrium toward a continuous increase in integration and organization.

Guidano's constructivist contributions to clinical cognitive theory and to cognitive psychotherapy have had extraordinary relevance and have significantly influenced the development of an important and original Italian school of cognitive constructivist psychotherapy (Bara, 2005).

His proposals have, however, generated strong resistance on the part of many authors in standard cognitive psychotherapy, who have criticized the progressive distancing of Guidano's approach from more traditional clinical praxis and the growing interest in the promotion of awareness in subjects with generic existential difficulties.

In reality, at the clinical level, the abandonment of behavioural and cognitive techniques appears debatable, since such a choice does not permit the treatment of serious pathologies, but restricts the field to intervention in minor disorders. Thus one risks what Carlo Perris (1996) described as "throwing the baby out with the bath water!"

The renunciation of various behavioural and cognitive techniques has led Guidano to substantially neglect schizophrenia and personality disorders. These constitute an extremely important area of clinical practice because of the level of hardship that such pathologies create for the patient, the family, and the entire social network.

In the last years of his scientific career, Vittorio Guidano, together with some of his students, increasingly turned his attention to the problem of schizophrenia. In 2001, Mannino and Maxia, (2001) summarized and discussed Guidano's work on this subject.

A focal concept of Guidano and his students on psychosis is identifiable in the conviction that psychosis, neurosis, and normality are placed along a continuum and can be traced to themes of personal meaning for the individual.

The psychotic condition is ascribable to an alteration of the processes that attribute meaning to emotional experiences.

In short, the reflections of Guidano and his collaborators on schizophrenia focus on delusional thought, which does not constitute the central topic of schizophrenia, but is present in many other psychopathological conditions.

The therapeutic procedure proposed, consisting solely of the reconstruction of contexts and the sequences of the patient's experience, appears to be a therapeutic method useful for the delusional patient, but inadequate for the schizophrenic subject.

All reference to the hallucinatory experience and its treatment is lacking and other aspects of the schizophrenic condition are neglected, including the psychophysiological and neurophysiological gaps and the deficit in communication skills and social competences.

In conclusion, Guidano's proposal, taken up by his students, is linked to the correction of processes of delusional thought, rather than to treatment of the schizophrenic patient, who would be very difficult to treat using only Guidano's intellectual approach. More acceptable, however, is the consideration that only a constructivist and narrative orientation can provide the key to the reality of delusional thought that is conceptualized by Anglo-Saxon authors in the standard cognitive therapy tradition as a set of computational errors to correct with the simple substitution of the logic of the therapist for that of the patient.

Returning to the cognitive-constructivist movement, Mahoney (1991) has focused on what he considers to be the five fundamental aspects of the cognitive-constructivist approach in psychotherapy:

- activity;
- order;
- identity;
- social processes;
- dynamic and dialectic development.

Activity. Human beings are described as active, not only in exploring the environment, but also in their continuous tendency to self-organize. They incessantly search to elaborate an internal order that is opposed to the disordered and chaotic flux of external reality.

Order. Internal order, which is pursued because of the constant activity of the processes of reorganization of the self, does not refer only to the conceptual dimension but to emotional equilibrium. Emotions thus occupy a crucial role as an organizing process. This highlights the importance of the emotional dynamic that should be considered not simply as a symptom to eliminate, but as a sign to interpret.

The evolution toward a higher order condition can begin solely through transitory states of disorder. The evolution of a system of human knowledge is, therefore, realized through the fluctuation of phases of order and conditions of disorder that often coincide with clinical symptoms.

The task of therapy is not to bring the patient to a condition of preexisting order before decompensation, but to help the patient's system of knowledge evolve toward conditions of greater integration.

Identity. This third aspect refers to the crucial topic of the self. The self is conceptualized, in the constructivist approach, as a central process of the mind, able to ceaselessly organize the complex flow of information from the nervous system in a dynamic and constantly integrated order.

The process of organization and development of the self is not described as internal to a solipsistic dynamic, but within the sphere of complex, relational interactions which characterize the life and development of humans as social beings.

Social processes. Constructivism attributes great importance to cultural, social, and political dynamics, tying the structure of the self to a historical context which determines an increase in freedom to explore new and novel evolutionary scenarios.

Regarding this, it is interesting to note that recently the attention of psychiatrists and cognitive psychotherapists using a constructivist approach has moved to the processes of globalization and to the meaning and value of local cultures.

Dynamic and dialectical development. The fifth principle of the constructivist epistemology is found in the conception of the development of the life cycle of humans as a dynamic and dialectical process.

Dynamic means being animated by an unavoidable evolutionary need for greater integration; dialectical means the need to consider human development as irrepressibly tied to the order-disorder dynamic that characterizes the organizational prerogatives of complex systems in a non-equilibrium state.

The life cycle is characterized by a continuous development of periods of increasing disorder and greater order and integration.

The fluctuation and the bifurcation that characterize the clinical event should not be seen as necessarily negative, but rather as a preface for an evolutionary progression toward more integrated forms of order and complexity.

Mahoney's conceptual systematization of the constructivist model (Lyddon, 1987), offers a great number of suggestions for a new psychopathology of schizophrenia. This constructivist model of schizophrenia, oriented to the logic of complex systems that I have developed, is presented in the second part of this monograph.

Within the constructivist approach, two recent therapeutic orientations should be mentioned because of their relevance for the comprehension of schizophrenia: *cognitive narrative psychotherapy and brief relational therapy* (Goncalves, 1994; Safran, 1998).

The development of the narrative orientation in cognitive psychotherapy constitutes a recent topic in the constructivist movement.

Posing determined opposition to the classic cognitive positions, which they accuse, without mincing words, of rationalism, authors in narrative psychotherapy have identified the following fundamental aspects as distinctive of their own epistemology (Russel & Waldrei, 1996):

- human beings are, above all, narrators of stories;
- mental activity is primarily metaphorical and imaginative, rather than rational and methodical;
- the continuous reworking of thought is the result of a fundamental process of the construction of meaning;
- reality as perceived by the patient, is described as a set of themes which the therapist can access only through a narrative and hermeneutical method.

From this conceptual position, an approach to psychotherapy based on the following points can be derived:

- knowledge (epistemic level) and reality (ontological level) are inseparable and organized on the base of a narrative process. Essentially all human beings live immersed in a reality that they have constructed through the development of a story and its protagonists;

- comprehension of the problems of the patient must begin with identifying and interpreting their narratives. Patients construct the meaning of real events based on narrations produced during the developmental process. In order to modify this mode of comprehending reality, less recent narrative processes need to be identified and modified;
- psychotherapy, using a hermeneutical approach, must carry out the work of decoding the narrative process. We will see later how narrative and its necessary reconstruction assume a crucial importance in the *Negative Entropy* therapeutic protocol.

To conclude this *topos*, I will refer to the position recently presented by Safran (1998) and defined *brief relational therapy*.

Placing himself solidly within the constructivist movement, Safran has progressively developed an approach to cognitive psychotherapy in which the relational aspect, with reference to the therapeutic setting, plays a prevailing role.

Considerable emphasis has been given to the analysis of relational patterns which are implemented in the setting, with explicit reference to the psychodynamic tradition of brief therapy and to the thematic of transference and counter-transference.

The importance of the setting is stressed, not only as a didactic context in which to propose the operations for exploring reality that will subsequently be implemented by the patient as homework, but as a privileged cite for the exploration of patterns for the construction of reality and of the idiosyncratic relational modalities of the patient.

These aspects also constitute a crucial topic for the therapeutic and rehabilitative model of *Negative Entropy*.

Carlo Perris proposed a series of convincing cognitive clinical models of schizophrenia that are not entirely classifiable within the standard cognitive psychotherapeutic framework. In his book, *Cognitive Therapy of Schizophrenia*, presented at Oxford in 1989, he outlined the first, and still valid, proposal for a cognitive model of schizophrenia and its treatment (Perris, 1989).

The work of Carlo Perris on schizophrenia and, more generally, on the "difficult patient" continued to develop coherently and profitably during the 1990s (Perris & McGorry, 1998). Perris's model is collocated outside the rationalist perspective of the American standard cognitive approach, and within the great tradition of European clinical psychiatry, with particular attention to the phenomenological perspective. Subsequently, Perris (1966) developed a position closer to constructivism and the systemic procedural approach.

In Italy, a number of authors, active in cognitive therapy, have also proposed original conceptualizations of schizophrenia and of therapeutic models.

Lorenzini and Sassaroli (1995) have developed a model of delusion based on a constructivist conception that refers to the position of Kelly.

Semerari (1999) and his group have focused on the study of metacognition in the psychotic patient and on the analysis of the therapeutic relationship.

Rezzonico and Meier (1989) have proposed a constructivist approach to the conceptualization of therapeutic and rehabilitative work with schizophrenic patients.

Other Italian authors who have dealt with the problem of schizophrenia from a cognitive perspective are Mannino and Maxia (2001), Arciero (2002), Procacci (1999), Pinto, La Pia and Mannella (1999), while Cocchi and Meneghelli (2004) have focused on diagnosis and early treatment.

This brings us to what constitutes a recent evolution in the adoption of the logic of complexity and of dynamic systems which are the epistemological and doctrinal points of reference for this monograph and for the *Entropy of Mind* model described herein.

The cognitive psychotherapy model oriented to the logic of complex systems (Complex Cognitive Therapy – CCT) has been developed by me throughout the 80s and 90s and presented in numerous international scientific venues: Toronto, Philadelphia, Chicago, Acapulco, Copenhagen, Thessalonica, and San Paolo in Brazil. A series of articles have also been published (Scrimali, 2000, 2001, 2003, 2004a, 2005a).

I will briefly present the conceptual basis for this approach since it represents a point of reference for the development of models of etiology, psychopathology, and clinical schizophrenia described in this volume.

In the second part of the 1980s, in the Cognitive Psychophysiological Laboratory of the Psychiatry Clinic of the University of Catania, I began to develop a constructivist and motor approach to psychophysiology based on a systems-processes perspective. The work was subsequently presented my 1991 monograph, *Sulle tracce della mente* (Scrimali & Grimaldi, 1991).

My research experience has been focused, on one hand, on processes of the mind, experimentally studied through psychophysiological and neurophysiological methodologies, and, on the other, on cognitive psychotherapy of schizophrenia, while not neglecting other pathologies, including anxiety, mood, and eating disorders (Scrimali & Grimaldi, 1991; Scrimali & Grimaldi, 1996).

Beginning in the early 90s, I began to adopt the epistemology of complexity and the theories of complex and non-equilibrium systems (Scrimali, 2004a).

An important year, from this point of view, was 1992, when a new journal, *Complessità & Cambiamento* was founded by our group.

Since the conceptualization of schizophrenia and the clinical, therapeutic, and rehabilitative proposals contained in this book are informed by an epistemology of complexity and by the logic of complex systems, it is necessary to briefly explain some crucial aspects of this model.

With the development of a general systems theory elaborated in the 1960s by Von Bertalanffy (1968), a frame of reference for an important revolution in contemporary science was created. This revolution, in which epistemology is increasingly relevant, made it possible to pursue unification in the disciplines of matter and energy (physics and chemistry), the sciences of nature (biology and ethology) and the human sciences (psychology, sociology, and philosophy).

The unifying potential of systems theory is in contrast with the reductionist perspective of the classical scientific approach and with the disjunctive thought of positivist epistemology.

The methodology no longer consists of isolating variables in order to discover and describe characteristics and behaviour, but rather to look for unifying approaches able to link together and holistically understand the largest possible number of phenomena.

The dream of classical physics, to achieve total understanding of the universe, beginning with the study and explanation of elementary phenomena and simple laws, in a deterministic and generalizable manner, has gradually deteriorated over the course of the 20th century.

In the first part of the 20th century, the second great doctrinal revolution in physics (after Newton and Galileo) began. This revolution, involving the theory of relativity and the progressive elaboration of quantum theory, helped to develop a less deterministic vision of reality.

Einstein articulated the theory of relativity, within the different components of restricted relativity, including general and unified relativity (Einstein, 1975).

The work of the great German physicist exercised considerable influence in the field of the theory of knowing.

One of the most important aspects in Einstein's elaboration concerns the analysis of the space and time variables that cannot be considered absolute entities, but must necessarily be evaluated in the relativistic space-time dimension.

Space-time cannot, however, be considered a separate entity from the processes that are created by matter.

The Euclidean critique of physical space is important. The geometrical behaviour of masses and the continuous movement of clocks depend on gravitational fields which are also products of matter. The epistemological consequences of Einstein's thought are clear when he states that:

> "In the measure in which the propositions of mathematics refer to reality, they are not certain, and in the measure in which they are certain, they cannot be applied to reality" [Einstein, 1975].

Quantum mechanics introduced, with Heisenberg, the principle of indeterminacy according to which it is not possible to contemporaneously determine the exact position an atomic particle occupies in space and its velocity. Thus, doubts and uncertainty intrude upon the physical description of the tiniest sub-atomic particles. Quantum theory is probability-based and its laws cannot disregard the laws of chance. Besides that, the concept and application of complex numbers assume enormous importance at the quantum level (Heisenberg, 1985).

In this way, the dream of achieving a full, generalized understanding of "all" phenomena, based on unequivocal and universal laws, is shattered.

A single particle, an electron, for example, according to classical physics, can occupy position A or position B in space. But because the electron is a tiny particle, subject to the laws of quantum physics, complex numbers appear in the equations that describe its position.

In this way the position of the electron can no longer be calculated in absolute terms.

Another important aspect that has not been entirely resolved in quantum theory is that of the observer; in fact, the very same operations of observation and measurement of quantum particles modify their behaviour.

With the advent of relativity and quantum physics, a change in the way of studying natural phenomena has been achieved, introducing a relativistic and probabilistic vision of the universe, from the very large to the very small.

But during the second half of the 20th century another revolution in the world of physics emerged: the complex systems.

With phenomena that involve enormous quantities of elements, animated by disorderly motion, such as gas molecules, the applicability of methods and laws of classical mechanics seems impossible. Thus, the themes of *probability and statistics*, capable of furnishing interpretive and predictive behavioural models of complex, chaotic systems, emerged.

During the 1960s, together with the music of the Beatles and the Rolling Stones, the youth movement, and social and economic unrest, the increasingly clear and documented perception in physics of what the great mathematician Henry Poincarè had anticipated at the beginning of the century was also emerging.

Any physical system, even if relatively simple and subject to the deterministic laws of Newtonian physics, can suddenly begin to exhibit chaotic behaviour, thus removing itself from the dominion of the two preferred activities of reductionist science: *prediction and control* (Poincarè, 1893).

It happens that apparently similar systems begin to evolve along enormously divergent lines, leading to different outcomes.

The complex approach, directing its interest to a greater number of levels of possible integration, indicates the necessity of a global, rather than linear, understanding of systems, of their organization, and of the relations of circular causality that connect them.

Ilya Prigogine (1997), one of the protagonists of the complexity revolution, after having elaborated a new discipline in physics—the thermodynamics of non-equilibrium systems—arrived at an epistemological synthesis that probably constitutes the most emblematic challenge of our time: *the end of certainty.*

An important aspect of complexity theories is the critique of determinism and the proposal of a probabilistic logic in which uncertainty constitutes a base variable.

If the laws of physics, in their classic formulation, describe an idealized, symmetrical, stable, and predictable world, the interest of authors like Prigogine focuses on a world considered unstable, uncertain, capable of evolving.

The understanding of chaotic systems can, therefore, only be pursued in probabilistic, non-deterministic terms (Prigogine, 1997).

From probability theory, the fundamental dimension of irreversibility was developed. This arose from classical thermodynamics, in particular, the second principle of Clausius, whereby the entropy of the universe is constantly increasing (Clausius, 1867). The continual increase in entropy delineates a line in time, an irreversible directionality of dynamic processes, from the past to the future.

The non-linear physics of non-equilibrium systems is the physics of unstable processes, of bifurcations, of probabilistic behaviour, of multiple choice, and of self-organization.

Another fundamental aspect to consider, elaborated by Prigogine (1980), is the substantial differentiation between closed and open systems. These latter systems exchange matter and energy with the outside. Thanks to this constant flux, open systems are able to maintain, unchanged through time, their level of entropy, because the continual disintegration of their structures are compensated for by the activity of reconstruction and reorganization.

Biological systems are open systems, operating in non-equilibrium conditions.

We human beings are made of atoms and molecules, but we are also highly complex, open, organized systems, that constantly exchange matter, energy, and information with the outside world.

Our existential situation is subject to the laws of particle physics, including both the second principle of thermodynamics and the laws of thermodynamics of non-equilibrium processes.

Our brain is, after all, the most complex system known to us today, even if it is made of atoms and molecules.

Based on the second principle of thermodynamics, our bodies and brains are constantly subject to an increase in entropy that causes the molecules and atoms that form them to become disorganized.

But because we are open self-organizing systems, we continuously oppose the increase in entropy, activating organizational processes and transforming matter from the environment into energy.

Thus the life cycle slowly sorts itself out between two antithetical instances; our body degrades, subject to the second law of thermodynamics, and our body is restructured according to the laws of non-equilibrium processes.

Heraclites' aphorism is to the point (Diels-Kranz, 1983):

> You live with death; you die from life.

The match is, however, unfair because the processes of reorganization lose ground daily; entropy increases imperceptibly and so we age and die. The molecules that make us up won't stay together, being so well organized and subject to an ironclad order: *pulvis es et in pulverem reverteris!*

Even the brain knows this melancholy parabola. But the mind, no; the mind is not subject to the second law of thermodynamics, the mind is constituted by *information* and as long as its physical support survives, it develops without stopping, it organizes, evolves, becomes articulated, and grows stronger.

Then suddenly without warning, a blackout. It is enough to interrupt the energy flow to the brain for a few minutes for this to become a closed system, a mere piece of flesh, subject to the second law of thermodynamics.

The Krebs cycle stops, the sodium-potassium pumps stop, the ions freely disperse, according to the concentration gradients, organization falls apart: *pulvis es et in pulverem reverteris.*

And the mind? No, it can, in part, survive beyond its physical support.

Where are the molecules that made up Homer's brain? A part of his mind has survived, for millennia, passed down from generation to generation.

Hector, Achilles, Ulysses represent information, and as such they take root in every new generation, in other brains, and so it will be as long as *homo sapiens* continue to live, reproduce, memorize, and read the *Iliad* and the *Odyssey.*

The mind survives in other physical supports. The books we write, for example.

The things we think are transferred with language and action outside our brains; they live in the minds of our children, as long as their brains support them, and then in our children's children, until entropy has dispersed them as well.

From the caves of prehistory to the skyscrapers of the third millennium, the mind of *homo sapiens* has never ceased to develop, transferring information from one generation to another.

Human societies are also dynamic non-linear systems.

The evolution of such a system is the result of the interaction between the behaviour of individuals and the barriers imposed by the environment. The behaviour of every single member is, in turn, determined by projects and desires that interact with the social system.

An important question to be asked is: do all human beings self-organize complexity based on environmental limitations (physical and cultural), according to rules that can be described as *a priori*?

By knowing the past, in substance, is it possible to predict the future? Or is the meaning of the human experience, understood as a dynamic process that evolves in a situation of non-equilibrium, to be looked for in higher levels of indeterminacy and unpredictability?

The actual developments of the physics of non-equilibrium systems and of self-organization seem to suggest the second option.

In the specific area dealt with in this monograph, the crucial question then becomes:

Will a complex and self-organized system, constituted by *homo sapiens* interacting in a social *milieu* (for example, in an industrialized country like Italy and an urbanized environment like Catania) that suddenly exhibits the chaotic behaviour of a schizophrenic individual, follow a predictable evolution (relapse, chronicity, disability, solitude, poverty, etc…), or could the system be facing open scenarios that lead to random, stochastic, evolutionary destinies?

The aim of this monograph is to identify adequate answers to this question.

One important aspect of contemporary science is the interaction of information theory with the second law of thermodynamics.

In the field of cybernetics, entropy is characterized as corresponding to a rate of indeterminacy or of contingency in a framework that describes the relationship of causal factors.

Because of a fundamental axiom of cybernetics—the sum of three rates, *indeterminacy* (entropy), *determinacy*, and *organization*, remains equal to 1—if the level of indeterminacy is increased in the system (i.e., entropy understood in an informational sense as uncertainty), there is a proportional diminution in the rates of determinacy and organization.

Systems theory and the thermodynamics of non-equilibrium systems offer a new interpretive key for human events and for psychopathology.

As an open system, the brain tends to maintain itself in a state of energy and elevated information, evolving towards new conditions of non-predetermined, increased organization.

It is the evolutionary indeterminacy of open systems that makes a flexible and teleonomic construction of evolutionary scenarios possible for humans.

In the course of this evolutionary parabola, unexpected occurrences can emerge in which the transactions between humans and the environment are altered.

According to this monograph, schizophrenia constitutes one of these occurrences, as I will try to demonstrate in the second part of this book.

Complexity theories entail new modalities of categorization pertaining to the fields of brain biochemistry, molecular biology, genetics, biological and cultural evolutionary theory, psychology and ethology.

I will briefly illustrate these implications.

In the central and peripheral nervous system, an important role is played by certain chemical substances able to promote or inhibit the transmission of information from one neuron to another.

The discovery of neuronal synapses has demonstrated that nerve cells communicate through a specific, highly specialized structure. Chemical mediators play a very important role in these synaptic mechanisms.

The transfer or blockage of information from one neuron to another is mediated by physical or chemical events. The former are constituted by mechanisms of depolarization or hyper-polarization, while the latter are referable to the liberation of mediators able to interact with the appropriate post-synaptic receptors, provoking the bio-electric phenomena of depolarization and hyper-polarization.

In the case in which alterations of the bio-availability of the different mediators (adrenaline, noradrenalin, serotonin, dopamine,

GABA, etc...) occur, the functioning of the information transmission mechanisms at the synaptic level are altered.

Thus, administering substances able to interact with the activity of neuro-mediators can provoke pharmacologically dynamic action in the nervous system that sometimes can be used therapeutically (Mosher & Burti, 1994).

In the case of depression, it is believed that some of the symptoms of this pathology can be traced to the reduction of catecholamine, with specific reference to serotonin.

In schizophrenia, an alteration in the functioning of nerve centers and pathways, with dopamine as the prevalent mediator, has been hypothesized.

The discovery of some biochemical mediators of synaptic transmission and the introduction in therapy of substances that interact with the biochemical mechanisms of the synapses, have provoked, beginning in the 1960s, an excessive enthusiasm, leading to the development of a reductionist logic in psychiatry.

The reasoning behind this can be summarized as follows.

The symptoms of schizophrenia improve if neuroleptics are administered.

These act on the level of the dopamine synapse. Thus schizophrenia, from an etiological point of view, is tied to a gap in these synapses.

A similar paralogism has been effectively criticized by Burti and Mosher (1994) who, by extrapolation, constructs an equivalent paralogism whose groundlessness appears immediately evident.

Digitalis improves contractibility and, therefore, the efficient functioning of the myocardium. Thus heart failure is caused by a lack of digitalis in the myocardium!

Some reductionist psychiatrists maintain that depression is primarily a biochemical illness, like diabetes. In the case of diabetes, insulin is administered, with depression, a serotoninergic drug is enough.

It is clear, however, that the biochemical mechanisms of information transmission, at the synaptic level, operate in an open system and are closely linked to the flow of information transiting the nervous system.

Thus, information input can modify a synaptic set, just as the modification of a synaptic set can alter the emotional state of a person.

If I participate in a psychotherapeutic session, my morale is lifted and, in correlation to this, the serotonin synapses are activated. If I take antidepressants, however, I might feel equally relieved because the same synapses are activated.

The basic problem is that the change in the biological (i.e., biochemical and structural) patterns of the brain does not assume real therapeutic value if it is not associated with a modification in the processes of the mind, thanks to the evolution of the entire system of knowledge.

Thus, the acts of reducing anxiety using benzodiazepine, elevating the emotional tone administering antidepressants, and reducing hallucinations using neuroleptics assume, in my opinion, therapeutic meaning only if such actions are part of a restructuring of the system of knowledge of the patient through the modification of cognitive, then emotional, patterns.

The excessive enthusiasm tied to the indiscriminate use of neuroleptics mentioned earlier, has been amply reconsidered. Based on experimental findings, many authors today believe that neuroleptics only act on symptoms and do not substantially modify the course of schizophrenia (Mosher & Burti, 1994; Warner, 1985; Ciompi, 2003; Scrimali, 2005).

This important argument will be discussed in depth in the third part of the book.

Another relevant theme, important for understanding schizophrenia, is the role genotype and environment play in determining the disorder.

The discovery of the structure of DNA by Watson and Crick, has shown how the double helix structure of nucleic acids is particularly adapted to preserving huge quantities of information which can be transmitted to progeny (Watson, 1968).

The *nature/nurture* problem becomes an issue, especially when referring to the central nervous system. In this complex and plastic system, it is difficult to determine whether the patterns of functioning (or malfunctioning) are due to genotypic or environmental causes.

The genetic program, regarding the central nervous system, constitutes a kind of outline on which information input coming from the environment continuously acts, modulating and reprogramming information and the ways of processing it.

The modalities of character transmission that determine cerebral functioning and, therefore, the functioning of the mind, are traceable to the so-called multi-factorial and polygenetic heredity. In this case, every phenotypic character trait is not determined by a single gene but by a large number of genes. Statistical approaches have been elaborated to study the specific typology of genetic inheritance, and a new discipline called *quantitative genetics* has been developed.

We shall also see how a considerable amount of experimental data unequivocally demonstrate that in schizophrenia, a certain rate of genetic determinism is present (not as high as many still believe), consisting of a predisposition upon which emotional experiences and cognitive activity act in the early developmental phases of the life cycle and during subsequent life events.

Evolution is an important topic in contemporary biology and psychology, and has, as we will see, important implications for schizophrenia Darwin's theory delineates a conception of phylogenetic development as a plastic and not deterministic process, which is subject to the laws of chance through mutation (Darwin, 1968).

A few of the most recent disciplines, including ecology and ethology, have many of the axioms and themes of evolutionary logic in common.

One of the most important is the historical approach, according to which biological, psychological, relational, and social realities are the result of millions of years of evolution.

In light of this historical perspective, it seems impossible to understand the *hic et nunc* without referring to the processes of phylogenesis and of biological and epistemic ontogenesis.

Every human being, to use Monod's effective metaphor, is a type of *living fossil* on whose organism, on the whose nervous system, is clearly written the history of evolution (Monod, 1970).

Another fundamental aspect that stems from an evolutionary perspective is individual variability in a population, since without such variability, no factor could to act to modify the general characteristics of a species.

Biological evolution is possible because of the characteristics of the genetic code, DNA, and its way of replicating and transferring itself from one generation to the next.

Even if DNA permits the accurate transmission of information, this process can be disrupted by genetic mutations.

A mutation provokes a modification of the phenotype that can be transmitted to offspring. If it is beneficial in terms of environmental adaptation and reproductive capacity, it will gradually spread through the population. In the structural organization of the human brain, traces of very complex evolutionary processes are observable in the transition from the reptilian brain to that of the more primitive mammals, to primates, and eventually to the development of the executive brain (frontal lobes) with its hemispheric specialization and correlated linguistic ability. This, by far, has constituted the most important evolutionary leap in the course of human development (MacLean, 1973).

In recent years there has been an impressive increase in research regarding the origin and biological evolution of humans, language, and knowledge.

Crow (2000) has gone so far as to affirm that the evolutionary acquisition of language has caused a specific vulnerability to schizophrenia.

Language is closely tied to self-consciousness, which is one of the most, if not the most, outstanding characteristic of human beings, and constitutes a true *evolutionary event* in the process of humanization.

We will also see how the processes that constitute the idiosyncrasies of schizophrenic pathology (the exclusive prerogative of humans) must be sought at this level.

The appearance of self-consciousness is an evolutionary process that characterizes ontogenesis in accordance with the well-known principle in which *ontogenesis recapitulates phylogenesis*.

One aspect of development, both phylogenetic and ontogenetic, that precedes self-consciousness, is constituted by the recognition of the self in reflected images and in the awareness of one's specific identity. In chimpanzees, the recognition of the self in the mirror is not present, but can be taught to the animal, as many studies have clearly documented (Canova, 2003).

Children also do not recognize themselves in the mirror until they are 18 months old. Before that age, they behave as if they were seeing another child.

A relation between the ability of different animals to recognize their reflection in the mirror and the level of evolutionary development has been demonstrated. Primates easily learn to connect their reflection to themselves, but only after the age of three years.

As we will see later, the behaviour of a schizophrenic patient in front of the mirror is critical and constitutes an observation that supports an evolutionary context for the psychopathology of schizophrenia.

Self-awareness is evolutionarily higher than the capacity to represent the world of physical objects and still higher than the ability to recognize one's own physical identity in the mirror.

Frith and Done (1989) proposed a neuropsychological theory relative to self-consciousness, distinguishing two well-differentiated types of cognitive processes, defined as *low and high level* functions.

The first type is automatic and routine, the second is conscious, intentionally controlled, and strategically oriented.

Higher level cognitive functions are associated with consciousness and awareness. From an anatomical and physiological perspective, these cognitive functions, linked to consciousness, originate from the prefrontal lobes, while lower order cognitive activity is linked to the posterior cortical areas.

The capacity to refer to oneself, and thus perceive higher order cognitive processes, is crucial to the functioning of the mind. This capacity is altered in schizophrenia. Hallucinations, in fact, characterized as dysfunctional processes deriving from the nervous system of the subject, are not recognized as such, but are interpreted as information coming from the external world.

Frith and Dolan have hypothesized that a functional disconnection in the different cerebral areas concerned with first and second order processes is at the base of schizophrenia. I shall return to this point in the second part of the monograph.

The thesis that schizophrenia constitutes a type of regression to a prior evolutionary state that characterized the human development up until the historical period described in the *Iliad*, has been advanced by Julian Jaynes in his fascinating book, *The Origin of Consciousness in the Breakdown of the Bicameral Mind* (Jaynes, 1976, 1996).

According to this American author, early civilized humans (up until the second millennium b.C.) were characterized by a certain functional autonomy of the right hemisphere and by the systematic presence of hallucinatory phenomena, ascribed to the relationship with divinity and political power, typical of theocracies.

Jaynes places the decline of the bicameral mind and the disappearance of hallucinatory phenomena around the end of the second millennium b.C.

Jaynes advances the suggestive hypothesis that schizophrenia can be considered a type of return to the bicameral mind, in which the activity of conscious thought is gradually replaced by hallucinations.

We will see how the study of psychophysiological parameters, including electroencephalographic potentials tied to the (P300) event, can help understand the functioning of first-order cognitive processes. We will also see how, through the use of these techniques, it is possible to document the alteration of these processes in schizophrenic patients. Moreover, many psychophysiological and neuropsychological studies have begun to furnish experimental evidence of damaged patterns of functional and hemispheric coherence in schizophrenic patients.

The ability to consciously make different choices and monitor one's strategies in the pursuit of goals, constitutes an important trait of self-consciousness.

As we will see, this is equivalent to saying that the self must possess evolutionary skills.

Another crucial aspect of self-awareness is the construction of a theory of one's mind. This evolutionary boundary that children reach by 5 years of age appeared phylogenetically during the course of human evolution, reaching its evolutionary acme in *homo sapiens*.

Given what has been stated here, it is clear that modern human beings represent a synthesis of a potent symbiosis between biological and cultural evolution.

From the moment in which the first hominids were able to communicate with each other, not only about the outside world, but also about subjective experience, the doors to a new reality—the world of culture—were opened.

From that moment on, biological and cultural evolution constituted two dynamic processes, tightly linked together, that have led to the current biological and epistemological dimension of humans today.

For thousands of years, a process involving an increase in cultural capacity, an increase in the encephalic mass, and an increase in the complexity of the cerebral structure has taken place.

The result of this evolutionary process has been enormous power in the face of the environment, beginning from *homo erectus*. Probably even the Neanderthals did not fear rivalry from the other mammals that populated their territory.

Unfortunately, the search for domination over the other living species has created the considerable competition and intra-species aggressiveness that has become an outstanding peculiarity of the human species. This has sadly culminated in actual genocides that may have, in fact, been initiated by *homo sapiens* against the less developed Neanderthals.

The progressive development of increasingly articulated and complex social organization has led humans to drastically modify—thanks to cultural evolution—the terms of biological evolution. The capacity to adapt and dominate in different historical periods and in different social and anthropological contexts appears closely correlated to the characteristics of social organization.

This important aspect can help us understand how schizophrenic subjects appear more suited to live in less developed societies than in industrial, urbanized ones, in accordance with their particular level of biological and cultural evolution that, as we will see later, is affected by a process of regression at both the biological (vulnerability) and epistemic (parenting and the organization of personal knowledge) levels.

Thus, a schizophrenic patient who is not positively integrated in an ecological niche permeated by elevated emotions and hostility, can adapt to a new niche characterized by a less intense emotional climate.

We will see, further along, how these considerations have operational consequences at the clinical level and in terms of familial and psychosocial intervention.

After having delineated the scientific background and the epistemology of the complex cognitive orientation which is at the base of *Entropy of Mind* approach, I will describe what I call the model of the *modular brain* and the *coordinated mind*, which constitutes another important perspective for understanding the dynamics of the schizophrenic process and the rationale for its treatment contained in this book (Scrimali, 2001).

In recent decades, a vision of the brain characterized as modular has been proposed and developed by numerous authors in the field of neuroscience (Goldberg, 2001).

According to this conception, the nervous system is said to be organized in modules, each exhibiting a certain autonomy and able to process entry information and produce output for other modules. The exchange of information between modules is constituted by limited capacity channels. Every module is organized in a specialized, genetically determined manner.

Another more recent conception sees the brain as an immense network of small units that are not organized in preordained terms, but on the basis of an evolutionary process. This process is developed in the course of ontogenesis and influenced by self-organization that is modulated by information input from the outside (Nesse, 2002).

Goldberg (2001) has called this possible mode of functional organization of the brain, "organization by gradients".

In reality, both the modular conception of the brain and the emergent organization based on information flow seem applicable to the human nervous system.

The more archaic structures, including the thalamus, exhibit a clear modular organization, while more recent ones, e.g., the cerebral cortex, appear to be responsible for very complex, probability-based self-organizational processes, tied to information flow.

Goldberg has pointed out that modular organization determined by genetics, based on stochastic evolutionary processes, constitutes an optimal response to each different evolutionary level.

Reptiles and birds exhibit brain organization that is rigidly modular. Mammals, endowed with a considerable cerebral cortex, seem to be dominated by teleonomic, self-organizational processes, implemented on the basis of informational flow.

The human brain is provided with a huge amount of cortical matter and exhibits a random, evolutionary dynamic that is stochastic and teleonomic.

In order that a unitary functional direction emerges from this enormous complexity, structures for coordinated control are necessary. These structures seem to be located in the frontal lobes (Goldberg, 2001).

The conceptualization of the mind as constituted by a coalition of multiple processes that are articulated at different levels was proposed by Fodor (1983).

This author has formulated the hypothesis that humans are endowed with "multiple minds", each specialized in specific functions and characterized by a functional dynamic, a different evolutionary meaning, and a distinctive course of development.

Robert Ornstein (1992) has subsequently proposed the interesting concept of the *"mind in place"*.

According to this conception, environmental needs determine the most appropriate module, chosen from a coalition of the specialized modules, to carry out the computational tasks required.

If the environmental contingencies are modified and the "active mind" is not the most appropriate one to carry out the task, this mind is placed in back-up, and a more suitable module is recruited.

In order for the comprehensive dynamic of the mind to be at its best, working in a flexible and generative manner, it is essential that the different modules are all active and functioning.

The processes of knowledge described by Guidano and Liotta (1983) as originating from two levels of knowledge, tacit and explicit, have become four levels in my conceptual elaboration:

- *Tacit level* (tacit knowledge);
- *Explicit level* (explicit knowledge);
- *Procedural, executive, and problem solving level* (procedural and executive knowledge, problem-solving skills);
- *Relational level* (social or Machiavellian intelligence).

The system of human knowledge, in light of this model, is a complex structure in which the different activities are carried out in coordinated terms, involving simultaneously a substantial part of the central nervous system.

Every conscious activity implicates the acquisition of information, its selection, elaboration, the involvement of structures for memory, and the use of the information for plans and strategies, in order to interact with the environment and with others.

Each activity of knowing is sustained by specific nervous structures and functions according to distinctive neuronal, computational, and biochemical mechanisms.

As we will see, in the schizophrenic patient all the diverse forms of knowing are affected by malfunctions, but it is the coordination of the different activities that is most altered in this pathology.

To conclude, the so-called *coalitional processes* must be mentioned (Scrimali, 2003).

The amount of information derived from the continual flow of experience from the external world and from the perception of the internal world—information that is constantly elaborated and re-ordered in the system of knowledge—is integrated into a complex and self-organized process: the Self that constitutes the unifying expression of the mind.

The human brain, an extremely complex, non-equilibrium biological system, is organized in multiple functional units, endowed with decentralized control mechanisms. This means that each one is provided with autonomous and peripheral processes of regulation.

As we have already seen, the more archaic structures exhibit a notable genetically-determined modularity. More recent structures, from a phylogenic and ontogenetic point of view, are modulated by the information entry flow and show considerable ability to self-organize.

From the many brain units, either modular or gradient, emerge patterns of elaboration of specific information that recognize different computational codes (analogue, digital, mixed).

Although every module and, therefore, every brain process exhibits self-organizing activity and is endowed with decentralized control, it should still be pointed out that in humans, complex processes of coordinated control emerge and are able to emulate a sense of oneness and cohesion among the many centers and varying processes.

Every human being, regardless of the incessant activity of the systems of differentiated and specialized knowledge, and regardless of the vertiginous quantity of data that is continually acquired during interaction with the world, has a sense of self as definite, unique, and stable over time.

It is this continual sense of self, always recognizable even during constant physical, psychic, and relational changes, that constitutes a central dynamic of the self. Damage to the self in schizophrenia provokes, according to the conceptualization proposed by this book, a significant increase in disorder that I have defined as *Entropy of Mind* or *Phrenentropy*.

This disorder is a pathology of the self, rather than a single activity of the mind or the brain (many of which are, in fact, altered).

The problematic of the self has seen, in recent years, a renewal of interest on the part of numerous authors, some from the cognitive field, others from the neurosciences.

In the work, *The Self and Its Brain*, Popper and Eccles (1977) observe that a peculiar human characteristic is the systematic awareness of one's identity for the entire life span, even after periods of interrupted physiological or pathological consciousness, such as occurs in sleep or in coma.

The sense of self is not, for Popper, a physical reality, however. In fact, the physical structure of the body changes during a lifetime, thus the self must be a process tied to consciousness and memory (Popper & Eccles, 1977).

Popper (1972) denies that the self is constituted by the simple activity of self-observation. He says that it is, rather, the result of processes of knowing that organize information acquired from the environment, as well as innate and biologically predetermined programs.

Popper and Eccles (1977) conclude that even if there is a constant process of the distribution of tasks between structures and different activities taking place in the brain, every human being, at all times, knows him or herself to be unique and unrepeatable.

After being an object of Popper's epistemological reflections and Eccles' neurophysiological studies, the self has recently become central to the field of clinical cognitive theory.

Many authors have focused on this critical problem (Bandura, 1971; Bowlby; 1988; Goncalves, 1994; Mahoney, 1991; Guidano, 1988, 1992).

With differences in articulation and argumentation, the following three topics are fundamental to the different theoretical approaches in the cognitive field:

- firstly, the self is a process of unification and internal coherence that arises from an incessant activity of abstraction, based on multiple personal experiences;
- secondly, the self constitutes an entity able to influence the development of both the individual and those whose share the same ecological niche;
- thirdly, the self, once developed through the evolutionary phases of the life cycle, reaches a certain stability during adulthood.

Within this cognitive paradigm, the self is considered a subjective entity, structured to begin from human information processing with attributes of autonomy, independence, and stability, though still exhibiting a considerable evolutionary capacity.

One of the authors who has significantly influenced the understanding of the self in the field of clinical cognitive theory is Vittorio Guidano. Guidano (1988, 1992) placed an evolutionary epistemology and a constructivist conception of the relationship with reality at the center of his thinking.

This author did not consider the self as a structure but, rather, as an organizational process in continual becoming. According to Guidano, the self is articulated on two levels which correspond to different processes that constitute, respectively, the acquisition of experiential data (experience) and the explicit decodification of the same data through language (explanation).

Guidano's conception of the self can be defined as "bi-level".

The sense of self, specific and unique to each human being, arises from a continual dynamic process between *experience* and *explanation*. The distinctive modalities of perception of reality and the equally idiosyncratic abilities and explanatory skills, constitute the specific connotation of each different self.

According to the conceptualization I proposed earlier, regarding the four processes of knowledge, i.e., *experience, explanation, action, relation,* the self assumes a *multi-level connotation*.

Unity of the self comes from two distinctive attributes of biological systems, the brain and the complex system of knowledge that is constituted by the mind.

According to the theory of auto-poieses, living beings are systems able to constantly maintain or limit themselves within a restricted field of values, which are the fundamental variables which define them.

In the case of the system of human knowledge, the variable that is constantly maintained, regardless of constant perturbations, is personal identity.

Self-reference is a process in which all new information is inserted into the system.

The formation of the self and its continual becoming is implemented in an inter-subjective dimension, in relation to important persons who, during the developmental phase of the life cycle, were nurturing figures and in adult life are members of one's personal network.

Regarding the self, William James originally described two *polarities* (James, 1997).

- *"I" (the I-Self)* which is constituted by the self as protagonist that elaborates information.
- *"Me" (the Me-Self)* which is constituted by the self as object of self-reflection. James also described a series of components of the protagonist Self (I-Self).
- *Self-Awareness* or the monitoring of one's:
  - internal physical states;
  - needs;
  - thoughts;
  - emotions.
- *Self-Agency*
  - sense of being the protagonist of one's own processes.
- *Self- Continuity*
  - perception of continuity through change.
- *Self-Coherence*
  - construction of non-incongruous meanings.

The distinction between the self and the non-self constitutes a crucial aspect in the functional dynamic of the self. This is an aspect which finds correspondence in other complex systems which make up the human body.

For example, from this point of view the immune system exhibits considerable similarities to the nervous system.

In fact, in the course of the life cycle, the immune system evolves, self-organizes, and continually modulates its functions and processes.

An important aspect for the working of the immune system is identifiable in the constant ability to distinguish between what is part of the same organism (the self) and what is foreign (the non-self).

Everything that is recognized as foreign is attacked and destroyed, maintaining, in this way, the integrity of the biological system constituted by the human body, when confronted with anything external that could compromise the complex organization of the individual.

It is in this sense that Antonio Damasio (1999) pointed out the centrality of the distinction made by the self between entities and processes that belong to the entity, and entities and processes that are external to the entity's physical and psychic boundaries.

This American neuroscientist, of Portuguese origin, has recently elaborated his conception of the self which is of considerable interest, because it is based on experimental research.

One fascinating aspect of this model is the distinction between the different levels of the self which include:

- proto self;
- core self;
- autobiographical self.

The proto self is constituted by the collection of all information coming from the internal biological world. The information usually does not reach consciousness.

Damasio indicates the threshold of human consciousness at the boundary between the proto self and the core self.

The core self is made up of the patterns of knowledge, activated by the external world, that modify the state of the central nervous system.

The core self is made up of shared information and is able to recognize an analogue code.

The core self is animated by a "here and now" dynamic and permits the identification of the person in transactions with the external world.

The autobiographical self emerges from the activity of memory processes that organize informational patterns coming from the external world in definitive mnemonic structures.

For Damasio, this component of the self is able to reflect on the past and anticipate the future.

Studying Damasio's model reminded me of the motto found in King Tut's tomb discovered by Carter and Carnavon. Each pharaoh chose a motto and Tut's is perfect for Damasio's autobiographical self: *I know the past, I envision the future.*

Damasio's model is very close to my idea of coalitional mind, which is traceable to the dynamic of the multi-level self, to the continual activity of narration, and to the conception of the proactive, rather than reactive, brain.

In certain circumstances, similar to what happens with the autoimmune diseases, for instance, the capacity to accurately discriminate between the "self" and the "non-self" deteriorates. The autoimmune system suddenly no longer recognizes as part of itself, entire cellular systems, that are attacked and neutralized, thanks to sophisticated destructive mechanisms.

Something similar occurs with schizophrenia when the modules and coalitional processes of the central nervous system no long recognize one's own activities and processes, considering them as disturbances coming from the outside and treating them as such.

That is what seems to happen during hallucinations, which are linked to nervous system activity. These are mistakenly codified as external processes, considered threatening for the integrity of the "mind system", and thus become the object of neutralization and coping processes.

According to Guidano, the dynamic of the self-construction derives from the base activity of motivational and biological processes, onto which the so-called *nuclear* or *prototypical scenes* are precociously superimposed.

They are formed from the earliest important emotional experiences, which are systematically repeated through interaction with nurturing figures, and tend to gradually structure an early, constant modality for perceiving the self.

A subsequent evolutionary phase is constituted by the so-called *writings*, that is, a series of explicit rules that permit the integration of analogue material from prototypical scenes into an explicative dimension.

Beck (1971) has also described a very similar process in his theory of schemas. For this author from Philadelphia, schemas are units of complex, emotional, and cognitive information that operate as both memory processes and heuristic instruments for the analysis of reality during the course of the life cycle.

According to Beck (1963) every individual orients him or herself in space and time and attributes a meaning to the experiences that occur based on the gradually structured schemas.

There are some rigid and dysfunctional schemas, constructed around negative experiences that took place during the developmental phase of the life cycle, that connote the dysfunctional mechanisms of information processing in neurotic or depressed patients. The self as a process produces, feeds, and maintains a structure that can be identified in *personal identity*.

Guidano (1988) defines *personal identity* as a process, similar to the self, and as a *structure* constituted by an ordered whole of explicit information.

Personally, I prefer to consider *personal identity* as a *system* (a system of knowledge allocated in the structures of memory), constructed and continually reorganized by the procedural activity of the self. The interface between personal identity, the self, and the external world is identifiable, in my opinion, in another process that is ascribable to narrative.

Narrative has assumed increasing relevance in the cognitive field and, above all, in the constructivist *milieu*.

Personal narrative can be described as a heuristic program through which each individual makes explicit his or her own life experience, illustrating personal identity.

The heuristic program, constituted by personal narrative, permits the unification of thoughts, motivations, memories, and the most disparate life experiences, in such a way that the inevitable components of ambiguity and uncertainty, linked to reality, are reduced. In this way internal coherence, thus order and the negentropy within the mind, can grow.

The narrative is structured progressively, during the developmental history of each individual, beginning with a background of heuristic needs that occur dramatically during infancy.

As Bettelheim (1984) pointed out, a series of problematic questions appear to the child:

- Who am I?
- Where do I come from?
- Who created humans and animals?
- What is the point of existence?
- What will I become?

Children, perturbed by these questions, will ask them in order to escape from a situation of indeterminacy, if they can rely on benevolent influences. Specifically, they will turn to their parents as a source of certainty and security.

It is important that the need to create order from uncertainty and disorder, that rises from abstract thought can find support from parents and the network that surrounds and sustains the child.

Some begin to create a positive story, centered on the sensation of being able to control reality and being able to live serenely in the condition of mystery that surrounds human existence; others, less fortunate, insert themselves into a story populated by uncertainty, phantasms, and negative power that heightens a sense of chaos and threat posed by existence.

The personal narrative of each individual is constantly conditioned by actual life experience and by the process of identity formation under way.

The relationship between personal identity and the heuristic narrative program must be considered as bijective and dialectic. In fact, even if personal narrative is determined by the actual identity of the subject, it is still being constantly remodeled by actual experience.

The heuristic program constituted by narrative tends to create sense and give order to reality, based on past history. Every new event must be able to insert itself into the script that is being recited, just as every new person or event introduced in a novel must find their collocation within the plot being elaborated by the author.

Russel and Waldrei (1996) define narrative as a fundamental instrument that has assumed increasing relevance in the cognitive field, above all, in the constructivist *milieu*.

As we will see, in schizophrenia we witness an evident and dramatic disintegration of narrative competence; one critical objective of therapy, therefore, should be the reconstruction and reactivation of the personal narrative of the patient.

Even if the narrative is aimed at maintaining order and coherence in the mind, it exhibits an openness to uncertainty, ambiguity, and disorder that can provoke temporary states of disequilibrium. These states are subsequently overcome, thanks to the activation of new evolutionary processes and the control of entropy.

Narrative has recently been the object of reflection by neuroscientists such as Siegel who, in his *La mente relazionale*, proposes a interpersonal neurobiology of narrative processes (Siegel, 1999).

A nervous structure that has a relevant role in the dynamics of narrative is, according to Seigel, the hippocampus which he defines as a "cognitive organizer" able to create a sense of self, both synchronically and diachronically, integrating active as well as past, present, and future processes.

Narrative processes, even if fed by memory systems of the hippocampus, involve numerous other structures of the two hemispheres.

The right hemisphere, with its analogue representations, provides images and scenarios for the stories to be narrated, while the left hemisphere implements a logical and linear elaboration, according to computational digital codes, making the sharing of personal stories possible.

Narrative activity is, therefore, the result of complex integrative processes between posterior, ventral, and bilateral regions of the two hemispheres. In this case, the functional and material recursiveness of the processes of the mind and systems of the brain, materialize.

Narrative activity stems from the integrity and perfect functional coordination of the multiple cerebral structures. This process then produces integration among the diverse modules of the brain in a positive recursiveness that nourishes the organization, that is, the Negative Entropy of the human mind.

We will see later how the breakdown of personal narrative constitutes one of the fundamental aspects of schizophrenic psychopathology, according to the *Entropy of Mind* or *Phrenentropy* model.

If the elaboration of reality and the actions that one exerts towards the eternal world are the result of processes of signification, and if these processes operate under the unifying aegis of narrative, then the current transactions with reality necessarily constitute the goal of a personal story. I will illustrate how the idiosyncratic modalities of the schizophrenic patient's interpretation of reality must be considered the result of a narrative story developed in a dysfunctional mode over the entire life cycle.

It may be useful at this point to recount an episode stemming from work with a patient suffering from paranoid schizophrenia.

He was assailed by delusions of persecution and firmly believed he was at the center of a complex secret service operation that controlled his every step in order to incriminate him.

After getting through the critical phase of the illness, we began to work with the specific hypothesis that the patient was afflicted by an idiosyncratic tendency to be suspicious of everyone, and that this tendency, linked to the patient's developmental history, derived from his parents and from his cultural and emotional *milieu*.

The patient was assigned the task of gathering elements that could corroborate or contradict the hypothesis proposed by the therapist. After some time, the patient recounted the following episode.

> "My father, from when I was little, would say to me that I should never trust anyone, and he would read me a fable that soon became my favourite".
> A father says to his child: "Climb up on top of the closet and jump off".
> "I'm afraid father", protested the child. "Don't be afraid", reassured the father kindly, saying, "I will be right here under the closet to catch you. That way you will not hurt yourself".
> "OK", said the child and obediently climbed up.
> "Catch me, Dad", begged the child, before jumping.
> "Of course", answered the father, readying himself to catch his son.
> The child then jumped, and he father deliberately remained immobile, while the child crashed to the ground.
> "Ouch, that hurts" cried the child. "Father, why didn't you catch me?"
> And the father said, "See, son, I wanted to teach you an important thing about life. Never trust anyone! If your father, who loves you, lets you fall, imagine what strangers might do to you!"

It is easy to understand how such a fable could be incorporated into the personal narrative of a patient. Thus, if one begins with a biological vulnerability and arrives the point of decompensation, the psychotic episode seems to be a coherent development of a life lived constantly in fear and mistrust of others.

Personal narrative responds to the irrepressible need of the mind to construct a sense of reality that is coherent with the past stories and with current cultural schemas of the individual.

Narrative theorists have also proposed a *narrative* paradigm for language, which they often distinguish from a *rationalist* one (Russel & Waldrei, 1996; Lyddon & Schreiner, 1998).

In the rationalist paradigm, language is considered to be a complex system of signs that are used to reflect reality and communicate the state of things among persons.

In the narrative paradigm, language is assumed to be the active creator of reality, rather than a simple mirror of already existing states. Moreover, students of narrative point out that human word games can lead to new levels of signification that transcend the original function.

Thus, these authors have challenged the rationalist paradigm and its tendency to exclude modalities of knowing that are not exclusively associated with logic and reason. They see narrative as an appropriate form of knowledge to express the wealth, diversity, and complexity of human lives (Russel & Waldrei, 1996).

In light of this perspective, reinterpreted hermeneutically, even the narration of a schizophrenic patient tells a coherent story.

This first chapter of the book concludes here. I have tried to delineate the basis of a complex orientation for the study of the mind that integrates biological, psychological, relational, historical, and social aspects and upon which a new scientific model of schizophrenia and its treatment, can be founded.

We are not yet ready to immerse ourselves in the *Entropy of Mind* which is what the second part of the book is about. First we must review the *physical traces of the Entropy of Mind*, the psychophysiological parameters able to furnish objective indications about the dysfunctional processes of the mind and the idiosyncrasies of schizophrenia.

CHAPTER TWO

On the Trail of the Entropy of Mind

1. Introduction

The title of this chapter echoes that of my earlier publication, written together with Liria Grimaldi, and called *Sulle tracce della mente* (Scrimali & Grimaldi, 1991).

The publication of that book in 1991 marked the end point of a huge project regarding the conceptual and methodological development of a complex constructivist orientation in psychophysiology.

Psychophysiology is the discipline devoted to the study of the physical signs of the mind, i.e., those biological indicators able to furnish objective information about the state of psychic, cognitive, emotional, and relational processes.

The work, carried out during the 1980s, at the Department of Psychiatry of the University of Catania allowed me to create and develop a cognitive psychophysiology laboratory aimed at both theoretical research on processes of the mind and clinical applications in terms of assessment and therapy in the context of integrated therapeutic programs.

The crucial and innovative aspect of the research was constituted, above all, by the development of a new theoretical and epistemological orientation in psychophysiology, informed by motor theories of the mind, by the logic of complex systems, and by the epistemology of complexity.

The methodologies and the entire system of implementation of the psychophysiological techniques described in this chapter should not be read in reductionist terms, but interpreted with an eye toward complexity.

The level of psychophysiological interpretation must not be considered or studied in reductionist terms and thus separated from the clinical context, but rather analyzed in a multimodal and multicontextual dimension.

The research, carried out in the 1990s by a group coordinated by me at the Department of Psychiatry of the University of Catania and presented in this chapter, permits the delineation of a fairly complete profile of the psychophysiology of schizophrenia articulated in three topics: the study of biological markers, processes of human information processing, and clinical psychophysiology.

As we shall see, research on schizophrenia, from a psychophysiological point of view, though still in a developmental phase, is already able to make an important contribution both to theoretical understanding of the *Entropy of Mind* or the *Phrenentropy* model and to the therapeutic and rehabilitative work of *Negative Entropy.*

2. Biological Markers of Schizophrenia

During the development of the DSM-III and its revised version DSM-III-R, the problem of establishing if, given the present state of knowledge, it is possible to use biological markers as diagnostic instruments, has been posed for the first time.

In reality, this objective has not been seized upon because the lack of homogeneity and standardization in psychophysiological research techniques has prevented the identification of pathognomonic markers for the various pathologies.

In the field of schizophrenia, a series of experiments has provided encouraging results regarding the validity of monitoring some parameters in order to obtain trait and state information correlated to the condition of the disorder.

Thus, the Associated Laboratory Findings of the DSM-IV affirms that even if specific biological markers for schizophrenia have not yet been identified with certainty, specific parameters can provide useful indications, at least for research (American Psychological Association, 1994).

The objective to identify these markers, it remains to be said, appears important enough not to be ignored.

Research on trait markers, present from infancy, may constitute a useful tool for primary prevention, while the availability of state markers would permit the accurate monitoring of the clinical condition, improving the efficacy of therapeutic and rehabilitative protocols.

But what should the characteristics of a biological parameter be so that it could be used as a marker of schizophrenia?

An initial distinction should be made between state and trait markers.

A biological marker means an indicator of illness, easily monitored and possibly quantifiable, which may have a causal meaning or which may only be phenomenal.

A trait marker is a biological parameter present in subjects who will develop schizophrenia or who are in a state of remission or recovery. Also, it is tied to some base characteristic of the functioning of the central nervous system, rather than to conditions of clinical decompensation.

If the biological parameter is present during a clinical phase of the illness, it should be considered a state marker. The parameters that, up until today, have emerged and may be excellent candidates for biological markers, are (Gruzelier, 2003):

- smooth pursuit eye movement dysfunction;
- electroencephalographic potentials elicited by acoustic patterns;
- spontaneous and evoked electrodermal phasic activity.

Regarding state markers, the most interesting parameters are:

- smooth pursuit eye movement of a moving target;
- potentials tied to the event, evoked by visual patterns;
- tonic electrodermal activity (Skin Conductance Level).

2.1. *Smooth Pursuit Eye Movement*

Monitoring smooth pursuit eye movement of a mobile visual target constitutes one of the most interesting psychophysiological parameters in the field of the psychophysiology of schizophrenia.

The alterations of eye movement in following a moving target with regular movement in the visual field of the patient constitutes, among possible trait markers of schizophrenia, the one that, until today, has produced the most unequivocal experimental evidence (Scrimali, Grimaldi, Cultrera & Di Stefano, 1994).

The importance of the evaluation of smooth pursuit eye movement (SPEM) in schizophrenia (movements of the eye following a target moving in the visual field), was pointed out by Holzman and collaborators, who demonstrated that 50-80 % of schizophrenic patients and about 45% of their close relatives show abnormalities in these movements. SPEM abnormalities are, therefore, considered to be a possible specific marker for schizophrenic disturbances of a genetic origin (Holzman, Kriglen, Levy & Haberman, 1980).

2.2. *Evoked Electroencephalographic Potentials*

In recent years the recording of evoked potentials has become one of the most common methods of study in psychophysiological laboratories.

In the field of evoked electroencephalographic potentials, three responses are distinguished: *a) visual response; b) somatic/sensory response; c) auditory response.*

Based on the study of the different typologies of evoked electroencephalographic potentials, two possible markers for schizophrenia have been identified: P300 and N50.

P300. In the area of long latency components of the evoked potentials, P300 holds particular interest for clinical psychophysiology because of its positive polarity and its average latency of about 300 milliseconds, with a range that varies from 250-400 milliseconds (Pritchard, 1981).

The recording of P300 in psychotic patients has proven to be a promising line of research, both for its heuristic implications and for its possible clinical applications.

At the psychophysiology laboratory at the University of Catania, our team has carried out experimental research to document the pathological characteristics of the modality of sensory information processing in schizophrenic patients (Scrimali & Grimaldi, 1991).

The results of the studies have demonstrated that the P300 of schizophrenics are significantly reduced in amplitude (Scrimali, Grimaldi & Rapisarda, 1988).

Many studies have demonstrated that the P300, elicited according to visual sensory modalities, can constitute a "state" marker of a psychotic condition, in that it changes along with clinical improvement.

Contrarily, the P300 evoked during a pattern of acoustic stimulation appears to be a probable "trait" indicator, in respect to the psychotic condition.

The evolution of P300 has been related to neuroleptic treatment, and Duncan (1988) has identified a significant correlation between clinical improvement, provoked by the administration of neuroleptics, and the increment in amplitude of visually elicited P300.

Also interesting is the fact that some patients, clinical non-responders to neuroleptics, have demonstrated a persistent reduction in amplitude of the visual P300.

Acoustically elicited P300 is not modified substantially, even after clinical improvement resulting from neuroleptic treatment. This concords perfectly with the persistence of acoustic hallucinations in cases of clinical remission after visual hallucinations disappear.

N50. This specific potential evoked early is tied to the "filter" processes on information entry patterns of the central nervous system (Hansen & Hillyard, 1980).

Its alteration in schizophrenic patients is traceable to the compromised filter competencies of entry information that afflict schizophrenic patients (Friedman, 1991).

The evocation methodology can be summarized in this way. The patient listens to two clicks, 500 milliseconds apart.

If evoked electroencephalographic potentials are recorded at each click, in normal subjects the positive wave that appears after 50 milliseconds, diminishes at the arrival of the second click.

English language writers describe this phenomenon as gating.

From the neurophysiological point of view, the diminution in amplitude of the response at the second click is tied to the loss of stimulus novelty and to a specific form of "learning".

In schizophrenic patients, a particular effect of this stimulation procedure is that in the recording of the N50, on average, the response to the second stimulus does not decrease in amplitude, but sometimes increases.

This may be interpreted as a difficulty of the central nervous system of the schizophrenic patient to recognize the second click as something "already noticed" (Hillyard, Hink, Schwent & Picton, 1973).

2.3. *Quantitative Electroencephalography*

The study of quantitative electroencephalography is a recent development in psychophysiological research that is creating interesting possibilities in schizophrenia regarding diagnostics, therapy, and rehabilitation, thanks to its use as a neurofeedback technique (Duffy, Hughes, Miranda, Bernad & Cook, 1994).

The QEEG (Quantitative EEG) is not substantially different from classic electroencephalography. The computerized quantitative analysis does permit, however, the calculation of parameters that can then be compared to different databases, developed over the years and based on studies with healthy control subjects.

In this way, it is possible to evaluate how much the functioning of one brain differs from another "normally" or "optimally" functioning brain. Numerous efforts, throughout the years, have been made to produce this EEG database.

Among the most used databases are those developed by Duffy and collaborators (Duffy, Hughes, Miranda, Bernad & Cook, 1994). These databases are the only ones to cover most, if not all, the life cycle of an individual, from birth to senescence.

Despite the many studies that have found statistical correlations between the QEEG data and some clinical syndromes, in reality, the use of the QEEG as a diagnostic tool in various pathologies is still limited.

Quantitative electroencephalography has been successfully used, however, in the field of EEG-biofeedback, or as it is more commonly known, neurofeedback (Demos, 2005).

Specifically regarding schizophrenia, there is little data in the literature, but the systematic application of computerized electroencephalography seems to be a useful tool for the functional and longitudinal clinical evaluation of the patient, as well as for initiating neurofeedback methods (Evans & Abarbanel, 1999).

Quantitative electroencephalographic recordings have permitted the identification, in schizophrenic patients, of a condition characterized by a greater presence of *theta* and *delta* rhythms in the anterior regions of the encephalon, with a concomitant decrease in *alpha* frequencies (Fenton, Fenwick & Dollimore, 1980).

Particularly interesting, even if not sufficiently corroborated by experimental proof, is the possibility to document, through QEEG recordings, dysfunctional conditions in the patterns of inter-hemispheric functional coherence, in order to begin neurofeedback therapy (Davidson, 1988).

At our Clinical Psychophysiological Laboratory, research has been carried out to evaluate the quantitative EEG in the assessment phase of a schizophrenic patient and in the use of neurofeedback to improve the neuropsychological functions of attention and concentration (Scrimali, Grimaldi, Sambataro, Petriglieri & Polopoli, 2001; Scrimali & Maugeri, 2004).

2.4. *Electrodermal Activity*

This parameter is one of the most interesting and easiest to use in psychophysiology, not only for the wealth of information it furnishes about psychic processes, but also because of its simplicity in reading and monitoring.

For these reasons, over the course of the 20th century, an enormous quantity of data and research on illnesses, including schizophrenia, has been accumulated.

In the context of studies on electrodermal activity, the phasic and tonic components must be considered (Prokasy & Raskin, 1973).

The phasic responses are usually indicative of rapid activation movements, following anxiety, emotional disturbance, or conflictual situations.

The monitoring of the phasic responses are carried out in various clinical and experimental circumstances.

From the clinical point of view, recording the response to anxiety is particularly interesting, because it allows the objective evaluation of the actual emotional resonance in stressful situations (Davis, 1929).

The "skin conductance level" (SCL) parameter is an index of the general state of activation and vigilance. A decrease in the SCL indicates progressive psychophysical relaxation, following the learning and practice of different self-control techniques.

Paul (1969) demonstrated that the condition of psychophysical distension, produced by brief training in relaxation techniques, is in perfect accord with changes in the SCL.

The daily monitoring of the SCL furnishes reliable indications of stress levels in a subject.

The parameter that has been studied the most in the field of electrodermal activity is the monitoring of evoked phasic responses through the administration of random tonal acoustic stimuli patterns (typically 20) (Boucsein, 1992).

Besides the extinction trend of the orientation responses, which is recorded in this type of trial (habituation), the recording of the SCL and the spontaneous phasic responses (Skin Conductance Responses: SCR) also assume importance (Prokasy & Raskin, 1973).

But what information can the monitoring of the skin conductance parameters furnish in schizophrenic research, and what relevance do they have for clinical practice?

The answer is that this parameter merits special attention. The information it provides about patients and their relationship with reality is extremely important and potentially very useful because its methodological simplicity makes it accessible in the clinic as well as in the lab.

The most significant current data regarding schizophrenic patients are the following.

Much research unequivocally demonstrates that while in healthy control subjects only a small percentage (5-10%) do not exhibit an orientation response to tonal stimuli, 40-50% of schizophrenic patients do fail to exhibit this response. This lack of response originates from an alteration in human information processing.

But even the schizophrenic patients who have an orientation response, show anomalies in electrodermal activity. In fact, even when the orientation responses are present, they are extinguished either too early or too late when compared to healthy control subjects. At any rate, the patients with an orientation response show unusually high SCL, compared to the controls.

The differentiation of patients into responders and non-responders, during a trial to elicit electrodermal orientation responses, has an interesting correlation with clinical presentation. Responder patients show a primarily positive symptomatology, while non-responders almost always suffer from negative symptoms (Gruzelier, 1984).

The recording of electrodermal activity, during the acute phase of psychotic decompensation, might constitute a useful parameter for prognosis and monitoring of the clinical response to treatment with neuroleptics (Spolin, Theyford & Cancro, 1971).

Regarding the significance of the "skin conductance" parameter on the predictability of the course of schizophrenia, research has shown that high skin conductance at the end of the symptomatic phase, indicates a limited recovery capacity. Also, a progressive increase in the SCL can signal the approach of a new crisis. (Zahn, Carpenter & McGlashan, 1981).

Another interesting aspect of electrodermal activity was studied by Raine and Venables (1984), who showed that this activity revealed a biological vulnerability, not only for schizophrenia, but also for other schizotypical disorders.

This study analyzed the electrodermal activity of children aged 3-11 years old, when the subjects had not yet manifested signs of schizophrenia. These recordings were compared with schizotypical personality evaluations carried out on the same subjects, aged 17-23.

The results showed that the electrodermal activity recorded in the 3-11 years old was significantly different in those who later manifested signs of schizophrenia.

This research shows anomalies in phasic and tonic patterns in electrodermal activity well before a clinical condition is manifested.

In our laboratories, I conducted experimental research in order to evaluate the level of skin conductance in patients with various forms of schizophrenia, in conditions of clinical compensation. These results were compared to a group of patients with neurotic-type disorders and to a group of normal control subjects (Scrimali, Grimaldi & Pulvirenti, 2004).

I also wanted to test whether, during clinical decompensation, the SCL would, in the psychotic patients, become particularly elevated.

There were 89 control subjects, 23 patients with schizophrenia, and 27 patients with different types of non-psychotic pathologies, who were referred to as "neurotics".

All the patients in the two groups were on medication. The schizophrenic patients were treated with neuroleptics, antidepressants, and anxyolitics; the "neurotics" with antidepressants, anxyolitics, and sometimes with low doses of neuroleptics.

We also studied five patients who arrived at the Department of Psychiatry of the University of Catania in conditions of acute decompensation. The patients were all suffering from paranoid schizophrenia.

Measurement of skin conductance was carried out prior to the beginning of any specific drug therapy.

The data from the first phase of the research show that there are no statistically significant differences among the three groups regarding the SCL parameter, during conditions of clinical compensation.

During phase II of the research, the mean values obtained were compared to those recorded from the controls and from the neurotic and psychotic patients in the decompensation phase.

All these latter comparisons showed highly significant differences.

The results of the research indicate an unequivocally clear picture of the behaviour of the SCL parameter in psychosis.

In conditions of clinical compensation, and while on medication, the skin conductance values were normal or decreased significantly. During the phase of acute decompensation, and in the absence of neuroleptic treatment, the conductance values tended to go up drastically.

Our research shows that SCL measurement constitutes a state marker for schizophrenia, exhibiting high levels only during clinical decompensation, and gradually returning to normal once medication begins to control the positive symptoms.

Subsequently, I planned and carried out further research to evaluate if evoked exosomatic skin conductance activity might constitute a specific marker for schizophrenia.

The study involved the three following groups:

- control group: 50 subjects;
- first experimental group: 19 "neurotics";
- second experimental group: 21 patients with schizophrenia.

The control group consisted of volunteers, contacted in varying contexts. The patients were recruited and tested in three different clinical settings: the Department of Psychiatry at the University of Catania, a private practice, and a therapeutic and rehabilitative community. The control subjects were administered the Middlesex Hospital Questionnaire in order to insure that they were free from psychiatric disorders. No one tested positive for any of pathological values on the six scales of the test.

The diagnosis, relative to the experimental groups, were carried out according to the DSM-IV-TR.

In the "neurotic" group, the subjects were affected with the following pathologies:

- panic attacks: 4;
- dysthymia: 3;
- depression: 5;
- eating disorder (anorexia): 1;
- generalized anxiety: 1;
- obsessive-compulsive disorder: 1;
- hypochondria: 2;
- conversion disorder: 1;
- bipolar disorder: 1.

The patients in the schizophrenic group had long suffered from paranoid or undifferentiated schizophrenia; they were all being treated with neuroleptics and were all in a phase of relative clinical compensation.

Both experimental groups of patients were subjected to pharmacological treatment with benzodiazepine, antidepressants, sedative hypnotics, and neuroleptics.

The fact that both groups were medicated, balances the eventual effect of this variable; if, in fact, the differences observed between the groups were ascribable to a bias due to drug therapy, a difference between the untreated control group and both the experimental groups would have emerged.

Instead, as we will see later, statistically significant differences between the "neurotics" and controls did not emerge.

It is, therefore, plausible to affirm that the differences identified in the controls and the psychotics, and in the neurotics and the psychotics, are not attributable to the medicines administered, but presumably to the specific characteristics of the pathological process.

The results of the research can be summarized in the following terms.

Range of response. No statistically relevant difference emerged regarding the range of response among the three groups studied.

Number of responses observed. This parameter is the focus of the research, in that it is correlated to processes of human information processing, altered in psychotic patients.

The comparisons demonstrate a substantial homogeneity between the controls and the neurotics, but show a significant difference between the psychotics and the other two groups studied.

The results demonstrate that the parameter "number of evoked phasic exosomatic electrodermal responses to acoustic stimuli" is a biological marker for schizophrenia.

Considering that all the psychotic patients tested were affected with schizophrenia over a long period of time, we can hypothesize that this is a trait marker for schizophrenia.

3. *Clinical Psychophysiology of Schizophrenia*

After having described the principal biological markers, both trait and state, for schizophrenia, I will now indicate psychophysiological procedures and methods that contribute to the construction of the clinical psychophysiology of schizophrenia.

It should be stated, however, that the development of a true clinical psychophysiology of schizophrenia can be realized only if we have methodologies that are easy to use outside of research laboratories and applicable in common treatment settings.

I have pursued this objective over the years by developing a tool and software named *MindLAB Set* and *MindSCAN*, as well as another instrument for the patient's use called *PsychoFeedback* (Scrimali, 2005a).

3.1. *Psychophysiological Profiles and Prognosis*

A series of experimental research has documented a certain number of characteristics of psychophysiological parameters, including the EEG and skin conductance, that permit the formulation of a prognosis at the time of the base evaluation of the patient and before beginning therapeutic and rehabilitative treatment.

Based on the literature, it is possible to tentatively trace a *psychophysiological profile of the schizophrenic patient*, with a good prognosis or with a more problematic prognosis, using patterns of central nervous system functioning and, therefore, of the gravity of biological vulnerability.

Concerning the EEG, it has been observed that graphs nearer to the norm and that tend to maintain the same patterns of activity over time without notable changes, after the beginning of neuroleptic therapy, might be indicative of a more problematic prognosis.

Arrhythmic graphs, with alterations in the alpha rhythm, because of the presence of rapid or slow rhythms that, above all, any change following medication, seem to suggest a better prognosis.

Based on these considerations, I introduced the systematic use of quantitative electroencephalography (QEEG) in the evaluation of schizophrenic patients, which we carry out in our laboratory with the instrumentation, Olotester (GW Elektron, 2004).

Regarding electrodermal conductance, a more favourable prognosis is correlated to the prevalence of phasic activity, recorded in the left hand, as opposed to the right.

Other aspects, detectable by the monitoring of electrodermal conductance, and indicative of a better prognosis, are the following:

- less latency in the orientation response;

- more rapid installation of the evoked extinction response to monotonous acoustic stimuli;
- greater electrodermal reactivity to stress.

The recording psychophysiological parameters, to formulate a prognosis and to monitor treatment, does not yet constitute an option routinely adopted at the clinical level.

3.2. *Evaluation of Treatment Response*

A recent, particularly interesting aspect in psychophysiological research is identifiable in the use of psychophysiological parameters, including indexes of clinical improvement of the patient, that are ascribable to the therapeutic protocols adopted.

At our laboratory, I carried out research to evaluate the validity of the SCL parameter as an indicator of clinical remission.

The patients who participated in the initial study were hospitalized at the Institute of Clinical Psychiatry at the University of Catania. The patients were enlisted in the project on the first day of their hospitalization.

The sample we monitored consisted of eight men and four women with an average age of 44.25, SD±15.74.

All the patients at the time of admission in the ward, presented acute psychotic decompensation and were diagnosed with schizophrenia, based on the diagnostic criteria of the DSM-IV (American Psychological Association, 1994).

Seven patients were affected with disorganized schizophrenia and five with the paranoid subtype.

The patient was informed of the possibility of participating in this research project, which was aimed at monitoring all the phases of clinical improvement, through the daily recording of skin conductance values, used as a psychophysiological parameter connected to arousal. A clinical evaluation was also carried out through an interview with a physician.

Once adherence was obtained, the *Brief Psychiatric Rating Scale* was compiled by the psychiatrist, following a clinical interview with the patient (Morosini & Roncone, 1994).

At the end of the meeting, the monitoring of the skin conductance values, through bipolar recording, was initiated.

The *Brief Psychiatric Rating Scale* was administered to the whole sample, on the baseline corresponding to the day of hospital admission and in ten days after hospitalization.

The psychophysiological monitoring of the electrodermal activity occurred daily. All the subjects were treated with 4 mg of haloperidol per day.

Measurement of the Skin Conductance Level was achieved by using the *MindLAB Set* of Psychotech (Psychotech, 2004).

The data obtained demonstrated that in the period under consideration (one week), a decrease in the comprehensive clinical symptoms was recorded along with a significant reduction in electrodermal conductance.

The research demonstrated that, relative to our sample of schizophrenic patients, the electrodermal parameter, SCL, can be used as a state marker in conditions of acute schizophrenia, and that it covaries with the clinical condition, as measured by a standardized instrument of assessment such as the *Brief Psychiatric Rating Scale*.

The method of measuring skin conductance can be administered easily and can, therefore, be applied on a large scale.

It is, thus, possible to hypothesize that this research, carried out on larger samples, can lead to validation of a biological state marker, that is easily monitored in both the clinic and by the patient at home, during the post-symptomatic phase.

3.3. *Monitoring Warning Signs of Relapse*

Since schizophrenia is an affliction, characterized by high levels of relapse, the identification of parameters that furnish premonitory indications of possible relapse, is particularly important.

In accordance with the model of schizophrenic stress and psychotic crises, which I describe in the second part of the book, it is possible to tie an increment in arousal with the progressive increase in the risk of relapse.

In this regard, even if some psychophysiological parameters seem good candidates for this role, indisputable experimental evidence still does not exist.

In our experimental and clinical psychophysiology laboratory, I recently began to develop a new area of research focused on field psychophysiology.

This is a new methodology, concerning the monitoring of psychophysiological parameters during day-to-day life. In this way, it is possible to gather information, in real time, on the clinical condition of the patient during daily life.

Accomplishing this is correlated to recent developments in electronic micro-components that permit the use of small, manageable devices.

The first methodological problem I had to resolve was the design and realization of a compact, robust, trustworthy, and, above all, user-friendly device, that could be used at home by the patients themselves, to measure skin conductance.

The original device, which I called *PsychoFeedback*, was intended to be compact, economical, and easy-to-use, by both the patient and staff (Scrimali, 2005; Psychotech, 2004).

The device, after a series of trials, proved to be valid and efficient for the scope of the research, both in terms of its cost and ease of use. After the device was completed, I created a form to be filled in by the patients to register the different daily readings of electrodermal conductance.

After finishing the instrumentation, I worked on the self-monitoring form to record positive symptoms, particularly correlated to conditions of stress.

In doing this, I referred to Andreasen's (1990) protocol for the evaluation of positive symptoms.

After the creation of the materials and techniques, I designed, together with some collaborators, the specific study (Scrimali, Grimaldi, Foti & Damigella, 2000).

Patients with schizophrenia, diagnosed according to the DSM-IV, would be admitted to the project. The patients were chosen among those hospitalized in our Department of Psychiatry.

The patients who participated in the study also had to self-monitor for arousal using the *PsychoFeedback* and self-evaluate for warning signs, using the forms created for this end.

Once home, the patients in the study were expected to continue the recording themselves.

In this first phase of the study, two patients participated for whom we are able to report findings.

Patient no. 1. Carmelina M., 33, single, health care worker.
Diagnosis, according to the criteria of the DSM-IV (American Psychological Association, 1994): paranoid schizophrenia.

She was hospitalized for three weeks in the Department of Psychiatry because of a decompensation characterized by auditory hallucinations, delusions of persecution, forced affect, and volition disorder with socio-occupational dysfunctions.

The disorder persisted for many years and had provoked past hospitalizations.

After three weeks of hospital care, and treatment based on 4 mg per day of haloperidol, the patient improved and was released after having been provided with a *PsychoFeedback* device and a sufficient number of forms, in order to continue the self-monitoring at home.

Patient no. 2. Marisa Z., 65, single, teacher, retired.
Diagnosis, according to the criteria of the DSM-IV (American Psychological Association, 1994): paranoid schizophrenia.

The patient was hospitalized for two weeks in the Department of Psychiatry because of a decompensation characterized by the presence of auditory hallucinations, delusions of persecution, referential ideas, thought derailment, ideational incoherence, and volition disorder with socio-occupational dysfunctions.

The patient suffered from this disorder for many years and had a medical history of hospitalization.

After two weeks in the hospital, with treatment based on 4 mg per day of haloperidol, the patient improved and was released.

During the hospital stay, the patient began to effect self-monitoring twice a day.

Upon release, the patient was furnished with a sufficient number of forms to continue the self-monitoring.

Of the two patients, the first showed excellent compliance, while the second exhibited greater difficulty in carrying out the experimental procedure. In fact, she did not fill out the self-evaluation forms for symptoms, limiting herself to the self-administration of the *State and Trait Anxiety Inventory* (STAI) (Spielberger, Gorsuch & Lushene, 1970. She did, however, measure the electrodermal activity for five weeks.

The second case can be used only partially, because the self-monitored data were not recorded during the phase of clinical decompensation, since the patient was inserted into the study at a point when her clinical conditions were already improving.

During the first phase of the hospitalization, she was very agitated and refused to undergo the psychophysiological recordings.

Only after overcoming the acute clinical decompensation phase, was it possible to obtain a certain level of compliance and begin the experimental program.

The patient began monitoring electrodermal activity and anxiety through the STAI upon release, when her clinical conditions were significantly improved.

The electrodermal parameter and the STAI scores show positive improvement that from a psychophysiological and psychometric point of view. In fact, the electrodermal conductance values were low, as where the values regarding the state anxiety.

In this way, a relation between the positive clinical improvement and the self-monitored electrodermal parameter has been documented.

This observation is encouraging but incomplete because data regarding the period of decompensation are lacking.

The data in case no. 1, however, present a more comprehensive picture because they cover a complete phase of clinical transition that began during a symptomatic period and concluded in an asymptomatic phase.

There is a correlation between the values of the self-monitored electrodermal activity and the clinical condition. Both the parameters, in fact, were significantly modified after the first week of hospitalization. The measure of anxiety changed more slowly, while the trend followed of the other two parameters.

The observations regarding the fourth week are particularly interesting. In that period the patient experienced one of the best periods in recent years, going to visit a friend in another part of Sicily. The work carried out has furnished encouraging preliminary data. The most interesting conclusions can be summarized as follows.

The device developed and called *PsychoFeedback*, works perfectly and can be used without difficulty by schizophrenic patients during the period of clinical remission.

The monitoring of electrodermal activity seems to furnish reliable data regarding the condition of emotional activation and, therefore, the risk of relapse, and may, in fact, be a candidate to become an important "warning sign".

In the context of a psychotherapeutic and rehabilitative approach within the cognitive and complex orientation, psychotic patients are able to effect the self-monitoring of warning signs in a phase of relative clinical compensation.

This procedure can limit the risk of relapse and help the patient achieve an elevated sense of self-efficacy, that contributes to the process of self-evolution, which is part of the therapeutic and rehabilitative project.

This project will be complete when it is possible to produce, at low cost, the *PsychoFeedback* device in order to permit its widespread experimentation and diffusion.

3.4. *Psychophysiological Parameters of Expressed Emotion*

In our psychophysiology laboratory, I developed a procedure to assess familial interpersonal relationships, consisting of evaluating the electrodermal activity of the patient, in the absence and in the presence of relatives, in the course of a performance of self-control of arousal through biofeedback. I have called this procedure the *Family Strange Situation* (Scrimali, 2005b).

In the context of the *Family Strange Situation*, two trials are carried out according to the following modalities:

- *I Trial*
  - the patient receives a succinct description of the biofeedback dynamic;
  - the patient tries to lower the acoustic biofeedback relative to the SCL (5′);
  - the electrodermal measurements are recorded.
- *II Trial*
  - the procedure is repeated, as in the first trial, but with relatives present.

In this phase the directions are given.

- *To the patient:*
  - repeat what was done earlier, trying to reach the best result possible.

- *To the relatives:*
  - a brief explanation of what the patient is attempting to do (*your relative must try to lower the sound of the instrument*);
  - they receive specific directions: observe his/her performance (*if you wish, you may express comments*).

The trials are executed using the *MindLAB Set* device connected to a personal computer with the software *MindSCAN* by Psychotech (Psychotech, 2004).

- *After the trial*
  - the experimenters ask the relatives their opinion (positive or negative) of the performance of their family member.

Another interesting aspect regarding the use of psychophysiological techniques studied in our lab stems from the evaluation of arousal in the relatives of the schizophrenic patients.

The hypothesis appears plausible that relatives with a high emotional response are characterized by elevated levels of arousal, measurable through the recording of electrodermal activity.

An important variable regarding the relatives of the patients we studied was their behaviour during the test performance of the patient, which was monitored through video-recording.

Based on the study of the numerous tapes, we codified the behaviour of the relatives in the following way:

- *participatory behaviour:* when the relative interacts with the patient in terms of verbal communication (messages or comments) or behaviors (for example, hugs or physical contact, in general);
- *non-participatory behaviour:* when the relative does not interact in any way with the patient.

If the relative is classified as participatory, he or she can receive two diverse classifications:

- congruous behaviour (as regards the direction and the goal of the trial);

- incongruous behaviour (as regards the direction and the goal of the trial).

We define congruous behaviour as communication that favours the relaxation of the patient (for example, a positive comment, or bland encouragement).

Incongruous behaviour is behaviour during the trial that disturbs the performance of the patient, including being too close, or even exaggerated physical contact. Naturally, hostile or critical comments are considered part of incongruous behaviour.

Also the total absence of involvement in the trial by the relative, either ignoring the order to cooperate in the successful outcome of the trial, or placing oneself outside the visual field of the patient, are considered incongruous behaviors.

In the course of our research, ten schizophrenic patients were tested with an average age of 22.11 years (SD:±7.32). The family members involved were 23 in number.

The recording were effected within the fifth day of hospitalization in the Department of Psychiatry of the University of Catania, after having initiated treatment with thioridazine (on average 100 mg per day).

So that the relatives of the schizophrenic patients would be faced with a homogeneous sample (gender, age, culture), a control group was formed of volunteers recruited from the staff of the Institute of Clinical Psychiatric of the University of Catania.

To members of the control group, we administered the Middlesex Hospital Questionnaire (Crow, 1966) and monitored for SCL through the *MindLAB Set* device, connected to a microprocessor, using the *MindSCAN* software (Scrimali, 2005a).

The first data analyzed regarded a comparison of the results of the electrodermal parameter, during the test of self-control by the patient, first in the presence of the experimenter and, subsequently, in the presence of the relatives. In this case, statistically significant agreement was recorded between the increase in arousal and the presence of relatives with high expressed emotion.

A subsequent analysis regarded the behaviour of the relatives of the patient while the patient was being tested.

A statistically significant association between the high expressed emotion variable and the emission of "incongruous behaviour" during the patient's performance was also observed.

This information assumes considerable relevance from the point of view of pathogenesis of the critical exacerbations of schizophrenia.

In fact, the behaviour of the relatives, during the trial, might be indicative of their actual behaviour in real life, just as the increase in arousal of the patient might be in relation to vulnerability to stress.

Another aspect of the work, pertinent to the study of the electrodermal conductance in the relatives, was the observation that those with high expressed emotions showed statistically significant higher levels of conductance than those relatives with low expressed emotions. In this case, their values appear similar to those of the healthy control subjects.

This experimental experience, carried out in our laboratory, together with the development of the *MindLAB Set* and the software *MindSCAN*, permit the adoption of a routine psychophysiological and behavioural evaluation of schizophrenic patients and their relatives at the clinical level. This approach has been inserted into the assessment procedures of the Negative Entropy protocol.

3.5. Biofeedback

Biofeedback is probably one of the most interesting new therapeutic techniques to emerge in recent years.

The innovative power of this technique for psychotherapy hasn't yet been completely explored on the theoretical or epistemological level. In terms of practical application, however, the judicious use of this technique can constitute an efficacious and manageable instrument of change.

In the cognitive field, biofeedback has solicited many studies, reflections and applications (Meichenbaum, 1977; Lazarus, 1971; Scrimali & Grimaldi, 1982).

Even if for many years, it was believed impossible to use these techniques with schizophrenic patients, this prejudice has been disproved by the work of Breier and Strauss (1983).

These authors, developing the idea that some schizophrenic patients were able to or could learn to control some symptoms in the schizophrenic spectrum, described a self-control process articulated in three stages.

In the first stage, called self-monitoring, the patient begins to monitor psychotic symptoms.

In the second stage, self-evaluation, the patient learns to recognize the negative implications of the symptom on behaviour.

Once these symptoms have been identified and recognized as such, the third phase sees the enactment of the mechanisms of self-control.

The diminution of arousal can be considered a method to reduce the state of anxiety and, therefore, mitigate psychotic symptoms, including hallucinations.

To reduce anxiety, Breier and Strauss proposed training that aims to implement a greater or lesser degree of involvement in the activity.

Personally, I have accumulated a great deal of experience with the biofeedback of electrodermal activity, used with schizophrenic patients during the phase of clinical remission.

The control of arousal, through feedback, can become an important method to increase the sense of personal competence of the patient and permit him or her to progressively construct coping behaviour for some psychotic symptoms.

A specific technique, collocated in the context of biofeedback, that is widely used in the treatment of schizophrenic patients, is video-monitoring and video-feedback (Ellring, 1991; Grimaldi, Frasca & Scrimali, 1993).

In this case, the entire behaviour of the patient is monitored in different areas, including problem-solving, verbal and non-verbal communication, and social relations.

The possibility of monitoring behaviour and furnishing feedback to the patients, so they become aware of the dysfunctional patterns and can correct them, is a particularly interesting in schizophrenic psychosis because the abilities of conceptualization, self-observation, and meta-cognition in these patients are considerably impaired.

PART TWO

Entropy of Mind or Phrenentropy

CHAPTER THREE

Etiology and Pathogenesis

1. The Complex Biopsychosocial Model

The medical model, because of its success in the treatment and prophylaxis of numerous, especially, infectious diseases, has developed within an interpretive framework that has become progressively (and erroneously, in my opinion) generalized and dominant in contemporary biological and reductionistic medicine.

Regarding psychiatry, however, a complex approach to the etiology and pathogenesis of the different psychiatric disorders has been proposed (Perris, 1996).

According to this new orientation, these disorders and their symptoms, observed at the clinical level, are the final result of a complex chain of events that begins with the conception of the individual.

It is interesting to note that a genotype malfunction often does not emerge in the absence of specific environmental factors.

A classic example of this is the affliction called *phenylketonuria*, an illness that develops because of the impossibility of metabolizing the amino acid, phenylalanine.

If the subject affected by this serious genetic disorder does not ingest phenylalanine, the ailment will not appear and the alteration in the genome will go unexpressed, though will still be passed on to the offspring.

It is possible that some psychiatric ailments, conditioned by a certain psychobiological predisposition, will not show for the entire life cycle of an individual, even though a specific vulnerability is present.

In this case, it is useful to analyze eventual non-clinical markers, correlated to the psychobiological vulnerability in question.

When a family medical history is taken from patients with psychiatric pathologies, for instance, obsessive-compulsive disorder, it can happen that the rest of the family seems apparently untouched by the presence of this affliction.

If, however, certain behavioural, emotional, or cognitive markers are investigated, including: *a great love of order, rules, and cleanliness, as well as extreme moral rigor, and the presence of scarce affect*, these markers will systematically emerge as present in the ancestors and often in collaterals of the patient.

In this case, it can be hypothesized that these subjects were able, thanks to their abilities or to fortuitous factors, to maintain an ecological niche safe from specific stress that could have led to clinical decompensation.

Obviously, some biological gaps, conditioned by genotype, have a greater probability to emerge than others.

For example, agoraphobic behaviour can be maintained, with a certain ease, in a state of compensation for one's entire life. A niche is constructed that keeps innovation and change out, making all attempts at exploration unnecessary and improbable.

In schizophrenia today, the probability that a decompensation does not occur before adulthood is low. Creating an ecological niche adapted to a subject with such a vulnerability, a subject who needs a situation of low stress and low information input, seems highly improbable, given today's lifestyles.

For example, today there exists a certain *noxa* able to decompensate any individual afflicted by a biological vulnerability for schizophrenia, because of its enormous potential to transmit information. That *noxa* is television.

It is a common observation that one of the most frequent psychotic symptoms, i.e., being at the center of another person's interest, in negative and dangerous sense, emerges in the patient's relationship to this medium.

It is extremely frequent that patients who have experienced psychotic decompensation claim to have begun to feel acutely uncomfortable watching TV.

Even the early signs of an eventual relapse are identifiable in an altered rapport with this medium. This is a rapport that many patients, after psychotherapy, are able to identify.

In conclusion, in the patient who exhibits clinical decompensation, we see a critical episode characterized by a increase in the entropy. This constitutes a chaotic transition in the course of a long story, which was begun many years before: at the moment of meiosis, when the genetic patrimonies of the parents met to create a genotype.

We can hypothesis that in this genotype, specific factors of vulnerability are present, based on the non-optimal functioning of some gene systems.

During the period in the uterus, during gestation and during birth, the environmental *noxa* begin to act on this genotype, adding pre- and post-natal influences to the genetic factor.

Immediately after birth, and for a long time to come, the maturation, development and programming of the nervous system takes place, with the contemporaneous construction of the system of personal knowledge.

In this phase important elements, including parenting and environmental factors such as social, cultural, economic, and life events, occur.

This interaction between genotype and environment, lead to development of a specific brain organization and a system of personal knowledge, more or less vulnerable to certain situational factors.

Stressful events that interface, like a key in a lock, with the structure of the system of knowledge vulnerable, provoke a crisis that coincides with the condition of the illness, characterized by an increase in entropy in the mind of the patient and in the diminished capacity to elaborate information.

Therapeutic interventions that reduce the problematic interaction between psychic mechanisms and environmental *noxa* decrease the level of entropy and, therefore, the symptoms. If the level of stress, activated by the pathogens, goes below a certain level (different for every individual) the symptoms disappear. This is what happens, much of the time, in the course of treatment with medications.

Since, however, the system of knowledge remains afflicted by a gap in functioning that constitutes vulnerability, the crisis can re-present itself if the level of stress increases once again.

A similar model has not actually been corroborated by unequivocal experimental evidence for any psychiatric disorder, even if today's research seems promising.

For schizophrenia, the complex model, delineated above, has been amply studied and documented by a series of research experiments that tend to support it. But the proof is still not established.

In this chapter, I will summarize experimental evidence that seems to support the etiological and pathogenic complex model for schizophrenia. I also cite research that has been carried out at the Department of Psychiatry, University of Catania .

This model, though still immature, and needing further, more robust experimental confirmation, furnishes a series of important conceptual bases for the programming of scientifically founded, and experimentally documented, therapeutic and rehabilitative treatment. The cognitive approach, outlined in the third part of the book is based in this conceptual model.

In this model, the *noxa-pathogenesis* of schizophrenia constitutes a stochastic process, with a multi-factorial etiology and teleonomic outcome.

The complex biopsychosocial model takes into consideration the biological vulnerability factor based on genetics, and genotypic interaction with environmental factors. These are able to condition the construction of a system of idiosyncratic knowledge in each and every individual.

Among the environmental factors that influence the development of the brain and the system of knowledge, great relevance is given to parenting and to the social, cultural, and economic conditions in which life develops.

Acute decompensation seems to be activated by a series of life events able to move the level of stress above a certain threshold (which is rather low for the vulnerable subject).

Also, the course of the illness, once the apophany (a change with the first appearance of psychotic symptoms) occur, is deeply influenced by environmental determinants, including the social, economic, and cultural situation, as well as the emotional climate, of the family.

Understanding the etiology and pathogenesis of schizophrenia, just as in any illness, constitutes a key passage for the development of treatment protocols and effective prevention.

I have never been much of a fan of *ex iuvantibus* criteria, and I have always believed that every protocol must be backed by a robust rationale, based on falsifiable theories and experimental corroboration.

As Basaglia (1968) used to say, it does not seem wise to adopt therapeutic methods like electroshock—citing the excuse, *"Anyway, it works"*—without knowing the rationale for its use.

This is equal to saying that if the television loses its audio which, by pure chance, is restored with a punch to the box, then hitting the TV ought to constitute a rational practice for repairing the machine!

Such a comparison might seem exaggerated but, unfortunately, it's not.

In fact, in psychiatry it often happens that authors propose therapeutic methods that are not experimentally documented or fully supported by an articulated rationale.

What's worse is that some authors seem uninterested in furthering understanding of the mechanisms of action and the processes at work in the protocols they propose, because, as they say, *"Anyway, it works!"*

I'm not a fan of shortcuts, either. They often lead you astray.

My problem is to convince you, my readers, that the choice of a complex approach constitutes a valid option and is, therefore, worth plowing through this book, in order to master a series of heuristic and operative instruments, that have been integrated and experimentally verified, but destined, in a few years, to become obsolete (I will, in the meantime, have written other books).

If I have convinced you, move to the next section; if not, I suggest you go back to chapter one and wait two turns, not forgetting that I clearly declared my intentions on the cover, so no one can say you weren't warned!

2. *Biological Vulnerability*

The topic of vulnerability is important to psychiatric theory in both the etiological and clinical contexts.

In modern psychiatry, the first author to use the term vulnerability was probably Canstatt (Stanghellini, 2002).

He hypothesized that exaggerated vulnerability, leading a subject to react to environmental factors in excessive terms, could constitute a generic predisposition for developing psychiatric ailments.

In ancient times, Galeno already hypothesized that illness stemmed from the interaction of external factors with an individual, whose physical and psychic make-up made this interaction, in positive terms, impossible (Galeno, 1986).

The stoic notion of *proclivitas* seems particularly close to the actual conception of vulnerability.

Proclivitas is a type of diathesis that predisposes perturbing factors (*effectus*) to action. The interaction of *proclivitas* and *effectus* leads to *morbus. Aegrotatio inveterata*, the outcome of *morbus*, coincides with the actual concept of chronicity, or a return to pre-existent conditions. In this case, however, *proclivitas* remains as an unavoidable character trait, subject to resurgence (Riva, 1998).

One of the first neurophysiological models, elaborated specifically for schizophrenia, was proposed by Zubin and Spring (1977).

The key points of this model can be summarized in the following way.

Psychotic apophany occur when vulnerable subjects are exposed to perturbing factors that raise the level of stress above the individual threshold, which in this case is rather low.

These perturbing factors can be varied: some act from the outside, in psychological ways, e.g., stressful life events, a highly emotional family climate, or a negative social environment.

Others can be of a biochemical nature such as the chronic use of hallucinogenic substances.

A critical episode can occur, not only if perturbing factors are present that act on the vulnerable individual, but also if the positive modulating processes such as social support, family relations, and a flexible structure of the Self, are inadequate.

The episode concludes after exposure to the perturbing situation ends. It is then possible for the individual to return to a level of stress and arousal below the threshold for clinical decompensation.

The conclusion of the episode necessarily leaves its mark on emotional, cognitive, behavioural, and relational frameworks. The residual effect, in this way, determines a considerable impairment of the sense of self-efficacy and self-esteem, further increasing the vulnerability of the patient.

Nonetheless, if maintenance behaviors of psychological equilibrium, prior to the development of psychotic apophany, were sufficient, from a clinical point of view, we can talk of *healing*.

If the prior level of functioning was already problematic, homeostatic maintenance behaviors, subsequent to recovery, will also be precarious.

This observation assumes considerable relevance. In fact, if psychotic apophany appear in subjects whose level of pre-morbid functioning was not satisfactory, thus vulnerable, it is evident that the outcome of clinical decompensation, characterized by the permanence of negative factors, should not be understood as an evolution toward chronicity, but rather as a return to an already unfavourable pre-existing condition.

Zubin and Spring's (1977) model is critical of the concept of chronicity. According to Zubin and Spring (1977), schizophrenia is not characterized by the permanence (therefore, chronicity) of the clinical symptoms, but by the persistence of vulnerability.

Determining chronicity, therefore, depends on the inability to insure the patients' living conditions that keep them below a specific (unfortunately low) threshold of vulnerability to stress.

Based on this conceptualization, it is also evident that the development of rehabilitative and therapeutic techniques to improve coping capacities and problem solving abilities in the face of problematic situations and stressful events, can change the illness's course, in positive terms.

During the 1980s, in light of developments in the field of human information processing, a new interactive model of vulnerability to stress was elaborated by Neuchterlein and Dawson (1984).

In view of these new theories, advances in the psychophysiology of schizophrenia have assumed considerable importance.

This new framework, delineated by Neuchterlein and Dawson, is actually an elaboration of the theories by Zubin and Spring. This new work analyzes and describes, in more detail, the psychological, biological, and psychophysiological processes that can explain the modalities of interaction between stressors and the vulnerable individual.

Four principal characteristics of vulnerability are described in light of a biopsychosocial complexity. They regard psychic and biochemical processes, human information processing, and the psychophysiology of the autonomous central nervous system. These characteristics can be monitored and measured through specific techniques, in the context of a multidimensional approach.

The four factors of vulnerability described by Neuchterlein and Dawson are (1984):

- schizotypical personality traits;
- anomalies in responses of the central nervous system to informational input;
- reduced capacity to serially process information;
- dysfunction in dopamine cerebral systems.

Regarding these factors of vulnerability, favourable conditions of personal and social *protection* exist. The former include coping abilities and a sense of self-efficacy; the latter include good problem-solving abilities in the family and the possibility to have a supportive and tolerant network at one's disposal.

Environmental factors that interact negatively on the vulnerable individual are, however, a hypercritical, hostile, emotional climate within the family, characterized by emotional hyper-involvement or by a competitive and hostile social environment.

Based on vulnerability and the favourable or unfavourable modulating action of the factors described above, it is possible to register an increase in entropy in a system that nears, but does not supersede, the threshold correlated with a full-blown clinical decompensation and, therefore, with psychotic apophany.

In this way, a premonitory condition is established that is difficult to identify, but is characterized by specific patterns, including an overload of information processing systems, an increase in autonomous arousal, and a worsening of the elaboration and management of psychosocial stimuli.

This premonitory condition entails the presence of specific neuropsychological, psychophysiological, and autonomous warning signs, that can be monitored and quantified with specific assessment techniques.

I have already spoken about the use of biological parameters that function as state markers in schizophrenia.

This problem assumes considerable relevance in clinical practice, helping to monitor the condition of vulnerability and, therefore, reveals an eventual breaching of the threshold that would create conditions for a new decompensation.

Regarding biological vulnerability, new studies have focused attention on the possibility that schizophrenia might be tied to an alteration in the processes of neuronal apoptosis (Thompson, Vidal & Giedd, 2001).

The presence of a defective gene, in the neuronal cells, would induce biochemical anomalies, responsible for nervous cell dysfunction.

This would lead to the process of apoptosis, i.e., a progressive "wilting" and elimination of the dysfunctional neuron from the active neuron population.

While necrosis is pathological, due to external *noxa*, apoptosis is a substantially functional process, beneficial for the nervous system.

When the process of apoptosis is not adequately regulated, there is an anomalous loss of neurons, with accompanying dysfunctions.

This model is compatible with the temporal dynamic of the psychotic process, which remains hazy and merely "hinted at" in infancy, only to emerge in adolescence when the phenomenon of neuronal pruning is more active because of a new functional organization of the brain.

It is interesting to point out that biological vulnerability is one of the strong suits of the biological therapeutic approach to the treatment of schizophrenia.

Numerous authors consider that if schizophrenia were due to a degenerative biological process, because of genetic factors, it would be possible to cure or prevent the affliction by identifying the substances able to impede or control the expression of the anomalous gene.

Obviously things are neither so simple nor unequivocal.

In fact, the modulation of neuronal activity and the expression of eventual defects can be conditioned, not only by medication, but also by cognitive, behavioural, and relational measures.

The strengthening of cognitive processes, the maintenance of good relationships, and the continual promotion of adaptive behaviors seem to be equally promising, but without biochemical shortcuts or genetic manipulation, that are not only *not* yet available, but are still ethically debatable.

Studies in neuroimaging show that the realization of a cognitive-inspired psychotherapeutic program modifies the functional and organizational patterns of the cerebral cortex as much as the administration of psychoactive substances (Paquette, Levesque, Mensour, Leroux, Beaudoin, Bourgouin & Beauregard, 2003).

3. Genome

A consolidated trend in contemporary literature on schizophrenia points to the importance of genetic factors in the emergence of this disorder (Gottesman, 1991).

This position stems from observations that even if 80% of subjects who are closely related to schizophrenic patients, do not develop the disorder, there are data, derived from family studies, conducted over the last 70 years, that show the risk of this illness in relatives is much higher than in the general population.

In fact, if the presence of persons with schizophrenia in the whole population is about 1 %, data from the family studies show the following percentages (Weinberger, 2002):

- monozygotic twins: 48%;
- dizygotic twins: 17%;
- siblings: 9%;
- half-siblings (one relative in common): 6%;
- first cousins: 2%.

This prevalence demonstrates the considerable influence of genotype, given the clear correlation between an increase in genetic similarity and an increase in the risk of the disease. These facts suggest, however, that the genetic factor is not decisive.

In fact, monozygotic twins exhibit 100% genetic concordance, i.e., their genomes are identical, but only in 48% of the cases does schizophrenia appear in both twins.

The usual epidemiological approach to evaluate the weight of the genetic and environmental factors includes:

- family studies;
- twin studies;
- adoption studies.

The following is a brief summary of these types of studies.

Family Studies. The data presented above, relative to the presence of the illness in the families of patients with schizophrenia, are the result of the now classic literature review by Gottesman and Shields (1972) based on 40 studies carried out in Europe between 1920 and 1967. More recently, a very careful study by Kendler and Gruenberg (1982) has mostly confirmed Gottesman's findings.

Twin Studies. Twin studies represent one of the most useful methodologies in epidemiological research (Bulmer, 1970).

The logic behind twin studies is based on the presupposition that monozygotic twins have an identical genetic complement and are exposed to the same prenatal risk factors. Birth, as a stress factor, also generally assumes the same characteristics in twin births.

Dizygotic twins share 50% of the same genetic complement, while prenatal and birthing factors are similar. If schizophrenia were a disorder in which the determining factor were genetic, the rate of concordance would be 100% in monozygotic twins and 50% in dizygotic twins.

The rate of concordance indicates the percentage of homogeneous copies for schizophrenia in twin samples.

Imagine having identified a group of 20 schizophrenic patients, each with a monozygotic twin. If we evaluate the siblings' twins for psychosis, the number of these twins also with psychosis, referred to the total sample, and related to 100, gives us the percentage rate of concordance.

If all twenty twins in our hypothetical group were afflicted with schizophrenia, the concordance rate would be 100%, if there were only ten, the rate would be 50 percent.

Studies on the prevalence of schizophrenia in twins demonstrate that the genome has a role in determining schizophrenia, but it is not of absolute determination, which points to the importance of the environment (Fischer, 1971).

To evaluate environmental factors, adoption studies have been very useful in epidemiological research.

Adoption Studies. Studies of adopted children permit us to separately consider the impact of genetic and environmental factors.

It is always surprising to me how many authors correctly identify particular characteristics of parents, not only in schizophrenic patients, but also in those persons afflicted with other pathologies, only to reach the hurried conclusion that the casual factor in determining the illness is parenting, or disturbed modalities of communication, or, at any rate, psychological factors.

When a series of similarities, in the parents of the patients, is identified, the only affirmation that is legitimate is that there exists a "family factor" in determining the illness under study.

The transmission of the disorder and, therefore, of altered information to one's progeny, can occur through two diverse mechanisms; one is biological, occurring during meiosis, the other regards the transmission of emotions, beliefs, behavioural frameworks, and relational models that takes place during development.

The only research strategy valid for evaluating the weight of these two factors is that of adoption studies.

The first controlled study of this type was conducted by Heston (1966). The results of this study were confirmed by Kety, Rosenthal, Wender, Schulsinger, and Jacobsen (1978). The principal findings of these studies are summarized as follows:

- children, born to schizophrenic parent(s) and raised by normal parents, present a rate of schizophrenia equal to 32%. This is significantly different from adopted children born to normal parents, who have a schizophrenia rate of 1.8% (still much higher than the normal population);
- half-siblings, who have the same father as the schizophrenic patients, but were adopted into another family, show a rate of schizophrenia higher then an adopted half-sibling with a consanguine not affected by schizophrenia (the rates are, respectively, 13% and 2%). This specific result tends to exclude the importance of factors tied to pregnancy or birth, given the siblings have different mothers.

Essentially, a subject with a schizophrenic half-sibling, through the father, will have in the genome certain information able to condition a considerable vulnerability for schizophrenia. In this way, even if the child is adopted into a family with positive nurturance, the genetic inheritance will have more influence than in the general population and than in adopted half-siblings without schizophrenic relatives.

All things considered, it is possible to affirm that the genome does play and important role in determining schizophrenia.

Very recently, studies have begun to explain the mechanisms of genetic transmission and alterations in the genome that condition vulnerability for schizophrenia.

Given the actual state of the research, the tendency is to hypothesize that the biological cerebral mechanisms at the base of a vulnerability for schizophrenia are genetically determined through a polygenic modality with differentiated *loci,* rather than imputable to a single gene (Tsuang, Stone, & Faraone, 1998).

There is multiple experimental evidence in support of this hypothesis.

- the risk of developing schizophrenia is proportional to the number of schizophrenic ancestors present in the family tree;
- the risk of the illness grows with the increase of the seriousness of the syndrome which afflicted the ancestors;
- these observations are not in accordance with the classic Mendelian model of heredity. In fact, if schizophrenia were imputable to a single dominant gene, then 50% of the offspring of a single schizophrenic parent would show the disorder. Similarly, if schizophrenia were caused by a single recessive gene, all the progeny of two schizophrenic parents would have the disorder.

Epidemiological studies do not demonstrate this, but, in both cases, show much lower risks rates in developing the disorder.

Mechanisms of multi-factorial and polygenic determinism have been hypothesized, and some authors have identified a limited number of loci (about 10), while others have posited a greater number (up to 100).

The multi-factorial, polygenic, threshold model was proposed for the first time in the 1960s by Gottesman and Shields (1972).

Regarding the identification of the location of the gene cluster responsible for the expression of vulnerability, research has recently been carried out indicating the mechanism of so-called linkage. Even if this research is still in the early stages, attention of the researchers has focused on chromosomes 3, 22, 6, and 8.

These studies will probably furnish more exhaustive information in the next few years, thanks to the rapid progress being made in the study of the human genome.

An important element that stems from present understanding of multi-genetic and multi-factorial determinism of schizophrenia, and is of great heuristic and practical importance, is the so-called "schizophrenic spectrum".

The concept of the schizophrenic spectrum was introduced by Kety et al., in 1978, following the observation that the biological children of schizophrenic mothers, adopted into normal families, not only had a greater incidence of schizophrenia, but also a greater incidence of schizotypical personality traits, as compared to controls (Kety, Rosenthal, Wender, Schulsinger & Jacobsen, 1978).

The schizophrenic spectrum comprises a series of disturbances correlated to schizophrenia, but with differences from the traditional clinical description of schizophrenia.

Among these afflictions, personality disorders in cluster *A* and the schizo-affective disorders are particularly important.

The disorders of the schizophrenic spectrum are significantly more prevalent in the family members of schizophrenic patients, than in the general population (Gottesman, 1991).

This data relates to the genetic model of the transmission of schizophrenia, described above, as multifactorial and polygenic.

The number of the genes inherited would determine a greater or lesser genetic vulnerability along the spectrum. A very low vulnerability means that traits are only barely evident in the personality structure. An increasing level of vulnerability conditions the possible appearance of personality disturbances and schizophrenia.

This has led to the suspicion that the same genetic constellation predisposes, not only the full-blown illness, but also a group of character traits that do not get to the point of manifesting themselves as actual schizophrenia.

The concept of the schizophrenic spectrum as a series of variations of the same genetically-conditioned disorder has been broadened to include schizotypal, schizoid, and paranoid disorders, as well as other disorders with psychotic symptoms that are not classifiable as schizophrenia or as an affective disorder (Lowing, Minsky & Pereira, 1983).

The schizophrenic spectrum model is useful in psychopathology for describing disorders that do not have the typical characteristics of schizophrenia, even if they are connected.

The principal problem is that the validity of the spectrum model, even if theoretically interesting, has not yet been proven.

The schizophrenic spectrum model is actually based primarily on clinical experience and still requires genetic, neurophysiological, biochemical, and psychometric evidence as a means of confirmation.

Until now, the attempt to identify particular characteristics of cerebral functioning in children "at genetic risk for schizophrenia" has provided interesting results, but is still short of convincing.

A series of specific aspects have been identified in children at risk for schizophrenia (Remschmidt, 2001), which are summarized in the following list:

- cognitive disorders:
  - alteration in test performance on measures of abstract thought;
  - reduction in IQ test scores;
- perception:
  - documented deficits in the ability to organize visual information;
- neuropsychological disorders:
  - poor performance on tests of visual attention;
  - reduced capacity to discriminate stimuli;
- working memory:
  - appears reduced;
- language:
  - poverty of speech;
  - poor coherence in the development of narrative;
- behavioural traits:
  - greater tendency towards social isolation;
  - higher than the average scores for aggressiveness;

- "soft" neurological signs:
  - difficulties in visual-auditory integration;
  - reduced motor coordination capacity;
  - reduced orientation;
  - perceptive dysfunction;
  - difficulty in reading;
- evoked electroencephalographic potentials:
  - increase latency variability;
  - reduction in amplitude of the initial negative and final positive components.

The following is a description of the hypothetical history of a subject who, beginning with biological vulnerability, develops a schizotypical personality, prone to schizophrenia, and subsequently experiences psychotic apophany.

- From birth to 2½ years old:
  - delay in acquisition and development of language and a persistent qualitative deficit in speech;
  - delay in motor development, e.g., in ambulation;
  - gap in fine motor coordination.
- From 2½ to 6 years old:
  - problems with language;
  - poor scholastic performance;
  - frequent, persistent daydreaming;
  - hyperactivity;
  - impulsiveness;
  - difficulty concentrating;
  - extreme changeability in mood;
  - inappropriate tendency to physically grasp onto adults;
  - sudden, unexplainable outbursts of anger.
- From 6 to 8 years old:
  - slight disorder in logical thought;
  - emotions are frequently inappropriate.
- From 9 to 11 years old:
  - hallucinations may appear;
  - delusions may appear.

- From 12 to 18 years old:
  - poor scholastic performance;
  - difficulty socializing with peers;
  - considerable relationship difficulty with parents;
  - difficulty in communication and relationships in general.

Along with Liria Grimaldi, at the Department of Psychiatry, University of Catania, I have personally conducted experimental research comparing patients with schizophrenia and patients with cluster *A* personality disorders (Scrimali & Grimaldi, 1998).

We investigated biological aspects of the ailment, monitoring a series of psychophysiological parameters tied to human information processing abilities, including evoked potentials tied to the event and the discrimination of noise signals. We also assessed parenting by administering the *Parental Bonding Instrument* to the patients (Parker, Johnston & Hayward, 1988).

Comparison with a control group of patients was also carried out.

The results of the research can be summarized as follows.

Common features are found in the schizophrenic patients and patients with cluster *A* personality disorders.

Both types of patients showed a deterioration of information processing abilities, which was more accentuated in the schizophrenic patients.

Parenting seemed to play an important role as parenting scores were lower in the schizophrenic group as compared to the cluster *A* personality disorder group.

These data suggest that biological vulnerability is present in patients of both groups, even if at different levels of malfunctioning (greater in the schizophrenic patients). The characteristics of parenting are important factors in determining one or the other pathology.

Recently, a series of neuro-imaging studies on adolescents with schizophrenia, has permitted the reconstruction of morpho-structural alterations in the brain that might be responsible for the gap which was just discussed (Thompson, Vidal & Giedd, 2001).

These images show a 10% loss of superior cortical material, localized in the frontal and temporal regions of the brain that are involved in crucial cerebral functions, including memory, acoustic perception, and attention.

4. *Prenatal, Perinatal and Gender-Related Factors*

The hypothesis that schizophrenia is provoked by factors that act during gestation and birth has been the object of theoretical and epidemiological research.

Researchers have also focused attention on the impact of gender on the difference in prevalence of the disorder, at different times in the life cycle.

One fact that has impressed researchers is that schizophrenics have a rate of birth in winter or early spring that is statistically higher than in the other months of the year (Hare, 1988). In reality, this higher birth rate during winter and early spring pertains to the general population as well, even though among schizophrenic patients the tendency is considerably greater.

The seasonal trend for births of schizophrenic patients is very similar to that of patients with other grave pathologies of the central nervous system, such as mental retardation.

Hypotheses have been formulated to explain this epidemiological observation.

The first hypothesis is related to family-relatedness in schizophrenia or, more broadly, on the schizophrenic spectrum, assuming that the parents of the patients also suffered from some form of the disorder.

Since babies born in winter were conceived during the summer, when social and sexual relationships are easier and more frequent, it has been assumed that schizophrenics will more often produce children conceived in the summer (and born in winter) who will have a vulnerability for schizophrenia.

A series of studies, however, has examined the birth dates of schizophrenic patients without finding any statistically significant difference when compared to the distribution of births in the normal population (Wynne, Singer, 1965).

Even if these studies involved only small samples, they do not support the hypothesis that the cluster of schizophrenics born more frequently in winter, has something to do with heredity.

Also, as I explained earlier, heredity for schizophrenia, though important, is not the determining element in the emergence of the illness.

At the end of the 1980s, another hypothesis was formulated suggesting that the winter and early spring birth rate for schizophrenics could be correlated to the flu epidemics that are particularly frequent in these months (McNeil & Kaij, 1978).

Recent research, however, has reassessed this position. Today the idea that infection during gestation by the flu virus (especially the A strain), is a causal factor in schizophrenia, receives very little support.

Another line of research has hypothesized that schizophrenia may be related to slight cerebral damage occurring during gestation or birth (Cantor-Graae, McNeil, Rickler, Sjoström, Rawling & Higgins, 1994).

This hypothesis has been related to the previous belief that males exhibit a higher rate of schizophrenia than females. Since males show a higher level of cerebral damage during gestation and birth, it has been suggested that these two facts are related.

Today, however, we know that schizophrenia does not show a significant difference in prevalence according to gender. If we look at the life cycle we see that women simply tend to develop the disorder later in life (Wynne & Cromwell, 1978).

In conclusion the state of research does not support the conclusion that prenatal and perinatal factors, either infective, metabolic, or traumatic, are at the base of the etiological and pathogenic mechanisms of schizophrenia.

5. *Parenting*

The theory of attachment is particularly important in the context of the *Entropy of Mind* and the *Negative Entropy* models. As we will see, I have conducted experimental research to study the role of parenting in determining the organization of the mind prone to entropy.

Beginning with the classic studies of Mary Ainsworth, attention has been focused on the modalities of attachment exhibited by children, in order to describe a relationship between these attachment modalities and pathologies developed later in life (Ainsworth, 1989; Ainsworth, Blehar, Waters & Wall, 1978).

Based on the biological vulnerability described, a negative social environment and a dysfunctional nurturing dynamic could lead to the development of problematic emotional, cognitive, and communicative behaviors.

These include chronic hyper-arousal, difficulty about separating noise from signals in informational patterns, qualitative and quantitative deficiency in one's social skills and behavioural repertoire.

Contrarily, a positive family environment and a favourable psychosocial situation constitute protective factors.

Among the numerous theories that have tried to explain the etiology of psychotic disorders such as schizophrenia, those that affirm the family's fundamental role in the patient's condition have long had an important place in psychoanalysis.

Frieda Fromm-Reichmann (1950) was the most important exponent of this position in psychoanalytic circles in the mid-twentieth century. She argued that the style of parental nurturance, in particular, that of the mother, was the principal etiological factor in the genesis of schizophrenia.

The first studies carried out were focused on the characteristics of the mother-child relationship.

In a small percentage of schizophrenic patients, Levy (1931) described a pattern conditioned by "maternal hyper-protection" and by a series of behaviors (excessive contact, prolonged infantile attitude, impeding independent behaviour, control and excessive power) which he felt contributed to the development of mental disorders.

Many efforts were made to identify similar patterns in the families of schizophrenics.

The concept of the "schizophrenogenic mother" was thus derived and, needless to say, was one of the most deleterious products of these efforts.

Despert (1938) analyzed the stories of 29 children, aged 7-13, with disorders along the schizophrenic spectrum. He observed that approximately 50% of the mothers in these stories were described as aggressive, excessively anxious, too solicitous, and were considered the "dominant parent", while the father was portrayed as weak, immature, calm, passive, and inadequate in his role within the family.

Kasanin, Knight, and Sage (1934) identified *hyper-protection* as the principal characteristic of relationships in 60% of the 45 cases they considered. They were, however, among the first to suggest the possible interactive participation of the child in the process of hyper-protection.

A study conducted by Reichard and Tillman (1950) was based on information gathered from 13 patients, in which they identified three categories of parents.

The first category included mothers who clearly manifested a rejection of their children and threatened their children's self-confidence with constant reprimands and shows of disapproval.

The second category was for mothers who hid their sense of rejection. They behaved in an oppressive and sadistically hostile way; they concealed their sentiments behind hyper-protective behaviour, impeding their children from becoming independent. This category, according to the authors, represented the most frequent relational typology in schizophrenia.

The third category regarded the figure of the "schizophrenogenic" father: oppressive, sadistic, and openly expressing rejection.

Despite the numerous descriptions from the mid 20th century literature regarding the behaviour of mothers and schizophrenic subjects, it is evident that psychoanalysts have tended to use brutal and stigmatizing language and an uncritical generalization, based on experience with only a few patients.

Arieti (1969), for example, coined the expression *monstrous being* to describe the mothers of schizophrenic patients. Rosen described these mothers as dominated by a *perverse sense of maternity* (Reichard & Tillman, 1950).

Besides the inopportune use of such brutal terminology, the lack of interest in why these "perverse" mother acted the way they did regarding their children, is surprising.

Rosenthal et al., conducted interesting research in 1975 on adopted children in order to evaluate how much of a role hereditary factors and nurturing style played in the appearance of psychopathological disorders in children (Rosenthal, Wender, Kety, Schulsinger, Welner & Rieder, 1975).

The study included 258 subjects, divided into four principal groups:

1. adopted subjects with a natural parent with a schizophrenic or manic-depressive disorder, and who gave up the child for adoption in the first months of life;

2. persons adopted in the first months of life, but whose natural parents did not suffer from psychiatric disorders;

3. persons who did not have natural parents with schizophrenic or manic-depressive disorders but were adopted and raised by persons with such disorders;

4. persons who were not adopted but had a schizophrenic or manic-depressive parent and were raised in the house of their parents for at least the first 15 years of life.

At the conclusion of the research, the authors affirmed that there was no difference in the quality of the parent-child relationship in the first two groups. On the contrary, however, the third and fourth groups both showed a worsening in the parent-child relationship when compared with the first two groups.

Regarding the psychopathological disorders in the "genetic" group (groups 1 and 4), these appeared significantly more often than in the "non-genetic" group (groups 2 and 3).

The results obtained seem to confirm that the style of nurturance and hereditary factors favour the development of psychopathological disorders. Among the two factors considered, however—genetics or parenting—the role of parents seems to exert less of an influence.

Heilbrun (1973) pointed out that the behaviour of persons who develop schizophrenia is governed by the same laws that regulate normal behaviour. This is based on the premise that all normal or abnormal behaviors can be explained by the same principles, and this has important implications for the study of the development of schizophrenia.

Heilbrun was aware of the impact of other interactive variables, such as genetics, that could contribute to schizophrenia or to an effective change in behaviour. In his studies, he said that the maternal educative attitude is not tied to genetic causes but, rather, to social influences that theoretically could depend on schizophrenic behaviors of individuals with any type of genetic complement.

The instrument used to evaluate the level of maternal control was the PARI (*Parent Attitude Research Instrument*). The *Parent-Child Interaction Rating Scales* was used to evaluate maternal nurturing capacity.

The author noted that subjects with a background of "aversive behaviour" in the mother, manifested an impairment of their cognitive faculties. Moreover, subjects with "high-control/low–nurturance", were inhibited in their capacity to take the initiative. They also reacted excessively to criticism.

The author determined two styles of adaptation to the aversive behaviour of the mother: one, the "closed style" was characterized by shy behaviour, to protect oneself from negative maternal stimulation; the other, the "open style" looked to the social environment as a source of approval.

Essentially, with the open style, children seem to use relational modalities in order to attract positive attention denied by the mother. The children's relational behaviour, however, did not function effectively to obtain the rewards necessary to increase self-esteem.

The danger that the open style behavioural pattern will deteriorate into a schizophrenic reaction is tied to those events that can be interpreted by the person as a sign of failure or a threat to safety.

Recently, there has been renewed interest in the role of parental nurturing in the different psychiatric illness, including schizophrenia, even if there is no longer a focus on a single cause to explain the appearance of the disorders.

Parker and his collaborators, in particular, reported data gathered with the questionnaire *Parental Bonding Instrument* (Parker, Johnston & Hayward, 1988).

The results of this study demonstrate that patients did not consider either parent to be particularly kind and, significantly, they considered their fathers to be more protective.

Parker noted that the experience of a bad style of parental nurturing was correlated with the first time a patient was hospitalized and with the high risk of relapse after being released.

Khalil and Stark (1992) used EMBU (Egna Minnen Betràffande Uppfostran) to evaluate the first memories of nurturing they received during their childhood in 53 patients diagnosed with schizophrenia.

The schizophrenic patients of both sexes judged the experience of rejection by their parents as high and the expressed affective warmth as low. Khalil notes that low nurturance influenced the age at the first hospitalization and the level of anxiety the patients manifested.

Subsequent work (Orhagen, 1992; Bebbington, 1993) supports the hypothesis that a high level of expressed emotion, i.e., a high level of emotional involvement on the part of relatives and the degree of criticism expressed by "key figures", would be predictive of a relapse or a new hospitalization for the schizophrenic patient.

Some years ago, together with Liria Grimaldi and Antonio De Masi, I carried out an experimental study on parenting in schizophrenic patients using some questionnaires we developed and administered to both patients and their parents (Grimaldi, Scrimali & De Masi, 1996).

The research involved a sample of families of schizophrenic subjects compared with families of neurotic subjects and families of subjects not affected by psychic pathologies. A questionnaire was administered separately to the patient (or control subject), to the mother, and to the father.

The period under consideration was from infancy to adolescence.

The sample consisted of eleven schizophrenic patients (diagnosed according to the criteria of the DSM-IV-R), eleven neurotics, and twenty controls—all of similar age and cultural background.

The three questionnaires were identical, except for the questionnaire administered to the mother in which the first three items concerned feelings during pregnancy.

All the items were presented so they referred exclusively to the personal experience of each individual tested.

The questionnaire was formulated to obtain information on the behavioural repertoire of parenting, on the ability of the parents to understand the motives for the difficulty of the child, on the self-image of the child, and on the idea that parents have about their child.

Themes concerning exploratory behaviour and the ability to understand and control emotions also were analyzed.

The last items of the questionnaire investigated the propensity to elaborate fantastic ideas and the characteristics of the feed-forward.

The first element of note, that emerged from the data, was that the statistically significant differences only occurred in the comparison between the psychotics and the controls. The neurotic group scores were at an intermediate level.

In the psychotics, the experience of nurturance was judged poor and inadequate.

Self-image in schizophrenic patients during infancy, childhood, and adolescence appeared confused and only rarely positive.

Memories of intense and disturbing emotions were described by these subjects and they were not able to formulate any type of critical evaluation.

Interaction with the maternal figure was generally poor.

During the period of development, psychotic subjects already demonstrated an explicit mode of thought which attributed logical causation to arbitrary events.

The mothers of psychotic subjects described their children as restless, exhibiting considerable difficulty in exploring the environment.

The children were remembered as closed to the outside world and characterized by limited interaction with the mother.

The behavioural repertoire of nurturing was described by the mothers themselves as inadequate.

Also, some mothers of the psychotic group had trouble describing the characteristics of their children at an early age.

The fathers of the psychotics lacked involvement in the nurturing of their children, which was demonstrated by the frequent absence of answers in their questionnaires.

The families members of the psychotics also responded to the questions in a manner that shows strong discord in the family.

In recent years, some new studies have appeared in the international literature on parenting in schizophrenia.

One study by Perris (1994) reached that conclusion that a negative experience in parenting undoubtedly constitutes an important factor contributing to determining a psychobiological vulnerability to schizophrenia.

Nonetheless, today there still does not exist sufficient experimental evidence that can unequivocally demonstrate the negative influence of dysfunctional parenting on the appearance of schizophrenia.

The scope of another study carried out by my group at the Department of Psychiatry at the University of Catania was to experimentally investigate if it was possible to document the elevated presence of dysfunctional nurturance in a sample of schizophrenic patients (Scrimali, Grimaldi, Cultrera & Russo, 1998).

An experimental group was created composed of schizophrenic patients diagnosed according to the DMS-IV (American Psychological Association, 1994).

These patients, hospitalized at the Department of Psychiatry of the University of Catania, were studied after they reached a sufficient state of clinical compensation.

The group was composed of 40 patients (25 males and 15 females, average age: 38.45 SD 12.8) diagnosed according to the following criteria: undifferentiated schizophrenia: 15; paranoid schizophrenia: 13; schizoaffective disorder: 8; residual schizophrenia: 4.

A control group composed of medical students was formed (19 males and 21 females, average age: 23.26, SD 1.61) to test the hypothesis that patterns of dysfunctional nurturing in schizophrenic patients are significantly more common then in a sample of healthy subjects,

We also included another control group of patients with other psychiatric pathologies, including: 4 with panic attacks; 3 with agoraphobia; 10 with generalized anxiety; 4 with obsessive-compulsive disorders; 2 with eating disorders; 17 with mood disorders (major depression: 14; dysthymia: 3). The group was composed of 19 males and 21 females, with an average age of 41.75 SD 14.5.

The *Parental Bonding Instrument* (Parker, Johnston & Hayward, 1988) was used to evaluate the parenting experienced. The Italian version by Grimaldi and Scrimali (2001) is validated for an Italian sample and used at the Department of Psychiatry at the University of Catania.

Parenting, evaluated as functional or dysfunctional, was significantly different between the patients and the controls for both the mothers and fathers.

Significant differences did not emerge between psychotics and patients with other pathologies.

Subsequently, a comparison of the three typologies of dysfunctional parenting in the three groups was carried out.

In this case there was a significant difference among patients and controls regarding mothers, but not among schizophrenics and patients with other pathologies.

For the fathers there was a significant difference between schizophrenics and subjects with other types of psychopathology. In the fathers of psychotics group the "absence of ties" was most common, while in the other psychopathology group the most common clusters were "control with affect" and "absence of ties".

The results emerging from the research show that the schizophrenic patients experienced higher rates of dysfunctional parenting on the part of both mothers and fathers than did the control group subjects.

This observation is also valid for many other pathologies, as our other control group showed.

I can, therefore, conclude, in light of the research carried out by our group, that parenting cannot be considered a definitive factor in schizophrenia.

An interesting line of reflection and research has been developed by Jeri Doane beginning in the 1970s. She analyzed the relational patterns in the families of schizophrenic patients in terms of attachment theory and studies on expressed emotion (Doane, 1978).

In particular, Doane, West, Goldstein, Rodick and Jones, (1981). investigated how much high expressed emotion of family members influenced their behaviour towards the patients, and how family members communicated such emotions to the patients

Doane (1978) developed a method of measurement called *affective style*.

Affective style can be considered a transactional measurement that evaluates the level of criticism, intrusiveness, or guilt-inducing behaviour that parents exercised over the patient during a highly emotional family discussion. This method of measurement classified the families as "AS benign" or "AS malignant".

Despite the many points of contact between expressed emotion and affective style, there are important differences.

Affective style, unlike expressed emotion, does not directly measure emotional hyper-involvement, but differentiates the types of criticism.

Studies that have used affective style as a method for the evaluation of family member interaction have demonstrated that this measure constitutes a good predictive factor for relapse in schizophrenic patients (Doane & Diamond, 1995).

These results have led some researchers to investigate relational behaviors that constitute affective style and personality traits of parents that feed the negative attitudes at the base of expressed emotion.

Mary Dozier and colleagues (Dozier, Stovall & Albus, 1999) observed that adults with serious psychic disorders tended to have parents evaluated as hyper-involved.

More specifically, subjects from hyper-involved families have more probability of using disturbed attachment strategies.

From these results, it is possible to deduce the importance of the type of attachment in the emergence and prognosis of psychiatric disorders.

Not only do the classifications of attachment in infancy and adolescence place an individual at risk for developing a psychotic pathology, but also the intra-familial patterns of attachment among adults and their internal representations can constitute a risk factor for relapse (Parker, Johnston & Hayward, 1988).

In recent years, the interest of researchers studying the communicative process and its alterations in schizophrenic patients, has turned to the analysis of dyadic interaction during development.

A particularly interesting study in this regard was conducted by Haack-Dees (2001). The aim of the study was to look for specific markers in non-verbal affective behaviour of schizophrenic adolescents and their parents and to explore whether there was a specific relationship between facial expression and the level of expressed emotion.

Particular attention was placed on the identification of positive patterns of affective regulation in contrast to maladaptive patterns.

In order to assess these patterns, 10 minutes of discussion between young schizophrenics and their parents were recorded. Discussions of a control group of healthy subjects and their parents were also recorded.

The index of expressed emotion of each parent was evaluated using the *Five Minute Speech Sample* (Magana, Goldstein, Falloon & Doane, 1985).

The emotional facial behaviour was described using Eckman's (1993) system of facial coding.

Additional information was evaluated including visual contact and para-verbal behaviour.

Detailed analysis of facial behaviour revealed, specific styles of dyadic emotional regulation for the different groups.

One surprising result was that the parents of schizophrenic patients were different from parents of healthy subjects in a clearer and more obvious way than were the patients from the healthy subjects.

Greater interactive distance was observed in the facial affect during the discussions between adolescent schizophrenics and their parents than in the discussions between healthy subjects and their parents.

Both the schizophrenics and their parents showed a reduction in the comprehensive frequency of facial activity and in the frequency of affective expression.

The facial expression of positive emotions (smiles and laughter) were substantially reduced, and the facial activity of the schizophrenics seemed to be dominated by negative emotions. A more balanced relationship between positive and negative emotions was observed in healthy adolescents.

Regarding the interaction between facial and para-verbal behaviour and visual contact in the schizophrenic group and their parents, a style that tended to maintain a strong emotional distance was observed.

The modest level of synchronized reactions of expressed facial emotion indicated a certain dulling of affect. The facial activity of the parents of schizophrenics with high expressed emotion was variable and, therefore, more active than the parents with low expressed emotion.

The parents of schizophrenics with high expressed emotion showed fewer negative facial emotions but higher verbal expression of negative emotions than parents with low expressed emotion, as always happens in conditions of high expressed emotion.

In the adolescent patient-parent dyad, characterized by emotional hyper-involvement and criticism, specific patterns of para-verbal behaviour, visual contact, and facial synchronization were found.

These patterns indicate a deficit of expression of hostile emotions in the dyad with high expressed emotion for hyper-involvement of parents and a gap in the expression of positive emotions in the dyad with high expressed emotion for criticism.

The research showed a fundamental difference in emotional communication between schizophrenic adolescents and their parents when compared to healthy teen parent dyads.

The dyadic pattern of emotional regulation varied with the index of expressed emotion of the parents. In each group a diverse organization of maladapted and protective communicative behaviour was observed.

In summary these findings support the great importance of parenting in determining the development of schizophrenia and influencing its course.

Controlled experimental research, carried out in recent years, has reassessed the preponderant role that was attributed in the past to the parental relationship in the development of schizophrenia.

There is no doubt, however, that parenting strongly modulates the expression of the genotype, profoundly influencing the development and organization of the central nervous system and, therefore, the processes of the mind.

To summarize the data available today from the literature and from the work of our group, it is possible to affirm the following statement.

Patients afflicted with schizophrenia have, more often than not, received dysfunctional parenting.

Such parenting is characterized by high levels of control and by an excessive emotional involvement, especially on the part of the mother.

Verbal and non-verbal patterns of communication and the relational processes are frequently dysfunctional. This prevents the patient from developing the skills associated with Machiavellian intelligence.

The nuclear family is characterized by poor social relationships.

The dominant belief systems in these families are based on diffidence, fear, and a sense of danger due to an expectation of negative events that could appear, even in magical and mysterious ways. These family belief systems frequently include:

- superstitious beliefs;
- external control;
- low self-efficacy;
- belief in harm by others;
- poor social relationships;
- tendency to use deceit and mystification as a relational instrument within the family;
- low cooperation;
- a vision of existence based on conflict and competition..

Vulnerable children are closed into themselves, speak little, and show inadequate relational patterns.

These children are often unreasonably afraid of strangers and show marked avoidance expressed with excessive and disorganized behaviour; they show frequent and sudden explosions of anger.

From a neuropsychological point of view, they appear easily distractible and do not adequately plan behavioural strategies.

The lack of well-defined relational boundaries makes the institution and harmonious development of the *self/non-self* dynamic difficult.

The presence of multiple and dysfunctional nurturing behaviors produces models of the self and of reality that are equally multiple and contradictory, interfering with the development of adequate meta-cognitive competences.

The cognitive processes tied to self-efficacy malfunction and contribute to maintaining a low and problematic self-esteem.

During adolescence the vulnerable subject shows evident difficulty in establishing romantic attachments.

The ability to initiate and maintain intimate relationships appears deficient and the delusions experienced will further compromise an already problematic self-esteem.

The mnemonic and cognitive deficits become accentuated as the terrible apophany approaches.

6. *Social, Cultural and Economic Factors*

The hypothesis that schizophrenia is a disease provoked by conditions of social hardship began take root at the end of the 1930s after the publication of the now classic study in Chicago by Faris and Dunham (1939).

These authors studied admissions to a psychiatric hospital, carefully analyzing in what areas of the city the patients lived.

They found a much higher prevalence of schizophrenic patients coming from the poorest, run-down areas of Chicago rather than from the residential neighborhoods, home to the well-off.

Other research focusing on the social stratification of the population, and not geographical location, confirmed the findings of Faris and Dunham.

Dividing the social classes into groups, we see the presence of schizophrenic subjects is three times higher in the lowest group, than in the highest group.

From these studies the *sociogenic* hypothesis was elaborated in which the negative conditions of gestation and birth and subsequent bad nurturing of the child, together with numerous and painful life events tied to poverty, are considered to be the basis of the etiology of schizophrenia.

Years later, however, other research has proven this hypothesis false.

As noted above, the identification of statistically significant clusters does not unequivocally corroborate a theory, but rather permits the elaboration of a set of theoretical possibilities. This simply means that further research must be conducted to choose which theories are more strongly supported by the data.

Often a program of research is conducted by a researcher who is motivated ideologically and trying to corroborate a particular theory because his or her professional career is tied to it.

In this case, the presence of unusually high clusters of schizophrenic patients in the poorer classes was interpreted as proof that social hardship was the sole cause of schizophrenia.

It seems, however, that schizophrenia is the most democratic and egalitarian of illnesses because it afflicts people of all social classes, races, cultures, and probably historical epochs, equally.

Schizophrenia is not an illness of some people, but it is the illness *par excellence* of *homo sapiens,* the dark side of our wonderful self-conscious mind.

So, if schizophrenia identically afflicts all social classes, why did Faris and Dunham identify the clusters discussed above?

The answer becomes clear in a subsequent study by Goldberg and Morrison (1963).

These authors studied the social position of fathers, uncles, grandfathers, and brothers of schizophrenic patients and found that they were uniformly distributed throughout the various social classes.

A new theory was developed based on these findings to explain the Faris and Dunham's data. This new theory was called *social drift* and it held that schizophrenic patients are born in all social classes but, subsequently, because of the cognitive, emotional, relational, and behavioural problems that accompany the illness, they tend to progressively slide down to the lowest levels of the social spectrum.

The consequence is particularly dramatic in a country like the USA which lacks a social safety net and is characterized by an climate of extreme competitiveness.

In these conditions, schizophrenic patients find it impossible to maintain the family's lifestyle and tend to migrate down the social ladder, reaching a condition of homelessness, and maybe a bench in Central Park.

A beautiful exemplification of social drift in New York is the well-narrated and magnificently photographed film, *The Fisher King*.

The two protagonists, before Entropy of Mind destroyed their lives, are a university professor (played by Robin Williams) and a famous radio personality (played by Jeff Bridges), who are filmed in gorgeous apartments and luxurious restaurants. After the apophany of the mental illness (schizophrenic psychosis for the first, and alcoholism for the second), one becomes homeless and the other lives in a poor neighborhood of New York.

The whole episode concludes symbolically in Central Park, the place of choice of many of the "Big Apple's" homeless.

In conclusion, today economic and social stress constitute a trigger for psychotic apophany and can be determinants of more serious manifestations of the illness, rather than its cause.

Recently, it should be noted that some authors have again taken up the idea of a possible *socio-genesis* of schizophrenia (Stanghellini, 2002).

The arguments of these authors are based on the differences in the incidence of psychosis in urban and rural settings.

Even though this is a position that is receiving attention in the literature, it should be noted that the differences observed regard not the prevalence, but incidence of the disorder, thus not the real presence of the biological problem in the population, but its manifestation and diagnosis. This may be related to the fact that in urban areas, as I have often pointed out, not only is the course of schizophrenia more serious, but the patient is also more likely to come to the attention of psychiatric services.

7. Life Events and Clinical Decompensation

Psychotic apophany, or a new crisis that interrupts a period of remission, can occur because of the arrival of precipitating factors that are either biological, such as drug use, especially hallucinogenics or stimulants, or psychosocial.

Experimental evidence suggests that repeated and significant changes in the social *milieu* of a subject vulnerable to schizophrenia, like excessive, stressful solicitation, can provoke acute decompensation (Dohrenwend, Shrout, Link & Skodol, 1987).

Even if there is agreement in the literature regarding the increase in ambient stress as an important cause of clinical relapse, there does not yet exist unequivocal experimental support for this conclusion.

Retrospective and comparative control group research has been carried out to try and demonstrate the role of stressful events in triggering psychotic crises.

The hypothesis being examined is whether clinical decompensation is preceded by a cluster of critical events, and if similar events in non-vulnerable subjects provoke particular pathological conditions.

One of the first controlled studies on the effects of life events in schizophrenia was carried out by Brown, Birley, and Wing (1972).

These authors identified a significant increase in a series of powerfully emotional life events in the three weeks before clinical decompensation.

A World Health Organization study has furnished interesting epidemiological data regarding this topic with data from nine areas around the world (World Health Organization, 1979).

The results of this research are important, even though no control group was used. The study examined 386 cases and the criteria for identifying a critical episode were carefully defined in well-structured and standardized terms, as were the chronological factors. The time period under consideration was the three months before the crisis.

Since the research in question did not include a control group, a comparison between the period preceding the crisis and one of equal length during the phase of well-being was conducted.

A greater frequency of stressful events was found in the six month period preceding the crisis, but a particularly important cluster of events occurred in the three weeks before the clinical decompensation occurred.

In conclusion, it is possible to affirm that research data corroborates the clinical evidence that stressful life events are capable of provoking an acute crisis in vulnerable subjects.

This lends credence to the complex biopsychosocial model of the etiology and pathogenesis of schizophrenia which assumes an enormous relevance for the planning of therapeutic and rehabilitative treatment of this affliction.

8. Environmental Factors and Illness Course

I have already pointed out that social and economic factors do not constitute, in themselves, an etiological factor crucial for development of schizophrenia, contrary to what was believed for many years.

It is still important, however, for the development of therapeutic and rehabilitative projects, to ask in what measure these factors are able to influence both the psychotic apophany and the course of the disorder.

Richard Warner (1974) conducted a literature review on just such a topic, examining 85 studies on the course of schizophrenia in Europe, Japan, and the USA, carried out from 1904 until publication of the article.

One of the conclusions reached by Warner was that economic factors are closely tied to the course of the illness and its final outcome.

In particular, one fact that assumes great relevance for therapy is unemployment.

Warner, in fact, was able to show a clear and significant association between rates of unemployment and the worsening of the illness course, through his careful analysis of the literature.

The effect of unemployment appears particularly evident, in light of data on the course of schizophrenia during the global economic depression between 1929-1940. In this period, with unemployment rates high, the percentage of positive outcomes for schizophrenia was particularly low.

On the contrary, if we consider the 1941-1955 period, characterized by a very low rate of unemployment despite the catastrophic event of the Second World War, it is possible to observe the best percentages of positive clinical outcomes in the century.

It is important to note that the use of neuroleptics had not been introduced in this last period, thus this improvement in the course of the disorder cannot be attributed to new medicines.

Other important factors that influence the course of schizophrenia are family and social support.

Some experimental data demonstrate the positive role played by the family in maintaining improved living conditions and, therefore, a less stressful situation for the patient.

Hare's (1988) Bristol study demonstrates that the phenomenon of social drift toward the poorer classes is prevalent for patients who do not have family support.

Strong social support is more widespread in less developed countries than in industrialized ones, and in small towns compared to large metropolises.

A good method for studying the eventual influence of social factors on the course of schizophrenia is through comparison of the course of the disorder in different parts of the world and in different environmental settings (e.g., urban or rural) of the same country.

Two important studies conducted by World Health Organization address these questions. The *World Health Organization Pilot Study of Schizophrenia* and the *World Health Organization Ten-Country Study* (Jablensky, Sartorius, Ernberg, Anker, Korten, Cooper, Fay & Bertelsen, 1992; World Health Organization, 1979). The conclusions reached by these studies were unequivocal: in developing countries, schizophrenia has a better course and prognosis than in developed countries.

The better prognosis is correlated to the presence of social support and lower levels of stress in everyday life. There is also less chance of social drift and less stigma attached to the illness in underdeveloped or developing countries.

For example, the authors of the World Health Organization study report that schizophrenic patients in Cali, Columbia had a particularly positive illness course which was linked to the level of tolerance and acceptance that relatives and friends expressed toward psychotic patients and their symptoms.

On the contrary, stigma felt toward a psychotic patient in developed countries is very high.

This factor is quite important in treatment protocols that involve family members of the schizophrenic patient, since these relatives also suffer the social stigma attached to the disease.

When the patient lives in an extended family (many relatives living together in the same household) as is typical in developing countries, the family provides greater support to the psychotic patient and the risks tied to the progressive development of hostility and criticism are reduced.

In this way, the family burden, associated with the presence of a schizophrenic relative is divided among many persons, lessening the stress and hyper-involvement of each individual.

Research has also documented a better prognosis for schizophrenia in women than in men (Salokangas, 1983; World Health Organization, 1979).

This improved prognosis has been associated with the fact that women with schizophrenia are more often married than are men with the same diagnosis. This may be explained by the fact that the illness manifests itself in women at a later age.

Because marriage offers possible support from a spouse, this support improves the prognosis of schizophrenic patient.

In industrialized countries, social and familial support for the schizophrenic patient are low, while the level of stigma, on the contrary, is very high.

The sociologist, Scheff (1966), has pointed out that, when a society attributes stigma to the role of the psychiatric patients, these patients will embark on a career of chronic mental illness.

Some experimental support exists regarding this observation.

Derek Philips' (1966) study concerning the behaviour of inhabitants of a city in New England analyzed the problem of stigma.

The research demonstrated that when a person, possessing all the attributes of an ideal average citizen, spoke of having suffered from mental problems in the past, he or she was discriminated against more than actual schizophrenic patients who exhibited behavioural problems, but who kept their condition of mental illness hidden.

In a famous study by Rosenhan (1984), a group of volunteers went to a psychiatric hospital pretending to have hallucinations. All were hospitalized and even though, in a few days, they resumed behaving normally, saying they no longer were having hallucinations, they were diagnosed with schizophrenia.

The hospital staff described the conduct of the pseudo-patients on the ward as clearly pathological; no one was released in less than a week, and one was kept for two months.

These results demonstrate that the beliefs of the physicians can themselves determine the prognosis and clinical course of schizophrenia.

In my experience, I have continually observed the positive role of social support and how this support is greater in small, not overly-developed towns, than in the large urban areas with life styles and rhythms typical of a metropolis.

In fact, my professional activity is divided between the large city of Catania and the small town of Enna.

Two anecdotes I would like to cite seem particularly pertinent.

The first regards the endemic difficulties my colleagues, responsible for the residential rehabilitative facilities, have encountered in trying to find places to locate therapeutic facilities such as group housing.

Systematically, neighborhood groups undertake action to block the establishment of these facilities, or to have them removed, if they already exist.

The difficulties are enormous in a big city like Catania, but there is much less resistance in small towns like Caltagirone, which is on the cutting edge in terms of intermediate facilities.

I would like to narrate an episode that illustrates this situation.

An elderly lady made an appointment to see me in my Enna office.

As soon as she met me she said the appointment wasn't for her but for an unfortunate soul suffering from schizophrenia. The fellow was living in a condition of social isolation and indigence in an unhealthy hovel in a poor neighborhood of Enna.

The women of the parish became interested in the fate of this man and wanted my help; so the enterprising woman asked me what she could do for him.

I said immediately that there was much that could be done, and the first step of a therapeutic strategy would be for me to meet the patient for an initial evaluation and, if necessary, begin the therapeutic and rehabilitative protocol including a brief period of hospitalization at the Department of Psychiatry of the University of Catania. The goal was to effect a complete evaluation of the physical and psychological condition of the patient and develop the appropriate therapeutic and rehabilitative strategy.

The woman enthusiastically approved and made arrangements to accompany the fellow to an appointment.

At the end of our meeting, the woman turned to the secretary to pay for the visit, adding that all the neighbors of the patient made small donations to create a fund to pay for his medical expenses.

Moved by this lesson in civility and the true Christian spirit of this community from little Enna, I decided to forgo my usual fee. I told the woman that I also wanted donate something to the therapy and rehabilitation of this patient, so I decided I would treat him for free.

The episode didn't end there. The following Sunday a beautiful cake was delivered to me with an Old Testament verse from the Bible inscribed on it: *The honour of one's name is worth more than any amount of riches!*

The patient subsequently followed the therapeutic and rehabilitative protocol of *Negative Entropy.*

Today he is well and has reached a good level of functioning and an almost complete social rehabilitation, in that he is able to maintain an autonomous and positive life style. He continues to see me in my office for monthly monitoring, while his neighbors occasionally check in to let me know of any problems.

Warner has traced the modalities through which stigma can negatively influence the course of schizophrenia to the theory of cognitive dissonance (Festinger, 1957).

According to this theory, individuals perform different mental operations to reduce the level of dissonance in their own belief systems because this dissonance is a cause of emotional discomfort.

If a person receives a stigmatizing diagnosis, this will create a dissonance with beliefs related to self-esteem.

In an effort to reduce dissonance and distress, the patient will tend to refute the diagnosis or assume behaviors that lead them to social isolation so as not to be further exposed to stigma. But in this way the deviant behaviour is accentuated.

This emerges with great frequency in clinical experience.

"Am I crazy?" ask the schizophrenic patients insistently when drug therapy is proposed. In this way an anguished alternative is created: accept the treatment and hospitalization or return to the stigmatized typology of being crazy.

To not undergo the treatment means to try and escape the fate being crazy.

But to not be aware of the illness and refuse treatment constitutes one of the clinical conditions which we label "crazy" and can create the premise for obligatory hospitalization.

Another illuminating example of the influence of stigma on the behaviour of patients and their family members is to be had by spending a morning as the receiving physician in the reception of two departments: Neurology and Psychiatry, as happens to me (unfortunately) a few times a month. The patient and family members arrive and ask that the patient be hospitalized in the Department of Neurology. As the physician, I explain that this decision does not constitute the beginning of a medical evaluation, but the end.

After having conducted the exam and diagnosing, for instance, depression, I propose hospitalization in the Department of Psychiatry.

Immediately the complaints and recriminations of the patient and family members begin (we are, after all, Sicilians and notoriously inclined to noisy theatricality).

"What, on the Psych ward? Do you think I'm crazy? I want to be in the neurological unit, I'm not setting foot in that crazy bin… You must be kidding!"

A certain amount of the stigma is also automatically transferred from the illness and the patient to the psychiatrist. In this context, there is an actual scale to stigmatization.
For example:

- medium-low level stigma: the psychologist;
- medium level stigma: the neurologist;
- high level stigma: the psychiatrist.

This, in my case, created a mini-tragedy in my family when my parents discovered that I wanted to become a psychiatrist; they had always dreamed of a heart specialist or surgeon in the family. They even begged me to at least choose neurology!

But back to the problem of stigma and its influence on the course of schizophrenia. Experimental evidence shows that accepting the diagnosis, which is already stigmatizing, constitutes a factor that can produce a negative prognosis (Sartorius, 2000).

The schizophrenic condition provokes a reduction in social contacts and the progressive isolation of schizophrenic patients; this fact is more marked in developed than in developing countries (Warner, 1985).

To conclude, it seem rather obvious that once psychotic apophany occurs, the course of the illness and the positive outcome of the therapeutic program cannot be separated from social factors.

CHAPTER FOUR

Psychopathology

1. Introduction

Psychopathology is a fundamental aspect of the study of all psychiatric disorders.

If clinical psychology describes the phenomenal aspects of diverse psychiatric problems, psychopathology aims to identify the mechanisms that underlie the dysfunctions.

Regarding schizophrenia, however, we are a long way from an exhaustive psychopathological explanation.

One particularly weak area is clinical cognitive theory because most people working in the field have only recently begun to be interested in this illness. Their approach, prevalently pragmatic, is aimed at therapy and rehabilitation instead of understanding the psychopathological mechanisms of the disorder.

The identification of the dynamics that produce the clinical symptoms of a disorder is closely tied to understanding the psychological mechanisms which govern the various psychological functions. These functions should then be linked, using a complex perspective, to the biological functions of the brain.

The attempt to formulate a psychopathological, cognitive and complex model of schizophrenia is an objective that begins with the identification of the dysfunctional cerebral processes which contribute to the development of the clinical situation.

The goal is to develop a heuristic that acts as a bridge between what *appears* (clinical phenomenology) and what *happens* (the biological processes of the brain and the psychological processes of the mind).

This heuristic still does not exist except in very preliminary formulations and the scientific data available does not yet appear sufficient to elaborate anything sufficient to describe schizophrenia.

In the rest of this chapter I will try to develop, even if still in a preliminary form, a psychopathology of schizophrenia inspired by constructivism and informed by the logic of complex systems.

I will begin with the clinical symptoms whose phenomenal aspects can most likely be traced to the alteration of the processes of the mind and the activity of the brain delineated in the preceding chapters.

According to for the DSM-IV-TR (American Psychological Association, 1994) schizophrenia is characterized by the presence of a cluster of signs and symptoms that must be present over a reasonable length of time (at least six months) and lead to significant impairment of function.

The characteristic symptoms listed in DSM-IV-TR are:

- delusions;
- hallucinations;
- disorganized speech;
- grossly disorganized or catatonic behaviour;
- negative symptoms, i.e., flattening of affect, alogia, and abulia.

The ICD-10 (World Health Organization, 1992) on the other hand, specifies the crucial aspects of schizophrenia are ascribable to alterations in the ideational and perceptive processes as well as the deterioration of the emotional dynamic.

The ICD-10 also notes how one of the most characteristic aspects of schizophrenia must be identified in the impairment of the sense of individuality, of uniqueness, and of the capacity to indisputably manage one's own psychological life.

As we will see later, the conceptualization of the psychopathology of schizophrenia, that I have developed and defined *Entropy of Mind*, is very close to that proposed by the World Health Organization.

Towards the conceptualization of the psychopathology of schizophrenia that I am formulating in this chapter, I will propose a different list of symptoms re-ordering and integrating the various seminal aspects of the disorder. In accordance with the multi-level processes of knowing, presented in the first part of the book, the schizophrenic symptoms can be outlined as follows.

- Symptoms related to perception:
  - hallucinations.
- Symptoms related to explicit knowledge:
  - delusions;
  - deterioration of cognitive functions:
    - memory;
    - attention;
    - learning;
    - recognition of faces and facial expressions;
    - planning strategy;
    - impairment of meta-cognition.
- Symptoms related to the sphere of Machiavellian intelligence:
  - disturbance of language and communication;
  - impairment of social skills;
- Symptoms related to the procedural sphere:
  - executive functions;
  - motor capacity.
- Symptoms related to the emotional sphere:
  - psychotic anxiety;
  - flattening of affect.
- Symptoms related to neuropsychological variables:
  - impairment of attention, memory, and concentration.

As it is easy to note, there are some differences between this formulation and the diagnostic criteria for schizophrenia listed by the DSM-IV.

For instance, regarding symptoms related to the impairment of the cognitive sphere, besides delusions listed by the DSM-IV-TR, I have included topics from the cognitive literature such as meta-cognitive disorders and the deterioration of cognitive functions. These include memory, attention, learning skills, recognition of faces and facial expressions, planning strategies, and meta-cognition.

Among the symptoms relative to the sphere of Machiavellian intelligence, I have included not only speech disorders, but also social skills impairment, which overlaps with the criterion labeled *social/work dysfunction* in the DSM-IV (American Psychological Association, 2000).

According to the DSM-IV, the diagnosis of schizophrenia cannot be made on the basis of clinical description alone. Some non-seminal criterion must be met, including the social/work dysfunction (disability criterion) and the length of the clinical episode (anamnestic criterion).

I have already pointed out that all the symptoms, including criterion *A* of the DSM-IV, do not seem to be pathognomonic to this disorder.

In this way, a neo-Kraepelinian approach is utilized, defining a disorder not by the clinical description, but by complications (social/work dysfunction) and chronological evolution (the length of the critical phases).

The limits of the Kraepelinian vision already appeared evident in the work of Eugene Bleuler who tried to define the disorder identified by Kraeplein as *dementia praecox*, based on the fundamental psychopathological mechanisms specific to the disorder and to the related symptoms. He coined a new term, schizophrenia, a reference to the schism present in the psychological functioning of the mind of the schizophrenic patient (Bleuler, 1950).

I believe that Bleuler's position is the best because of its attempt to delineate a complex description of schizophrenia.

Bleuler formulated the hypothesis that a primitive, fundamental disorder was present in this ailment, ascribable to the loss of coordination of the different psychological functions. It was not yet possible, however, to describe the neurophysiological and biological dynamics behind the affection.

Even though today similar goals are still not entirely attainable, it should be noted that we are getting closer.

My conceptualization of the schizophrenic condition, which is the basis of the *Entropy of Mind* model, can be summarized in the hypothesis that schizophrenia is a disorder based on psychopathological mechanisms traceable to an alteration in the functioning of the diverse typologies of the activity of knowing described in the first part of the book. These include the impairment of the mechanisms of memory and the presence of dysfunctional coalitional processes linked to an etiological, multi-factorial, and complex dynamic.

Within the context of this meta-theory, I believe that the clinical and nosological approaches must include identifying the idiosyncratic elements of the disorder in question.

I have already mentioned how none of the symptoms described in the DSM-IV-TR can be considered pathognomonic.

Based on the observation of hundreds of schizophrenic patients diagnosed according to the criteria suggested by the DSM and evaluated in terms of both social and occupational skills and episode length, I have elaborated the following position which might be called neo-Bleulerian.

I believe that a *specific clinical condition* exists definable as schizophrenia, or to use the neologism I have coined, *Phrenentropy,* recognizable in the DSM-IV, or better, the ICD-10 criteria.

I also think that some symptoms linked to specific cerebral mechanisms are absolutely pathognomonic to this condition and when they are present, make a diagnosis possible.

These symptoms are ascribable to what I want to define, echoing Beck (1979), as the *constructivist triad of schizophrenia* and include the following:

- impairment of personal identity;
- alteration of the sense of uniqueness and continuity of the self;
- rupture of personal narrative.

Before illustrating my theory of the psychopathological processes of schizophrenia, a brief summary of cognitive contributions to the psychopathology of the disorder might be useful.

The first attempts to elaborate psychopathological models of schizophrenia began with human information processing in the 1960s when McGhie and Chapman (1961), using the now classic theory of Broadbent's filter (Broadbent, 1958), hypothesized that a deficit in this mechanism is at the base of cognitive dysfunctions in schizophrenic patients.

A series of more systematic studies and research regarding cognitive approaches to schizophrenia began in the 1970s.

In that period, researchers in information theory became interested in schizophrenia in the attempt to apply this new model of human information processing to the disorder (Shiffrin & Schneider, 1977).

Over the decade, many studies were carried out to evaluate aspects of the various information processing activities in schizophrenic patients. Attention was focused on both the unconscious and automatic parallel processes as well as on the intentional and conscious serial processes.

Koh, (1978) a researcher from Chicago, argued that schizophrenic patients use inadequate strategies for processing and elaborating information before the information is memorized.

According to Hemsley (1977), the fundamental problem of schizophrenia is abnormal perceptive experiences, with delusions deriving from the attempt to rationalize these experiences.

Gray and others have tried to formulate a neuropsychological model of Hemsley's theory. They hypothesized that the conflict between what is expected, based on past experience, and stimuli coming from the individual's internal and external environment occurs because of the interaction in the subiculum between the "central monitor", located in the hippocampus septum system, and the "behavioural control system" which includes the caudate and the accumbens nucleus. In schizophrenia an interruption in the connection between the subiculum and the accumbens may determine the defective integration of stimuli coming from the individual's internal and external environments and the memory of prior experience (Gray, Feldon, Rawlins, Hemsley & Smith, 1991).

The neuro-anatomical model Weinberger, Berman and Zec, (1986) differs from Gray's model in the localization of lesions within the relative circuits. Based on neuro-histological evidence, Weinberger has, in fact, proposed that the lesion are located in the entorhinal cortex.

Elkhonon Goldberg (2001) has suggested that the dysfunction, linked to frontal sub-cortical circuits, primarily involves the left hemisphere; and this could, reconcile the hypotheses of Gray and Weinberger with theories of schizophrenia based on an anomaly in hemispheric lateralization according to Goldberg.

The Hemsley and Gray model only considers positive symptomatology and presumes negative symptoms to be epiphenomena.

Both models hypothesize that anomalies in the processes of hemispheric lateralization are at the base of schizophrenia.

According to Nasrallah (1982) although the two cerebral hemispheres exchange a continual flow of information they have separate spheres of knowing integrated in a single self.

In schizophrenic patients the integration between the two hemispheres may be impaired, leading to the loss of the unity of consciousness. Thus, the left hemisphere might perceive information coming from the right side of the brain as from an external source.

This mechanism would explain the conviction that thoughts, sentiments, or intentions are either imposed by "external forces" (input from the right hemisphere is the source of the experience of being influenced, of passivity, and of thought insertion), or come from the outside (output from the left hemisphere to the right).

The ambivalence and incongruence of affect, often present in schizophrenia, is the result of a poorly integrated state of consciousness. The formal thought disorder is due to the emergence of a modality of thought typical of the right hemisphere.

Evidence produced by neurophysiological, neuropsychological, and neuro-anatomical studies supports the hypothesis of functional impairment of the left hemisphere which may be the result or the cause of an inappropriate functional prevalence of the right hemisphere.

Frith and Done (1989) maintain that two modalities of behavioural control exist. The first is based on "willed intentions", i.e., on self-generated plans; the second is "stimulus driven", tied to the external contingencies of the individual.

In schizophrenia, a fundamental deficit in the use of the first control modality, i.e., a deficit in the production or monitoring of intentional action, exists.

This would explain the presence of perseverance, stereotypes, and slowness in patients in which negative symptoms are prevalent.

In this case, positive symptoms are traceable to the non-recognition of the intentionality of acts guided by the system of "willed intentions". The cognitive deficit, then, is represented by the incapacity of internal monitoring of self-generated actions.

The disorganized symptoms (including affective incongruence and incoherent language) are due to the prevalence of the "stimulus driven" behavioural modality because of a deficit in its inhibitory processes.

According to Frith and Done, the negative symptoms of schizophrenia derive from a dysfunction in the connections between the system that is comprised of the prefrontal lateral cortex, the supplemental motor area, and the anterior part of the cingulum and striate cortex.

The same dysfunction may be at the base of stereotyped perseverance and inappropriate behaviors in subjects with verbal incoherence and affective incongruence who are incapable of inhibiting *stimulus*-driven responses. The authors also maintain that a less serious disorder in the same circuit leads to a deficit in the monitoring of intentional behaviour and is thus responsible for the positive symptoms.

Frith (1992), using the so-called "theory of the mind", further developed his model which focused the ability to explain the behaviors of the self and others based on inferring intentions or, more generically, mental states.

Hallucinations constituted by voices that speak in the third person come from the attribution to others of one's own inferences regarding their mental states. For example, if I think that my interlocutor is criticizing me, this thought assumes the characteristics of a strange voice that is insulting me.

Patients with negative symptoms might be afflicted by a serious deficit in the ability to represent and know their own mental states.

From the neuropsychological point of view, the functions that underlie the theory of the mind depend on vast cortical-limbic circuits.

In particular, the areas that seem to be implicated include the frontal orbital regions (which are involved in the capacity to entertain social relationships), the amygdala (involved in the recognition and elaboration of emotions), and the superior temporal area (involved in the recognition of faces).

The representation of the intentions of the self and others is carried out in a circuit that consists of the caudate and the frontal and supplemental motor areas.

Schizophrenia may be conceptualized as a syndrome of disconnection between the prefrontal regions and specific cortical areas, whose interaction requires complex frontal sub-cortical circuits.

In the model proposed by Edelman (1992), schizophrenia is considered to be a disorder of consciousness, in a Jamesian sense, i.e., an integrative process characterized by individuality, intentionality, and unity.

According to Edelman, the morphogenesis of the brain is not predefined by a genetic program but represents an epigenetic process that is developed during the course of the lifetime of an individual through the selection of neuronal groups ("neuronal Darwinism").

In this theory the initial phases of ontogenesis—the so-called "primary repertory"—is activated through the processes of cell division and migration and the development of redundant and meta-stable neuronal connections. These are not unequivocally specified in the genetic program and are different, even in homozygous twins.

Over the life span of an individual, the neuronal connections undergo a process of remodeling which gives rise, through synaptic selection, to the so-called "secondary repertory".

In Edelman's theory, all the mental functions, from perceptual categorization to higher order consciousness, are emergent properties of the activity of the so-called "global maps", or ample neuronal populations, selected by experience and correlated through the reentry circuits.

Categorization is an emergent property, as demonstrated in the robot, Darwin III, which consists of a rich network of connections (neural network) and is endowed with an eye and an arm (with sensory and motor functions).

In human beings the value circuits in charge of maintaining basilar homeostatic functions are represented by the centers of the encephalic trunk, the hypothalamus, and the autonomous centers, while the neuronal network for perception and movement is constituted by the specific primary cortexes.

The value circuits and the sensory and motor maps are connected by a reentry circuit located in the hippocampus, in the amygdala, and in the septum; when value circuit activity and the maps are concomitant (correlated), the reentry circuit promotes experiential synaptic selection.

Moreover, in humans an associative memory system of the correlations between the perceptive categories and value systems (conceptual memories) is developed; this system is located in the frontal, temporal, and parietal associative cortex.

Primary consciousness is an emergent property of the reentry circuits that connect the systems of conceptual memory and those of perceptual categorization.

Higher order consciousness (secondary consciousness) develops in an inter-subjective context with the establishment of symbolic communication and the construction of the self.

In the Edelman model, therefore, consciousness is seen as a property or emergent function that involves extensive neuronal connectivity.

Consciousness is also structurally heterogeneous since it emerges from the interaction of many levels of integration (perceptive, conceptual, and symbolic categorization).

Secondary consciousness is closely tied to the construction, in an inter-subjective context, of a symbolic model of the self. As such, secondary consciousness requires not only the epigenetic development of individual neuronal circuits, but also a personal history of affective interactions with meaningful others.

In this model schizophrenic syndromes are conceptualized as a pathology of reentry. This may be caused by an alteration in the maps or in their reentry connections at any point, and as a consequence of any mechanism (from neurotransmitter alteration, to neuronal loss, to precocious attachment disorders).

For example, an alteration in the reentry circuits between the areas for language and the centers for conceptual categorization and/or the cortical appendages that preside over temporal order would explain formal positive thought disorders. Whereas the lack of synchronization in the reentry between the phases that execute perceptual categorization can induce confusion in perceptive anticipation and perceptive input. This would result in the attribution to the outside of internal events (anticipation of a critical comment can be perceived as a critical voice coming from the outside).

At the end of the 1970s, Frith (1979) formulated an hypothesis that the symptomatology of schizophrenia was referable to an alteration in the mechanisms of awareness of the peripheral processes of information processing, with an excessive increase in the symptoms.

According to this English author, in the schizophrenic patient a series of unconscious activities are monitored by the active control of consciousness.

Auditory hallucinations, according to Frith's initial elaborations, are the result of listening to sub-vocalizations that usually accompany ideational activity.

Furthermore, Frith maintained that when a person hears a sound, this information pattern becomes the object of a series of elaboration processes that normally do not draw on consciousness. In this case, psychotic patients become aware of these cognitive processes which then give rise to hallucinatory phenomena.

This author has continued to study the neuropsychology of schizophrenia, publishing a 1992 monograph entitled, *The Cognitive Neuropsychology of Schizophrenia,* that still constitutes an important contribution to the cognitive approach to the psychopathology of the disorder (Frith, 1992).

Frith is convinced that the symptomatology of schizophrenia derives from a specific cerebral dysfunction whose mechanisms he has tried to identify and describe through experimental research.

According to Frith, the most important cerebral dysfunction in schizophrenic patients is ascribable to a deficit in the processes which govern the representations of mental activity.

Schizophrenic patients are not able to attribute a self to their own intentions and, because of this, feel controlled from the outside.

The altered processes are located, for Frith, between the prefrontal and temporal cortex.

Another particularly interesting aspect of this 1970s cognitive-inspired research was the attempt to corroborate theories about dysfunction in human information processing with data from research in psychophysiology and neuroscience.

At the beginning of the 1980s, Callaway and Naghdi (1986), two researchers from San Francisco, proposed an articulated model of the psychopathology of schizophrenia influenced by human information processing and corroborated by much experimental psychophysiological data.

The authors described two typologies of information processing. The first was constituted by automatic processes, actuated in a parallel modality, while the second consisted of serial activity, controlled consciously.

According to Callaway and Naghdi, the processes of serial elaboration are altered in schizophrenic patients, while the parallel functions worked normally or at levels even higher than the norm.

A series of experimental data was presented to support this theory, including an analysis of reaction time, a study of the blockage of cerebral *alpha* rhythms, and the registration of evoked electroencephalographic potentials.

The work of Callaway and Naghdi influenced my own theoretical reflection and experimental research in the 80s, leading me to develop a constructivist model of the mind. This model is based on hemispheric specialization, on the functional differentiation in analogue and digital modules, and on a psychopathological model of the schizophrenic condition, and focuses on an alteration in patterns of functional hemispheric coherence.

In the 80s, a group of researchers from Los Angeles, most notably Nuechterlein and Dawson (1984), also began to elaborate another model of the psychopathology of schizophrenia using human information processing.

Starting with the hypothesis that there would be a reduction of attentive resources and information processing in schizophrenic patients, they tried to identify and describe the characteristics of this type of disorder.

In this way, they identified at least two specific characteristics of the cognitive activity of schizophrenic patients: a deficit in the most elementary components of information processing, and a deficit in the mechanisms of memory, with a particular reference to working memory which oversees the acquisition and systematization of perceptual data.

This latter aspect has been evidenced through a test to discriminate noise signals that requires the active participation of working memory. This anomaly might render understandable the tendency of the schizophrenic patient to focus attention on often irrelevant details instead of paying attention to contextual data.

In the years between the 1960s and 1980s, there was considerable interest, even from the non-cognitive circles, in the dysfunctions of thought activity studied from a cognitive perspective.

I am referring to the important work of Silvano Arieti (1978), who elaborated an interpretation of schizophrenia that, along with the classic drive mechanisms of the psychodynamic approach, gave ample attention to the cognition of schizophrenics.

Much of Arieti's work, which is evolutionary in its perspective, can be included in the cognitive approach to schizophrenia.

The principle of teleological regression, the theme of paleological thought, and the problematic of teleological causality, just to cite a few key aspects of Arieti's work, seem particularly interesting to me and have attracted my attention since the 1980s.

If, in the 1970s, the systematic interest of cognitive researchers in dysfunctional mental processes the underlie schizophrenic symptoms was manifested for the first time, we would still have to wait until the 1980s for Carlo Perris's cognitive elaboration (after many years of work with schizophrenic patients in Sweden) of a precise clinical proposal.

In 1989, the monograph, *Cognitive Therapy with Schizophrenic Patients*—a milestone in the cognitive approach to schizophrenia—was presented at Oxford during the World Congress of Behavioral and Cognitive Therapy (Perris, 1989).

Perris's proposal proved comprehensible, innovative, and coherent. A heuristic framework was clearly delineated that brought the etiology of schizophrenia closer to a complex model, beginning with biological vulnerability and taking into account life events and patterns of nurturance. Considerable emphasis was given to attachment theory and to dysfunctional mechanisms in the patterns of nurturance experienced by schizophrenic patients.

In an equally clear and coherent manner, he described the dysfunctional dynamic that governs the information processing with reference to both emotion and cognition. For the next ten years, Perris continued to study the mechanisms through which negative modalities of nurturance interacting with a biological vulnerability lead to the typical emotional and cognitive dysfunctions of schizophrenia.

In the 1990s, there was an intensification of research in schizophrenia on the part of English cognitive psychotherapists represented by the work of Kingdon and Turkington (1994), Garety, Kuipers and Fowler (1994); Fowler, Garety, Birchwood and Tarrier (1992), Wykes, Parr and Landau (1999), Chadwick, Birchwood and Trower (1996) and others.

In Europe, considerable attention was given to the proposals of Falloon (1985), in the therapeutic field, and to Liberman (1994) in rehabilitation.

The cognitive approach to therapy in schizophrenia, excepting the better articulated and complex conceptualization of Perris, comes from classic rationalist cognitive therapy, with particular reference to sensory functioning of the mind.

Recently, Aaron T. Beck has manifested a considerable interest in schizophrenia, publishing, together with Rector, a number of articles on the argument (Beck & Rector, 2000, 2003, 2004).

The heuristic frame of reference is Beckian, with a significant emphasis on the well-known mechanisms described by the author from Philadelphia including arbitrary inference, selective abstraction, excessive generalization, etc…

The role of emotions and the processes of tacit knowledge in the determination of the psychopathology of schizophrenia have still not been thoroughly studied.

In the area of etiology, the role of nurturance and attachment has not been adequately taken into consideration.

The approach proposed is merely psychological, informed by the conception of human information processing, without reference to the biological aspects of cerebral functioning.

Research carried out by my group at the Department of Psychiatry at the University of Catania has led me to develop a different heuristic framework, influenced by constructivism and personal narrative, as well as by the motor theories of the mind (Scrimali, 1994).

The model I have adopted is based on the fundamental concepts of attachment theory. As we will see, this different formulation assumes significance for clinical work, and I will approach this issue again in the third part of the book.

At this point, I would like to address the key aspects of the psychopathology of schizophrenia, beginning with the cognitive literature.

2. Human Information Processing Disorders

2.1. *Hallucinations*

Hallucinatory phenomena are one of the most characteristic manifestations of schizophrenic pathology.

Kurt Schneider included hallucinations among the most important symptoms of schizophrenia, and both the DSM-IV-TR and the ICD-10 consider perceptual distortion phenomena to be a crucial aspect of schizophrenia (Schneider, 1954; American Psychological Association, 2000; World Health Organization, 1992).

The *International Pilot Study of Schizophrenia* (World Health Organization, 1997) has shown that 73% of schizophrenic patients report hallucinations in the acute phase of decompensation.

It should be noted, however, that even if hallucinations constitute an important element in schizophrenia, they are also present in other psychiatric pathologies including depression, bipolar disorder, and post-traumatic stress disorder.

In the field of clinical cognitive theory, beginning in the 1980s, much research regarding hallucinatory phenomena has been carried out with the aim of identifying and implementing effective treatment methodologies as well as formulating an adequate conceptualization to promote new theoretical models of perceptual distortion phenomena.

Considering that cognitive psychotherapy developed from a computational conception of the mind, based on information theory, and taking account of the fact that hallucinations are a dysfunction of human information processing, the interest of cognitive authors in this topic becomes clear.

Though the sequential exposition of the data in this monograph requires the separate treatment of hallucinations and delusions, it must be stated that in schizophrenia the two topics are closely connected.

Both these psychopathological aspects are, in fact, ascribable to a deficit in the information processing. Also, a close relationship exists between the two phenomena because the hallucinations feed the delusions while the delusions facilitate the activation of hallucinatory phenomena.

Both the hallucinations and the delusions are linked to the malfunctioning of cognitive schemas and internal operative models. This constitutes a dysfunction in the executive brain, making it unable to recognize and use data coming from the internal and external worlds in an appropriate manner.

Obviously, from my point of view, hallucinations and delusions cannot be considered only in terms of cognitive functioning, but must be studied in light of the comprehensive organization of the system of human knowledge, without neglecting emotional and rational components.

We will see in this section, and the section dedicated to therapy, how the standard cognitive orientation has created a real revolution in both the conceptualization and the treatment of hallucinatory phenomena. In my opinion, however, this approach is not wholly adequate because it is based on a digital logic that neglects the analogue processes of the emotional and relational spheres.

The following is a brief summary of the most important contributions from clinical cognitive theory regarding hallucinations.

Carlo Perris, in his fundamental work on the cognitive psychotherapy of schizophrenia, does not propose a new or articulated theory of hallucinatory phenomena, but bases his reflections on the concepts already formulated by Arieti (Perris, 1989). The approach is mostly descriptive. He points out, following Arieti, that hallucinations appear when the patients expects them, demonstrating, therefore, that hallucinations are produced in particular emotional conditions. Based on classic psychopathology of Jasper and Schneider, Perris also notes that hallucinations are attributed to external world when, in fact, they are the result of cognitive activity that is actually part of the processes of the mind.

Kingdon and Turkington, in 1994, proposed a more original interpretation of hallucinatory phenomena drawing on the work of Asaad and Shapiro (1986) and hinting at a possible neurophysiological mechanism linked to a dysfunction in the system of cerebral control.

Fowler, Garety, and Kuipers, in 1995, in their conceptualization of hallucinatory phenomena, return to the work of Slade and Bentall and cite the neuropsychological studies of Frith (Fowler, Garety & Kuipers, 1995). These three authors introduced the concept of meta-cognition, ascribing hallucinations to a gap in meta-cognitive processes.

Based on a review of the epidemiological and psychophysiological research, Bentall proposed a cognitive model of hallucinatory phenomena with the following salient aspects (Bentall, 1990; 2003).

Hallucination as a possible experience in individuals not affected by mental disorders. Hallucinations are also present in the experience of persons not affected by schizophrenia and even in people with no mental disorder whatsoever. Based on research carried out in Great Britain, Johns et al., reported that 25% of the people studied mentioned having had hallucinatory experiences at some point in their lives. This figure is in accordance with the findings of Slade and Bentall (Johns, Nazroo, Bebbington & Kuipers, 2002; Slade & Bentall, 1988).

Hallucination as an experience tied to culture. Another interesting aspect emerging from the work of the English authors is the role played by cultural belief systems in the appearance of hallucinations. In fact, Johns noted that hallucinatory phenomena were described with higher frequency by British residents belonging to Caribbean communities than by people of Anglo-Saxon descent (Johns, Nazroo, Bebbington & Kuipers, 2002).

Hallucination as a process related to levels of arousal and stress. The increase in arousal and the presence of conditions of chronic stress can activate hallucinatory phenomena.

Hallucination as a process provoked by non-optimal information input. In predisposed subjects, hallucinatory phenomena are activated when informational patterns are characterized by a lack of input or, contrarily, by the excessive presence of noise.

Auditory hallucinations as a process linked to sub-vocalizations. In this case acoustic hallucinations are related to sub-vocalizations. Therefore, the perception of voices is a malfunction in the processes of monitoring an internal dialog.

Hallucination as an actively controllable process. Bentall notes that hallucinations can be made to stop by engaging the individual experiencing them in verbal activity, including reading out loud or speaking.

In 1996, Chadwick, Birchwood, and Trower proposed an interpretation of hallucinations using the acronym ABC (*Activating Event, Belief, Emotional and Behavioral Consequences*), based on the rational-emotive perspective of Albert Ellis (Chadwick, Birchwood & Trower, 1996).

In this framework hallucinations are conceptualized as an activating event to which the patient attributes a meaning which provokes emotional and behavioural consequences. The work of these authors contributed to interesting and innovative developments in the therapy and rehabilitation of psychotic symptomatology.

The models proposed, however, are still more descriptive than explanatory and are not sufficiently linked to recent developments in neuroscience.

One important aspect of hallucinations that, in my opinion, must not be neglected is related to biological vulnerability. Such vulnerability is ascribable to specific dysfunctional behaviors tied to the functioning of systems of representation, including internal dialog and the production of mental images. Regarding the biological aspect already discussed, the important role of stress and emotional disturbance has likewise been identified. Clinical observations demonstrate that hallucinations appear with greater frequency in periods or situations of stress.

Many patients are able to pinpoint the beginning of the voices to a specific moment in their lives, which is almost always linked to a traumatic episode or a period of particular emotional stress.

In line with these observations, psychophysiological research had demonstrated that the hallucinations occur concomitant with an increase in arousal, measurable by the recording of psychophysiological parameters.

This opens important prospects regarding the use of the methods of clinical psychophysiology for the monitoring and maintenance of optimal levels of arousal.

A biopsychosocial model of hallucinatory phenomena that I would like to propose can be articulated according to the following points.

- base characteristics of the central nervous system tied to the genome;
- factors relative to development, connected both to parenting and cultural and social factors;
- conditions which lead to the stabilization of the hallucinatory experience.

According to this conceptual framework the following occurs during the developmental history of individuals subject to psychotic apophany. Bias in the formation of systems of internal representation and of schemas for the elaboration of a relationship with reality can be added to biological vulnerability. This vulnerability is related to idiosyncratic patterns in the functioning of the central nervous system typical of these subjects.

The formation of these schemas seem to be more common in the more archaic cultures in which the role of transcendent, magical, and numinous factors play a greater role.

In conclusion, in the emergence of hallucinations, the biological factors connected to the malfunctioning of the brain interact with more specifically psychological determinants tied to the organization of the system of knowledge.

Beck and Rector (2003) examined data produced by cognitively oriented English authors and articulated a "cognitive model of hallucinatory phenomena". This is obviously a "Standard" cognitive model tied, as we will later see, to a rationalist logic.

According to the two authors, a condition of the system of knowledge exists that predisposes one to hallucinatory phenomena and that can be traced to the following factors:

- predisposition for auditory imagination;
- dysfunction in cerebral processes for perception;
- presence of hyper-active cognitive schemas.

According to Beck and Rector, in persons prone to hallucinations, the processes of internal representation of external reality are excessively active. Also, since every perception is the result of information coming from the external world, but also from the activity of internal cognitive processes, in some individuals, in certain circumstances, the internal processes could be activated without any stimulus coming from the outside.

In conditions of emotional stress or of poor sensory input, hallucinatory phenomena would appear, in these subjects, in all its strength.

At this point, the American authors asked why, while many subjects have hallucinations episodically, in patients afflicted with schizophrenia, do the hallucinations last for longs periods of time and provoke acute discomfort.

To answer this question Beck and Rector provide factors that might be responsible for the indefinite self-perpetuation of hallucinatory phenomena in psychotic patients. These factors are:

- delusional beliefs regarding the hallucinations;
- the development of inefficient coping and safety behaviors.

As soon as the hallucinations begin in the psychotic patient, a system of delusional beliefs is activated based on feeling at the mercy of the external world full of numinous and magical influences.

The presence of hallucinations and the activation of a delusional belief system, in turn, motivate attempts at coping and safety which consist of trying to interact with the voices or images in order to limit their danger. Other coping mechanisms include diminishing social contacts and spending more time at home watching television.

Besides this, psychotic patients develop elevated levels of vigilance, in expectation of the voices, in order to feel ready to react. These coping behaviors are, nevertheless, inefficient and are responsible for the stabilization of the psychotic condition.

Social isolation, the loss of relational references, and the condition of continual fear and hyper-vigilance increase the hallucinatory phenomena, maintaining a self-perpetuating vicious circle.

An important aspect of Beck and Rector's conceptualization is identifying the key passage in the activation of psychotic experience; it is not the presence of the hallucination itself, but its insertion into a delusional system of interpretation that is important. This results in the activation of mechanisms of self-maintenance.

This observation is taken from the studies of Van Os and Krabbendam (2002) who state that the presence of hallucinations in and of itself does not create the psychotic experience, but psychosis develops when the patient attributes hallucinations to external factors. These then become part of the delusion of being harmed, persecuted, and influenced.

Chadwick, Birchwood, and Trower (1996) also note that it is not the hallucinations that create the schizophrenic condition, but rather the system of delusional beliefs in which they are inserted. It is then the mix of hallucinations plus delusion that determines the psychotic condition and related behaviors.

These observations assume considerable importance in the treatment of hallucinations.

We will see how the initial therapy entails trying to interrupt the loop between hallucinating and delusional thinking. The hallucinations will become immediately more acceptable and less disturbing if it is possible to place them within a new conceptual system, proposed by the therapist, thus removing them from the delusional interpretation.

The conceptualization of hallucinatory phenomena, developed by Beck and Rector, based on the work of the English cognitive psychotherapists, finally constitutes a position that is not only descriptive, but also explanatory.

From my point of view, however, this conceptualization is still inadequate. As an initial consideration, it is interesting to note that Beck and Rector describe perception as a process constituting the acquisition of data from the external world, from the activation of information, and from activity internal to the nervous system. In this way, this position approaches a constructivist, cybernetic, and motor vision of the mind.

They employ, however, the usual pragmatic and clinical approach, without renouncing the idea that such processes are only valid for the psychotic mind and do not constitute the base mechanism of the human mind.

The fact is that the standard clinical orientation still remains strongly anchored in the logic of human information processing, without applying the principles of the cybernetic revolution of the motor mind in which the mind is conceived as able to systematically control its own input.

Another aspect that is lacking in the theory of Beck and Rector is related to the exclusive focus of attention on explicit cognitive processes.

No mental process can be understood without, in my opinion, considering emotional and relational logic and computational analogue codes.

Beck and Rector relate hallucinatory phenomena to the hyperactivity of cognitive schemas connected to the perception of the external world (Beck & Rector, 2003).

But the perception of the external world is not only a computational digital process, tied solely to cognitive schemas. These schemas constitute the interpretive framework for perception, in other words, they are the structures of meaning of the executive mind and are not directly connected to perception.

Perception is a mental process with its own specific computational codes. Thus hallucination cannot be considered a process linked only to the hyperactivity of cognitive schemas, but must be interpreted as the incapacity of those schemas to impose adaptive meanings on excessively active and chaotic tacit activity.

Therefore, hallucination is not a dysfunction of cognition, but a defect in the interface: experience-explanation-relation-action.

A similar point of view is now sustained, not only by a different epistemological and theoretical vision, but also by much experimental data.

Important references can be found regarding this in the research and conceptual models proposed by Teasdale and Barnard (1993).

The two English authors, with their conceptualization relative interacting cognitive subsystems, have pointed out that different brain modules use specific computational codes that operate together.

The codes relative to the elaboration of information are the following.

Sensory and proprioceptive codes. These are related to the perception of acoustic, visual, and proprioceptive information.

Code for the structural recognition of informative material. This permits the recognition of constellations of sounds and visual information in patterns of meaning, for instance, the phonemes and relative visual information for the recognition of a human face.

Codes of propositional and implicated meaning. These constitute the highest processes of meaning, able to identify and conceptualize the informative material and to construct a personal meaning in relation to one's own story as well as current experiences.

Codes related to effectors. These are implicated in cybernetic processes of control over output. Every action is monitored and the information that comes from the activity of monitoring must be kept distinct from information coming from the external world.

In conclusion, Teasdale and Barnard describe:

- a sensory process;
- an intermediate process of recognition;
- a meaning process;
- a cybernetic process of output control.

These different processes use, in a specific way, the analogue and digital computational codes.

The conceptualization of the two Cambridge authors constitutes an optimal conceptual frame or reference for a complex model of hallucination.

It is evident that with distorted perception, the "hyperactivity of the processes of meaning" is not present, as Beck and Rector think, but we are faced with an inadequacy of these processes, while the sensory processes, relative to tacit knowledge, are unusually active.

Beck and Rector refer to the example of a person who anxiously waits for an important phone call and who, at a certain point, has the sensation of having heard the phone ring.

The same example that the two authors from Philadelphia propose seems to demonstrate that, in these conditions, the analogue processes of tacit knowledge are particularly active (i.e., the processes of experience), rather the digital processes of explanation.

The fact is that Beck and Rector remain tied to the paradigm of the primacy of cognition, considering emotion as a mere by-product. In this case it actually seems that the opposite is true. The tacit processes of experience, as in the example of someone anxiously waiting for the phone to ring, are very active, producing an error in explanation!

Further opportunity for reflection regarding a complex conception of hallucinatory phenomena comes from the work of Robert Ornstein who has proposed a modular and complex logic of the brain and the mind, pointing out the important role of the right hemisphere in the normal life of homo sapiens and in mental disorders (Ornstein, 1997).

Ornstein underlines how schizophrenia should be considered a pathology of the right cerebral hemisphere which begins to malfunction, altering one's sense of relationship with reality.

Ornstein, who is not a clinician, but a neuroscientist, only touches on the problem of hallucination, locating, nonetheless, the interpretive key in the malfunctioning of the analogue processes of the right hemisphere.

In reality, hallucination is a complex process in which understanding, or at least the attempt to understand, must not neglect a similarly complex vision of all the processes of knowing, including emotion, cognition, relational processes, and the regulation of action.

A series of observations on the structural and functional organization of the nervous system, in the field of motor theories of the mind, permits the construction of a complex frame of reference that is useful for the development of a constructivist and motor model of hallucination, rather than a rationalist and sensory one.

At this point, I would like to introduce my own conceptualization of hallucinatory phenomena. This constructivist and complex interpretive model also includes, as we will see later, delusion and takes into account the following aspects:

- a cybernetic and motor conception of the mind;
- modularity of the brain and complexity of the mind;
- the presence of a number of computational codes in the human brain;
- the necessity of systems of interface among the various modules and vulnerability of the processes of analogue-digital conversion and vice versa;
- a complex vision of the disorder, relative not only to the single malfunctioning of specific modules, but also, and above all, in terms of coherence and organization or, in other words, *entropy;*
- an evolutionary conception in which hallucination and delusion are forms of the paleo-gnostic resettling of the human mind, from both an ontogenetic and phylogenetic point of view;
- the crucial importance of relational factors for the understanding of hallucinatory phenomena.

The different points in this interpretive framework will now be discussed synthetically.

Within a motor approach that regards the working of the nervous system and the mind, it is necessary to underline that every input that "enters" the nervous system, through any sensory modality, is constantly "controlled" by a process of central origin.

Rodolfo Llinàs (2001), in his interesting contribution, *I of the Vortex: from Neurons to Self,* describes the human brain as a processor that is particularly talented in the role of "emulator" of reality, rather the recorder of external data.

Llinàs, in agreement with Maturana and Varela (1980), states that the fundamental nature of the human brain is that of a autopoietic system, in which sensory input, rather than inserting itself into the nervous system, simply constitutes a transitory disturbance.

Another crucial characteristic of the human brain is, according to Llinàs, that of being pro-active and not reactive with regard to information coming from the outside world.

The neurophysiological reflections of Llinàs are an important contribution to the motor theories of the mind to which the models presented here refer.

The sensory receptors are independently active of every excitation coming from external reality, and this activity is continually modulated by nervous activity from control centers allocated throughout the central nervous system.

The most paradigmatic example is that of extension receptors present in muscle. These receptors, called neuromuscular spindles, are controlled in the degree of extension by efferent fibers called *gamma* that are attached to similarly named motor neurons.

The efferent informational pattern depends on the degree of muscle extension and, therefore, on stimuli coming from the outside world. They also depend on the level of activity of the gamma motor neurons which are controlled by the central motor systems.

In conclusion, the highest level processors of the central nervous system, in order to establish the effective level of muscular extension originating from outside stimulation, must take the degree of activation of the gamma motor neurons into consideration.

An increment in this activity that is not recognized as such and is removed from the higher order processes of coordinated control of the central nervous system could create an anomalous perception of corporeal stimulation in the absence of actual information coming from the external world.

A common experience we have all had can help explain this idea. It often happens at the onset of sleep to clearly and frighteningly perceive *the sensation of falling.* Such a sensation is, in reality, an actual proprioceptive hallucination, comprehensible thanks to what was just described regarding the motor functioning of postural perception.

While falling asleep the level of gamma motor neuronal activity diminishes drastically. Since the higher order processes of coordinated control are beginning to change to a modality of functioning that is very different from what it is when one is awake, these can, in this delicate phase of a transition of state, make an error in interpreting information that arrives from the neuromuscular spindles. In this case, the support of the bed is not perceived, and there is a sense (hallucinatory) of falling.

Obviously this type of interpretation is more complex in more sophisticated and evolved sensory systems, such as the acoustic or visual systems.

Regarding sight, for example, there are multiple and diversified mechanisms of central control for input.

In the 19th century, Helmotz had already noted that every time our eyes moved, the image on the retina also moved; but despite continually modifying the position of our eyes, we still perceive the world as stable (Fulton & Howell, 1971).

This means that a system of central control able to discriminate if movements of the virtual image on the retina are due to a movement of the eyes or to external reality.

This mechanism must carry out a continuous comparison of data coming from the various sources, including the centers that determine ocular movement, information relative to working memory, and images actually present on the retina.

These control systems are systematically tricked by a technique that has permitted one of the greatest revolutions in art and communication, i.e., the possibility of representing movement in the cinema and in the different visual mediums.

In this case the perception of movement is a mere illusion.

In reality the images that form on the retina are fixed photographs and all we are seeing is a series of images, each one a slight bit different than the others, but each one absolutely stable.

We, instead, very realistically perceive movement.

This phenomenon was explained, until recently, by the sensory theory of the mind, based on the so-called "persistence of the image on the retina".

Today it is thought that the illusion of movement is actively created by a central processor that elaborates a sequence of moving images coming from working memory.

The process follows this dynamic: if, in each image, the background remains fixed, and the person appears each time in a slightly different point, that means the person has moved.

In this interpretation, the illusion of movement is not produced *peripherally* by the working of the retina, but is *constructed centrally* by processors, systematically tricked by a program written and evolved on the genome, in order to identify movement in the environment.

Now, if it is true that visual hallucinations are a typical symptom of schizophrenia, it is also true that one of the most characteristic biological markers in schizophrenic patients and in their relatives is an alteration in the smooth pursuit eye movements. This data can be read, for now, only in speculative terms, in the following way.

A deficit exists in the central control processors designated to coordinate the images coming from working memory and employed in the decoding of visual patterns, just as an analogous deficit is present in the control of eye movement.

In the case of a more profound malfunctioning, these processors trick the system of visual image elaboration, exchanging information coming from outside, for informative patterns that are allocated in the central mechanisms of memory.

In order to illustrate this concept more clearly, I would draw the reader's attention to experimental data related to the psychophysiology of the orientation reflex that is particularly appropriate for introducing the following considerations.

A certain number of tones, identical in frequency and intensity are administered through headphones, at the same rate—for instance, every five seconds.

The orientation reflex is recorded through the monitoring of electrodermal activity.

During the repetition of the stimulus, the electrodermal response tends to be reduced, until it disappears. The number of repetitions varies from subject to subject. If at a certain point we omit the stimulus at the moment it was expected, what would we observe?

Paradoxically a new orientation reflex would appear.

This simple experiment demonstrates some of the crucial aspects important for a motor theory of perception and, therefore, the hallucinatory distortion of perception.

The presence of a "signal" can lose relevance for the central nervous system if it is monotonous because the mind of a person is constantly looking for variant aspects of reality; invariant aspects tend to be neglected since they are less relevant to environmental survival and adaptation.

The absence of a "signal" triggers a new series of central information processing that causes the orientation reflex to reappear.

This type of experiment clearly demonstrates the presence of mnemonic mechanisms called working memory. It is evident that after the appearance of the monotonous stimulus, a "copy" is constructed that is temporarily housed in the working memory.

A model is thus created of what is happening in virtue of the considerable proactive tendencies of the human brain.

The model, provisionally elaborated in the brain, goes something like this: a stimulus of 1,000 hertz at 70 decibels, every 5 seconds, is being administered.

Every five seconds an exploration of reality is carried out in order to check the (provisional) model that has been created.

In the case in which no sound is presented at the 5 second interval, the model is invalidated and the central processors begin working to reformulate a new theory of the transactions in progress.

This chain of events necessitates the presence of a "virtual" model of the informative acoustic pattern in some of the cerebral modules which support that part of short-term memory that re-enters the so-called working memory.

From this emerges the hypothesis that hallucinations are nothing more than informative patterns coming from central cerebral modules which have been removed from the coordinated controls of the higher order centers of perception. In this way, one may say that the higher order centers of perception are tricked.

This conception is supported by the classic experiments regarding sensory deprivation such as those conducted by Bexton, Heron, and Scott (De Benedetti, 1976).

Subjects were made to lie down and were exposed to a series of visual, acoustic and proprioceptive stimuli which maintained a condition of perceptive isolation, permitting only monotonous stimulation (a soft white light, a constant noise), effectively blocking all sensory information.

This condition was only interrupted for the few minutes each day necessary to eat and evacuate. Among the volunteers recruited for the experiment, only a few lasted for more than 2 or 3 days.

Of extreme interest, however, is what happened during the first crucial days of sensory deprivation. Early on a spasmodic search for any new input to interrupt the monotony of the experimental setting was manifested. In this situation, modifications of one's critical abilities appeared. Any type of discourse, however inconclusive or incoherent, was greeted with joy and readily believed. During the experiment cognitive abilities also deteriorated. Simple problems could not be solved. Vivid acoustic, visual, and sensory hallucinations also appeared.

A similar result was reached by provoking sensory deprivation with drugs. For instance, an anesthetic substance such as phencyclidine blocks the sensory afferents without directly acting on consciousness (Gelhorn & Loofbourrow, 1963).

Administered in appropriate doses, phencyclidine makes every proprioceptive and tactile stimulus disappear. Even visual input is no longer recognized.

Shortly, hallucinations appear and slow potentials are recorded at the electroencephalographic level.

To conclude, similar phenomena have been described during the course of "natural experiments" in which speleologists have been forced to remain in deep caverns where there is a natural lack of visual and acoustic input. In these cases acoustic and visual hallucinations also occurred.

These experiments clearly suggest, as my esteemed colleague Gaetano Benedetti (born in Catania such as me) intuited many years ago, that optimal functioning of the central nervous system requires an adequate amount of information (De Benedetti, 1987).

The functions of the brain and the processes of the mind degrade rapidly when the flow of information is altered, in terms of either excess or privation.

From this data we can draw the hypothesis that in the schizophrenic patient the range of optimal stimulation is unusually constricted because of biological vulnerability. Also, the flow of information is established in chronically negative terms because of either an under-stimulation, due to social isolation, or an over-stimulation, traceable to disturbed relational patterns of control and communication, tied to a negative emotional climate within the family.

This conceptualization, which will be further discussed later, has a crucial implication for therapy: the mechanism for therapeutic and adaptive coping regarding hallucinations must be identified in the development of the patient's ability to maintain the flow of information at an optimal level.

An experiment conducted many times in our lab seems to support this position.

A test regarding the interception of different acoustic stimuli is carried out. The pattern is constituted by "rare" stimuli with specific tonal characteristics that are defined as "targets".

These stimuli are inserted in an input pattern with some others, called "decoys", that are very frequent and more numerous. During the test there are also brief intervals free of stimuli. The patient receives instructions repeated orally five times about the "target stimulus" and the "decoy stimulus" in order to recognize them.

The subjects are then given a switch and told to click each time they hear the "target" and not to click when they hear with the "decoy". The trial begins as soon as the instructions are terminated.

An electronic device created by our lab is able to quantify the number of exact, wrong, and missing responses, as well as responses not contingent on any stimulus. The possible errors in this type of trial are various.

Clicking in the presence of a "decoy" is a false positive; not clicking in the presence of the "target" is a miss.

It happens (and this occurs primarily with schizophrenics) that the patients click in the absence of any stimulus. It is as if they were perceiving a greater number of target stimuli than actually exist.

In a certain sense this is an hallucinatory phenomenon, i.e., perception without an object.

Our results show that normal and neurotic subjects rarely err in this type of trial, and they never make the false positive errors.

In the end, I would like to formally propose that hallucinations are constituted by the activation and utilization of sensory material allocated in the systems of memory and that this informational pattern, present in some modules of the brain, escapes from the coordinated control of the executive brain to be perceived as coming from external reality.

This position does not arise solely from my research but has also been present in the literature for some time. Stephens and Graham have recently proposed a similar conceptualization (Stephens, Graham, 2000).

For these two American authors, acoustic hallucinations are constituted by processes coming from inside the nervous system that are misunderstood and experienced erroneously as sensory input coming from the outside world.

Julian Jaynes (1996), in his beautiful book on the *bicameral mind,* also arrived at similar conclusions, posited in terms of an evolutionary and anthropological perspective.

According to Jaynes, up until the third millennium b.C., the process of hemispheric specialization and the perfect coordination between the right and left sides of the brain had not yet been reached.

Humans continually heard hallucinatory voices that, according to Jaynes, depended on a still not perfected ability of the processors of the left hemisphere to discriminate whether the informative patterns were coming from the external world or from the other hemisphere.

According to Jaynes, the schizophrenic condition is a regressive backslide toward modalities of central nervous system functioning similar to those that existed before the decline of the bi-chambered brain and the emergence of a unitary consciousness of the Self.

More specifically, this American author sustains that the hallucinatory voices stem from memorized admonitory experiences coming from the temporal lobe of the right hemisphere.

The arguments to corroborate this interesting point of view are certainly suggestive, if difficult to prove. They refer to a few studies on coherence patterns of electroencephalographic rhythms recorded in schizophrenic patients who seemed to demonstrate a greater activity in the temporal lobe, while the exact opposite was recorded for healthy subjects.

Besides this, Jaynes cites some data relative to epilepsy in the temporal lobes. He refers to statistics which show that when a patient has epilepsy sustained by a *focus* present in the left temporal lobe, massive acoustic hallucinations are recorded because of hyperactivity in the right hemisphere and a diminished efficiency in the left.

When the epileptic *focus* is located in the right hemisphere, however, hallucinations are only very sporadic.

More pertinent and richer experimental evidence is present in the neuropsychological perspective of Frith (1992).

This English writer, after having distinguished between the "input" and "output" theories of hallucination, supports the second.

He, in fact, denies the existence of convincing experimental evidence able to corroborate the idea that hallucinations are a type of anomalous processing of data present in reality, even if in different times and modes from those perceived.

Frith supports a theory of output which is, in fact, a motor theory of the mind. In light of much experimental evidence, he believes in the central control of the processes of sensory information acquisition and in the possibility that this central control is altered in schizophrenia.

In this way, information that leaves from inside the central nervous system, or better, from some of its modules, is erroneously understood as coming from the outside world.

This deficit is due to the systematic impairment of the central activity of control and of awareness that Frith places at the center of the cognitive psychopathology of schizophrenia.

Recent studies have been carried out that attempt to clarify the functional processes that underpin hallucinatory phenomena using techniques of neuro-imaging, including *positron emission tomography* (PET).

Specifically regarding perceptual distortion phenomena, frontal-temporal functional relations have been studied, since the two areas are involved, respectively, in the control and production of internal representative processes.

During tasks involving the creation of verbal material, Silbersweig and Stern (2001) used tomography and positron emissions to show notably different patterns in control subjects compared to patients suffering from schizophrenia.

In the former, during the generation of words, activation of the left frontal regions and a diminished activity in the temporal areas were observed.

This diminution of the activity in the temporal areas was not evinced in the psychotic patients. This would seem to indicate a deficit in the executive control processes of the frontal lobes, as compared to the temporal lobes that generate the processes of internal representation.

The functional pattern, documented tomographically, seems to confirm the hypothesis that auditory hallucinations are generated by hyperactivity of the modules responsible for representation as compared to those for coordinated control (Weinberger, Berman & Zec, 1986).

Other research, also using tomography and positron emissions, studied cerebral activity during the course of the hallucinations (Musalek, Podreka & Walter, 1989).

During these studies, the presence of hyperactivity in the associative visual cortical areas was ascertained in patients with visual hallucinations, while there was greater activity in the auditory-linguistic areas during acoustic hallucinations (Cohen & Servan-Schreiber, 1992).

This specifically demonstrates the involvement of systems of internal representation, both visual and auditory, in determining perceptual distortion phenomena.

The cooperation between cognitive science and neuroscience permits the creation of a coherent and explanatory scenario for perceptual distortion phenomenology.

Based on all that has been said, hallucination constitutes, together with delusion, an epiphenomenon of a comprehensive maladjustment of the system of human knowledge and should be considered, in schizophrenia, as one of the signs of increasing disorder in the nervous system and of its partial disorganization.

Hallucination and delusion constitute, nevertheless, only partially successful attempts to manage entropy, activating safety procedures that change the nervous system into a more archaic modality of functioning that I have defined paleo-gnostic.

The complex framework I have just delineated for a new understanding of hallucination has great potential for the development of efficacious therapeutic procedures, as we will see in the third part of the book.

In conclusion, it seems possible to affirm that the mystery of hallucinatory phenomena may be solved thanks to the adoption of a motor conception of the mind, based on a complex model of the modular brain and the coordinated mind. A lot of water under the bridge!

I remember clearly, when I was still a student of medicine studying hallucination for an exam in psychiatry, I felt a sense of frustration and annoyance at the complicated and crazy conceptualizations of hallucination based on *ad hoc* hypotheses (as Popper would say) like the *so-called anti-dromic conduction*, supposedly activated in pathological conditions of the central nervous system (Rossini, 1969).

Now, however, after many years of study, clinical work, and experimental research, I am savoring the fruits of the revolution created by the development of the epistemology of constructivism and of the cybernetic conceptions of the "relational" and "motor" mind.

2.2. *Delusion*

Delusions constitute one of the key problems in schizophrenia and concern both psychopathology and therapy.

In the cognitive field, delusions have catalyzed the efforts of many researchers, even if we are still far from possessing sufficiently articulated theories, supported by convincing and unequivocal experimental data.

The classical approach to delusions developed by Jaspers (1982) described this symptom as a morbid process, particular to psychopathological conditions.

This author established his view of all the salient aspects of delusion in the following three points:

- the absolute subjective conviction of the patient;
- the inaccessibility and non-modifiability in the face of logical confutation;
- the implausibility of content.

We will see, further on, why Jasper's work is debatable, and why such a position, which negates the value of therapeutic efforts, must be overcome.

In fact, a crucial objective in therapeutic and rehabilitative protocols for schizophrenia is the modification of the patient's absolute belief in the delusions. This will lead to the falsification and progressive abandonment of the delusional contents.

Thus, the assumption of "inaccessibility and non-modifiability" in the face of logical confutation must be drastically reappraised.

The implausibility of content appears obvious only in terms of descriptive clinical research, but often this implausibility disappears if we adopt an explanatory and hermeneutical approach. A typical case that occurs continually in clinical practice is the following.

The patient does not want to eat, convinced that someone is trying to poison him or her. Usually the patient bilieves that some family members are secretly administering poison.

Obviously such an affirmation will cause the psychiatrist to label this behaviour delusional with all the attached stigma.

Very often, a brief interview with the relatives of the patient is enough to discover that they have been putting considerable doses of haloperidol in the patient's food or drink.

Now it is clear that the patient has perceived something real, and even if he or she "jumped" to absolutist conclusions, these conclusions are not entirely in contrast with reality.

As we will see later, a constructivist and complex approach toward delusion not only permits overcoming the position of Jaspers, but opens new and important therapeutic possibilities.

The first theories of delusion elaborated in the psychotherapeutic field were motivational.

Bentall and Corcoran (2001) pointed out how the first hypotheses about delusion, formulated by Freud, referred to feelings of insecurity regarding the relational condition of the patient with significant others.

In psychoanalysis delusion is considered a defense mechanism against a possible violation of self-esteem in individuals whose self-esteem is fragile (Freud, 1950).

In situations in which the individual's self-esteem is threatened, this defense mechanism, consistent with the delusion of being the object of hostile actions by others, is invoked.

Early cognitive research on delusions, however, was primarily oriented towards information processing, rather than towards possible emotional and motivational dynamics.

An important hypothesis, emerging from cognitive research is that the characteristics of ideation in normal and delusional subjects represents a continuum rather than a qualitatively distinct process (Blackwood, Howard, Bentall & Murray, 2001).

Delusions, therefore, represent not a pathological process, but a dysfunctional state that can emerge in non-psychotic conditions related to human information processing.

The systematic interest in delusional thinking by writers in clinical cognitive theory began in the 1980s.

Jacobs (1980) formulated a conception relative to the relationship that normally occurs between the activity of thinking and the process of consciousness. He pointed out that the activity of thinking usually precedes that of consciousness because thinking constitutes the primary activity through which meaning is assigned to reality.

Some of the important aspects of the work of these authors from Liverpool are discussed below.

Life events and relational and social context. Delusions develop in relation to life conditions, both past and present, that have made the individual feel humiliated, frustrated, abused, and neglected.

This point is corroborated by studies of delusional patients and by sociological considerations which show that delusional symptoms are reported to be particularly present in immigrants to foreign nations who have not integrated into their new environment well.

Factors relative to perception and attention. Different lines of research have demonstrated that dysfunctions in perception set off delusions (Beck & Rector, 2004).

Subjects suffering from delusional beliefs, especially delusions of persecution, tend to excessively select and amplify information relative to threatening phenomena (Bentall, Kinderman & Kaney, 1994).

This helps us understand the difficulty patients with schizophrenia exhibit in recognizing the diverse emotions and, in particular, positive emotions on the face of persons with whom they interact. Attention is focused on negative information while positive information is neglected.

Memory bias. Bentall and Corcoran (2001), and their collaborators underline how delusional patients have a bias in the recall of memory; they selectively remember all the episodes in which they have been the object of humiliation or persecution and have difficulty recalling or focusing on memories of positive relational events. This memory bias seems to play an important role in the genesis and maintenance of delusional beliefs.

Dysfunctions in logical inference. Bentall and Corcoran note that a variety of research has demonstrated how a style of attribution of external locus of control plays an important role in determining delusion. In particular, paranoid patients tend to overestimate the potential influence of significant persons who are considered powerful (Kaney & Bentall, 1992).

Meta-cognition. Disturbances of meta-cognition have been identified in delusional patients. These patients have difficulty formulating flexible and falsifiable hypotheses regarding the thoughts of those to whom hostile intentions are attributed.

Tendency not to modify beliefs on the basis of new facts. Numerous studies have shown experimentally that patients suffering from delusions have a particular tendency to incorrectly elaborate all information in a new setting and jump to conclusions without taking new elements into account.

The recursive cycle of the processes of attribution of meaning and of self-representation. Bentall and collaborators have described the recursive dynamic between the processes of attribution of meaning and of self-representation.

This dynamic means that the attribution of negative meaning to an event leads to impairment in the perception of the self. This makes it more likely that later events will be interpreted as negative for one's self-esteem.

Regarding the etiology of delusion, Bentall, et al., have formulated a multi-factorial model linked to the following aspects:

Biological and genomic vulnerability. Different studies have documented that delusional behaviour is a functional process of the brain that begins to form precociously and is based on biological vulnerability, probably tied to the genome.

Specific studies of children of schizophrenics show them to have dysfunctional styles of causality attribution and information processing from infancy. These then become straightforwardly delusional in adulthood.

Factors relative to developmental history. Parenting and the emotional climate of the family are considered of maximum importance. A series of data shows that mothers, in particular, influence the developmental modality of meaning attribution in children (Fonagy, Redfern & Charman, 1997).

Though this model appears exhaustive and subject to experimental verification, these English authors stress the need to follow up on the research in order to reach increasingly adequate corroboration.

Blackwood, Howard, Bentall, Murray (2001) have proposed a cognitive and neuropsychiatric model of delusions.

associative areas, identifiable in the border zone between the occipital and parietal temporal lobe and in the prefrontal cortex (Chen, 1994).

To conclude, each of the areas cited above is connected to subcortical structures responsible for emotional memory, including the limbic system and the base ganglia.

These secondary associative areas have been identified as the seat of the processes of schematization and categorization of reality, that is the "creation of meaning" related to perceptive data.

Likewise, a posterior system (temporal, occipital, parietal, and limbic) and an anterior system, consisting of base ganglia, the limbic system, and thalamic structures that project to the frontal cortex, are involved.

Hemispheric specialization also influences the processing in this very complex network (Grossberg, 2000).

Thus, the centers in the right hemisphere are responsible for the representation of reality regarding spatial, temporal, and non-verbal patterns, while the modules of the left hemisphere are oriented to semantic categorization.

In this accurate anatomical and functional description, a coherent neurophysiological base can be identified for the functional dynamic of "experience" and "explanation" articulated by Guidano.

To summarize:

- *a posterior system* comprises the associative areas for perception and the limbic system. It is responsible for collection and processing, according to an analogue and parallel computational logic, and for the interpretation of data from reality;
- *an anterior system* that includes the base ganglia is associated with the motor cortex and is responsible for the control of action;
- *a system* based on the prefrontal associative areas is responsible for monitoring and controlling behavioural sequences.

The perfect functioning of the mind stems from the balanced coordinated dynamic of these systems. If a functional disconnection and a loosening of coordinated ties occur, specific problems emerge.

If the posterior (temporal, occipital, parietal, and limbic) system becomes excessively active, the self is pervaded by emotions and schemas related to harm, danger, deception, and disaster.

If the anterior motor system, responsible for the generation of language, becomes excessively active, on the other hand, the self perceives the sensation that its behaviour and cognitive activity are being controlled from outside.

This description of the neuronal networks, which constitute the anatomical and functional conceptualization of the higher processes of the mind, is a prelude to an explanatory proposal for delusion that stems from the study and integration of numerous neurophysiological models present in the literature, including the works of Hoffman (1997), Cohen and Servan-Schreiber (1992), Vinogradov, Poole, and Willis-Shore (1998), of Chen (1994b), and of Rappin.

The model proposed by Vinogradov, Poole and Willis-Shore (1998) seems to me to be very interesting and can be synthetically summed up in the following points:

- the functional disconnection of the various modules responsible for the superior processes of the mind, due to the alteration in neuronal communication;
- the redundant role and the impairment of memory processes;
- the dysfunction of emotional processes responsible for self-protection that become hyperactive;
- the dysfunction of cognitive and semantic processes that become under-active;
- the role of dopamine synapses in determining these dysfunctions.

After having presented their model, the three authors propose a series of questions that constitutes a challenge for future research on delusion.

Specifically:

Developmental history. What is the role of emotional experience during developmental history in determining a dysfunctional basis of the cerebral networks which constitute a vulnerability for delusion?

Emotion. What is the importance of emotion in provoking and maintaining delusion?

Coping. Why does delusion cause a feeling of relief in the patient and is reinforced as a coping mechanism?

Determinism. Why with delusion does the system of consciousness become rigidly deterministic, rather than probabilistic?

Dopamine. In relation to the role of dopamine-based cerebral systems, which are hyperactive thus creating a continual and painful sense of novelty and extraneousness, delusion may be a coping mechanism that lowers the level of uncertainty.

Psychophysiological laboratory data. Experimental proof exists that documents the alteration of the processes of information acquisition and its construction in schizophrenic patients.

The framework delineated by Vinogradov, Poole and Willis-Shore represents a workable synthesis from which I have developed a personal set of conceptualizations, though still preliminary and incomplete.

Now I will describe my own elaboration of the psychopathology of delusion, in the context of schizophrenia, initially listing a series of nodal points which stem from what has been amply presented in the first part of the book.

Delusion is the result of complex processes of knowing that involve, not only the cognitive sphere, but also emotions. Machiavellian intelligence is also fully involved.

The conceptualizations which try to discriminate whether the emotional component is primary or secondary are, in my opinion, fundamentally unproductive since experience (emotional level) and explanation (cognitive processes) are synchronized activities, occurring in unison.

Emotions are not a sub-product of cognition but constitute a potent and efficacious form of knowledge, constantly in direct contact with reality, from which they are able to rapidly and simultaneously process billions of bits of information. With delusion, tacit knowledge grasps an intrusive, hostile, and pressing reality that actually exists, at least within the family, even if its proposition and communication, in explicative and explicit terms, is defective.

Delusion does not constitute a dysfunctional phenomenon that presents itself unexpectedly and suddenly during schizophrenic apophany, but appears to be the result of patterns of knowledge and schemas that are constructed gradually during developmental history, beginning from biological vulnerability.

Individuals, prone to schizophrenia are afflicted by systematic deficits in the separation of noise from signal; they often feel confused and incompetent in social relationships, and sometimes they are not able to make sense of interactions with reality and with others.

In the determination of delusion, the processes of memory play an important role.

In particular, mnemonic schemas developed from recurrent episodes in which the individual was persecuted, mistreated, or abused are crucial.

For example, having experienced, over the course of development, continual betrayal by one parent and scenes of jealousy by the other, an individual constructs an interpretative schema of relationships in reality, necessarily tinged by betrayal.

So if the patient begins a romantic relationship with another, his or her system of knowledge does not freely and flexibly elaborate the data about the actual behaviour of the person in question, but evaluates the other's behaviour based on negative personal memories.

The vulnerable individual grows and develops in a family climate characterized by dysfunctional communication and altered social competences.

The vulnerable individual has been raised in a family climate in which continual intrusiveness (where boundaries and privacy are not respected), hostility, and criticism prevail.

The individual prone to delusion develops weak explicative competences and poor meta-cognition, while his or her channel of tacit knowledge is always active and perhaps too open.

In delusion, patterns of Machiavellian intelligence have strong implications, in schizophrenia, however, they systematically appear inadequate.

Delusion can be understood starting from its component of tacit knowledge, rather than its explicit explicative content.

Delusion should be re-contextualized within a positive emotional climate of acceptance of the patients, of consideration of their rhythms, and of their ways of relating to others. Background noise and other sources of stress should also be reduced within the environment.

Delusional beliefs are intensified by hostility, criticism, and attempts at rational confrontation based on explicit logic. This point will be further developed in the third part of the book dedicated to therapy and rehabilitation.

Delusion cannot be adequately understood in terms of a rationalist epistemology. Useful heuristic instruments, however, can be found in the hermeneutic approach that takes into account personal narrative.

Delusional expression or conviction are reduced by administering neuroleptics. This points to the role of dopamine in systems that become hyperactive and must be adjusted.

Starting from these nodal points, it is possible to propose a sufficiently well-developed conception of delusion.

Delusion is constituted by a disorder of knowing that originates in a series of concurrent and contemporaneous malfunctions of tacit knowledge, of explicit knowledge, of Machiavellian intelligence, and of the processes of memory.

Delusion originates at the level of the *interface*: *experience-explanation-interaction.*

Delusion has its biological foundation in an alteration of the functional coherence of various cerebral modules with particular reference to hemispheric specialization.

Delusions appear in the presence of the following critical factors:

- hyperactivity and entropy of the tacit analogue channel;
- a deficit in the explicit digital channel;
- malfunctioning of coalitional processes;
- a deficit in information processing regarding social interaction, for example, the difficulty in recognizing facial emotions;
- difficulty in formulating conjectures regarding the mental states of others;
- hyperactivity of memory in guiding the interpretation of reality;
- presence of negative social and relational situations.

Delusion is the state of decompensation and of an increase in entropy in an already dysfunctional system because of the presence of a specific biological vulnerability and of the inadequate construction of processes of knowing, born from very negative nurturing experiences.

The decompensation originates from stress due to an increase in the complexity of the environment.

Hostility, criticism, control, emotional hyper-involvement, limitation of social contacts with the outside world, and the systematic experience of others as intrusive, threatening, and devious are the elements that generate the following "emotional experiences:"

- being controlled from the outside;
- thinking one's thoughts are being read by others;
- being spied on;
- being harmed by others, even close friends or family, who do, in fact, systematically deceive the patient.

These emotional experiences are structured in dysfunctional schemas, constituted by emotional, cognitive, and relational patterns. These are present in the personal cognitive organization of the patient well before the psychotic apophany and are also found in other family members.

These dysfunctional schemas are activated more intensely during the psychotic decompensation because of the increase in stress.

Delusion is not inaccessible, *tout court*; it is only inaccessible to an explicative logic of rationalist confrontation.

Delusion can be understood in light of a hermeneutics which considers the personal narrative of the patient and not an abstract truth criterion, disconnected from individual personal events.

My proposal for the psychopathology of delusion refers to the following evidence, in good part, already presented.

The schizophrenic patient shows a deficit in digital explicative processes and a hyper-functioning of the emotional analogue processes.

The patient suffers from a serious dysfunction in the social interaction-experience-explanation process used to understand reality and social interactions with others (Callaway & Naghdi, 1986).

A systematic and in-depth survey into the ecological niche of the patient, including the reconstruction of developmental history, permits the identification of the modalities for the formation of dysfunctional schemas at the base of delusional phenomena.

Delusional behaviour is activated in relation to stress and the increasing complexity of reality.

This conceptualization of delusion, which is sufficiently well-developed and coherent in and of itself, is particularly useful for clinical practice.

In the third part of the monograph, we will see how abandoning the rationalist conception of delusion and adopting a constructivist and complex approach, opens up new possibilities of therapeutic and rehabilitative intervention.

To conclude this section, I would like to narrate a rather interesting personal episode that has led me to reflect on the relationship between information processing and the delusional interpretation of reality.

Some time ago I contracted conjunctivitis from an adenovirus, which quickly developed into keratitis, with tiny opaque foreign bodies under the corneas of both eyes.

I suddenly found myself living in the painful condition of drastically reduced sight and a confused and indistinct vision of reality. I endured some terrible months, having enormous difficulty affecting day-to-day living and my numerous work-related activities.

Nonetheless, this experience was useful in that I was a participant, as it were, in a natural experiment.

I was suddenly thrown into a situation in which I could not recognize the identity of people at more than a meter away. Even in face-to-face conversation, I could not completely discern facial expressions.

I found myself living, because of an infetious illness, and not (fortunately) because of malfunctioning cerebral processes, in a condition similar to that in which patients afflicted by *Entropy of Mind* habitually live.

I had to resolve the problem of expressing relational behaviour with a neutral facial expression when I was unable to recognize the person who was coming toward me.

Because of this, I kept a serious and anonymous look on my face, only to be replaced by a more appropriate expression when I recognized the person in front of me.

I soon realized that I was blocking my facial expression for fear of committing errors, and one day I had the impression of seeing the exact same expression of many of my psychotic patients on my "frozen" face.

Besides this, something else happened in this period of eyes illness that amounted to another precious natural experiment, this time regarding delusion.

I was in Syracuse holding a conference for physicians and psychologists on the cognitive and complex treatment of schizophrenia.

The faces in the auditorium appeared to me, because of keratitis, confused and indistinct.

At a certain point I began to speak of expressed emotion and as always happens to me in these circumstances, I asked myself if I wasn't giving a negative picture of parents with high expressed emotion by recounting numerous episodes from my clinical experience.

Suddenly, I had the total sensation of recognizing a person present in the hall—the father of a psychotic patient I was treating.

I thought: *Look there is Piero's father. He must have heard of the conference and came to be better informed regarding his son's problem!*

I began, however, to note a critical and hostile expression on his face, and I had the painful sensation of having offended him with my talk of parents with high expressed emotion.

I remember feeling inadequate and guilty, not being able to make it clear that parents with high expressed emotion are not at fault for the problems of their children.

I then thought to remedy the situation by repeatedly pointing out that the expressed emotion construct must not be construed as stigmatizing; rather, parents who exhibit this relational dysfunction develop it probably as a response to having a psychotic individual in the family.

All my efforts were for naught: the father of my patient continued to glare at me hostilely.

The conference broke for a coffee break, and I was lucky enough to have the opportunity to conclude this experiment.

While I was having coffee, I saw *Piero's father* at the counter. I went over and said: "I'm happy you came to the conference, even if you had to travel from Catania!"

"No!"—he said—"You're mistaken: I'm from Syracuse!"

I drew close, I looked as best I could, and finally I figured out that he was not, in fact, the father of my patient, but a perfect stranger.

I tried to clear things up and continued the conversation only to discover that he was a fellow psychiatrist whom I had never before met.

To summarize: *The presence of a deficit in the recognition of faces and emotion's leads one to construct information in a dysfunctional mode.*

I did not recognize the face of the patient's father; I more or less constructed it from memory because of a lack of informative visual input.

Emotional states influence the construction of reality. The vague sense of guilt I feel every time I speak of parents with high expressed emotions activated an internal dialog and the question: *What if there is a parent in the room with high expressed emotion?*

This cognitive and emotional set led me to construct the features of a parent in the face of a stranger. An actual case of invented reality! It seems important to state that luck helped me in this circumstance. In fact, the falsification of the dysfunctional elaboration of reality I constructed was possible through the chance encounter with the person in question.

Fortunately for me, my difficulty in recognizing faces was resolved in a few months because my inability to see and recognize people was linked to a reversible problem affecting the cornea. The right therapy was a simple eye-drop solution of cortisone. Psychotic patients, however, can return to "seeing" only if the central processes of information are restored, and chemical substances are not enough to obtain this result! In this case, the therapeutic program is not as simple as a few drops of cortisone in the eyes, but is definitely achievable, even if in complex terms, as we will see in the third part of the monograph!

3. Neuropsychological Disorders

3.1. Introduction

The deterioration of cognitive functions has been considered relevant in schizophrenic pathology since the observations of Kraeplein (1919).

The first reflections on the meaning of cognitive dysfunctions tended to consider them a secondary to other aspects thought more important to schizophrenia such as hallucinations, delusion, and emotional and motivational disturbances.

More recently, a different approach to the problem of cognitive dysfunction in schizophrenics has been developed, positing it as a primary deficit, specific and pathognomonic to schizophrenia. A series of experimental data demonstrate that the cognitive skills of schizophrenic patients seem altered, even before psychotic apophany (Frith, 1992).

The appearance of acute symptomatology brings a abrupt increase in cognitive dysfunction that continues to worsen during the course of the illness. It seems that the deterioration of the cognitive functions persists even during clinical improvement, remaining with the patient for the rest of his or her life.

Based on these data, it is possible to hypothesize that the cognitive deficits of schizophrenia constitute a trait marker and are probably ascribable to biological vulnerability. The cognitive deficits most systematically observed and studied in schizophrenic patients pertain to the following areas:

- memory;
- attention;
- learning;
- recognition of faces and facial expressions;
- meta-cognition;
- strategic planning.

I will now briefly describe each of these different areas.

3.1.1. Memory

Memory deficits in schizophrenia have been the object of systematic studies since the 1970s (Green, 1996).

Regarding the nature of this deficit, different research has shown a greater impairment of long-term episodic memory, which is a deficit encountered in all the phases of the syndrome (Tamlyn, McKenna, Mortimer, Lund, Hammond & Baddeley, 1992), while marked and specific deficits in implicit memory have not been reported.

A certain difficulty in organizing and filtering events and communicating them comprehensibly has been noted in patients with schizophrenia; the inability to remember is ascribable to this difficulty in organizing material (Docherty, Hawkins, Hoffman, Quinlan, Rakfeldt & Sledge, 1996).

Studies on verbal fluency show that semantic memory is also impaired (Kolb & Whishaw, 1983).

The visual-spatial deficits seem to involve the parietal-prefrontal connections, while the deficits underpinning the use of episodic memory involve the limbic-prefrontal connections (Goldman-Rakic, 1992).

Other authors have identified deficits in working memory and in the capacity to recall and recognize information (Baddeley, 1986).

The discrepancy of findings supports the hypothesis advanced by Saykin, Shatasel, and Gur (1994) in which there may be different types of deficits in different patients.

Numerous studies have noted poor performance on tests which explore long-term and episodic memory in patients with schizophrenia, whereas deficits regarding implicit or procedural memory have not been reported (Stip & Lussier, 1996).

Other data would seem to indicate a more marked impairment of verbal memory as compared to visual-spatial memory (Tamlyn, McKenna, Mortimer, Lund, Hammond & Baddeley, 1992).
More recent studies indicate that deficits in long-term episodic memory are present in all phases of the syndrome, even if its severity is positively correlated to the length of the illness (Duffy & O'Carrol, 1994).

Some experimental data show a greater impairment of recollection (for example, remembering words from a memorized list) as compared to recognition (saying which words the subject reads from a list were already presented previously) (Goldberg, Wienberger, Pliskin, Berman & Podd, 1989).

This finding seems to indicate that it is not the capacity to remember that is impaired but, rather, the ability to organize material in a way favourable to later recall.

Some authors, using studies of verbal fluency, find that in schizophrenia, semantic memory is also compromised (Tamlyn, McKenna, Mortimer, Lund, Hammond & Baddeley, 1992; Duffy & O'Carrol, 1994).

Schizophrenic patients perform poorly on tests which ask the subject to produce the greatest number of words that begin with a certain letter in a limited amount of time, or indicate objects belonging to the same category.

Kolb and Whishaw (1983) have documented, however, that the performance of schizophrenic patients on verbal fluency tests is altered when the rule to follow is that the words begin with the same letter, while there is no change when they are asked to produce words that refer to the same category (e.g., fruit).

Similarly, Chen (1994) found that the recognition of semantic categories is not altered in schizophrenics and believes that the difficulty in verbal fluency comes from the strategies of recollection and not from semantic impairment.

Rund and Landro (1995), after comparing memory function in affective disorders and in schizophrenia, concluded that the performance of schizophrenics on long-term memory tests was inferior to performance of a control group, and the difference between the two test groups was clearly significant.

In the context of studies on memory, semantic priming (or facilitation) research should also be mentioned (Gabrieli, 1992).

Priming is distinguished in two categories: semantic and episodic or perceptive. The first is the facilitation of recognition or of categorization of a target stimulus when it is preceded by semantically similar stimuli. The second is the facilitation of recognition observed for a repeated target stimulus compared to non-repeated ones.

Semantic priming is increased in schizophrenic patients compared to healthy control subjects (Kwapil, Hegley & Chapman, 1990).

The expression, short-term memory, refers to the ability to maintain in memory, for a limited time, a certain amount of information that does not require active manipulation on the part of the subject. The tests that are used most often to evaluate this function are the *Digit Span* and *Block Span*. During these tests, the researcher presents the subject sequences of numbers or cubes of increasing lengths which must be immediately repeated in the same order. Short-term memory in the schizophrenic patients appears altered (Gruzelier, Seymore, Wilson, Jolley & Hirsch, 1988).

Working memory includes the functions that maintain memory for a limited period of time, i.e., information that must be used in a specific context to carry out a task (Baddeley, 1986).

Parker, Derrington, and Lackmore (2003) evaluated cognitive deficits regarding working memory and attention in three samples representing schizophrenia, bipolar disorder, and healthy controls. The results show poor performances in patients with schizophrenia as compared to the other two groups.

After studies on 34 patients, who were followed for a period of four months, Paul, Puschel, Sauter, Renthsch, and Hell (1999) affirmed that the alteration in working spatial memory can be a reliable marker of schizophrenia.

Recent research concludes that patients with schizophrenia present a selective deficit in verbal memory (Wexler, Stevens, Bowers, Sernyak & Goldman-Rakic, 1998).

In the end, a meta-analysis of 70 studies on long-term memory (free memory, memory with cued recall, and recognition of verbal and non-verbal material) and on short-term memory (digit span) documents the impairment of the mnemonic functions of memory in schizophrenia (Aleman, Hijman, DeHaan & Kahn, 1999).

The severity of the alterations in memory in patients with schizophrenia is not related to non-specific factors including age, drug therapy, length of the illness, conditions of the patient, severity of the pathology, or positive symptoms (Feinstein, Goldberg, Nowlin & Weinberger, 1998).

Other research conducted at the Department of Psychiatry of the University of Catania has documented serious problems in the different types of memory in patients with schizophrenia, particularly short-term memory (Scrimali, Grimaldi, Salimbene, Sambataro & De Leonardis, 2002).

3.1.2. Attention

The distractibility and, therefore, the difficulty in focusing attention is a critical aspect in schizophrenic patients that was noted in the early observations by Kraepelin (1919). A considerable amount of research points to a systematic deficit in the attention span of schizophrenics. This important aspect in the psychopathology of the ailment has been recently reinterpreted in light of human information processing, and various explanatory hypotheses have been formulated.

One theory holds that the deficit in attention processes is related to an impairment of the filter that selects the information to process Another model called "relative to information processing ability", has appeared, (Breier, 1999). This model has two critical features: the resources for processing and the procedures of allocation.

The first feature refers to the quantity of performance that can be carried out simultaneously without causing interference. It has been observed that schizophrenic patients have reduced capacity for simultaneous processing (Docherty & Gordinier, 1999).

Attention is directed toward the patterns of stimuli moderated by the importance of those patterns derived from long term memory. In the context of attention processes, one must distinguish between intentional attention (active) and automatic attention (passive). Numerous studies have demonstrated that both types of attentive processes are altered in schizophrenic patients.

Typical schizophrenic patients show a deficit in intentional attention constituted characterized as easy fatigue in the processes that sustain attention (Gray, Feldon, Rawlins, Hemsley & Smith, 1991).

Therefore, when the schizophrenic patient initially tries to focus attention on a task that must last for a certain amount of time, the patient succeeds in beginning the task but quickly starts to perform poorly and must interrupt the trial (Heinrichs & Zakzanis, 1998).

3.1.3. Learning

Patients with schizophrenia show considerable difficulty in learning during both the phase of clinical decompensation and the course of the illness (Frith, 1992). This marked impairment in learning competences is linked to the malfunctioning of important cognitive functions already described, including attention and the capacity to identify the important information to be learned and to organize it hierarchically.

A pathological process that hinders learning in schizophrenic patients is the perseverance that inhibits the identification of new responses when the demands of performance are modified.

This malfunctioning of the learning process in schizophrenics is traced to the incapacity of the central processors to opportunely modulate lower level operators when a new type of response is required. This deficit is attributable to the malfunctioning of the cortical areas in the frontal region.

A very interesting fact regarding learning in schizophrenic patients comes from experimental research conducted by Dominey and Georgieff (1997). These authors have tested the hypothesis that in schizophrenics, learning is altered more at the explicit than at the tacit level.

The learning process was studied in a group of schizophrenic patients using a specifically designed test. The task was divided into two components. The first was tied to the comprehension of information immediately available in a pattern presented to the patients, thus depending on tacit learning. In the second part of the test, the patients had to identify abstract relationships among elements that could only be found using explicit cognitive abilities.

The authors concluded that the learning processes that require a high level of abstraction are more severely impaired in schizophrenic patients. This finding is extremely important for therapeutic and rehabilitative strategies.

In the psychotherapeutic process, it is important to render every concrete element that must be acquired in a complex situation comprehensible to the patient rather than use approaches that necessitate high levels of abstraction, at least in the early phases of treatment. With rehabilitation, as we will see in the third part of the monograph, the strategy of cognitive empowerment assumes considerable importance.

3.1.4. Recognition of Faces and Facial Expressions

The recognition of faces and of diverse emotional facial expressions is a competence of crucial importance for the dynamics of good social relations.

Thanks to the pioneering work of Ekman (1993), facial expressions connected to base emotions have been identified and described in standardized terms across cultures. Based on this, researchers have carried out a series of experimental studies of the ability to recognize the emotions of the human face.

Recognition of faces and emotions by schizophrenic patients has only recently become the object of systematic research. Diverse studies have investigated the problem of facial recognition using brain imaging methods including the fMri and the Pet (Johnston, Katsikitis & Carr, 2001).

Research in functional and behavioural neuroimaging suggest that the processes implicated in the recognition of faces can be strongly influenced by socially relevant information. Experimental observations have indicated the presence of a deficit in the schizophrenic patient's ability to recognize faces. This information is consistent with everyday clinical experience and is a serious obstacle in the implementation of therapeutic and rehabilitative strategies designed to increase social competences.

It thus seems that the deficit in the recognition of faces and facial expressions and, more generally, of tacit signals connected to relational patterns is a deficit that has a powerful impact on the impairment of the functions underlying Machiavellian intelligence.

These deficits constitute a trait deficit, as I have already pointed out, and persist despite the lessening of acute symptoms. Thus the clinical assessment is of paramount importance when planning and executing a therapeutic and rehabilitative project, as we will see in the next part of the monograph.

In research projects designed to identify better therapeutic strategies for schizophrenics, our group carried out a study using a new instrument for evaluating the performance of facial recognition in psychiatric patients developed by Rehacom, and distributed in Italy by Ems of Bologna (Rehacom; Scrimali & Fisichella, 2003).

Twenty-five patients suffering from schizophrenia and diagnosed according to the DSM-IV were involved in this study. The patients, residents in a therapeutic community, were in a state of clinical compensation and being treated with neuroleptics and benzodiazepines. Two control groups were formed. One consisted of 25 patients with various pathologies was called the "neurotic" group. The second included 25 normal subjects and was defined the "control" group.

The patients with "neurotic" pathologies were contacted for assessment at the Department of Psychiatry of the University of Catania or at a day clinic. All received drug treatment, including antidepressants and benzodiazepines.

The assessment methodology used for the research included a computerized tool created by Rehacom that contained packets for neuropsychological assessment. In particular, the study in question was carried out by using the program "Memory of Faces" (Gesi) for Windows (Rehacom, 2003).

The results obtained at the end of the study can be summarized as follows.

The patients appeared diffident and even reluctant to participate in the trial before beginning the test and during its execution. They were afraid, *a priori,* of not being able to perform the task. This correlates to low levels of self-efficacy and self-esteem normally present in psychiatric patients. However, during the course of the test, generally speaking, they become more confident with the task and the work proceeded well.

The test of facial recognition, "Gesi", showed a significant deficit in the psychiatric patients compared to the healthy controls in most of the trials. The psychotic patients, in particular, exhibited poor results when compared to the neurotic patients. This is clear from the significant difference recorded between the two groups of patients on the first level of the test.

The psychotic patients showed a notable difficulty passing on to the second level of training compared to the group of neurotic patients.

At this level, the significant difference manifested by the psychotic patients in matching faces with professions demonstrates the deficit in semantic memory tied to the memory of faces.

To conclude, our research on the recognition of faces shows that patients with schizophrenia have an elevated and specific deficit in the recognition of faces and in matching faces to semantic data.

This data constitutes a precious base for the planning of training aimed to improve performance.

This training, which can be conducted using the same computerized program used for assessment (Rehacom, 2003), and appears very promising for psycho-social rehabilitation.

It is evident, in fact, that the disability relative to social and relationship competences cannot be resolved if the patient is not helped to improve the ability to recognize faces and emotions. This disability, in turn, prejudices self-efficacy, motivating dysfunctional coping behaviors based on avoidance.

In the context of more recent research carried out at the University of Catania in the Department of Psychiatry, I evaluated the ability to recognize facial emotions in a sample of patients with schizophrenia and compared their performance to control subjects and to patients with neurotic disorders.

To conduct this second study, the *Test Pictures of Facial Affects* (Ekman & Friesen, 1969) was used. The test is composed of 24 faces (12 women and 12 men) who represent the six base emotions described by Ekman. The 24 photos were selected by Ekman and Friesen from Ekman's original 1976 catalog (Ekman, 1993).

The test was conducted on a personal computer using a program developed by Sambataro at the Laboratory of Cognitive Psychophysiology at the Department of Psychiatry of the University of Catania.

Three groups were formed: a control group of 100 subjects between the ages of 20-60; a second group of 29 patients diagnosed with neurotic disorders including depression, anxiety, and eating disorders; a third group of 21 patients with schizophrenia and schizo-affective disorder.

The diagnoses were made in accordance with the criteria of the DSM-IV-TR.

The patients were contacted through different institutions. In particular:

- the Department of Psychiatry of the University of Catania;
- the Sant'Antonio Assisted Living Therapeutic Clinic, Piazza Armerina;
- two private psychiatric practices, one in Enna and one in Catania.

The control subjects were administered the *Middlesex Hospital Questionnaire* (Crow, 1996) in order to exclude the presence of psychopathology. The control subjects were chosen to represent diverse educational levels (middle school, high school, college). The working hypothesis was confirmed at the high levels of statistical significance ($p<0.001$).

The mean "total errors" in the recognition of emotions committed by the group of psychiatric patients was higher than in the control group. When the neurotic and psychotic patients were compared, the difference was statistically significant; the psychotic group made many more errors than the neurotic patients. The emotions that differentiated the patients from the controls in statistically significant terms were:

- joy;
- fear;
- surprise.

The psychotic patients were differentiated from the neurotics on five out of six emotions. Only sadness did not reveal any differences between the two groups of patients. This study has permitted me to confirm the hypothesis in which facial recognition of emotions is deficient in schizophrenics not only when compared to the controls, but also compared to the neurotic group. The emotion that psychotics recognize best seems to be sadness, and that which they recognize least is surprise.

3.1.5. Meta-Cognition

As I have already said, the awareness of self constitutes the acme of the functions of the central nervous system and also the highest step in both biological and cultural evolution.

Schizophrenia, among the various psychic disorders, most affects the capacity to consciously reflect on oneself.

Flavel (1979) first formulated a systematic conceptualization of meta-cognition, defining it as: *a cognitive process that focuses on other cognitive processes.*

Meta-cognition is, therefore, *consciousness of the processes of consciousness* and describes a function of self-reflection about processes and about the state of the mind.

Frith (1992) has also dealt with this theme in a systematic fashion with particular reference to schizophrenia. He suggested that all the cognitive dysfunctions that make up the substratum of the psychopathology of schizophrenia are traceable to a fundamental mechanism identifiable in an alteration of known experience. This alteration of meta-cognition is manifested, above all, in social interaction. In this context, the problem of the deficit in meta-cognition becomes the difficulty, or even the inability to represent and decode the mental states of others.

In this condition, schizophrenic patients exhibit difficulty in managing on-going relationships, because they are limited to using information derived from the explicit communication of their interlocutor. Referring to this aspect, Frith proposed the theory that schizophrenic patients develop delusions based on the incapacity to formulate correct inferences about the mental states of others.

I am not entirely in agreement with Frith on this point. If it is, in fact, true that the schizophrenic patient is not able to correctly represent the mental state of others, why does the patient systematically attribute negative attitudes to others?

I think that schizophrenic patients are definitely afflicted with a deficit in the processes of abstraction relative to the explanation of on-going experience, but I also believe that they perceive the emotional experience of others through the tacit channel, even if the cognitive deficit of explicit knowledge prevails. This would lead the patients to elaborate emotional experience in terms that are too drastic, dichotomous, and absolutist. In my opinion, the patients are victims of a complex set of dysfunctional processes. Their disorganized behaviour, ambivalence, and sloppy and unfriendly appearance, elicit tacit behaviors of rejection by others that are perceived and indeed magnified by the hyperactive system of emotional knowing of the patients. The explanation of current experience occurs in one direction, using rigid, internal operating schemas and models that are connected to negative convictions about social interaction and based on diffidence and the necessity of not trusting others.

We know, in fact, that schizophrenic patients develop a series of dysfunctional schemas in social contexts because of a family situation characterized by an emotional climate with high levels of hostility and criticism and also because of the social segregation of these families.

One further reflection has been proposed by Uta Frith and Christopher Frith (2004) regarding the neuropsychology of mentalization which is the ability to imagine what is in the mind of another person. Based on studies of neuroimaging, they have identified the areas involved in the mentalization process in the medial prefrontal cortex, in the temporal lobe, and in the posterior-superior temporal sulcus.

Recent studies have documented the neurophysiological and neuropsychological bases of the considerable ability of small children to imitate the expressions and social behaviour of adults (Decty, Chaminade, Grèzes & Meltoff, 2002).

Rizzolati and collaborators have developed a theory of "mirror neurons" which are a population of cells specialized in the activation of imitation behaviors (Rizzolati, Fogassi & Gallese, 2000).

Gopnik, Meltzof and Kuhl (2001) underline how the development of a sense of self is also tied to the complex interaction involving imitation between parents and small children. The two English authors affirm that the progressive structuring of the appropriate emotional reactions stems from the continual imitation of the nurturing figure.

In light of these neurophysiological findings, and of the poor social, relational, and emotional competences that one often encounters in the patients and their families, it seems possible that something has not functioned in the processes of imitation and, therefore, the development of the self.

Leslie (1987) has proposed the idea of meta-cognition as a complex function sustained by three different cerebral modules.

The first module, called ToBy (*Theory of Body Mechanism*), develops during third and fourth months of life and supervises proprioception and bodily motility. This module assures the ability to monitor all movements and understand if they are caused by the brain or by external causes.

The second module, called ToMm1, develops around the eighth month and serves to monitor the effects of the actions of others.

The third module, called ToMm2, appears in the subsequent phase of development, and is aimed at recognizing attitudes people display in responding to different events.

The problem of meta-cognition emerges clearly when we want the patient to recognize the fact that his or her relational processes are dysfunctional, in order to correct them. To obtain this result the patients must observe their own cognitive processes, a very difficult task. It is clear, therefore, that the improvement of meta-cognitive functions is a crucial objective within the therapeutic strategy, as we will see in the third part of the book.

The subject of meta-cognition in psychopathology had been studied by a group from Rome coordinated by Antonio Semerari (Semerari, 1999). Carcione and Falcone (1999), in particular, define meta-cognition as:

> The capacity of the individual to carry out heuristic cognitive operations on one's own and other's psychological behaviors, as well as the capacity to use this knowledge for strategic ends to solve problems and to control specific mental states of subjective suffering.

The meta-cognitive function is developed and modulated in the context of relationship reciprocity with nurturing figures.

Research by Main (1991) has shown that the quality of attachment is influenced by the meta-cognitive abilities of the nurturing figure.

If these abilities are poor in the parents of the schizophrenic patients, then it seems likely that nurturance will also be compromised and, in turn, the patients will not be able to adequately develop their own meta-cognitive abilities.

Fonagy (1995) hypothesizes that the development of the meta-cognitive process is traceable to an inborn human behaviour, but its efficacy depends of the quality of nurturance experienced. The lack of a positive reciprocity and the experience of a negative climate, often characterized by unpredictability and mistreatment, are at the origin of impaired meta-cognition.

In the area of the meta-cognitive competences, Carcione and Falcone (1999) distinguish a series of sub-processes, including:

comprehension of the minds of others. This is the ability to analyze the mental processes of others during a relational exchange (on-line process);

decentralization. This refers to the capacity to analyze mental processes of others in the abstract, rather than when currently involved in the exchange (off-line process);

differentiation of own mental states. This meta-cognitive competence consists of being able to monitor and discriminate one's own emotional and cognitive states;

differentiation of the representation of internal states compared to external reality. This indispensable function allows the system of knowing to distinguish between internal representative processes and external reality at all times.

mastery. This is the capacity of the individual to conceptualize one's own mental states and those of others in the context of the actual situations to be managed and problems to be solved.

Maurizio Falcone underlines how a grave deficit in the meta-cognitive process of differentiation is active in schizophrenia. In this way, the system of knowledge tends to attribute an external origin to internal cognitive processes.

3.1.6. Strategic Planning

Strategic planning is one of the most important functions of the proactive human mind. This crucial function consists of the anticipation of reality and in the capacity to correctly identify and connect a series of tactics that permit the achievement of a strategically predetermined objective. In schizophrenia, we see the impairment of strategic planning abilities (Nuchterlein & Dawson, 1984).

In a problematic situation, the patient exhibits notable difficulty in identifying the useful parameters upon which to build a problem-solving strategy (Erickson & Binder, 1986). Once the criterion has been identified, the patient persists in maintaining it, even when the scenario changes. This behaviour is clearly demonstrated by a neuropsychological assessment tool called the *Wisconsin Card Sorting Test* that will be discussed in the third part of the book. Strategic planning is closely tied to executive functions.

In fact, the execution of an efficacious behavioural strategy necessitates both the identification of a strategic plan and the control over the plan in the executive phase. Strategic planning and executive functions are likewise influenced by other processes including attention and memory. This consideration, once again, points out how closely interdependent are the processes of the mind.

4. Impairment of Machiavellian Intelligence

Epidemiological research has long-documented the phenomenon of the so-called social drift of schizophrenic patients (Faris & Dunham, 1939).

This phenomenon consists of the considerable difficulty for the schizophrenic patient in maintaining his or her role and social position after the appearance of the disorder (Goldberg & Morrison, 1963).

In this way, schizophrenic patients tend to "slide" toward the lower social classes where psychotic patients tend to cluster (Turner & Wagenfeld, 1967).

This phenomenon demonstrates that schizophrenic patients exhibit a weakening of social competences relative to the so-called Machiavellian intelligence. Much research has tried to identify the specific characteristics of the gaps in Machiavellian intelligence in the schizophrenic patient (Mazza, DeRisio, Tozzini, Roncone, & Casacchia, 2003).

In light of the data gathered, it is possible to affirm that schizophrenic patients exhibit a notable weakening of the knowledge of social rules of the surrounding culture in which they live, as compared to patients afflicted with mood disorders (Sullivan & Allen, 1999).

Other research has demonstrated that schizophrenics perform more poorly than normal control subjects on tests involving identifying the emotional state of the protagonist on a videotape in social interaction situations (Kondel, Mortimer, Leeson, Laws & Hirsch, 2003).

If the social competences are reduced in schizophrenic patients in normal exchanges, the deficit is even more marked in problematic social situations which require specific problem-solving abilities. In order to correctly effect interpersonal problem-solving strategies, a subject must be able to identify and decode the salient aspects of the problem, carry out a series of evaluations, make decisions, and transmit them correctly to the interlocutors. It is clear that the communicative process assumes enormous relevance in the entropic dynamic of the mind. The problem of language and communication in the schizophrenic patient has, in fact, taken on crucial importance since the 1960s.

This can be traced to the birth of psycholinguistics and the work of Chomsky, the illustrious cognitive author (1985), and to the studies of the pragmatics of human communication and the dysfunctional communication of the schizophrenic patient by Watzlawick, Beavin, and Jackson (1971). These authors developed a position on schizophrenia which places the communicative disorder at the center of the illness's dynamic, identifying it as an idiosyncratic aspect of the communicative paradox.

Cutting (1985) summarizes the results of experimental studies on schizophrenic language up to the 1980s in the following points:

- the speech of schizophrenics is less comprehensible than that of normal subjects;
- schizophrenics use a weak vocabulary;
- the language of schizophrenics presents disturbed phonetics.

The linguistic anomalies of schizophrenic patients seem to relate to a pragmatic disorder in the sense that their discourse does not take into account the needs of the interlocutor. It has been asked if schizophrenic patients are aware of their difficulty in conversation. Clinical data have demonstrated that the answer to this question is affirmative and is what makes these patients anxious, contributing to their low self-efficacy and esteem.

More recently, language disorders in schizophrenic patients have been linked to the impairment of neuropsychological processes which are encountered in the psychotic condition, including impairment of meta-cognition and attention.

Frith (1992) maintains that the difficulty in communication is traceable to the fact that schizophrenics show difficulty in inference regarding the mental state of others, and this is attributable to a deficit in meta-cognition.

Elaine Chaika (1982), analyzing deviant discourse in schizophrenic patients, proposes that dysfunctional attention must be considered an important cause of the gaps in schizophrenic discourse. This author began with the consequences of the lack of attention in normal subjects and their effects on routine sequences and suggests that there is a need to look for analogies with the characteristics of schizophrenic discourse.

Chaika focused on the attention competence of the speaker, insisting on the fact that the crucial element in the impairment of discursive competence in schizophrenic patients is not due to a linguistic, but to an attention deficit. She, therefore, hypothesizes that attention plays a fundamental role in the process of construction of meaning and discourse.

A perspective based in mental neuro-development has been proposed by Leask, Done, and Crow (2002). They note the need for an evolutionary theory for schizophrenia and suggest that schizophrenia may be traceable to a disorder in the human capacity to use language which would be connected to problems of the institution of functional hemispheric dominance.

This hypothesis suggests that a failure in the efficacious development of the functional asymmetry of the brain leads to an alteration in the formation of hemispheric specialization.

Other authors write about conversational capacity in schizophrenia, analyzing the same type of disability in pre-schizophrenic children. They describe the results of an analysis of the pre-morbid precursors of schizophrenia with regard to the functioning of discourse and language (Walsh, 1997).

Walsh's study focuses on the need for a detailed analysis of children who might be at risk for mental illness such as schizophrenia, pointing out that these studies of pre-morbid development pose the question that a specific conversational disability, apparently pre-morbid, could be part of the development of schizophrenia.

Much research on linguistic disorders in schizophrenia has analyzed the deficits at the different levels of language, considered to be a system of representation governed by relational roles (France & Muir, 1997). In many studies, specific low level defects have not been found (Chaika, 1982). Therefore, among researchers the conviction has developed that the very highest levels of the linguistic process are impaired in schizophrenia. This does not mean that at the most elementary levels, one does not find errors, e.g., lexical, syntactic, and semantic. It means, rather, that in schizophrenia the dysfunction at this level can be explained as a consequence of errors that occur in higher order processes. Schizophrenic patients show problems evident in the inference of knowledge and intentions of their listeners and in the use of this information as a guide for conducting discourse (Lanin-Kettering & Harrow, 1985).
These problems can be summarized in the following way:

- deficiency in planning;
- poverty of discourse;
- poverty of discourse content;
- difficulty in controlling plans;
- difficulty in self-monitoring;
- difficulty in monitoring the mental state of others.

The ability to self-monitor was examined in an experiment in which the tone of the voice of the subject was distorted through an appropriate instrument (Frith, 1992). The schizophrenic patients said they heard strange voices every time they talked. From studies on animal and humans, we see that there are areas of the left cerebral cortex in which the difference between the sound of one's own voice and that of others is identified. The function of this area is altered in schizophrenic subjects (McGuire, Shah & Nurray, 1993).

The capacity to understand intentions and desires of others was studied recently by developmental psychologists. This ability, fundamental for the development of the "theory of the mind", has been found lacking in autistic children (Baron-Cohen, Leslie & Frith, 1985).

Without this capacity, the autistic child cannot understand that others have different thoughts, emotions and desires. This is considered a deficit in the mechanism that permits human beings to construct an efficacious theory of the mind or to "mentalize" (Premack & Woodruff, 1978).

Both these terms refer to the necessary perception that others have minds different from our own and to the awareness of our capacity to understand the desires, hopes, and intentions of others, in order to predict or anticipate their behaviour.

An inadequate capacity to represent mental states of others negatively influences the management of social interaction. Communication cannot be successful based on the simple knowledge of words given that words in different contexts assume different meanings. The most important context is that of the desires and intentions of the one who is speaking.

Schizophrenics know that others possess their own minds, but they have lost the ability to interact with them. Others appear to them as impermeable to possible understanding.

This lack in the capacity to represent mental states of others can be studied thanks to the administration of some simple tests like the following (France & Muir, 1997).

The following situation is described to the patient:

> John left 5 cigarettes in a pack which he places it on the table and then leaves the room.
>
> Janet enters the room and takes one of the cigarettes, without John knowing.

A first question regards memory. The experimenter asks:

> How many cigarettes are left in John's pack?

Immediately after the subject is asked a question to assess mentalization.

> When John returns, how many cigarettes does he expect to find?

Patients affected with paranoid schizophrenia respond correctly to the question that implies an efficient mnemonic process, but not to the one requiring mentalization because for them John must know what they know, that a cigarette has been taken from the pack. In conclusion, if the schizophrenic patient knows something, they believe that everybody else knows it too.

This observation is frequently repeated in clinical interactions. It often happens, in fact, that after having asked a patient afflicted with schizophrenia a question, they answer convincingly with: *Why are you asking me? You already know the answer!*

On the whole, therefore, research results have shown that language disorders in schizophrenic patients are only, in part, tied to thought processes and must be considered in terms of the deficits in the neuropsychological processes of attention and meta-cognition and to the features of pragmatic communication (Crow, 1997).

In the schizophrenic patient, it is not only verbal language that is altered, but a comprehensive impairment of the capacity to relate to others. Thus, it is necessary to extend the analysis of language and communication to include body language, posture, movement, facial expression, and gaze.

It should be pointed out that even if the psychotic patient demonstrates a considerable difficulty in expressive competence in communication, they appear extremely receptive on an emotional level. It is, therefore, indispensable that the therapist be well-aware that the patient will perceive every emotional nuance in attitude and tacit communication.

Specific dysfunctional relational styles have also been described for the different subtypes of schizophrenia. The paranoid patient assumes an authoritarian style that is rigid and intolerant. The disorganized patient is characterized by a greater disintegration of communicative patterns and by the introduction of a sort of noise made up of inadequate and confused signals (France & Muir, 1997). In simple and catatonic schizophrenia language appears particularly poor and forced.

In conclusion, it is possible to say that in schizophrenia the communicative disturbances constitute a very important aspect of the pathology and case history. Such disturbances concern the tacit and explicit levels, involving language as well as non-verbal communication. Communicative disorders are, therefore, responsible for the deficits in attention, memory, and executive functions.

5. *Deficits in Procedural Competences*

5.1. *Loss of Planning Skills*

In the schizophrenic patient the procedural competences are altered considerably, contributing substantially to determining the disorder. The procedural competences are articulated in a series of strongly interrelated skills with different tactical and strategic meaning.

The executive functions contribute to the ability to plan and carry out tactical procedures. Such tactics must, however, be linked in order to realize objectives that are increasingly articulated strategically.

The ability to plan strategically constitutes one of the most remarkable functions of human intelligence and is a function prone to significant deterioration in schizophrenic patients.

In this way, a considerable loss of planning skills emerges. This psychopathological problem constitutes a notable obstacle to treatment and rehabilitation and must be systematically taken into consideration when planning treatment.

5.2. *Alteration in the Executive Functions*

Executive functions are a series of skills necessary for carrying out intentionally programmed and controlled actions.

These skills are altered in schizophrenic patients because of the presence of the following problematic aspects:

- difficulty in planning;
- impairment of the ability to solve problems in which the solutions are not already available, but require abstraction and creativity;
- the capacity to choose between different behavioural options;
- regulation of attention functions during the execution of a task.

Norman and Shallice (1987) have proposed a cognitive model to explain the reduced capacity to act in schizophrenic patients in the areas of movement, language, and affective expression. They hypothesized that these dysfunctions can be determined by a deficit in the system of attention supervision.

The system of attention supervision normally modulates secondary level processor activity that controls the production of automatic actions. Norman and Shallice have named this system, "decision catalog". These processors are only capable of stimulus-guided behaviors; in the absence of new environmental stimuli, the system remains inactive or persists in the same modality of action.

The "decision catalog" system is normally modulated by the attention supervision system that can modulate the routines in competition; it can, for example, suppress action activated by external stimuli.

Because of this mechanism, the attention supervision system can promote a particular action when no *routine* from the environmental context has been selected; thus, the mechanism can predict persevering behaviors, can inhibit response to stimuli, and can generate new actions in situations in which no *routine* action is activated.

In absence of this modulation, it is difficult to exhibit adequate behaviour in situations in which no routine action is appropriate. This difficulty is expressed as a lack of spontaneous and intentional actions (poor volition). Moreover, routine actions are not easily interrupted, even when they do not seem to be the most appropriate (perseverance). Lastly, in absence of modulation on the part of the system of attention supervision, routine actions can be stimulated by environmental situations, even if inappropriate, thus causing distraction and incoherent behaviors.

At the Institute of Clinical Psychiatry at the University, I have carried out research oriented to identify and develop original instruments to assess the executive functions in schizophrenic patients. In this context, I became interested in a new computerized assessment tool called *Iter,* developed by Enea for the Antartide project.

Research aimed at evaluating if this tool could be used with schizophrenic patients was planned to see if it could indicate a specific profile in these patients when compared to a control group and to patients with other pathologies. A series of preliminary experimental tests convinced me of the possibility of using the *Iter* tool with psychotic patient. Modifications in the administration routine were necessary, however.

Subsequently, we began an experiment with three groups: the first group of 20 control subjects, the second of 20 schizophrenic patients, and the third group of patients with depression. The test, carried out on a computer, consists of representing a city map on the monitor. The topographic location of places on the map were presented using different numerical codes in and the patient carries out a series of tasks.

The presentation of the map is done preliminarily, using icons and graphics we developed in order to make the tasks clearer. Consultation with the examiner was permitted during the test. The city clock (placed at the bottom center of the screen) marks the virtual time that passes during the test. The subject has four and one quarter hours of virtual time to carry out the errands in the city.

The test is presented as a simulation of a situation that could emerge in real life and for which the elaboration of a prearranged, goal-oriented plan is necessary.

The subject is furnished with a list of the possible errands to carry out in order to reach a final goal the departure by plane for a three-week trip. For each errand, a number of corresponding locations on the map and the specific costs in terms of time allowed are set.

The test subject is asked to choose, in advance, the errands that seem most important. It is also possible to note them on paper, if desired. The subject is then asked to create an itinerary following rules and constraints that are clearly described with the help of icons and graphic material available.

The performance is recorded on a personal computer by using software developed for this purpose. Maximum real time allowed for the completion of the test is 60 minutes. The software *Iter* permits the subject to go ahead only when they comply with the rules and constraints present on the map. Any violation blocks the subject's progress, and progress requires return to compliance.

The administration of *Iter* took place in the Department of Psychiatry's laboratory at the University. The room, well-lit and silent, with the subject seated at a desk with a personal computer. The examiner, who assisted all the trials, was available to answer any questions. All the subjects performed the *Iter* test under the same conditions.

The measures that differentiated the three groups and that, therefore, delineate a clear profile of performance are: "the time needed for the errands", "performance on the test" (both absolute and weighted), and "the errors along the route".

These differences in performance appeared impaired in depressed patients, but were even worse in the schizophrenic group.

The three measures of performance on errands (completed, abandoned, and serious omissions) differentiated the schizophrenics from the depressed and control groups, but not differentiate the control from the depressed group. The results were that same for the measure, "errors along the route".

The research demonstrated that the capacity to plan and execute complex tasks in an orderly fashion is considerably impaired in the schizophrenic patients. For this reason, this difficulty in planning must be taken into consideration in the assessment procedures and especially in the rehabilitative protocols.

6. *Disturbances of the Emotional Sphere*

Even though the dysfunctions of the cognitive processes constitute the most relevant aspect of the psychopathology of schizophrenia, the alterations of affective expression also assume considerable importance in development of this illness (Flack, Laird & Cavallaro, 1999; Kring, 1999).

Luc Ciompi (1988) was the first to systematically develop the conception of schizophrenia as a disorder linked primarily to affective logic.

The concept "affective logic" was proposed by Ciompi in 1982 and, subsequently, developed and updated. It is based on an integrative orientation that brings together concepts from Piaget, from psychodynamic theory, and concepts derived from the neurosciences (Ciompi, 2003).

According to Ciompi, schizophrenia is attributable to a non-linear type of distortion of the normal emotion-cognition dynamic. The affective logic model has been systematically tested over the last 20 years at the Soteria Institute of Bern through the use of integrated therapeutic protocols. A series of controlled clinical trials have permitted Ciompi to demonstrate that a protocol based on psychotherapy and social support, implemented in an empathetic environment with low emotional stimulation, permits psychotic patients to re-establish a positive emotional, cognitive, and behavioural dynamic (Ciompi, 1994).

The affective logic model of Ciompi, with its emphasis on the emotion-cognition interface, seems to me the closest to my conceptualization of the *Entropy of Mind*.

Even if the disturbances of affective expression present in schizophrenia are numerous, those that assume the greatest specificity are substantially attributable to the triad: *flattening of affect, discordance, and ambivalence.*

Flattening of affect. This is manifested by a reduction in the normal modulation of the emotional framework in which a sort of inertia regarding emotional stimulation is exhibited and which leads the patient to react insufficiently with the environment. This flattening is clearly revealed in expression, gesticulation, and vocal intonation which appear to be poorly modulated.

Beyond this, a substantial decrease of exploratory activity is observed, as there is a notable reduction in the curiosity and interest expressed for the feelings of people who are close to the patient.

Affective discordance. This is a discordance between explicit and tacit communication. It happens, in this way, that the patient sometimes smiles in painful situations or relates joyful events with a pained expression.

Ambivalence. This is an very important and particularly pathognomonic aspect of the disturbances to affective expression in schizophrenic patients. It consists of the simultaneous presence in the emotional dynamic of the patient of contrasting sentiments, for example hate and love.

To conclude, it remains to be pointed out that schizophrenic patients frequently seem to be depressed. A pilot study on schizophrenia, carried out by the World Health Organization, was able to identify symptoms of depression in 81% of schizophrenic patients studied (World Health Organization, 1979).

The depressive state, which complicates the description of schizophrenia, would seem to be linked to the sense of loss of identity, the reduction of social relationships, and the deterioration of self-esteem, attributable to the stigma which derives from a diagnosis of schizophrenia.

7. Impairment of Self-efficacy

The behaviour of each individual is regulated, in a proactive sense, by the capacity to represent the consequences of all possible conduct. This capacity is linked to the important function of *self-efficacy*, a topic systematically studied by Bandura (1971) in the area of cognitive psychology.

The research experience of our group has shown both the systematic impairment of the sense of self-efficacy perceived by schizophrenic patients and the importance of correcting this dysfunction in the framework of the therapeutic project.

Central to the theory of Bandura is the concept of perceived self-efficacy. This refers to the belief in one's own ability to organize and effect the course of actions necessary to adequately manage the situation in which one finds oneself and to achieve predetermined results (Bandura, 1982). The conviction of efficacy influences the way in which people think, feel, find personal motivation, and act (Bandura, 1971). Five topics can be identified that are connected to convictions of efficacy.

- Psychological factors;
  - prior personal experiences;
  - known vicarious experiences;
  - convictions relative to personal self-efficacy;
  - emotional and physical conditions;
- Material factors.
- Psychological factors.
- Personal experiences of efficacious management.

These constitute, without a doubt, the best way to acquire self-efficacy, in that the subject maintains a memory of lived experiences and draws positive support from those experiences which have led to success. The experiences of efficacious management also permit the increase in future expectations, so the person will face new events with greater motivation and with the awareness of possessing the skills necessary to overcome any obstacle.

Vicarious experience. The consists in learning through imitation or through the observation of a model. Imitation, long studied by Bandura, is, in fact, a fundamental tool for learning through the successful (and unsuccessful) experiences of others. Observing a model is an excellent way of acquiring knowledge and new experiences. This becomes most effective when the subject can identify strongly with the model.

Imitation is the principal element in a child's development. A child learns language imitating sounds produced by adults and then learns to use the words repeated in the formation of sentences. Naturally, the same occurs for gestures, communication, behaviour, and the expression and experience of affection. The more positive the vision of reality furnished by significant figures the more secure the child will be in relating to the world and events.

Convictions Relative to Personal Self-efficacy. These are the basic convictions that all individuals possess regarding their abilities and possibility of positively facing the most disparate problematic situations. These convictions are strongly correlated to the actual efficacy of one's behaviors.

Emotional and Physical Conditions. When individuals experience a period of stress or a phase of tension and physical weakness, they tend to perceive the state of the moment as a sign of a possible failure. Just as with the physical state, the emotional state can influence the perception of the efficacy of the subject. Good mood increases the sense of efficacy, while a bad mood will reduce it.

- Material factors
  - economic insecurity;
  - absence of political experience;
  - lack of or inadequate access to information;
  - precarious economic support.

The conviction of efficacy works on the level of emotional processes, determining a positive image of the Self or, conversely, increasing tension, anxiety, and depressed feelings, tied to failure. When self-esteem, a fundamental element in the relational abilities of the subject, is too low, negative effects are produced. Low self-esteem damages these abilities which are a source of satisfaction and which help deal with elements of stress.

Thus, it is fundamental that during the developmental phase of the life cycle individuals develop a good level of self-esteem, a positive vision of reality, a sense of personal security, and the awareness of being able to manage events in a way that leads to the desired effects *(conviction of control).* The conviction of control is important because it is a fundamental requisite for the achievement of objectives and assumes a particular role in the construction of the image of the self. Already at the age of two, a child develops the motivation for success which is manifested by the will to do things alone.

Subsequently, the consciousness of success and failure is formed, accompanied by pride in the first case, and shame in the second. This continues for the period that goes from middle to high school, as the child becomes aware of the concepts of ability and inability.

It is in this phase that children must receive as much support as possible from the home environment which will permit them to understand the true potential of the abilities they possess. Patients afflicted by psychiatric disorders usually have experienced dysfunctional parenting, and their perception of self-efficacy is often reduced.

Schizophrenic patients who have multiple neuropsychological deficits associated with different operations, including attention, memory, executive functions, communication, and perception, seem to be characterized by a deficit of perceived self-efficacy. The leads to the creation of a vicious circle that feeds the disability.

Self-efficacy is also strongly related to the possibility of expressing relational and social behaviour. On one hand, the level of social competence acquired during development contributes to building a sense of specific adequate ability in the area of relationships. On the other hand, possessing an elevated sense of self-efficacy motivates the subject to explore more frequently and securely social situations, creating the possibility of further acquiring competences.

Based on the preceding considerations, the hypothesis was formulated that patients afflicted with psychiatric disturbances are characterized by a lower level of relational competences and, consequently, by lower self-efficacy, with less social competence than in healthy subjects. This leads to the creation of a series of vicious circles which must be identified and interrupted during the course of psychotherapeutic and rehabilitative treatment.

Because of the importance of self-efficacy in understanding the psychopathology of schizophrenia, but also for the considerable importance it plays in therapy and rehabilitation, I have recently conducted research regarding this topic. Together with my staff, I decided to experimentally evaluate if the levels of self-efficacy were significantly different in individuals with different pathologies, i.e., emotional, mood, and eating disorders, on one hand, and schizophrenic psychosis, on the other.

Using the term neurosis, we identified patients diagnosed, according to the DSM-IV, with:

- panic attacks with agoraphobia;
- obsessive-compulsive disorder;
- dysthymic disorder;
- eating disorders.

The following individuals participated in the research:

- 11 control subjects with an average age of 42.3 years, with 7 women and 4 men;
- 11 patients with psychosis with an average age of 43.8 years, with 4 women and 7 men;
- 11 patients with neurosis with a an average age of 43.7, with 9 women and 2 men.

The patients who participated in the research were either hospitalized in the Department of Psychiatry of the University of Catania, clients of a specialized private practice, or members of a therapeutic and rehabilitative community.

All the patients received adequate pharmacological treatment for their pathologies. The average age of the members of the different groups were not significantly different. The socio-cultural variables were not, however, homogeneous. In fact, the control subjects all possessed a higher level of education than the patients. Since this could constitute a source of bias this difference was kept in mind during the evaluation of the results.

In order to evaluate self-efficacy, two instruments were used: the Asp\A and the Apcis (Caprara, 2001). The Asp\A is a scale used to evaluate perceived social self-efficacy, i.e., the convictions of the subject regarding the capacity to easily fit in, feel comfortable, and perform a proactive role in new social situations.

The two scales were self-administered to the selected sample and took place, in part, in the presence of the test administrator, and in part, in the administrator's absence without a detailed explanation. All in all, the average time of administration was 15-20 minutes. The overall picture that emerged from the research can be synthesized in the following manner.

Regarding the Asp\A, there was a statistically significant difference in the appraised values between the group of neurotics and the control group and between the group of psychotics and the control. The difference between the psychotics and the neurotics was not, however, statistically significant.

Regarding the Apcis, there was a statistically significant difference between the controls and the psychotic patients and between the neurotic and psychotic patients. The first scale, which measures social competence in general terms, revealed an impairment in both neurotic and psychotic patients. The competence relative to interpersonal communication evaluated by the second scale was more impaired in psychotic patients than in neurotic patients. The difference between neurotics and the control group was not significant in this second scale.

These results can be interpreted in the following way.

In the two groups of patients, an impairment of self-efficacy was appraised relative to social competence. Regarding communication, self-efficacy was particularly compromised in psychotic patients and less so in the group of neurotics.

The fact that the differences in self-efficacy in communication for neurotic patients was not statistically different from the control group demonstrates that the socio-cultural variables did not create a salient bias.

This means that the perceived relational competences in the domain of communication were not substantially affected by the level of education.

This research showed the presence of low levels of self-efficacy for relational variables and communication in psychiatric patients. The psychotic patients perceived their own communicative performance was negative and particularly impaired.

These data have important consequences for therapy and rehabilitation. In fact, as already noted, the low levels of self-efficacy contribute to the perpetuation of the disability. Thus, the implementation of rehabilitative and psychotherapeutic programs must focus on improving the relational, social, and self-efficacy competences.

8. Negative Symptoms

The first formulation in descriptive terms of *negative symptoms* in the central nervous systems disorders was proposed by Pinel (1801).

This author identified the impoverishment of speech, the flattening of affect, social withdrawal, and cognitive deterioration as the principal presentation of negative symptoms that could be observed in mental disorders.

Many decades passed, however, before a conceptualization that was not merely descriptive, but also explanatory, was developed, and was applied more often to neurological and not psychic pathologies.

In 1875, Jackson (1932) proposed a dichotomous model for epilepsy in which the negative symptoms were defined as primary because they were attributable to a cerebral lesion. Other symptoms of a positive nature were traceable to the liberation of second order processes usually controlled by some other centers whose activity was compromised by a pathological process.

In schizophrenia, Bleuler (1950) was the first to fully identify the negative symptoms considered pathognomonic to the disorder, including the flattening of affect.

Subsequently, interest for negative symptoms declined so much that Schneider's (1954) classification of the symptoms of schizophrenia was based exclusively on positive symptoms.

This emphasis on the positive symptoms of schizophrenia was accentuated by the responsiveness of these symptoms to neuroleptic treatment, which has little effect on the negative symptoms of the disorder.

Only since the 1980s, with Crow's formulation, have negative symptoms returned to the forefront (Crow, 1980).

Today, the problem of negative symptoms in schizophrenia appears of great importance; they constitute a considerable part of the disability of the schizophrenic patient, they are difficult to treat, and they are able to negatively influence the course of the illness (Stolar, 2004).

Today, however, there still does not exist a uniform position on what should be considered a negative symptom of schizophrenia.

The following enjoy the largest consensus:

- flattening of affect;
- impoverishment of speech or of the content of discourse;
- loss of initiative.

Other negative symptoms that have gained an ample consensus in the literature but are not universally cited, include:

- social withdrawal;
- anhedonia;
- motor slowness;
- thought blockage;
- slowness of speech;
- carelessness in personal appearance and hygiene;
- impairment of work and school activities.

To conclude, other features that are not considered by all authors to constitute negative symptoms are:

- loosening of associative connections;
- affective ambivalence;
- catatonic behaviour;
- attention deficit.

From what has been presented here, it is clear that the evaluation of negative symptoms is still an open topic.

According to Kirkpatrick, Buchanan, Breier, and Carpenter (1993), the symptoms that can be included in the negative syndrome of schizophrenia, based on a large international consensus, include:

- flattening of affect;
- speech impoverishment;
- blockage of volition;
- anhedonia.

Kirkpatrick, Kopelowicz, Buchanan, and Carpenter (2000) point out how patients who show negative symptoms are differentiated in a significant way from those in whom the symptomatology is characterized, in greater measure, by the presence of positive dysfunctional phenomena. The variables which appear different are: the course of the illness and the presence of considerable neuropsychological deficits and specific characteristics noticeable in the brain through brain imaging.

Another very relevant issue in the conceptualization of negative symptoms is the persistent problem of whether to consider these symptoms primary or secondary. Primary symptoms are connected directly to the dysfunctional process which constitutes the schizophrenic affection, while secondary symptoms may be connected, for example, to treatment with neuroleptics or to the condition of isolation in which the psychotic patient is usually reduced. The correct evaluation of a schizophrenic symptom as primary or secondary is very important for any treatment protocol.

The scale most frequently used for this end is the *Positive and Negative Syndrome Scale* (PANSS), (Kay, Fiszbein & Opler, 1987).

In conclusion, the negative symptoms of schizophrenia which enjoy a large consensus are the following:

- flattening or dulling of affect;
- alogia;
- apathy;
- anhedonia.

Excluding alogia, which is a symptom correlated to explicit cognitive processes, it is evident that these are primarily symptoms of the emotional and relational sphere. In schizophrenia the emotional dynamic is dulled and socialization is reduced.

Neal Stolar (2004) formulated a cognitive conceptualization of the negative symptoms of schizophrenia which was then further developed together with Rector and Beck (Rector, Beck & Stolar, 2005).

This is the first complete attempt to produce a cognitively-influenced formulation of this problem area given that most of the traditional literature in the field has concentrated on delusions and hallucinations. Moreover, Stolar, points out most cognitive theorists hold the conviction that negative symptoms, identified principally as social withdrawal, are a type of coping mechanism activated by positive symptoms.

Stolar also notes that the negative symptoms of schizophrenia constitute a challenge to the standard cognitive conception which considers dysfunctional emotional processes as an epiphenomena of problems related to cognition.

For this North American author, negative symptoms have an autonomous origin separate from cognition and can be identified preliminarily in possible deficits in the central nervous system. According to Stolar, these deficits must be, in part, functional and remediable since both pharmacological and behavioural treatments are able to reduce their presence.

The negative symptoms of schizophrenia, according to Stolar, can either be secondary or primary.

In the first case, they must be traced to a different dynamic, for instance, the negative action of a medicine, the progressive loss of social relationships, the lack of gratifying situations, or the frustrating effect of hallucinations and delusions. Stolar, however, indicates that the negative symptoms of schizophrenia can constitute a primary symptomatology, attributable to complex neurophysiological and psychological causes, even if he does admit that in light of standard cognitive theory it is difficult to formulate an adequate conceptualization of these symptoms.

Stolar cites dysfunctional processes and morphological alterations of the areas involved in emotional dynamics, including the limbic system, the amygdala, the prefrontal areas, and the caudate nucleus. Starting with this prevalently biological gap, that is thought to be behind the negative symptoms, Stolar tries to formulate a conceptualization of the symptoms that fits the standard cognitive conception of emotions and cognition.

According to the author, besides the difficulty of thinking positively about how many good things occur in one's life, it is the lack of plans and projects and the gap of projecting oneself toward the future, that is the principal cause of the persistent lack of positive emotions in schizophrenic patients. The conceptualization of Rector is, by his own admission, rather immature and not supported by enough scientific evidence.

From my point of view, it seems that the greatest limit to this theory, typical of writers in the standard cognitive therapy tradition, is reasoning primarily in terms of cognition and then finding themselves in difficulty when confronted with emotional phenomena.

Also interesting, in this case, is the idea that when a gap in emotions is recorded for which no cognitive dynamic can be found, the explanation can be looked for in the biological realm.

As I have tried to show in this book, I believe that emotion is a primary process related to and not subordinated to cognition.

Referring to the processes of the multi-level self, amply described in the preceding chapters, it is possible to affirm that negative symptoms can be thought of as a problem that affects both tacit and Machiavellian knowledge, whereas positive symptoms regard the cognitive area of explicit knowledge and the behavioural area of procedural knowledge.

If we consider the phylogenetic and ontogenetic gradient, it is evident that negative symptoms affect the most archaic components of the brain as well as the oldest processes of the mind, including motivational, emotional, and relational processes.

These processes of the mind are altered in the schizophrenic patient, as has been amply discussed in this monograph, without it being possible or necessarily useful to establish if such an alteration is primary or secondary. This is a complex process that begins with biological vulnerability and is structured by parenting that tends to blunt or dull the emotional resonance of events the patient is exposed to during the life cycle.

In confronting negative symptoms, neither is it enough to activate behavioural processes that increase activity, nor is it sufficient to implement competences and social relations. Working at the cognitive level is not a solution, either.

I believe it is necessary, above all, to use relationships to reactivate or promote the exchange of emotions that can only be initiated in the area of interpersonal processes.

Once again, it is the process of re-parenting that is crucial and not just the specific techniques, be they behavioural or cognitive, as I will try to demonstrate in the third part of the book.

Rector, Beck and Stolar (2005) have developed their conceptualization of the negative symptomatology of schizophrenia, attributing it to the presence in the belief system of the patient of idiosyncratic "convictions", identifiable in the following points.

Conviction of the need for relational distancing. It is not important to maintain social relationships, in fact, it could be dangerous.

Negative convictions regarding one's own possible competences. My performance will be shoddy, compared to others.

Negative convictions activated by positive symptoms. Since I am threatened by strange phenomena and dangerous plots, it is better that I stay at home alone, avoiding all contact with the outside world.

Low expectations for gratification. Nothing can gratify me and so why should I bother with difficult activities?

Low expectations for success. I have difficulty succeeding in the tasks that are asked of me!

Pessimistic expectations tied to stigma. Given I am schizophrenic, I have no hope of getting better.

Idiosyncratic perception in decisions about limited resources. I don't have the basic competence necessary to undertake any type of task.

The presence of this dysfunctional belief system feeds and maintains through recursive vicious circles the processes of emotional flattening, of energy, of alogia, and the lack of volition that constitutes the negative syndrome of schizophrenia.

The identification of these dysfunctional cognitive aspects presented by Rector, Beck and Stolar stem from clinical observation and constitute the premise for psychotherapeutic and rehabilitative intervention that is an integral part of the Negative Entropy protocol, as we shall see in the third part of the book.

9. *The Constructivist Triad:* Entropy of Mind

As it has emerged from the previous study, schizophrenia is a pathological condition which seems to involve almost all the processes of the mind.

The various disorders which afflict the emotional sphere, the processes of elaborating information, cognitive and procedural activities, and Machiavellian intelligence are nevertheless not wholly exclusive to schizophrenia and can be found in other pathologies.

According to the position I have formulated in this book, the pathognomonic aspects of schizophrenia can be traced to a *triad* comprising the following topics: *impaired personal identity, alteration of the sense of unity and continuity of the self,* and *the breakdown of personal narrative.*

As Bleuler (1950) has already noted, the particularity of schizophrenia is not based on single symptoms and signs, but rather on the fact that in this pathology the unity of the psyche is broken as a result of a sudden and progressive deficit in unifying processes.

In the first part of the monograph I have stressed the fact that the brain works in modular terms and consequently the mind is constructed through coalitional processes such as *personal identity,* the *self,* and *personal narrative.*

In schizophrenia, it seems as if these processes, from which a unitary sense of self and a unified perception of one's identity emerge, undergo serious malfunctions. This leads to the dissolution of the sense of unity which derives from the coalitional processes and a fragmentation of knowledge into a chaotic multiplicity from which neither order nor integration emerge (O'Brien & Opie, 2003).

As I have already noted, the basic activity of the brain is the creation of order from disorder to which can now be added the creation of *unity from multiplicity* (Panksepp, 2003).

In schizophrenia, order slackens and unity dissolves, while entropy and the splitting of the mind emerge. The sense of self and its continuity are impaired (Vogeley, 2003).

The alteration of the unifying processes of the self and the dissolution of identity originate from a fragmentation and a disorganization of personal narrative (Gallagher, 2003).

The capacity of elaborating, in unitary and organic terms, the narration of life and its events is altered because of the intrusion of different rules and new scenarios which suddenly transport patients to another set where they feel extraneous (Phillips, 2003).

This conceptualization refers to the neurobiology of the integration processes of the human system of knowledge (Kircher & Davis, 2003).

The maintenance of an effective dynamic of the coalitional processes implies perfect communication and functional integration between the front and back cerebral lobes of the right and left hemispheres of the brain (Parker, Derrington & Blackmore, 2003).

As I have already thoroughly discussed, in schizophrenia a deficit of integration and communication between the different parts of the brain occurs along with the appearance of more disorganized and entropic modes of functioning. In this way, after the dramatic apophany personal history breaks down, and patients slip into an alien dimension, losing the fundamental reference points which derive from the unifying processes of the mind.

Patients no longer know who they are; they are not capable of recognizing the information coming from their brains as their own. Above all, they cannot describe and communicate to others the agonizing experience afflicting them. A truly pathognomonic sign of schizophrenia and its terrible apophany is the progressive incapacity of patients to recognize themselves in the mirror and the consequent horror which originates from observing an alien image looking back from a mirror that should be reflecting their own familiar figure.

The terror caused by the loss of one's own identity probably represents the peak of human suffering since this experience expresses the exact opposite of the most fundamental needs of the mind of *homo sapiens*: identification, categorization, and unity.

It is not a coincidence that one of the cruelest and most widespread forms of torture consists of denying prisoners their name and identity, reducing them to mere numbers, part of an infinite set, deprived of individuality.

On the contrary, epochal events which mark radical changes and dramatic narrative turns in a person's life, often drive people to assume new names and different identities.

A typical example is the *"nom de guerre"* that many members of the Italian Resistance adopted when they went underground. There was obviously a need for secrecy, but that was not the only reason, as I was once told by Pompeo Colajanni, a great leader of the Italian Communist Party, who took part in the war of liberation using the code name "Barbato" (Bearded One). Adopting a new name marked and confirmed a revolutionary change as well as the irreversible entrance into a new narration which broke with the past Fascist dictatorship.

The psychotic apophany breaks the continuity of personal identity, leaving no possibility of building a new one. "I don't know who

I am anymore", say the patients, terrified. "Who's that monster looking at me from the mirror?" they ask themselves, shattered.

Patients slowly lose their capacity to distinguish themselves from reality; they become a chaotic agglomeration of fragmentary experiences which remodels itself by chance every day, like the vivid but fleeting images in an entropic kaleidoscope. Since the patients are in the middle of a chaotic transition, they no longer seem capable of integrating the past with the present as events can no longer be arranged in an intelligible plot (Gallagher, 2003).

The progressive impairment of personal identity can also be attributed to the disintegration of autobiographical memory. These considerations have been corroborated by an experimental study carried out by Salame, Danion, Peretti, and Cuervo (1998).

These French authors showed the impairment of autobiographical memory and a corresponding deterioration of personal identity in a sample of patients affected by schizophrenia. In turn, the impairment of autobiographical memory is attributed to the deterioration of episodic and semantic memories. The progressive loss of coherence of the processes of self and the fragmentation of personal identity lead to the gradual dissolution of the ability to narrate.

Lysaker and Lysaker (2002) have experimentally demonstrated that in patients affected by schizophrenia the sense of self intended as actor and protagonist also collapses within their inner dialog.

The patients are not able to tell a story where they are both agents and protagonists, rather they are defenseless victims of overwhelming meanings. If personal narrative is the result of a program of self-explanation, losing one's identity breaks the narrative plot into a fragmentary series of different, disconnected, film-like scenes.

The schizophrenic condition, according to this conceptualization, assumes a completely different connotation with regard to the numerous other psychopathological disorders which can affect the human mind. In neurotic disorders, rigid and dysfunctional patterns are activated in difficult conditions. The sense of unity of the self and the specificity of personal identity is never significantly altered, nor does narrative activity ever stop. Schizophrenia is, therefore, a truly unique condition of the mind which probably derives from the impairment of coordinated systems activated by process of the hominoid development and the emergence of the self-conscious mind.

As it is written in Genesis, Adam and Eve eat the fruit of knowledge and they become creatures endowed with reflective self-consciousness who, like God, are able to tell good from evil. As to the expulsion of Adam and Eve from Paradise, which marks the beginning of the human adventure on Earth, the threat of God and punishment seemed to be the awareness of physical pain, fatigue, and death.

Things were not quite that way!

God proved to be, in that case, rather evasive. The real threat was not physical pain, fatigue, or death, but the *Entropy of Mind*, the terrible apophany which shatters our existence as human beings, driving us into an unbearable dimension.

Thus, after being driven from Paradise to wander the Earth, one bears a new punishment of being hurled into an alien dimension which is no longer the one prior to the birth of the self-conscious mind, and not even that of the completely functioning, self-conscious mind. It is just a terrifying *Entropy of Mind*.

I felt it would be interesting to quote a short passage written by a patient to describe the condition of clinical decompensation from which she had recently emerged.

> I heard a thousand noises amplified, the most bothersome were the birds; my surroundings were intolerable.
> I was at my sister's home, I was very sick, everything I looked at would immediately provoke in me a feeling of repulsion.
> I prayed like never before and feared I was going to die, it was an unbearable agony, that sense of death imprisoned my soul and on top of the sense of death came the sense of guilt. Terrible!
> I already felt I belonged to another world, a reality I didn't know.

10. Apophany, Phrenentropy, Paleognosy

In this concluding part of the chapter I will try to formulate an approach to the psychopathology of schizophrenia based on the trilogy: evolution, entropy-negentropy information. These three parameters can furnish a new interpretive key to the history of humanity and to the single individual.

Biological, cultural, and historical evolution has produced, and still continues to produce, an organizational process or, better, a process of negative entropy that progressively spread over the whole planet, even reaching our moon where there are signs of negentropy and human information. Even the planet Mars is involved, as highly organized and extremely negentropic human products have landed there.

From very early on, hominids began to impress information on the environment, reorganizing it according to their needs. Chipping a stone to make a spear tip constitutes an evolutionary process, negentropy and information. Using fire to light up the night constitutes an evolutionary process, negentropy and information. Cooking food constitutes an evolutionary process, negentropy and information.

Human development can be described as a progressive and increasingly exasperating process of evolution, negentropy and information, i.e., in opposition to the physical processes of decay, entropy, and loss of information. The transition from analogue to digital, marked by the hemispheric specialization and by the appearance of language and, subsequently, by phonetic, thus digital writing.

Recently, we have assisted an even greater digital revolution in the field of electronic commodities. Videocassettes and analogue players have been substituted by digital DVD's. We are living in a new historical and cultural period that can be defined, following Negroponte (1996), as the "digital" era.

Even in human ontological development, the individual passes from the analogue first stages of life, to the digital stages of spoken language (age two) and written language (age five).

The conception "evolution, entropy-negentropy information", which is part of recent developments in the thermodynamics of non-equilibrium systems, offers new possibilities to rethink Darwinian approaches to the psychopathology of schizophrenia in light of information and chaos theories. An evolutionary approach to the psychopathology of schizophrenia has been proposed by numerous authors.

Arieti (1978), with his formulation of paleological thought, has coherently developed a hypothesis that the schizophrenic subject undergoes a regression taking the shape of less evolved cognitive processes. This author points out how all psychiatric theories that propose the idea of regression for the psychopathology of schizophrenia use a Darwinian evolutionary perspective, as well as a Jacksonian concept of dissolution (Jackson, 1932).

This well-known principle developed by Jackson affirms that in nervous system disorders the functions that develop last, phylogenetically speaking, are the most vulnerable to noxious pathogens. In disorders that compromise these functions, secondary order processes are liberated from control activity. In this way, in disorders of the nervous system, negative symptoms that are referable to the lessening of the higher order functions and positive symptoms that are attributable to the emergence of lower order modulated or inhibited activities can be observed.

This perspective is suited to the psychopathology of schizophrenia, a disorder in which the most recent cognitive functions, from a phylogenetic point of view, including meta-cognition, the unifying processes of the self, personal identity, and the ability to narrate deteriorate. The modalities of emotion-based information processing, that are phylogenetically older, are, on the other hand, activated.

Arieti points out that while the process of human brain evolution has shown a continual rise from the concrete to the abstract, in schizophrenia concrete forms of thought re-emerge. These forms of thought are typical of archaic evolutionary stages from both an ontogenetic as well as a phylogenetic perspective.

According to the principle of *progressive teleological regression*, schizophrenic cognition is not merely illogical, but can be interpreted based on the hypothesis that the schizophrenic patient uses second-order cognitive processes compared to those used by normal subjects. Arieti develops the idea of *paleological thought* following the work of Von Domarus (1944), who previously described a typical alteration in the logic of schizophrenic patients.

According to this conception, while the normal individual accepts identity on the basis of a subject, patients with paleological thought accept identity on the basis of a predicate. Using an ontogenetic perspective, Arieti points out that, not only schizophrenic patients, but also little children tend to show a paleological logic that is progressively replaced by the Aristotelian logic of adults.

Maintaining that children from one to three years old show paleological thinking, Arieti provides the example of small children who, upon seeing an image of any man, will call it father. The logic behind this arbitrary affirmation is the following. Father is a man. The image represents a man. Therefore, because the predicates are equal (man), the subjects are also equal. The image thus represents the father.

The schizophrenic patients shows a similar mode of reasoning. In an example cited by Arieti, a schizophrenic patient says she is the

Madonna. The paleological reasoning behind this statement can be interpreted thusly. The patient thinks: *the Madonna is a Virgin.* Then: *I am also a virgin, so I am the Madonna.*

Arieti further developed the description of the characteristics of the paleological thought by adding the principle of *teleological causality,* i.e., for every event *there exists a unique and precise cause and a specific reason.*

The teleological causality is absolutely deterministic but is still applied by the patient using paleological thought to understand psychic events that are complex and do not respond to a logical linearity. Also, in this case, Arieti adopts an ontogenetic perspective citing the research of Piaget regarding small children. The great Swiss psychologist demonstrated how children attribute a specific intentionally to natural phenomena based on an animistic and anthropomorphic conception of the world (Piaget, 1954).

For small children things have a personality and natural phenomena assume a self-referential meaning. Typically, for children the moon moves in the sky at night in order to illuminate the street for those who are walking in the dark.

Furthermore, a tendency toward causal, unified, and imputable explanations and to an immature logic are also observed in cultural phylogeny. Arieti points out that paleological thought was the predominate of Homeric Greece and is still present today among peoples with very primitive cultures.

In conclusion, Arieti argues that paleological thought is present in early infancy and in dreams and, therefore, expresses a less integrated and evolved mode of thought (Arieti, 1969). Schizophrenia is a condition of regression that, from a phylogenetic and ontogenetic perspective can be defined as more primitive (Arieti, 1974).

Similarly, Jaynes (1976) has put forth a suggestive theory of schizophrenia as a condition characterized by the return of the mind to bicameral functioning.

In his book, *The Origin of Consciousness in the Breakdown of the Bicameral Mind,* the American author presents this provocative thesis, corroborated by historical and anthropological data. Until the third millennium b.C., patterns of hemispheric coordination in humans were different and the two brains functioned autonomously. The right hemisphere produced intense activity stemming from emotional experiences of a normative nature that occurred during the developmental phase of the individual.

In this way, the emotional schemas present in the right hemisphere, becoming activated in conditions of intense stress, are not recognized by the left hemisphere as activity coming from the same brain but, rather, as hallucinatory phenomena linked to divinity.

In the beginning of the second millennium b.C., according to Jaynes, a different coordinated dynamic arose between the two hemispheres characterized by increasing integration, and humans ceased to perceive the informational patterns produced by the right hemisphere as hallucinatory.

According to Jaynes, schizophrenia leads to a relapse into a condition similar to that of the bi-chambered brain. It is clear that this author has applied the logic of evolutionary thought to cultural evolution.

More recently Steven and Price (1996) have proposed an organic, evolutionary approach for psychiatry. In their book, *Evolutionary Psychiatry,* they propose a conceptualization of psychopathology that begins with a Jungian position, then integrates the most recent discoveries of neuroscience, human ethology, and the social sciences.

These authors consider schizophrenia as a psychopathological condition characterized by a deficit of higher order integrative functions and by the exaggerated activation of cerebral structures and functions that are usually subordinate. The Darwinian approach to the psychopathology of schizophrenia has been reconsidered in light of the preceding literature and presented by Crow (2000).

After an ample literature review, Crow discusses the most significant aspects of the modern evolutionary approach to the psychopathology of schizophrenia. The crucial points for Crow are the following.

A genetic mutation among hominids provoked hemispheric specialization. This specialization created an advantage in environmental adaptation which eventually spread through the human populations, entirely supplanting the preceding genotypes.

In the human population, therefore, the genotypic characteristics for lesser hemispheric specialization and for the manifestation of psychopathological conditions typical of schizophrenia have not disappeared. They tend to emerge in about one percent of the population.

In conclusion, the particular aspects of the evolutionary approach to etiology and to the psychopathology of schizophrenia can be summed up this way:

- schizophrenia is a specific affection of *homo sapiens;*
- schizophrenia needs to be understood in terms of its relationship to hemispheric specialization and the acquisition of language which are both unique characteristics of the human species;
- schizophrenia is a condition of regression or devolution, reversing biological and cultural evolution of the human species from both a phylogenic and ontogenetic perspective.

Regarding the regressive slippage of processes of knowledge to functioning modalities of the more archaic type, I would add a personal reflection to the positions of Von Domarus and Arieti regarding paleological regression (Von Domarus, 1944).

As we have seen, the two writers point out that in the individual afflicted by schizophrenia, there seems to be an devolution process characterized by the reappearance of archaic logical processes belonging to preceding phylogenetic and ontogenetic conditions. I would add that the regression does not involve only the formal logic of thought and cognitive conceptualization, but involves the entire system of mind, with implications for all the forms of intelligence that I have described: tacit, explicit, procedural, and Machiavellian.

Regarding this last point, I would like to cite recent research on primate ethology that shows how the amount of social relationship and the number of individuals that can be part of a group are related to the increase in the cerebral mass as we go up the evolutionary ladder (Dunbar, 1993).

Now it appears clear that the schizophrenic patient has an accentuated deficit in the relational processes and drastically reorganizes the number of persons related to, considerably reducing social contacts. As we have seen, the procedural competences are also impaired and the planning of complex strategies deteriorates as well, while affect becomes monotonous and flat.

We are not only in the presence of an devolution of logic, but rather a comprehensive and regressive reorganization of the entire system of knowing. For this reason I would like to propose the neologism, *paleognosy,* to describe this condition of the psychotic mind.

A patient afflicted with schizophrenia is a *paleognostic individual*. The comprehensive condition of the patient's mind, based on more archaic regressive functioning, can be defined *paleognosy*.

Very recently, in line with the thematic development of the trilogy, *information, entropy*, and *evolution*, some sporadic explanations of the schizophrenic problem using the thermodynamics of non-linear systems and chaos theory have appeared in the literature (Perna & Masterpasqua, 1997).

In this way, the concept of regression which, as we have seen, is one of the most interesting topics in the multiple approaches to the psychopathology of schizophrenia has begun to be interpreted in terms of chaos theory.

According to thermodynamics of non-linear systems and chaos theory, a regression can be defined as a condition that is a consequence of an increase in entropy during which the system moves away from a condition of equilibrium (Thelen & Smith, 2000).

According to chaos theory, regression does not necessarily assume an unequivocally negative meaning as something the deteriorates or re-establishes itself in a state of lesser integration or greater disorder. In physical terms, a regression is only a transition of state that can also be a sign of achieving new conditions of dynamic equilibrium that are even better integrated and stable than those from which the system diverged at the beginning of the disturbance.

The formulation of Perna and Masterpasqua (1997) is very interesting. It involves two larges systems in the nervous system that continually interact; one is chaotic and probabilistic, while the other is ordered and deterministic.

The former is characterized by a logic of associative functioning that is synthetic and syncretic, the second is tied to formal and logical sequential processes.

From the perspective of entropy (understood in terms of an informative indeterminacy), the chaotic and probabilistic system is a system of high entropy, while the ordered and deterministic system appears to continually create order from disorder, thus is a teleological system based on the goal of systematically reducing indeterminacy and, therefore, entropy.

In a condition of good integration, the two systems function in perfect harmony; in a pathological state, however, a discrepancy is created between environmental pressures with an excessive input of information and the capacity of the ordered and deterministic system to lower the level of entropy. In this way, the comprehensive level of entropy begins to grow dangerously. The system can no longer maintain the prior state of dynamic equilibrium and must implement a transition towards a new condition, characterized by a different set-up for the information processing systems. This different set-up may be represented by the schizophrenic condition.

According to Perna and Masterpasqua, in schizophrenia the level of entropy and chaos of the entire nervous system increase massively. This increase of disorder is reflected in the environmental niche which also enters a condition of turbulence with negative repercussions on the patient, instituting a vicious circle that continually increases entropy.

The formulation of Perna and Masterpasqua is extremely interesting and can be easily interfaced with an idea of Guidano (1992) regarding the two processes of the mind: experience (a chaotic and probabilistic process) and explanation (an ordered and deterministic process). The formulation also finds a basis in much psychophysiological research describing the two different systems of elaboration present in the central nervous system that are altered by the condition of schizophrenia.

Some recent experimental research has furnished data that support the hypothesis that schizophrenia can be considered a condition of high entropy and chaos of the mind.

Paulus and Braff (2003) have conducted experimental research using chaos theory in order quantify the level of entropy of the central nervous systems of schizophrenic patients. They then compared their results to a healthy control group. The working hypothesis, which constituted the basis of the research, is linked to a conception in which the schizophrenic condition is considered to be a state of complex disorganization of the entire nervous system, rather than a simple movement toward a less evolved and integrated state.

The data that emerge from this research demonstrate a higher average level of entropy in schizophrenic patients than in the control group.

This research represents one of the first attempts to apply nonlinear analytical methods to the condition of the central nervous system as compared to the normal measures of performance and integration of classical neuropsychology.

Another experimental contribution has been proposed by Tschacher and Scheier (1995) based on research that monitored the clinical condition of a group of schizophrenic patients for 200 or more consecutive days.

Methods of non-linear dynamic analysis were applied to the variations in the symptomatic condition. These authors demonstrated, with their sample group, that a significant majority of the patients showed a chaotic trend rather than a linear evolution in their symptomatic situations.

Even if research on schizophrenia inspired by chaos theory and non-linear dynamic systems is just beginning, it appears quite promising.

Regarding chaos and entropy, I would like to present a text written by one of my patients.

> Those magicians whom you have trusted to make magic with the devils, inserting them in the sex and the bladder, making it impossible to urinate and day by day ruining the kidneys of my family and friends for years making them go to the hospital to urinate with catheters for the sake of cruelty forcing them in this way not to speak to people because there was the Saint who cured with her pure and candid soul while I did not help her because of wickedness and presumption and everybody helped her because she was going crazy. The poor thing was going crazy because of the devils that were working against us with the presumption to say to the doctors that I was schizophrenic.
>
> Filling me up with medicine for years because I had understood everything and they were afraid that the truth would be discovered threatening my family, falling back on me, making me crazy with voices in my head for years and making my family crazy. While the bastard Saint for ten years had sex with my husband in his sleep making him impotent and irrecoverable because of envy and jealousy because he would have sex with me.
>
> Sending people in ultrasound with the complicity of an 800 number so that they attacked me to make me go crazy casting spells on my husband so he would love her and marry her, making me die from the brain that is making them go crazy in order to have children with my husband. Nine years ago she made me abort making my husband also go crazy because of jealousy.

Concluding this chapter I would like to mention again that I am a long way off from furnishing a exhaustive conception of the psychopathology of schizophrenia, even if the adoption of the complex perspective which I have been attempting to develop in recent years and am presenting here, marks a considerable advance.

Despite this, I feel able to affirm that many of the aspects presented here and corroborated by a considerable amount of experimental data, permit the formulation of an interesting hypothesis based on the following schema:

- diatesi;
- disontogenesis;
- apophany;
- Entropy of Mind and Phrenentropy;
- paleognosy.

Schizophrenia is a affliction that only affects humans and is not imputable to the alteration of individual processes of the mind and activity of the brain, but regards the entire system of knowledge and coalitional processes.

This condition is ascribable to a specific biological vulnerability (diathesis) and to the negative action of the dysfunctional processes of programming of the mind activated during developmental history and traceable primarily to parenting (disontogenesis).

Apophany emerges at the moment in which the resources for the creation of meaning and coherent narration are overcome by the challenges of reality.

Schizophrenia, in the critical phase that follows apophany, is a condition of chaotic transition, characterized by an increase in the Entropy of Mind. In fact, schizophrenia is, *par excellence*, the Entropy of Mind.

The individual who experiences Entropy of Mind activates coping mechanisms in the attempt to diminish disorder and recreate an acceptable meaning of existence.

This attempt at coping that regards all the processes of knowledge is activated through a dynamic that I have defined *paleognosic regression*.

The paleognostic individual may find an equilibrium in the human groups of less developed cultures, but enters into serious conflict with others in the so-called advanced societies. This is because of the enormous amount of information and the scarce relational and social support due to the limited time available for daily routines and the difficulties that characterize life in these so-called developed countries.

In neurotic and emotional disorders, the complex system constituted by the mind and the brain exhibits specific malfunctioning that does not disrupt the sense of self and personal identity. In schizophrenia, however, this is precisely what happens.

Patients, after psychotic apophany, are sucked into a chaotic spiral that constitutes the schizophrenic condition. They become something different from what they were before, they no longer experience, act or think like *homo sapiens*, though they still live among them. They quickly enter into conflict with others. In order to care for these unfortunates, we must reach the place they are and not wait for them to return to our world.

To treat a schizophrenic means courageously traversing a difficult boundary toward a different dimension in order to find the patient and interface with him or her in order to exchange information.

This interface must be established on an emotional level, which is the only level that still functions reasonably well in the schizophrenic patient. Only when the patients have "felt" us inside their world, and once the terror has been removed, will they have learned to trust. Only then can we begin the return trip that will bring us both back into the dimension of *homo sapiens*. As is clear, in this conception curing schizophrenic patients constitutes a challenge of incredible difficulty.

In the third and last part of the book, I will try to provide some directions, still provisional and approximate, for this incredible adventure. I will end this second part of the book with the words of a patient that express, with great clarity and strong emotional impact, this very difficult condition.

> I don't know how to stay in this world.
> I lack cleverness, while the others know how to reach their goals.
> I am like an automaton, piloted from the outside.
> I feel only negative thoughts, which then always come true.
> Reality is strange and foreign.

I feel like an animal, and it is impossible for me to reason
with my head.
I act on instinct and I can't make plans.
I feel useless and I depend on others.
I was wise, and now I am helpless.
Before, by myself, I constructed meaning,
Now I am the passive vessel of the thoughts of others!

This woman has returned from the desolate territory of the Entropy of Mind. Now she is well, she works, loves, evolves, lives again as a human being. But how did she overcome the phrenentropic condition?

To answer this question you must read the third and last part of the book! Don't worry, it's only 162 more pages!

PART THREE

Negative Entropy

CHAPTER FIVE

Conceptualization, Diagnosis, Assessment

Even though the first systematic conceptualization of schizophrenic disorders was formulated by Kraepelin (1919) at the beginning of the 20th century, today we are still discussing if a specific clinical condition that can be traced to a unitary illness definable unequivocally as schizophrenia actually exists.

Regarding clinical conditions characterized by psychic problems, we should also note that at least four different orientations in different classification or evaluation systems of the patient have been identified (Procacci, 1999). The four categories regarding schizophrenia are:

- categorical;
- dimensional;
- structural;
- functional.

1. *Categorial Approach*

The categorical models of schizophrenia are the best known and used today and will be dealt with at the beginning of the chapter. I will reserve discussion of the dimensional and functional categories for the section on assessment.

The categorical diagnostic orientation in clinical psychiatry derives directly from the methodology of biological medicine. Through "diagnosis" a series of individuals affected by a specific illness are identified. Important corollaries of this approach are constituted by the assumption that for every specific illness there are a corresponding, equally specific etiological pathogenic dynamic and a characteristic pathophysiologic state. Finally, this categorical model indirectly postulates that when faced with specific diagnostic situations there must exist just as many *ad hoc* therapies.

A classic example of this approach could be observed at the beginning of the 1980s in the DSM-III when a new nosological entity, "panic attacks", was created. A pharmacological treatment was immediately proposed specific for the new illness based on alprazolam. To paraphrase a political slogan of the past, in favour of universal suffrage—*one man, one vote*—could become the new slogan of the drug companies—*one diagnosis, one drug*!

A recent, brilliant example of such simplistic (but effective) marketing is the campaign by a French multinational that promotes that uses a specific therapy based on amisulpride for the disorder with the new diagnostic label "dysthymia".

In the categorical type of classificatory system, the different symptoms are gathered together in a specific illness entity that refers to an equal number of pathological conditions.

The most important categorical systems, internationally, are the *Diagnostic and Statistical Manual of Mental Disorders* (DSM) of the American Psychiatric Association and the *International Classification of Diseases* of the World Health Organization (ICD) (American Psychiatric Association, 1987, 1994, 2000; World Health Organization, 1992).

Regarding the first system, I will refer to the revision of the IV edition (DSM-IV-TR), for the second, I will use the ICD-10, relative to the classification of mental and behavioural disorders. A third categorical system of classification of schizophrenia is that proposed by Crow.

DSM-IV-TR. The Diagnostic and Statistical Manual of Mental Disorders is proposed as a merely descriptive approach and, therefore, atheoretical psychiatric nosology.

In reality, at least for schizophrenia, this diagnostic system is hardly atheoretical and espouses a very clear position. Two out of three crucial aspects for diagnosing schizophrenia treat it as a chronic and debilitating disease.

This impression is confirmed if we compare it to the ICD-10 classification system of the World Health Organization, which I will address shortly. For now it is enough to underline the fact that while the DSM focuses on the long duration of the illness and on the social and occupational dysfunction, the ICD-10 points out how schizophrenia, in many cases, can be brief and have a positive outcome, consistent with complete recovery.

The Diagnostic and Statistical Manual, IV edition—Text Revision of the American Psychological Association, requires six crucial criteria in order to diagnose schizophrenia. Of these, three constitute criteria of inclusion and three, exclusion, as is clear from the list:

- characteristic symptoms;
- social and occupation dysfunction;
- length;
- exclusion of schizoaffective and mood disorders;
- exclusion of substance use or a medical condition;
- distinction from a pervasive developmental disorder.

Now let's consider each of the preceding six aspects.

A) Symptoms. Two (or more) of the following symptoms; *5 symptoms,* each present for a significant period of time during a period of a month (or less if treated with success):

1. delusions;
2. hallucinations;
3. disorganized speech (for example, frequent incoherence or distraction);
4. grossly disorganized or catatonic behaviour;
5. negative symptoms, i.e., flattening of affect, alogia, abulia.

It should be noted that only one symptom of criterion no. 1 is required if the delusions are bizarre, or if the hallucination consists of a voice that continues to comment on the behaviour or the thought of the subject, or if two or more voices converse together.

B) Social and occupation dysfunction. For a significant period of time from the onset of the disorder, one or more the principal areas of functioning such as work, interpersonal relations, or personal hygiene is notably lower than the level reached before the illness (or when the onset is in childhood or adolescence, an incapacity to reach an expected level of interpersonal, scholastic, or occupational functioning is manifested).

C) Duration. Continuous signs of the disorder persist for *at least six months.* This period of six months must include at least one month of symptoms (or less, if treated with success) that satisfy criterion *A* (i.e., symptoms of the active phase) and can include periods of prodromal or residual symptoms.

During these prodromal or residual periods, the signs of the disorder can be manifested only by negative symptoms or by two or more of the symptoms listed in criterion *A* that present in an accentuated form (for example, strange beliefs or unusual perceptive experiences).

D) Exclusion of schizoaffective or mood disorders. Schizoaffective or mood disorders with psychotic features are excluded when:

- no major depressive, manic, or mixed episode occurs concurrently with the symptoms of the active phase;
- if episodes of mood alteration during occur the phase of active symptoms, their duration is brief relative to the total length of the active and residual periods.

E) Exclusion of substance use and of a general medical condition. The disorder is not due to the direct physiological effects of a substance (e.g., illegal drugs or medication) or a general medical condition.

F) Distinction from a pervasive developmental disorder. If there is a history of autism or other pervasive developmental disorders, the additional diagnosis of schizophrenia applies only if significant delusions or hallucinations are also present for at least one month (or less, if treated with success).

Concerning the course of the illness, the DSM-IV proposes the following distinctions:

- episodic with residual intercritical symptoms (the episodes are defined by the reappearance of considerable psychotic symptoms); specify also if: with relevant negative symptoms;
- episodic with no residual intercritical symptom;
- continual (considerable psychotic symptoms are present for the whole period of observation);
- single episode in partial remission; specify also if: with considerable negative symptoms;
- single episode in complete remission;
- different modality or not specified;
- less than a year from onset of the initial symptoms of the active phase.

To conclude, some subtypes are considered that are defined on the basis of the predominant symptomatology at the moment of evaluation. Paranoid and disorganized types tend to be, respectively, the least and most serious.

The diagnosis of a particular subtype is based on the case history that was determined by the most recent clinical evaluation and the presentation for treatment, and can vary over time. It is not uncommon that the illness presents with symptoms that are characteristic of more than one subtype. The subtypes identified by the DSM are:

- *Paranoid type*: this is diagnosed when there is anxiety with grandiose or persecutory delusions, the typical presentation includes hallucinations.
- *Disorganized type*: this is diagnosed when there is considerable disorganized speech and behaviour and flat or inadequate affect are present (unless the catatonic type is also present).
- *Catatonic type*: this is diagnosed when considerable catatonic symptoms are present (not considering the presence of other symptoms).
- *Undifferentiated type*: this does not satisfy the criteria for the catatonic, disorganized, or paranoid type.

- *Residual type*: this is applied to situations in which there is a continual manifestation of the disorder, but that do not satisfy the criteria for the symptoms of the active phase.

ICD-10. Classification of Mental and Behavioral Disorders. The *International Classification of Diseases* developed by the World Health Organization (World Health Organization), constitutes the codification system of all pathologies.

In this nosological system there is an exhaustive classification of mental illness, and the system is largely compatible with the DSM-IV.

This system is also based on a multi-axial evaluation methodology.

Regarding the diagnosis of schizophrenia, some considerations are relevant.

The minimum duration of the disorder must be greater than one month. In fact, while the DSM-IV specifies a duration of at least six months, the ICD-10 provides for a diagnosis of schizophrenia for a condition that exhibits the symptomatology described for more than one month.

Very important is the explicitly formulated consideration by the authors that the adoption of the brief one month limit stems from the need to confute the commonly held belief that schizophrenia is always a chronic and lengthy disorder.

World Health Organization studies carried out in many nations throughout the world have demonstrated that there are patients in every culture that exhibit symptoms typical of schizophrenia that last for less than six months.

Sartorius, therefore, wants to eliminate the criteria of chronicity and duration in favour of a vision of schizophrenia described as a syndrome that recognizes different causes and multiple scenarios for its course and outcome and that is influenced by an inextricable series of genetic, physical, social, and cultural factors.

The introductory paragraph on schizophrenia affirms that the course of this illness is varied and cannot be defined as inevitably evolving toward chronicity. It also clearly notes that in a certain proportion of cases, that varies in different cultures and populations, recovery is complete or almost complete.

ICD-10 points out the impossibility of identifying symptoms that are entirely pathognomonic in the clinical situation.

The following symptom clusters are listed as the salient clinical aspects of schizophrenia:

a. thought echoing and insertion, stealing, or transmission of thought;

b. delusions of control, where one feels passive about one's own body that it is controlled from the outside. Delusional perception;

c. hallucinatory voices that comment on the behaviour of the patient or discuss the patient among themselves, or other types of voices, for example, that come from parts of the patient's body;

d. persistent delusions that show inappropriate cultural, political or religious content, or belief in the possession of supernatural powers such as, for example, the power to control climate or be in contact with aliens from other worlds;

e. persistent hallucinations in any sensory mode;

f. blockage or interpolation of thinking that provokes incoherence or disorganized speech, or speech characterized by the presence of neologisms;

g. catatonic behaviour;

h. negative symptoms including apathy, under productive speech, emotional dullness or incoherent emotional responses, withdrawal or marked decrease in social activity, as long as these symptoms are not due to current depression or neuroleptic treatment;

i. a significant and consistent modification of behaviour including a distinct loss of normal interests, an attitude consistent with feeling a loss of goals and complete closure within oneself, with consequent social withdrawal.

The preceding clusters of symptoms do not hold the equal importance.

In fact, the clusters from *A-D* are considered more important than the *E-I* group. The steps to diagnosis suggested by the ICD-10 are notation of the following:

- The presence of at least one symptom, if marked and evident, or two, if more subtle, listed in clusters *A-D*, or if there are only symptoms from the *E-I* clusters, then there must be at least two clearly present.

- The symptoms must last at least one month. When the duration is less than a month, a diagnosis of a schizophreniform disorder is supported. This is changed to schizophrenia after the duration of a month.
- The duration of a month does not include prodromal symptoms but must include only the time period during which the evident symptoms are clearly present. According to the ID-10, schizophrenia, occurs the following subtypes:
  - *Paranoid*: characterized by delusions (especially grandiose or persecutory) and hallucinations.
  - *Hebephrenic*: characterized by fragmentary delusions and hallucinations. The most important aspect of this subtype is the modification of the affective sphere. Behaviour appears silly and fragmentary. There is a tendency toward isolation and hypochondria is common. This form of schizophrenia usually begins around 15-25 years of age and is characterized by a particularly severe prognosis.
  - *Catatonia*: serious impairment of the motor and postural sphere.
  - *Undifferentiated*: a subtype used when there are symptoms diagnostic of schizophrenia, but they do not fit a diagnosis of one of the three subtypes cited above.
  - *Post-depression schizophrenia*: is a form of depression which occurs after a psychotic episode.
  - *Residual schizophrenia*: a condition of long duration in which there is a progression from a more active first stage of the illness to a second longer lasting stage characterized by negative symptoms. Even if this condition lasts a long time, it must not be considered irreversible.
  - *Simple schizophrenia*: a rare form of the psychiatric disorder with an insidious and progressive development of behavioural eccentricity and a decline of personal performance in varied contexts. Delusions and hallucinations are not much in evidence.

– *Other forms of schizophrenia* which include:
  - cenestopathic schizophrenia;
  - schizophreniform disorder, not otherwise specified.

  And exclude:
  - schizotypal disorder;
  - cyclical schizophrenia;
  - latent schizophrenia.

– *Schizophrenia, non specified form.*

A final aspect regarding the illness course that must be added is the following:

- episodic with progressive deficit;
- episodic but with stable deficit;
- episodic with intercritical remission;
- with incomplete remission;
- with complete remission;
- another type of course;
- uncertain course due to a too brief observation period.

The classification of schizophrenia proposed by Crow. Among the categorical approaches to the diagnosis of schizophrenia, the system of classification of the psychotic condition proposed by Crow must be included. This system identifies two syndromes called positive schizophrenia (Type I) and negative schizophrenia (Type II).

The first clinical condition is characterized by the following aspects:

- symptoms: positive;
- response to neuroleptics: good;
- cognitive deterioration: absent;
- outcome: reversible;
- responsible biological processes: increase in active dopamine receptors.

Type II schizophrenia, according to Crow exhibits, the following characteristics:

- symptoms: negative;
- response to neuroleptics: poor;
- cognitive deterioration: present;
- outcome: irreversible;
- responsible biological processes: neuronal impoverishment, demonstrable structural alterations of the central nervous system.

2. *Dimensional Paradigm*

In the dimensional approach to pathological conditions and to schizophrenia, in particular, a system of evaluation is used that substitutes the study of a series of "dimensions" for diagnostic categorization.

This model derives from the research methods of psychology rather than medicine. The study of different dimensions permits the identification of a cluster of symptoms rather than a cluster of patients. The dimensional approach is discrete, not categorical, so it is possible to analyze many dimensions at the same time. The concrete actuation of such an approach is realized through the collection of information carried out through specific instruments of assessment on a certain number of variables.

A typical example of a dimensional orientation to the study of schizophrenia is furnished by Liddle (1987). This author has tried to classify the symptoms exhibited by a group of patients suffering from schizophrenia over a long period by using the *Present State Examination* and the Andreasen (1987) scale of positive and negative symptoms.

Analyzing the data obtained, Liddle has identified three dimensions traceable to:

- distortion of reality;
- psychomotor impoverishment;
- disorganization.

These dimensions lead to the following diagnostic orientations:

- distortion of reality: positive forms;
- psychomotor impoverishment: negative forms;
- disorganization: disorganized forms.

Nancy Andreasen (1987) has proposed her own declaredly dimensional orientation to the conceptualization of the schizophrenic condition. She also developed instruments of evaluation for the identified dimensions that can be grouped into two clusters: positive schizophrenia and negative schizophrenia.

Two dimensions emerge in Andreasen's positive symptoms: psychoticism and disorganization. Andreasen criticizes the schizophrenic typologies of Crow, which recognize two different etiological pathogenic mechanisms: organic and functional. According to Andreasen, both the syndromes are attributable to biological factors.

Negative schizophrenia constitutes a psychopathological and specific clinical entity with a profile characterized by:

- poor pre-morbid adaptation that begins in infancy;
- particularly severe negative symptoms, from dysphoria to thoughts of suicide;
- severity in the "disorganization" dimension;
- low hostility.

Patients diagnosed with negative schizophrenia have a high incidence of vague neurological symptoms.

Regarding risk factors and etiology, many possibilities have been investigated, including: familial, biochemical, and psychophysiological parameters assessed by means of brain imaging.

These data lead to the hypothesis that negative schizophrenia is a specific nosological entity related to the presence of precocious neuro-developmental dysfunctions that interfere with cognitive and social functioning from the first years of life.

The identification of the negative syndrome and, more generally, of negative symptoms is not merely a diagnostic and nosological problem, but, on the contrary, it assumes enormous importance for the planning of therapeutic and rehabilitative treatment, as we will see later.

3. *Structural Orientation*

If the categorical and dimensional models of schizophrenia are at the base of the more biological approaches, the structural model was introduced by standard and constructivist authors in the cognitive psychotherapy tradition.

Beck (1971), as we have seen, developed, the conception of processes of meaning which are organized in schemas that constitute the base structures of the system of knowledge. This type of conceptualization was applied to schizophrenia by authors such as Kingdon and Turkinton (1994), Fowler, Garety, and Kuipers (1995). The constructivist approach to the evaluation of the psychotic patient is part of both the structural and categorical models.

In fact, regarding the first aspect Vittorio Guidano (1988) described specific groups of constructs that identify a series of diagnostic categories called "organization of personal meaning".

In Guidano's conception, great emphasis has been assigned to the identification of the typology of the organization of personal meaning which applies to every patient, indeed, to every individual.

4. *Functional Model*

A functional approach to the conceptualization of the condition of schizophrenia can be seen in the model developed by Carlo Perris (1989).

This author identifies a series of altered functions in the schizophrenic patient, including the incapacity of decentralization and meta-cognitive difficulties.

Hans Brenner has also proposed a functional approach to schizophrenia, focusing on a series of neuropsychological deficits (Brenner, Bettina, Roder & Corrigan, 1992).

A further, primarily biochemical, functional model defines schizophrenia as a disorder characterized by fives symptom categories (Liberman, 1994):

- positive symptoms;
- negative symptoms;
- cognitive symptoms;
- aggressive symptoms;
- anxiety and depression.

Gruzelier (1991) has elaborated another functional and explicative model of schizophrenia based on psychophysiological research and rich in potential implications for theory.

The British author proposes two possible behaviors of the nervous system in schizophrenia. The first is characterized by social closure and withdrawal. The second is marked by relational and emotional behavioural hyperactivity.

The two syndromes are traced to an under-active left hemisphere in the first case, and an excessively active left hemisphere in the second.

The diverse set-up of hemispheric functional coordination present in the two syndromes is documented by psychophysiological data, including spontaneous and evoked electroencephalographic activity and the study of evoked bilateral electrodermal activity. The determination of the two different dysfunctional mental states is traced by Gruzelier to the first stages of ontogenesis.

The presence of the dysfunctional organization of the psychotic mind, structured in different terms in the various schizophrenic typologies, constitutes a basis for a therapeutic hypothesis proposed by Gruzelier and uses psychophysiological methods to promote new functional patterns and coherence of the cerebral hemispheres. In particular, Gruzlier sees great rehabilitative potential for neurofeedback.

The functional conceptualization of schizophrenia has always attracted my attention and much research has been conducted in our laboratory regarding the study of hemispheric functional coordination. This has been documented at the central level, through the study of quantitative electroencephalography and evoked potentials, and peripherally, through the monitoring of electrodermal activity (Scrimali, Grimaldi & Rapisarda, 1988; Scrimali & Maugeri, 2004; Scrimali, Grimaldi & Pulvirenti, 2004).

I will address this issue in the part of the book dedicated to therapy, but now I want to point out how functional models open more possibilities for therapy than the categorical approaches, which serve primarily for classification.

After this brief excursion into the problem of the conceptualization of the schizophrenic condition, I will now describe my personal point of view regarding this delicate question.

Here it seems useful to cite Michele Procacci who has placed me among the authors who have contributed to the functional approach to schizophrenia because of the research carried out by my research group regarding psychophysiological and neuropsychological parameters of the condition (Procacci, 1999).

Substantially, the model *Entropy of Mind* or *Phrenentropy* is a system-processes model that identifies a crucial aspect of the schizophrenic condition in the alterations of many functions of the mind.

As I have explained in the second part of the book, the most specific dysfunctional processes of the psychotic condition are, in my opinion: the impairment of personal identity, the alteration of the unity of the self, and the fracturing of personal narrative.

A series of disorders are present, however, that even if they do not constitute an exclusive presentation of schizophrenia, do produce a clinical situation.

In conclusion, the different approaches—categorical, dimensional, structural, and functional—described in this chapter, constitute different interpretive grids, useful in different circumstances, for understanding and working with the schizophrenic condition.

At this time, it does not seem opportune to discuss in the abstract which approach is "better" or more useful; I think that each one should be used in the appropriate situation. My own position on the problem of diagnosis can be summarized in the following way:

The conceptualization of the schizophrenic condition as *Entropy of Mind* or *Phrenentropy* refers to a *procedural psychopathological model, informed by the logic of complex systems.*

In the context of assessment aimed at the development of a therapeutic and rehabilitative plan, I believe that a functional and dimensional approach is very useful. The categorical diagnosis, which is a descriptive, not explanatory, should be used only later, after beginning treatment, when trying to classify the clinical condition of the patient for research, medico-legal or epidemiological ends.

I think that today the possibility to unequivocally represent the schizophrenic condition intrinsically does not exist.

Diagnosis and conceptualization do not describe actual characteristics of the patient but, rather, processes or schemas in the mind of the health worker. As I have tried to show in this chapter, the adoption of a diagnostic and conceptual approach influences the elaboration of the therapeutic protocol.

It is evident that I do not agree with the approach *"one diagnosis, one drug"* or for that matter, *"for every dimension, a molecule"*.

In this book I describe a heuristic model and a therapeutic protocol for schizophrenia informed by the epistemology of hypothetical realism and complexity. The model is, therefore, procedural, systemic, evolutionary, multi-dimensional, ecological, and multi-contextual.

Every psychopathological dimension of the schizophrenic condition, becomes an object of functional evaluation and of a therapeutic and rehabilitative intervention that is activated in different contexts and with different modalities.

The evaluation phase of the patient, the family and the network is a crucial topic in the context of any therapeutic and rehabilitative protocol.

The process of assessment is aimed at providing a solid and articulated base for the formulation, development, and implementation of a personalized therapeutic and rehabilitative plan.

The use of evaluation procedures repeated during the different phases of the protocol permits the accurate monitoring of changes in the condition of the patient, the family, and the network. In this way, valuable feedback is collected that can help to correct, *in progress*, the therapeutic and rehabilitative strategies adopted.

Besides this, the careful study of the process of change permits the systematic evaluation of the therapeutic protocol in terms of efficiency and efficacy.

The assessment process which is the base of the *Negative Entropy* protocol is articulated in a multimodal and multi-contextual dimension in accord with the epistemology of complexity. Information from the patient, the family, and the network is gathered and integrated. The patient is studied at different levels of systemic integration, including the biological, emotional, cognitive, behavioural, and relational levels. The procedures and the instruments of assessment adopted are the following.

- **Assessment of the patient**
  - Diagnostic: In accordance with the DSM-IV and the ICD-10 (American Psychological Association, 2000; World Health Organization, 1992);
  - Clinical and psychometric;
    - Brief Psychiatric Rating Scale (Overall & Gorham, 1962);
    - Scale for the assessment of positive symptoms (SAPS) by Andreasen (1987);
    - Scale for the assessment of negative symptoms (SANS) by Andreasen (1990).

An alternative to these the three scales is the Positive and Negative Syndrome Scale (PANSS) (Kay, Fiszbein & Opler, 1987).

This instrument of assessment permits the evaluation of positive and negative symptoms of schizophrenia as well as its most important psychopathological aspects. Use of the PANSS is spreading at the international level because of its reliability. Reliability is attained by use of the detailed manual which facilitates standardization by the health worker.

- **Psychophysiological**
  - Analysis of the exosomatic spontaneous and evoked electrodermal activity;
  - Quantitative computerized electroencephalography (QEEG);
  - Recording of evoked electroencephalographic potentials (in particular N50 and P300).

- **Neuropsychological**
  - Attention and concentration (Di Nuovo, 2000);
  - Visual analysis and cognitive strategies (Studer, 1998);
  - Facial Recognition (Rehacom, 2003);
  - Recognition of the facial expression of emotion (Ekman, 1993);
  - Meta-cognition (Carcione, Falcone, Magnolfi & Manaresi, 1997).

- **Disability**
  - Efesto Protocol (Scrimali, 2005c; Grimaldi, Scrimali & Sciuto, 1997).

- **Family assessment**

- **Multimodal evaluation and familial emotional climate**
  - Five Minute Speech Sample (Magana, Goldstein, Falloon & Doane, 1985);
  - Demetra Test (Scrimali, 2004b);
  - Relative Bonding Instrument (Grimaldi & Scrimali, 2001).

- **Study of the functional processes of the family**
  - Family Assessment Measure (Skinner, Steinhauer & Santa-Barbara, 1983);

- **Study of the psychophysiological patterns relative to the familial process**
  - Family Strange Situation (Scrimali, Grimaldi, Cultrera & Santagati, 1995).

- **Assessment of social support, of home environment, and of quality of life**
  - Social Adaptation Self-Evaluation Scale (Bosc, Dubinj & Polin, 1997);
  - Home visit;
  - Lancashire Quality of Life Profile (Oliver, Huxley, Priebe & Kaiser, 1997).

CHAPTER SIX

Prolegomena for Psychological Therapy of Schizophrenia

The scientific basis of the mechanisms of action and the rationale behind psychotherapy, as a treatment modality, have not been entirely understood and unequivocally documented to date. Still more controversial and problematic is the question of psychotherapy in schizophrenia, even if sufficient data does exist in the literature for an initial synthesis which I will try to delineate in this part of the book.

A preliminary consideration based on experimental evidence documents the efficacy of the psychotherapy in schizophrenic psychosis. In fact, numerous controlled studies and literature reviews have clearly shown that the psychotherapeutic cognitive behavioural treatment achieves the following objectives (Garety, 2003):

- stably reduce psychotic symptomatology;
- significantly reduce the number and severity of the relapses;
- improve adherence to drug regimes;
- render relationship patterns more effective.

The only type of psychotherapeutic intervention, besides the behavioural and cognitive approach, that has shown an unequivocal efficacy in treating schizophrenia is family therapy (Birchwood & Spencer, 1999) Obviously this does not mean that other psychotherapeutic orientations are less useful for schizophrenia, only that controlled data regarding their efficacy has not yet been produced.

Pilling, Bebbington, and Kuipers (2002) reviewed 18 controlled trials using family therapy and randomly chosen patients. In all, 1467 patients diagnosed with schizophrenia were involved in these studies. The crucial aspect that emerged from this study of the efficacy of family intervention therapy in schizophrenia is related to the lower rates of relapse that this type of psychotherapy produces. This leads us to affirm that both cognitive-behavioural psychotherapy and family intervention therapy in the treatment of schizophrenic patients are effective.

In particular, cognitive-behavioural psychotherapy excels in the resolution of symptomatology, while family intervention is especially useful in the prevention of relapse.

A more complex and advanced position concerns the psychotherapeutic process, in general and, above all, for this text, the psychotherapeutic process in schizophrenic patients. From research just cited, the unequivocal efficacy of the psychotherapeutic procedures emerges in these areas:

- modifying behaviors, permitting the patient to acquire new competences;
- modifying the cognitive processes of human information processing;
- improving the relationship patterns, thanks to the positive development of the familial emotional climate.

The role of other processes that have not been fully considered in both the standard cognitive-behavioural approach and in family therapy, include:

- the therapeutic relationship;
- the reactivation of neuropsychological functions;
- the reconstruction of personal history;
- the restoration of the self;
- the promotion of the proactive narrative function.

These aspects in, my opinion, constitute particularly important processes in the therapy of the schizophrenic patient and are an essential part of the *Negative Entropy* protocol.

The most important contributions to the development of these processes come from authors in ethological and evolutionary psychiatry, cognitive constructionist psychotherapy, systems-processes psychotherapy, post-rationalist psychotherapy, and the orientation developed by me using the logic of complex and dynamicsystems.

It should be noted that the fundamental contributions I will address can be applied to the schizophrenic patient, even though they have not always been intended for such use.

These topics will be discussed in the section on the Negative Entropy protocol, and, for the moment, I will deal with the rather difficult problem of the widespread prejudices and preventative mental health measures that still pervade the psychotherapy of schizophrenia.

After years of study, world-wide travel, and endless discussion about the Negative Entropy protocol, and after having participated in many congresses and debates on the psychotherapy of schizophrenia with important authors in the fields of psychotherapy and cognitive psychotherapy, I have matured the belief that in the fields of psychiatry and among psychologists and psychotherapists, the following points of view are well established:

- therapy in schizophrenia must be primarily biological, therefore, *pharmacological* (including electroshock, which is included in the guidelines of the American Psychiatric Association, 1997);
- pharmacological treatment is the most legitimate form of cure because schizophrenia is considered an illness with a strong organic basis and thus traceable to cerebral damage that only drugs can compensate for or repair;
- psychotherapeutic interventions should not be used in schizophrenia, unless flanked by drug treatment, often with the single declared intent of improving compliance with the pharmacological treatment;
- there is not sufficient experimental evidence able to demonstrate that cognitive psychotherapy can be effective by itself in the treatment of schizophrenic patients.

These beliefs are, in my opinion, essentially without foundation and the product of preconceived notions.

I have already discussed the evidence that denies neuroleptics the definitive status in resolving the pathology; they have been reduced to an important but not decisive role in the relief of symptoms. Sometimes there are negative side effects that outweigh the benefits, and there is the risk of irreversible damage. Many patients, moreover, are "non-responders".

I will agree with the criticism that there is not sufficient data on the effectiveness of cognitive psychotherapy, on one condition: we need to stop saying there is not yet enough scientific proof, then preclude the possibility of experimentation, claiming that depriving a patient of neuroleptic therapy is unethical. I believe that it is ethical, in fact, in many cases, it is healthy!

Phillipa Garety (2003) presented a series of clinically controlled studies at the annual American Psychological Association meeting in Denver, in which the effect of cognitive-behavioural psychotherapy in schizophrenic patients was shown to be as effective as the latest neuroleptic drugs, resulting in a 20 to 40 percent decrease of the principal symptoms, without any side effects.

Interestingly, the results presented by Garety provoked notable resistance in many therapists, even those of a cognitive-behavioural orientation.

Jesse H. Wright argued during a mailing list debate for the Academy of Cognitive Therapy that to present cognitive behavioural psychotherapy as an alternative to the use of neuroleptics in the treatment of schizophrenic patients could seriously damage the reputation of this type of psychotherapy in the eyes of American psychiatrists and psychiatrists from other countries (Wright, 2003).

The author's rationale for calling psychological treatment of schizophrenia with out pharmacological treatment unethical was based on the conviction that psychotherapy cures "functional" problems, while psychotropic drugs are effective in treating psychiatric disorders characterized by organic "damage".

Such a conceptualization appears, from my point of view, merely symptomatic and not truly therapeutic, if by therapy we mean an evolution in the processes of the mind of the patient. The most we can obtain from drug therapy is a relative and often crude modulation of some base brain functions (arousal, mood, human information processing, sedation, and sleep).

The central nervous system, contrary to what was thought until recently, shows a considerable ability of self-regulation, neuronal plasticity, and self-reparation (Cozolino, 2002). Thus, it is not correct to assert that damage to the biological structure cannot be repaired. Psychotherapy, in general, and the cognitive approach, in particular, constitute an effective therapy for all psychotic disorders, including those with a presumed presence of biological alterations. Psychotherapy can gradually modify mental processes and reprogram cerebral circuits (Schwartz, Stoessel & Baxter, 1999).

Evidence is accumulating that corroborates these claims which, I will admit, still do not enjoy the incontrovertible support of experimental data. Some research using neuro-imaging techniques, has demonstrated the presence of functional and morphological modifications in certain areas of the brain following cognitive therapy treatment of patients with depression or obsessive disorders. (Rosenberg, Benazon, Gilbert, Sullivan & Moore, 2000).

An example is the study of the phobic patients to cognitive behavioural therapy carried out using functional magnetic resonance imaging (fMRI) (Paquette, Lèvesque, Mensour, Leroux, Beaudoin, Bourgouin & Beauregard, 2003).

This group of Canadian researchers obtained fMRI recordings in patients suffering from spider phobia and a control group to while they watched films containing images of huge spiders.

In the phobic patients, the first series of recordings taken at the beginning of the psychotherapy that showed a significant activation of the back lateral prefrontal cortex (Broadman's area 10 or BA 10), of the para-hippocampus and, bilaterally, of the associative visual areas. In normal control subjects, only the left occipital circumvolution and the inferior temporal area of the right hemisphere were activated.

According to the authors of the research, the increment of activity of Broadman's area 10 in people with phobias seems to reflect the use of meta-cognitive strategies that attempt to regulate and mitigate the fright reaction to the vision of spiders. The activation of para-hippocampus areas, on the other hand, creates an intense and automatic reactivity of emotional memory that provokes avoidance behaviors and helps maintain the phobic reaction.

After having successfully completed the program of cognitive-behavioural psychotherapy, the patients who have overcome the phobia re-administered the fMRI while viewing the film. This time they do not show activation of Broadman's area 10 or the para-hippocampus.

This is significantly correlated to the extinction of the fright reaction and the elimination of avoidance behaviors. This demonstrates that cognitive-behavioural therapy can modify the activity and functional organization of certain cerebral circuits involved in phobic disorders.

Paquette et al (2003) conclude that an effective psychotherapeutic intervention not only acts on the mind, but also seems to "reprogram" the brain.

Another study has documented analogous data in depressed patients treated with medications and cognitive therapy.

Using tomography and positron emissions, Goldapple, Segal, Garson, Lau, Bieling, Kennedy and Mayberg (2004) have shown that cognitive psychotherapy leads to important and stable modifications in the functional patterns of the brain in persons suffering from serious forms of depression.

In particular, an increment in activity in the hippocampus and the dorsal cingulate was observed along with a respective decrease in the activity of some cortical areas, including the dorsal, ventral, and medial regions.

These patterns are typical found following the cognitive psychotherapeutic treatment and well differentiated from the functional modifications induced in the brain by a drugs like paroxetine.

Unfortunately, similar data do not exist for schizophrenia, but the increasing adoption of brain imaging methods and quantitative EEG's suggest that we may be close to overcoming the belief, with all its grave consequences, that schizophrenia is incurable.

A new approach to psychotic illnesses seems to be in order that could be called cognitive neuropsychiatry, following Panthelis and Maruff (2002).

It is interesting to note that this new orientation began with the study of schizophrenia and then expanded to other illnesses, including obsessive-compulsive disorder and depression. According to this model, we need to systematically analyze the biological markers of the psychiatric conditions in order to document functional changes after the introduction of the therapeutic processes.

A similar project is the focus of research and clinical applications I have been developing in Catania at the Laboratory of Cognitive Psychophysiology.

For example, when using the *Family Strange Situation* test, we might document a significant increase in electrodermal conductance in a patient in the presence of family members with high expressed emotion. If, after finishing the therapeutic program with the family, we then record a modification in skin conductance, we are essentially implementing the program recommended by Panthelis and Maruff.

Gruzelier has identified a new dimension in therapy for schizophrenic patients by documenting dysfunctional procedural patterns through the technique of quantitative electroencephalography (QEEG). He has also indicated in the adoption of the techniques, which include neurofeedback, a therapeutic procedure able to produce stable modifications in the state of cerebral systems (Gruzelier, 2003).

The mind intended as a dynamic set and flux of information is influenced by interpersonal experiences, not only during the critical years of development, but for the whole life cycle (Cozolino, 2002). Relational experiences, especially emotional ones, powerfully influence the mode through which our minds represent the internal and external world.

Based on the construction and development of a relationship of intense relational dynamics, psychotherapy uses a process of reparenting. This is specifically intended to modify the state of the human mind, favouring a better integration in a systematically controlled manner and, therefore, a more effective interaction with internal and external reality.

Through the continued and controlled flow of information which activates diverse channels and is mediated by analogue and digital computational codes, psychotherapy introduces new information to brain of the patient as well as sets of instructions to organize this information within pre-existing contexts. In this way, psychotherapy promotes novel, evolving structures of self-organization according to non-linear dynamics.

The aim of the conceptualization I have been developing over the years is to identify a particular set of complex information and the modalities to transfer, allocate, and integrate it into the system of knowledge of the patient. The goal is to institute and promote a renewal of the process of self-organization of the complex system that is the brain of the patient, toward the condition of negative entropy.

As we will see, the strategic objective of psychotherapy in schizophrenic patients is the reactivation of the unifying activity of the coalitional processes, with particular reference to the self. This means activating, promoting, and maintaining new integrative competences that will be corroborated by new functions for the autobiographical narrative structures. These structures will develop through the process of narrative rewriting.

Finally, the psychotherapy of the schizophrenic subject, intended as a complex process, can initiate, sustain, and direct a profound reorganization of the mind of the patient. This is more than a simple attempt to correct individual errors considered to be dysfunctions in human information processing by the standard cognitive approach to psychotherapy.

The tactical interventions activated thanks to the application of the multiple techniques described here must merge in a *strategic revolution,* consistent with the profound reorganization of the system of knowledge of the patient. This reorganization must integrate past, present, and future in a dynamic, historical and evolutionary dimension typical of complex non-equilibrium systems. This will involve the entire structure of the self, personal identity, and narrative.

The psychotherapeutic process does not generically avail itself of the relational context, but is constituted by the relational process of re-parenting which promotes the development of a new and novel self through an innovative and equilibrated situation, characterized by attachment and parenting typical of the *Negative Entropy* setting.

After delineating the conceptual basis that underlies a cognitive orientation in the psychotherapy of schizophrenia based on the logic of complex systems, I will now address some more specific aspects of the *Negative Entropy* protocol.

The logic of such a therapeutic program does not stem from a tactical dimension aimed merely at recovery of an acceptable emotional, cognitive, and behavioural equilibrium and at the institution of specific skills in the patient, but must be considered in light of a *strategic orientation.*

The different phases of intervention are designed to promote in the patients and their family members a progressive increase of the capacity to reflect about oneself and a new ability to narrate one's life in coherent terms, including a new organic and well-structured story relative to the illness.

The therapist, or better the medical staff, using the different cognitive and behavioural techniques must be able to assume the role of a "secure base". The whole therapeutic and rehabilitative project is conceptualized as a process that can promote a new dynamic of parenting created between the patient and the staff. The final objective of the work is the construction of a new *relational mind* in the patient. This objective can be realized, in my opinion, only in the dimension of *re-parenting* that the patient can experience, then explain, and, in the end, narrate.

The target of the therapeutic intervention in the schizophrenic patient must be constituted by the activation of new integrative dynamics able to first contrast, then resolve the process of mental fissuring typical of this psychosis.

Daniel J. Siegel (1999) has formulated some questions that seem particularly pertinent to the problem of promoting new integrative functions in schizophrenic patients characterized by coalitional processes of the self. The questions formulated by Siegel in his extraordinary book, *Developing Mind*, are the following:

- How are the integrative processes of the mind developed?
- What are the neuronal mechanisms that permit the integration of the functions of the mind?
- In what way do genetic factors, especially experiential ones, influence the maturation and the development of these processes?

The preliminary response of Siegel is that the development of new integrative processes in the human brain is the result of a flow of energy and information.

Siegel's conceptualization agrees with the theoretical basis described in this monograph. The exchange of information that occurs in the *Negative Entropy* setting permits the patient to progressively insert emotional, cognitive, procedural, and relational processes, previously disassociated and chaotic, in a set of greater functional integration. This occurs with a comprehensive increase in the levels of information, order, and integration which are characteristics of the physical condition of the reduction of entropy and typical of complex and dynamic systems that develop in non-equilibrium systems.

The dynamics of integration that must be promoted in the mind of the patient are both synchronic and diachronic. Synchronic coherence consists in tying together in a harmonic and functional complexity different processes that are carried out in unison. This target is pursued when we attempt to develop the meta-cognitive competences in the patients to help them to differentiate and better integrate the chaotic processes of the schizophrenic mind.

Coherence and diachronic synthesis refer to the integration of processes that are carried out at different times. To heal the schizophrenic mind, it is necessary to promote a process of integration between the past, present, and future. Obviously, the creation of coherence and integration among contemporary processes and processes that are staggered over time constitute a complex and multi-level dynamic.

Based on this, it appears clear that an important objective of psychotherapy, in general, and the psychotherapy of schizophrenia, in particular, must be the promotion of integrative functions of the coalitional processes. The development of these integrative functions appears closely correlated to interpersonal experiences of nurturance; for this reason psychotherapy cannot be carried out within a *generically empathetic* relationship but must be developed within an actual nurturing relationship.

Between the therapist or staff and the patient, a condition of stable functional pairing that Siegel defines as *interpersonal mental resonance* must be created. Only through a positive nurturing relationship can a particular condition be created that Csikszentmihalyi (1993) has called *optimal relational experience*. This new experience makes it possible for the system of knowledge to evolve towards a condition of greater integration.

Based on these theoretical and conceptual premises, I have developed a psychotherapeutic and rehabilitative approach that constitutes a strategically oriented unitary and organic project distributed through articulated and well-differentiated tactical stages.

The use of a group of health care workers is linked to the need for the specific competences and to the fact that therapy for the schizophrenic patient is, from the technical, emotional, and organizational point of view, more complicated than therapies for other types of pathologies. Also, work must be done with the patient, the family of the patient, and within the patient's social network.

Given the gravity of the problem, which is almost always associated with a condition of disability, the intervention must be structured in multi-contextual terms since the activity is carried out in hospital structures, out-patient clinics, and therapeutic group homes.

Part of the therapeutic and rehabilitative program is applied at the home of the patient and in the neighborhood. (For this reason I tell my students from the very first lesson that psychiatric and psychosocial rehabilitation therapists can forget about working behind a desk and should immediately procure comfortable sneakers and jeans).

In this case, the health worker will use appropriate techniques, not only at the home of the patient where intervening at the level of the family is possible. The therapy patient will be physically accompanied to the situations that the staff has identified as important for the construction and development of therapeutic intervention. In this way, the shared experience will permit the patient to face situations that have been avoided, reinforcing a sense of trust in the therapist.

The therapist assumes the role of mediator between the home environment and the patient, permitting the patient, thanks to the material and emotional nearness of the *secure base*, to evade the rigid behavioural limits that until now have been imposed by assumption of the sick role.

Because of the active presence in the field, the rehabilitation therapist becomes a privileged observer who can evaluate the emotion resonance of the patient created by the new life experiences. In this way, the therapist can contribute to the development of cognitive, emotional, behavioural, and relational performances that promote a condition of increasingly greater autonomy in the patient.

An important aspect of the rehabilitative program regards the neuropsychological competences that are systematically compromised in psychotic patients. The problems linked to the malfunctioning of short-term memory, attention, and strategic planning are certainly as important as social skills or communicative abilities. In fact, these latter skills can only be developed when an improvement is registered in the neuropsychological abilities.

All this has been concretized in a protocol of cognitive and complex inspiration developed at the Institute of Clinical Psychiatry at the University of Catania and at the Superior Institute for the Cognitive Sciences at Enna. I have chosen to call this protocol "*Negative Entropy*" because the name refers to the logic of complex systems that is crucial to the epistemological, theoretical, and clinical models proposed in this book.

Since the increase in disorder and disorganization within the system constitutes entropy, or in our specific case, *entropy of mind*, the attempt to reduce disorder and disorganization that is achieved in the therapeutic and rehabilitative work represents the objective to pursue, i.e., an increase in *negative entropy*.

The theory of the cure to which the new protocol refers is not the recovery of a pre-existing condition but is centered on the promotion of an evolutionary process and the incessant search for new dynamic equilibriums. This is pursued through a continual progression toward the future determined by the unidirectionality of movement through time and by the process of the organization of the mind realized through the constant search and institution of these new equilibriums.

The patients ask continually, "Will I be like I was?" The answer I give is always, "No!" This is because complex systems develop according to a logic of irreversibility and because, even if it were possible to return to a mental state similar to the one prior to the breakdown, we would find ourselves at the point where the psychosis began, just like in those films which portray an impossible "return to the past".

To better illustrate the concept, I use the same metaphor Prigogine used during an interview in an American scientific journal to make the concept of irreversibility clear.
Prigogine said:

> Let's start with the egg of a chicken and scramble it. We obtain a new condition regarding the state of the egg. This condition is irreversible. Try starting from the scrambled egg and then recompose the whole egg we had at the beginning of the experiment!

Doing therapy does not mean an impossible return to the past but the construction of a new present and the development of a teleonomic and stochastic scenario for the future.

The complex system constituted by the patient and by his or her ecological niche is organized according to unique and unrepeatable pathways that must be explored together with the therapist in the search for a new positive equilibrium. *Negative Entropy* constitutes the end of this search and the name of the therapeutic protocol I have developed. To use the Latin of ancestors: *Nomen, numen.*

CHAPTER SEVEN

The Setting

1. Introduction

The *Negative Entropy* protocol constitutes an integrated therapeutic program that is articulated in a succession of strategically interrelated stages. The various phases of the *Negative Entropy* intervention, even though developed in specific terms for schizophrenia, constitute obligatory steps, in my opinion, in any therapeutic and rehabilitative project.
These steps can be identified as follows:

- crisis intervention and treatment of the patient;
- development of the therapeutic relationship;
- progressive activation in the patient and the therapist of the motivational system of attachment between adults;
- construction of the *secure base* relationship;
- therapeutic and rehabilitative work with the patient on the behavioural, emotional, cognitive, and relational levels;
- suicide prevention;

- strengthening of meta-cognitive functions;
- improving neuropsychological performance;
- development of social and relational competences;
- construction and development of a new structure of the self;
- promotion of a positive personal identity with effective self-esteem;
- activation and implementation of the narrative function;
- institution of the therapeutic relationship with the family;
- activation, also with the family, of a *secure base* relationship;
- therapeutic and rehabilitative work with the family;
- finding employment;
- conclusion of the systematic phase of the psychotherapeutic and rehabilitative treatment;
- activation and maintenance of the counseling phase as well as the monitoring of warning signs and the prevention of relapse.

It is evident that we are not talking about a unique and specific setting, but rather a multiplicity of places and modalities in which multi-contextual and multimodal interventions take place. The therapeutic relationship assumes a crucial role in each phase of the treatment.

To underline this aspect, nothing seems to me more appropriate than the words of a girl who was my patient.

At only 23 years old, she had already experienced numerous psychotic breaks characterized by delusions, hallucination, and psychomotor agitation. I had successfully applied the *Negative Entropy* protocol. The girl was in the phase of monitoring and relapse prevention.

She had learned to recognize the warning signs and implement the safety procedures consisting of immediately taking 3 mg daily of haloperidol and calling me right away on my cell to set an appointment. In fact, one day she phoned, clearly anxious and agitated (I was driving my car in city traffic), saying:

"Doctor Scrimali, I'm really worried, I haven't slept for two days and my thoughts are confused and I'm afraid I am getting sick again. Yes, I know, I know, I must take Serenase immediately, but can we see each other as soon as possible?"

"Of course", I say, "Come to my office tomorrow afternoon".

The next day the girl explained the problem very competently. She had made love for the first time with her boyfriend, and then she had spoken to her mother about it, devoured by guilt. The mother was very critical and is now sure that everybody in the town knows of the "event". I reassured the girl, reminding her of the theory of arousal in which situations of intense emotional stress can reactivate the older, more rigid ways of thinking.

We agreed on the fact that a condition was created and that the possibility that everybody in town knew what happened was a mere hypothesis, not a fact. Then we began to discuss the problem that provoked the emotional decompensation.

The girl wanted to know from me if she really behaved badly, and what might be the consequences. I told her, calmly, that making love with one's boyfriend is the most normal thing in the world.

She responded, "But I want to live according to the Church and I teach catechism to children. How can I live in sin?" "Well", I said, "There's confession for things like this! If you consider making love a sin, then confess it as soon as possible and you will be forgiven".

"That's true", she said, "I didn't think of that!"

Then looking worried again, she added, "But what if I 'relapse'?"

"You see", I said, " When one confesses, it is not necessary to have the certainty that one will not sin again, in fact, because we are imperfect beings, it is probable that it will happen again. You must simply resolve not to repeat the 'sin,' if making love is actually a sin".

The girl suddenly brightened up, and a smile of relief spread over her face. Once again relaxed she said, "Doctor Scrimali, when I am having a crisis, I don't need Serenase. You are my neuroleptic! All I need is a brief meeting and I find a positive meaning to things. Thank you!"

"Thank you", I answered, "What you just said is not only beautiful, but you have given me a new page for my book! To be called a neuroleptic is actually the best compliment I have ever received!"

To affirm the centrality of the relationship in the therapeutic process may seem banal but, in reality, it is not so if we consider, for example, that each topic has been neglected by the behavioural psychotherapy and rarely studied in the standard cognitive approach.

If we consider as a reference the classic work by Judy Beck on Cognitive Therapy, it is possible to see how little relevance is attributed to the therapeutic relationship in both a conceptual and applied sense (Beck, 2003).

The relationship is considered as a frame, a general condition of psychotherapy, not a crucial process in the dynamics of change.

The position of other cognitive authors, Jeffrey Young and Jeremy Safran, for instance, who place themselves outside the standard approach, is different (Young, 1999; Safran, 1998). Young, Klosko and Wieshaar (2003) attribute a crucial significance to the therapeutic relationship within the dynamic of *schema therapy.* With the term re-parenting, they propose a conceptualization of the therapeutic relationship as a new process of parenting able to reactivate evolutionary dynamics in the personality of the patient, similar to those realized during development.

Still more central is the role attributed to the therapeutic relationship by Safran and Muran (2000). They propose a constructivist and systemic approach, underlining how the therapeutic relationship is the key instrument in the construction and development of the self.

I would like to point out that in the treatment of psychotic patients, the therapeutic relationship has constituted a crucial element in the psychotherapeutic and rehabilitative dynamic, more so than in any other disorder.

Freud (1978) already intuited how relational processes are activated during therapy that go back over the developmental steps in the prototypical relationships with parental figures, as experienced by the patient over the course of development.

Marguerite A. Sechehaye (1951), in her work on the psychotic patient, described the role of the therapist as a nurturing figure that the patient calls "mother". She noted that the psychotherapeutic process is substantially a dynamic of re-parenting, even if she used a psychodynamic terminology that predates the development of attachment theory.

Contemporary work in the cognitive field focusing on the therapeutic relationship are attachment theory and the theories of interpersonal motivational systems (Liotti, 2001). John Bowlby (1998) has clearly conceptualized the role of the psychotherapist as a nurturing figure, focusing on the five following points:

- the therapist becomes a secure base from which to explore what generates suffering and pain;
- the therapist encourages exploration of new situations;
- the therapist helps patients rediscover their own histories, in order to place actual processes in relation to experiences of nurturing and trauma experienced during developmental history;
- the therapist makes the patients progressively able to place their internal operative models in relation to negative experiences of the past.

Liotti (2001) has described the interpersonal motivational systems as unconscious processes that analyze and control the relationship in progress. Among these, motivation attachment, nurturing, and agonistic systems assume particular relevance for the therapeutic relationship. This last system is necessary for the negotiation and maintenance of social group hierarchies and for access to and use of resources.

In the psychotic patient or patients afflicted by personality disorders, the agonistic system is gravely dysfunctional, and this leads to the systematic adoption of tactics of confrontation and defense with interlocutors seen as hostile and intrusive.

Safran and Segal (1990) have pointed out how the patient manifests interpersonal cognitive cycles that are rigid, dysfunctional, and recursive. Patients systematically wait to be rejected, looked at, laughed at, and not loved because of the negative experiences of nurturing and the stigma tied to the illness. This leads to self-protection and relational tactics of defiance, confrontation, and closure.

In the therapeutic relationship patients exhibit their interpersonal motivational schemas. This permits their identification, analysis, and modification.

Semerari (1999) includes the therapeutic relationship in a cognitive theory of treatment and outlines the following roles:

- positive social influence;
- privileged context for new awareness;
- corrective interpersonal experience;
- experience able to increase self-knowledge;
- identification of role models.

I agree completely with the theory even if, in the relationship with psychotic patients, there is a further difficulty regarding the meta-cognitive deficits that this pathology provokes. The therapeutic setting constitutes an ideal training ground to develop improved meta-cognitive skills.

For example, patients often say, "I know what you think of me", implying a negative opinion. This is a great opportunity to get the patients to see their negative attitude and begin to work on learning to comprehend the mental states of others.

We ask the patients to verbalize what they think to be the mental state of the therapist at different moments during the session, inviting them to also verbalize the modalities through which these ideas were reached. Provided with suggestions and feedback (obviously always truthful), the patient is guided toward understanding the meta-cognitive skills that had been neglected over the course of his or her developmental history.

As I have already mentioned, many authors have pointed out the importance of the agonistic interpersonal motivational system in the therapeutic relationship (Liotti, 2001). I think that in the earliest phases of the therapeutic intervention, it is opportune to try and deactivate this motivational system in favour of one of attachment.

Essentially, if the agonistic system is activated, for example, during an acute crisis, it is very difficult to develop a therapeutic relationship. It is necessary to remove oneself from the negotiation in terms of power and defiance and try to activate, when possible, the system of nurturing, delaying the analysis and modification of the agonistic motivational system. This can be achieved by accepting the point of view of the patient and exhibiting an attitude of protection and caring.

The system of attachment with the affectionate, protective, or reassuring person is also activated in adults if they find themselves in situation of danger or weakness. It is exactly what one should try to achieve in a situation of crisis intervention, which is the topic of the next section.

2. *Crisis Intervention and Patient Care*

Crisis intervention is a topic addressed by some cognitively oriented English authors such as Birchwood, Fowler, and Jackson (2002). For effective crisis intervention, it is necessary for the staff to be able to intervene within 24 hours. The staff must include a specifically trained psychiatrist and a specialized nursing staff.

In the majority of the cases, the therapeutic interventions of the crisis unit are mostly pharmacological while the psychotherapeutic and rehabilitative treatments are programmed and conducted after the clinical conditions of the patient have improved. The dichotomy between pharmacological and psychotherapeutic treatment, though widespread and appears negative.

The two types of intervention constitute different tactics in a single strategy that unfolds in a multimodal and multilevel dimension. In the model of crisis intervention I am proposing the psychiatrist working in the crisis unit should also be the therapist who will later be responsible for the patient's program of cognitive and rehabilitative therapy.

When this is not possible because of logistical or organizational problems, it is important that the members of the crisis unit and those of the therapy and rehabilitation unit agree on the conceptual, methodological, and clinical approaches adopted.

It is a good idea that the psychiatrist on the therapeutic and rehabilitative staff assists the patient during the critical episode. This makes it possible to construct a nurturing relationship and a secure base for the patient. It is indispensable that the psychiatrist receives exhaustive information on the operative protocol to be followed and specific training regarding verbal and analogue communication. The nursing staff must also be trained. During crisis intervention, it is important to create a positive emotional climate in which everyone knows exactly what to do. Exchanges between members of the staff must be brief, calming, and incisive.

The setting. Regarding this topic, a preliminary question must be posed. Is intervention at home carried out by the staff more useful than hospitalizing the patient. Both options have advantages and disadvantages, and any decision must be based on the different situations.

On one hand, crisis intervention at home permits the non-de-contextualization of the patient, is cost-efficient, and keeps the support network of family and friends involved. On the other hand, hospitalization medicalizes the problem, moves the patient to an artificial environment, and is organized in rigidly hierarchical terms, but does provide greater security.

The most important variable to be considered is the family. In the majority of cases, with a patient suffering from a psychotic decompensation, high expressed emotion is characteristic of family members. In these circumstances, the physical distance of the patient from the family environment satisfies two synergistic objectives.

On one hand, the family burden is reduced This permits a period of reprieve from the very stressful conditions the presence of a psychotic person in the family creates. On the other hand, the patient will undoubtedly benefit from separation from an environment characterized by high levels of expressed emotion.

Imagine an agitated psychotic patient who refuses to participate in a therapeutic program. In this case two possibilities exist. In the first, the patient is at home and refuses to go to the hospital, in the second case, the patient has already reluctantly been accompanied to the emergency room of a hospital.

In the first situation the members of the crisis unit must go to the home of the patient and decide whether hospitalization is necessary, either accompanying the patient to the hospital, or continuing the treatment at home.

In both cases the key to the intervention is overcoming the patient's distrust, constructing a preliminary therapeutic alliance and initiating an appropriate pharmacological therapy.

We think that with this fundamental issue, a good part of the patient's future and possibility of recovery is played out. It must be pointed out that the schizophrenic patient is often extremely suspicious and distrustful of others, who are seen as hostile and threatening.

Coercive intervention, possibly with restraints, would aggravate the patient's beliefs, making further treatment problematic. Thus, every effort should be made to create at least a minimum of trust in the patient for the staff and avoid power-based authoritarian attitudes, which will help the patient accept the treatment.

This is a critical aspect of crisis intervention and linked to the staff's mastery of tacit communication and relational games.

These aspects stem from the creation of mutual cooperation based on a win-win situation of sharing mutual objectives, rather than the deployment of methods that coerce the patient, subdued but not convinced, to accept a condition against his or her will.

As I have said earlier in this chapter, social animals like humans have particularly active, genetically preexisting, motivational mechanisms to regulate social interactions.

There is, for example, a motivational mechanism that encourages cooperation and another that induces competition (Liotti, 1993). In humans, obviously these genetically preexisting motivational systems are amply modulated by learning during developmental history through the development of complex schemas in which emotional, cognitive, procedural, and social behavioural patterns are closely entwined (Panksepp, 1998).

In patients who show schizophrenic disorders, the schemas of distrust and competition are particularly active. Fellow human beings are perceived by the patient as threatening, treacherous, and intrusive beginning in childhood. The parents of the patient often behave as hostile and emotionally hyper-involved, always considering their own needs first, rather than caring for and satisfying the needs of the child.

A typical example is the following. A young schizophrenic patient in decompensation continues to repeat that his parents are secretly poisoning him. He refuses to eat and plans to get revenge on his relatives. These statements seem, at first glance, delusional. They do, however, represent how the patient narrates his situation, and every narration, no matter how fantastic, contains some relation to reality. Then the truth emerges. It is common in clinical practice to discover that relatives will often put haloperidol in the food or drink of the patient.

Another example that demonstrates the trans-generational passing on of dysfunctional schemas imprinted with distrust is the following. The patient does not want to take the medicine. He says they hurt him and are actually poison.

"What is he saying", his parents say, "Do you hear him, Doctor?" They add, "The poor thing is delirious".

Then, as soon as I prescribe drug therapy, they become excessively apprehensive:

"Which drug is it? It won't hurt him, will it? You know he was poisoned before by the wrong drugs prescribed by unscrupulous doctors!"

When patients are in decompensation, the mechanisms of distrust are at their maximum level and they see in others (including family members), persons who are potentially hostile and ready to take advantage of their position of weakness in order to hurt them. At this point the physician who is managing the first crisis intervention is faced with an obvious objective: to reassure and create a different relationship pattern, defusing competitive and defensive attitudes and triggering mechanisms of cooperation.

Substantially, a win-win situation must be promoted in order to achieve a mutual objective. This approach derives from game theory (Turocy & von Stengel, 2002).

Zero-sum games exist (in an algebraic sense: for example +1 and -1=0) in which only one person wins, while the other loses and suffers the consequences. *"Vae victis"*, thundered Brenno, when the defeated Romans criticized his improper application of the conditions of surrender.

Games also exist in which you win or lose together (in this case, the algebraic formula is +1 and +1=+2; or: -1 and -1=-2). These are zero-sum games of cooperation, and in an ecological context these games prevail.

A typical example is the equilibrium that exists among the animals of the savanna. Each one has a specific role and all survive. Imagine if the predators were able to increase their hunting abilities and thus kill more herbivores than usual. For a brief period their species would have an advantage and increase, but soon they would be faced with increasingly scarce food.

Another example, still more appropriate is the relationship in a human couple. The two members of the couple must cooperate, together achieving positive living conditions that permit the harmonious growth of the family. If, however, a dynamic of competition is triggered, the result will be destructive for both members of the couple.

At this point the problem is how to stimulate the cooperative dynamic in the patient. Some key aspects of this fundamental approach can be schematized in the following way:

- create a climate of trust through listening;
- do no react to the hostility and provocations of the patient (which often constitute a test to see if the therapist can be trusted);
- concentrate on the solution of the problems;
- look for proposals and solutions that embrace the requests of the patient;
- try to understand and share the point of view of the person in decompensation.

It is important, from my point of view, to avoid a rationalist attitude such as: *The patient is delusional; the "correct" logic must be restored.* More useful is a constructivist attitude: *The patient is narrating his or her construction of reality. To help I must, firstly, enter into and share the story.* It is important not to dispute the affirmations of the patient.

If the patient claims the Secret Service is after him, this hypothesis should be accepted (can we be sure it's not true?) and reassure that patient that in the hospital special security measures will be adopted. If the patients claims to have been poisoned, it should be explained that hospitalization is the best way to insure that the food is strictly controlled.

Initially, then, it is crucial to enter *into the world of the patient.* This must be done at an emotional level because psychotic patients in decompensation are afflicted by a hyper-functioning tacit channel. It is not possible to trick them. In fact, one must not *pretend* to believe the patients, *one must really believe them.*

This is achieved through training developed on an epistemological base that, in our case, is constructivist and narrative.

To facilitate the therapeutic alliance with the patients, it is necessary to take their part when family members are present and, subsequently, separate them from their families so the interview can continue with the patient alone. The presence of family members is almost always ruinous because they are often hostile and emotionally hyper-involved. Often their behaviour can trigger a crisis of agitation and dangerous acting-out in the patient.

The reality proposed by the patients is a mere construction, just like ours. It is not opportune to try and refute it and, at least during crisis intervention, share it. This applies to the whole staff.

It is unimaginable that a member of the staff, during crisis intervention, would laugh, wink, or make other signs of disapproval during the course of the narration. These could be interpreted by the patient as further signs of trickery or conspiracy. Persuasive communication is based on believing what one is saying. Thus, if we say we believe the patient, until proved otherwise, we must really believe it!

Another fundamental aspect in these circumstances is knowing how to listen. We must not stimulate the patient with too many questions but leave space for them to freely express themselves. They will feel more comfortable rather than pressed, as usual, by the hostile and inquisitorial behaviors of others.

At this point, the first phase of the negotiation needs to end with a preliminary agreement regarding the acceptance of therapy and, in particular, pharmacological treatment.

To achieve this goal, a medical approach adopted in an atmosphere of nurturance is a useful tactic.

After allowing the patients to speak freely and creating a climate of acceptance of their experiences and reassurance about the possibility of receiving help, I proceed in the following way:

I've noticed while you were talking that your color is a little pale. Could you be anemic? Let me get a better look.

Then: *Maybe it's a good idea to check your blood pressure and if necessary, do an electrocardiogram. Can I please measure your blood pressure and listen to you heart?*

These medical practices usually trigger, even in the most reluctant patient, an attitude of cooperation.

Immediately after: *Look, your pressure is too low and you seem anemic. All the stress you have been undergoing recently must have taken a toll on your body. A period of rest and some medication would be a good idea. And then there's your pulse rate. Don't you hear your heart beating hard? You are suffering from tachycardia. We should intervene; I would like to give you a shot.*

Essentially, it is necessary to initiate drug therapy based on an attitude of medical nurturance. This, however, is no mystification by the psychiatrist because the majority of psychotic patients in a state of clinical decompensation are in bad health and suffer from tachycardia and malnourishment.

The decision of the patient to adhere to the therapeutic and rehabilitative project should be developed through intermediary steps. The first step to be negotiated is the following: the patient accepts the medical care and assumes a cooperative behaviour while the physician and the staff offer to accept his or her point of view, to help them and protect them. Only once the crisis is over and a positive relationship with reality is restored, can the other steps in the therapeutic program be negotiated.

I am, by the way, absolutely against using force or instruments of restraint, and in 25 years of work with psychotic and agitated patients, I have never experienced (or provoked) an accident. Obviously, the staff must project a image of strength and confidence through relaxed but firm attitudes and behaviors.

The number of staff members must also be appropriate; *crisis intervention must never take place in the presence of only one staff member!* We must not forget that in the patient subject to psychotic decompensation, the logic of competition and aggressiveness is active. If alone with the psychiatrist, the temptation to attack might become overwhelming.

In the film *Mister Jones,* there is a convincingly portrayed, violent scene in which a patient in a state of decompensation attacks the young psychiatrist who, by herself and evidently fearful, is trying to calm him. That sequence could be entitled: *Everything not to do during crisis intervention.*

If the patient had been faced with a psychiatrist and three nurses stationed around the room and ready to react to every eventuality, any aggressive impulse would have been subdued.

What are the guidelines to follow for pharmacological treatment in the crisis phase?

The objectives are to control anxiety, agitation, and aggressiveness and create compliance. To achieve these ends it is appropriate to use strong a neuroleptic such as haloperidol. Based on research, the optimal dosage is less than to 7 milligrams per day (Bebbington, 2002). Higher dosages do not improve the efficacy and have side effects.

Benzodiazepines are particularly useful, administered via intramuscular injection: for example, 2 mg of lorazepam, up to three times a day. As soon as a relationship is established thanks to the medical approach already described, an intramuscular injection of 3 mg of haloperidol and 2 mg of lorazepam should be given. In this situation, I would note that even the smallest details count.

I use the deltoid muscle for these injections, asking the patients to simply roll up their sleeves. This may seem irrelevant, but it isn't.

Long experience has helped me understand that asking men to lower their pants or women to expose their legs can be experienced as a situation of subjugation and passivity, often tied to negatives episodes from childhood. This, however, does not happen when one receives the injection in the arm, maintaining eye contact with the doctor.

Immediately after this, the patient can be transferred from the emergency room for the treatment of the crisis phase of the disorder. They should settled in comfortable rooms with low sensory stimulation (pastel colors, absence of loud noises, and no machines and furnishings that can create a sense of trepidation).

In the crisis unit, medical personnel and qualified nursing staff will proceed to create an empathic relationship with the patient, at low stimulation, in order to assure continuance of the drug therapy and monitoring of the patient's medical condition.

In this phase, it is necessary to limit the presence of family members which almost always trigger anxiety and agitation. The therapy will be continued, using intramuscular injections, until the patient is able to take them orally. As soon as this is possible, haloperidol and lorazepam can be given in pill form, at a average dose of 6 mg per day for both, obviously taking into account the weight and general condition of the patient.

3. *Hospitalization*

Once the acute crisis is over, the patient can be accommodated in a room with other patients (two per room in our Clinic) and gradually begin socialization. This period of hospitalization in the ward must be used to pursue the following objectives:

- consolidation of compliance and progressive development of the therapeutic alliance with the staff;
- gradual stabilization and simplification of the drug therapy;
- comprehensive evaluation of the physical conditions that are almost always impaired and the institution of appropriate therapeutic measures;
- activation of assessment procedures;
- conceptualization of the case history by the staff;
- formulation and planning of the therapeutic and rehabilitative project.

Daily individual sessions are conducted in order to consolidate the cooperation of the patient and activate the motivational system of attachment. In this phase it is necessary to avoid all criticism of the patient's point of view. The sessions should be oriented primarily to the definition and solution of problems.

Concluding this phase, that at the Cognitive Therapy Unit of the Department of Psychiatry of the University of Catania can last for from 10 to 20 days, the patient is released. Ensuing treatment in a day hospital is arranged with the first visit scheduled for a few days after release from the hospital.

4. Out-Patient Structures

Semi-residential structures constitute an elective setting for the provision of the mid-period therapeutic and rehabilitative program which can sometimes last for a long while. Two specific formats can be identified: the day hospital and the day center.

4.1. Day Hospital

The day hospital is a semi-residential structure that, in the spirit of actual Ministry of Health directives, aims to provide diagnostic, therapeutic, and rehabilitative services, over the brief- and medium-term. It is open eight hours a day and serves, above all, to provide the management of the sub-acute phase of the serious pathologies, including schizophrenia.

Research has documented the efficacy and efficiency of this type of structure in the treatment of psychotic patients, especially when compared to hospitalization (Mosher & Burti, 1994). In my own personal experience, the day hospital constitutes the true fulcrum of the Cognitive Therapy Unit for the treatment of schizophrenic patients. This structure permits the accomplishment of all the steps of the *Negative Entropy* protocol, almost always avoiding medicalization and hospitalization.

From this point of view, the day hospital does not simply constitute a transition from the hospital ward to out-patient therapy but can be used for the management of future critical episodes and for the greater part of the therapeutic and rehabilitative therapeutic techniques.

4.2. Day Center

This is a daytime structure that is less medicalized than the day hospital and provides a point of reference over time for the social support of the patient and the accomplishment of rehabilitative programs focused on the maintenance and continual development of socialization processes. The center may be located in an urban context outside the hospital and is often managed by the private sector.

The day center, because it is set in the urban and social context of the city, can be an optimal instrument to combat the stigma and physical isolation that is imposed on the schizophrenic patient in the so-called advanced societies. In this way, the day center becomes a crucial part of treatment and rehabilitation, rejecting the idea of chronicity and avoiding the consequent tendency toward segregation.

Cocchi and De Isabella (1986) have identified some guide-lines for day center activities that constitute a reference point for my theoretical elaborations and for the actual work of our group.

They have, for example, noted that the different rehabilitative activities should not constitute a simple juxtaposition of techniques, for their own sake, while drug treatment and the medicalized setting remain the operative points of reference. The day center must:

- be characterized by high flexibility and personalization of the therapeutic and rehabilitative proposals;
- be collocated in an ample and well-articulated social support and occupational network;
- provide for the progressive reduction of therapy in favour of the construction an actual support network of the patient based on real human relationships, separate from medical praxis.

5. *Out-Patient Care*

When the patient can count on the support of family and their involvement in the therapeutic program, the setting can be progressively oriented toward the provision of a psychotherapeutic and rehabilitative plans according to guide-lines that will be articulated in the next section. In this case, the clinical setting is an out-patient structure that, in my own experience, can be developed in both a public and private context.

In some cases, however, this is not possible. Sometimes the family is physically absent or dispersed so that constructing a valid support network for the patient is not possible. Sometimes, because of illness or problems in the family, e.g., personality disorders or even substance abuse, the patient needs effective and prolonged support that family can not provide. In these circumstances, the residential rehabilitative structures, including the therapeutic and rehabilitative communities and group homes, assume considerable importance.

6. *Residential Care*

6.1. *The Therapeutic and Rehabilitative Community*

The therapeutic and rehabilitative community is the result of experimental activity begun in Great Britain right after the Second World War (Stein & Test, 1985). In Italy, the systematic development and experimentation with this type of community began with *Law 180*. The therapeutic and rehabilitative community constitutes the ideal setting for the phase of the therapeutic plan aimed at the achievement of the following objectives:

- construction of an atmosphere of acceptance of present needs, without encouraging stagnation, while activating a developmental process in the personality structure;
- activation of a socialization process that is constantly being improved, thanks to the learning and continual exercise of new emotional, cognitive, and communicative competences.

6.2. *The Residential Community*

This constitutes a still more advanced setting in respect to the therapeutic and rehabilitative community and is characterized by social support rather than a medical approach. Often these are found outside the structures of the Department of Mental Health in Italy and are run by the private sector. The staff is usually made up of social workers and rehabilitation therapists.

CHAPTER EIGHT

The Neuroleptics: Specific Therapy or Remedy for Symptoms?

The pharmacological treatment of schizophrenia dates back more than fifty years and has been the central part of clinical practice of treatment of schizophrenia on a large scale. It would, therefore, seem possible to realistically assess the results and identify data in order to render this treatment more rational and effective.

The pharmacological era in the treatment of schizophrenia, indeed, the pharmacological era, *tout court,* since neuroleptics were the first psychotropic drugs used in clinical practice, started in 1952 with an article by two French researchers, Delay and Deniker. They treated 38 schizophrenic patients with chlorpromazine, documenting significant clinical improvement (Delay & Deniker, 1952). This was a crucial step in the development of psychiatry. For the first time in the human history, we had finally created an instrument able to control, if not defeat, the curse of madness.

It seems legitimate to ask, even if it appears paradoxical and provocative, whether the advent of the neuroleptics and, subsequently, the tricyclics and benzodiazepines have been more useful for the psychiatrist or for the patients and, *apropos* of the patients, we should also ask in what way has drug therapy really helped them. We will see later that such a question is not actually as paradoxical as it might seem since many authors including Mosher and Burti (1994), Warner (1985), and Ciompi (2003) have addressed the issue. The question that should be posited is the following:

Are the prognoses for schizophrenia, depression, and anxiety disorders substantially different today than they were in the pre- pharmacological era?

In case of an affirmative answer, we need to ask, "Thanks to what process?" To respond unequivocally to such a question is not easy, even if the authors cited above have tried to in scientifically valid ways.

More recently, Colin A. Ross and John Read (2004) have discussed psychiatric myths, including those about neuroleptics. They stress how many of the beliefs of psychiatrists about the use of these drugs are based on assumptions that have not been scientifically proven.

In particular, the two authors describe the myths about neuroleptics in the following way:

- *Myth 1*: neuroleptics are prescribed only to patients with psychosis;
- *Myth 2*: the introduction of neuroleptics has permitted deinstitutionalization;
- *Myth 3*: neuroleptics are more effective than placebos;
- *Myth 4*: the therapeutic benefits of neuroleptics are more numerous than their side effects.

Drawing on many experimental studies and review articles, the two authors reach the conclusion that neuroleptics have not significantly influenced the psychiatric revolution of deinstitutionalization. They also conclude, these drugs need to be managed with extreme caution and should only be used for symptoms when strictly necessary. This position is also applicable to the most recent "atypical" neuroleptics. The opinions of Ross and Read may seem radical, but they are well supported. On my part, I would like to limit myself to a few personal considerations.

In my opinion, drug therapy does not modify the prognosis and course of any mental pathology since it does not permit the reprocessing of mental data or favour the development of new functional networks. It only modulates the base biological processes of the brain. The irreversible and developmental changes in the processes of the mind can only be accomplished by psychotherapy in the context of a secure base relationship.

The use of drug therapy can, however, help create the conditions necessary for the initiation of a psychotherapeutic and rehabilitative work. Essentially, in psychiatry the use of drugs constitutes a tactical stage in the therapeutic strategy.

Certainly the advent of psychopharmacology does deserve recognition since it is responsible (at least in Italy) for the progressive abandonment of shock therapy.

Frankly, I consider shock therapy a black page in the history of psychiatry. Even after many years, it still pains me to think about those poor patients treated with neurovaccine, a pyretic agent, feverish, shaking with terrible chills, and suffering horribly, due to this absurd and negative practice, which I can personally claim to have always contested and never used.

The idea of making patients suffer and provoking a physical illness, even though iatrogenic, seems a sort of revisitation of the demonic vision of mental illness. The psychiatrists who practice shock therapy in their starched white shirts seem to me to be the modern day heirs to those who tortured *the possessed*, i.e., the poor schizophrenics of a few years ago. The means are different, but the treatment is still for their own good—purging them of their madness through suffering.

A classic example of this is the representation of shock therapy in the film, *A Beautiful Mind*. The patient, tied up like a condemned man, receives a dose of insulin that provokes a terrible shock. It looks like an emphatic image, but it represents the pure and simple truth of psychiatry in the 1950s and of a certain more recent biological psychiatry.

But back to the neuroleptics. It is true that the advent of chlorpromazine generated enormous enthusiasm (perhaps because it helped reduce the use of shock treatment). It was possible to impart a new energy to the search for more positive methodologies in the treatment of schizophrenia which, up until then, consisted primarily of segregation through institutionalization and sometimes of treatment that constituted actual torture for psychotic patients.

Delay and Deniker (1952) wrote of a "cure", limiting their observation to the critical episodes they treated. In the following years, however, enthusiasm changed since chlorpromazine, though able to control some typical symptoms of the critical episode, including hallucinations, psychomotor agitation, and delusions, did not modify the course of the illness; it could not prevent relapse, cognitive deterioration, and the destruction of the organization of the mind.

With the expansion of experimentation, it became clear how the use of chlorpromazine was not free of problems and inconveniences. Many patients did not respond to treatment with the drug. Worrisome side effects also began to be observed in the extrapyramidal system with the manifestation of the triad constituted by pseudo-parkinsonism, akathisia, and dystonia. Besides this, a long period of treatment can lead to the appearance of serious tardive dyskinesia resistant to treatment with anti-cholinergics.

Over time, numerous other side effects due to chlorpromazine emerged, including hypotension, cloudy vision, urinary retention, hyperprolactinemia, and galactorrhea. Pharmacological research concentrated efforts on identifying more active and selective substances for psychotic symptoms in order to reduce the side effects.

Thus a new class of neuroleptics, including the phenothiazines, the thioxanthenes, the diphenylbutil-piperdines, and the benzomid substitutes were developed. Since it was thought that the pathogenesis of schizophrenia was already identified, i.e., maladjustment in the D2 receptors, a series of stronger neuroleptics were developed to block these receptors.

Haloperidol was the prototype of a new class of particularly potent psychotropic drugs that blocked the D2 receptors and controlled the positive symptoms of schizophrenia (Bellantuono, Balestrieri & Amaddeo, 1993).

The enthusiasm of the pharmacologists reached the sky in the 1970s, above all in the USA, where Ross Baldessarini (1977), in his treatise on psychopharmacology, proposed the name *antipsychotics* for this class of neuroleptics, considering them specific drugs capable of actually curing schizophrenia.

This enthusiasm was exaggerated and developed into a scientific myth for the end of the millennium that served to nourish the most reductionistic, pathogenic theories about schizophrenia. Meanwhile, a new generation of neuroleptics was being synthesized and gradually introduced in clinical practice, including clozapine, risperidone, and olanzapine.

These substances were characterized by a pharmacodynamic action involving not only the D2 receptors for dopamine, but also the 5HT2 receptors for serotonin. It was also demonstrated that intense action on the D1 dopamine receptors, associated with stimulation of the D2 receptors, could exert a therapeutic effect on the negative symptoms of schizophrenia (Wirshing, Marshall, Green, Mintz, Marder & Wirshing, 1999).

The advent of these new substances characterized by this new innovative pharmacological profile seemed to be real step forward in the pharmacological treatment of schizophrenia since they appeared to be so effective, especially on the negative symptoms of the disorder and with fewer side effects than the older neuroleptics.

In the first part of the 1970s, however, a dangerous side effect of clozapine was identified, following the death of a number of patients. As a result, the drug was taken off the market in a number of countries.

In 1988, the results of a careful study of this drug were published, involving 319 patients who did not exhibit a positive response to previous treatment with neuroleptics (Kane, Honigfeld, Singer & Meltzer, 1988).

The studied showed that the efficacy of clozapine was much greater than chlorpromazine, and in 1990 this drug was reintroduced in the USA with the requirement of monitoring the blood for indications of dyscrasia by means of weekly blood tests in order to kept possible agranulocytosis under control.

Risperidone, introduced in Great Britain in 1993, appeared to be one of the more manageable atypical neuroleptics (Bellantuono, Balestrieri & Amaddeo, 1994).

The drug seemed effective, not only on positive symptoms, but also on negative ones and did not cause excessive sedation or impair cognitive performance. One of the side effects produced compliance problems because the drug can cause significant interference with sexual function, especially in men.

Olanzapine, put on the market in 1997, has a therapeutic profile similar to clozapine but without the worrisome negative side effects of blood dyscrasia. It does, however, often cause considerable weight gain (Conley & Mahmoud, 2001).

After many years of experimentation with atypical neuroleptics, today it is possible to talk of the therapeutic profile and the advantages they have over the first generation neuroleptics.

I personally, believe that the so-called atypicals have not substantially modified the pharmacological treatment profile for schizophrenia. This is consistent with the findings reported in the CATIE study and similar reports (Stroup, McEvoy, Schwarts, Byerly, Glick, Canive, McGee, Simpson, Stevens, & Liverman 2003, Lewis, Davies, Jones, Barnes, Murray, Kerwin, Taylor, Hayhurst, Markwick, Lloyd & Dunn, 2006). There is one indirect positive effect, however, from their introduction; pharmaceutical marketing strategies now advocate an integrated psychoeducational approach to treatment for patients and their families.

All things considered, I do not have any doubts about the utility of neuroleptics during a critical episode, especially when positive symptoms prevail. The problem of what to do during the mid- and long-term periods remains open, however.

Based on a series of experimental studies, Loren Mosher and Lorenzo Burti (1994) criticize the long-term treatment of schizophrenic patients with neuroleptics.

One study by Davis (1980) analyzed the rate of relapse in a double blind trial in order to compare neuroleptics and placebos in two-year long, mid-term treatment program for schizophrenic patients. The rate of relapse after two years in this study was between 50-60 percent in patients treated with neuroleptics, and from 70-80 percent in those receiving a placebo. As is clear, the difference is not that great considering that the patients receiving the placebo did not receive psychosocial treatment of any kind.

Another study by Kane (1999) has demonstrated over the mid-term an incidence of tardive dyskinesia of 5 percent per year. This means that eventually one fourth of the patients treated for five years with neuroleptics could manifest tardive dyskinesia.

Based on this data, Mosher and Burti conclude that the risk/benefit relationship of mid- and long-term treatment with neuroleptics appears unfavourable.

Referring to studies on expressed emotion, Mosher and Burti call attention to the need to consider the emotional and relational variables of the patient and family before intervening with therapeutic and rehabilitative programs.

Richard Warner arrives at the same conclusions, identifying and recommending a series of options relative to the integration of neuroleptic treatment with psychosocial intervention. These can be summarized in the following points (Warner, 1985).

- Initiate the treatment with low doses of neuroleptics, increasing them very gradually;
- If a therapeutic response at medium doses is not obtained, dosage should not be increased, but benzodiazepine should be integrated into the therapy;
- Carefully consider every critical situation in order to avoid confusing, per example, akathisia due to neuroleptics, with an increase of anxiety;
- Try to identify, for mid-term treatment, the minimum dosage useful for the patient.

After referring to the literature, I would like to express my own personal opinion. I feel that the integrated use of neuroleptics with psychotherapeutic and rehabilitative therapy constitutes the most rational procedure available today. The first point to consider is the need to develop, together with the pharmacological treatment, an exhaustive psycho-educational program that involves the patient and cohabitating family members.

Clearly explaining the rationale for the pharmacological therapy, the importance of adherence, the aspects of therapeutic action, and, above all, the side effects can improve compliance. Thus in order to optimize therapeutic collaboration and dosage adjustments, the oral administration is preferable to treatment with depot drugs, usually administered parenterally.

Another guide-line in my approach to the pharmacological treatment of schizophrenia is to scale down the medicalization of the patient, proposing drug protocols that are straightforward and easy to follow, limiting the prescriptions to the minimum necessary.

As already noted, one crucial item in pharmacological therapy is its continuation over time.

Since neuroleptics carry out a single filtering action regarding stressful environmental situations, the possibility of suspending drug therapy, then reintroducing it based on indications from the monitoring of indices relative to patient arousal in response to an increase in environmental stressors, appears interesting.

This objective can be pursued by initiating psychophysiological monitoring of the patient. The recording of spontaneous and evoked electrodermal activity is a reliable index of the level of patient stress (Ohman, 1981).

Even if this procedure is not fully documented in the literature, recent data (presented in the next section) from our Clinical Psychophysiology Laboratory show its usefulness.

In the presence of a positive clinical evolution and an improvement in the familial emotional climate, it is possible to interrupt neuroleptic treatment.

The patient and family members are trained through psychotherapy to monitor the prodromal symptoms in a period of particular emotional overload; the therapist will register the exosomatic electrodermal activity during the weekly sessions. In case a marked increase in arousal is noted, the treatment will be reintroduced.

Obviously, the reinstitution of drug treatment is the object of a specific work in the psychotherapeutic setting; the resumption of the drug must be correctly understood by the patient and family, not in terms of a relapse—thus, failure—but rather as the reintroduction of "coping" behaviour in the face of a critical, but transitory, moment in the psychosis.

The contents of a brief cell phone call made to me by one of my patients during the summer vacation provide an example.

"Doctor, excuse me for bothering you, but I wanted to tell you that the hallucinations have returned. Today, on the bus I saw strange figures dancing on the roof. Perhaps it is too hot here in Catania, so I am sleeping little and working too hard! Do you think I should start taking Serenase again?"

I'm not ashamed to confess how much that phone call moved me. This patient, until a few months before, was reduced (because of the schizophrenia, but also because of electroshock and incredibly high doses of neuroleptics administered during repeated forced hospitalizations) to a kind of statue, without emotional expression or social skills, reduced to the status of a whining half-wit and considered chronically ill by the very physicians who had contributed to the development of this state of chronicity.

Besides the evident results of communication training that the patient had undergone (note the perfect form of the phone call), compliance and the ability to monitor the symptoms (recognized as such and not as terrifyingly real events), had also been impressively increased.

To conclude, it seems opportune to point out the use of biofeedback permits teaching the patient better management of anxiety and good behavioural control; this allows the reduction in the use of psychotropic substances.

Muscular tone biofeedback is also useful in combating akathisia and the tremors due to the neuroleptics.

Even though in the protocols used by me, the neuroleptic doses are always rather low, it happens that I treat patients who have literally been inundated and chemically restrained with neuroleptics. It is not unusual to encounter patients who have received injections of 100 mg of haloperidol and who take up to three different neuroleptics a day, as well as a robust dose of an antiparkinsonian drug. In these cases, biofeedback, associated with a program of wash out, are particularly effective for the management of tremors and akathisia.

CHAPTER NINE

Psychotherapy

1. Strategic Orientation

The psychotherapeutic and rehabilitative program, *Negative Entropy,* constitutes a protocol informed by the logic of strategic planning. *Strategic planning* is based on an interdisciplinary approach of programming and implementation of complex processes that develop in a *probabilistic scenario* characterized by *high levels of uncertainty* (Kelly & Allison, 1999).

Unlike *operative planning,* that includes a predictable environment subject to few changes, strategic planning faces situations characterized by an elevated number of processes, elements, and variables that are manageable only within a complex logic.

Operative therapeutic planning, even if long-term, is different than planning that is informed by strategic criteria. The following criteria are particularly relevant:

- *operative planning:*
  - consider the future predictable;
  - implement planning in periodic terms;

- consider actual tendencies as capable of developing indefinitely in the future;
- implement planning based on a vision of the future as a fixed scenario;

- *strategic planning:*
  - evaluate the future as basically unpredictable;
  - implement planning as an unceasing and continuous process;
  - consider the future as an uncertain scenario in which new events, innovative trends, surprises, and surprising dramatic turns materialize;
  - consider an ample range of different possible futures.

If we apply these parameters to the planning of a therapeutic and rehabilitative program for schizophrenic patients, we obtain the following outline.

Operative Planning. The future of the patient is predictable according to a reduced and dichotomous range of possibilities including recovery (considered improbable), discomfort, relapse, and chronicity (assumed to be a certainty). The planning of a therapeutic project is implemented at the beginning of the treatment, and it is up to the patient to change while the plan, until the moment of the final verification, remains unmodified.

The future of the patient, from this point of view, is considered a mere continuation of the present and thus necessarily characterized by the same cognitive, emotional, relational and procedural processes that the patient exhibits at the moment of assessment.

Strategic Planning. The future of the patient is not predictable and within this sphere of unpredictability, even recovery, often considered impossible in a diagnosis of schizophrenia, must be included. The planning of the therapeutic interventions is not implemented all at once but changes continuously as the scenarios gradually present themselves. The treatment team meets these new scenarios with the rapid reprogramming of settings and strategies, responding in a flexible manner to the complex challenges of the Entropy of Mind. Bearing in mind the teachings of Popper, the team is able to produce new tactical theories by continually allowing the previously adopted ones to "die" as they are gradually disproved. For example:

Relative X will be an obstacle to change, it was said at the beginning of the therapy. Relative X, instead, against all predictions, is participating positively in the evolving process of change.

Good, now relative X is an ally in this process!

But after this positive phase, relative X is now exhibiting new and unprecedented resistance to the change. *Unfortunately, once again relative X constitutes an obstacle to change!* The planning, then, is continually reformulated, in order to adapt to the process. Doesn't just the opposite occur when one forces the process into a straitjacket of rigid and schematic operative planning?

Strategic planning presents us with mostly positive surprises, refuting Murphy's law "everything that can go wrong will". Actually some things that should go well, don't, while many things that could go wrong, surprisingly, won't.

Fifteen years ago I found myself faced with a delirious, severely bipolar young woman at our clinic. In that period, this disorder, with its problematic prognosis, was considered the biologically-based affliction *par excellence,* to be treated exclusively with heavy medication.

This is the framework suggested by operative programming and accepted by the majority of colleagues (including some members of my staff). The future of this patient will include chronicity, symptoms treated with heavy drugs, and disability (predictability of the future).

Cognitive therapy does not have instruments to treat bipolar disorder (planning implemented according to actual tendencies). One needs to take into account probable scenarios (chronicity) and be realistic (read: don't do anything except prescribe drugs). I, however, did not want to give up and formulated a therapeutic project based on the strategic planning program outlined above.

In such an approach the future of the patient was not seen to be predictable and any therapy had to include new facts and possibilities, recovery included. I expected new trends, including the development of effective cognitive therapy protocols for bipolar disorder. So I went to work with my entire staff.

- The patient re-stabilized (disproving the scenario of chronicity).
- The patient graduated from college (disproving the scenario of disability).

- The patient married (constructing a valid personal network and disproving the prediction of social difficulties).
- The patient found and maintains a good job.
- The patient has benefited from new therapeutic protocols developed by our group and others (Lam, Jones & Howard, 1999). Based on what has been said, it is evident that the following description of tactics, strategies, techniques, and methods constitute an conceptual abstraction of a dynamic and complex process that characterizes the changing, stochastic, and aleatory scenario of the setting.

2. *Coping, Problem Solving, Self-Management*

When we take on a psychotic patient, in a condition of acute decompensation, the first tactical objective is to re-organize the daily routine beginning with the necessities of maintaining a minimum of well-being, including personal hygiene, nutrition, rest, and sleep. The phases to be implemented, often with the active participation of the rehabilitation therapist, are the following.

Planning and structuring of everyday activities. The daily routines negotiated with the patients are programmed by completing the appropriate written protocol. The rationale to be adopted is clearly explained to the patients. This is because in many clinical situations the planning and implementation of the behavioural programs normally carried out automatically are changed. In this way a negative loop may be instituted and consolidated as follows.

Activity planning is not possible and no routine is implemented because they have not been programmed. The human mind is not reactive but proactive. This means that the human mind is continually anticipating the future, which gradually takes shape. In the case in which this proactive response is compromised, human beings become reactive, exposed to the solicitations of the environment in a passive and casual manner.

The planning of everyday activities constitutes an initial attempt to restore proactive abilities to the mind of the patient. In many cases, when the clinical situation appears serious and the planning and implementation of everyday activities are compromised, it may be necessary to physically assist the patient in the execution of the programmed routine. In this type of therapeutic methodology, which can be positively carried out in a group, the rehabilitation technician plays a key role.

Every morning the patients are guided by the therapists, with patience, comprehension, and firmness, in the implementation of the various routines. These include getting up, washing, having breakfast, listening to the news on the radio, commenting on it, having the first meeting of the day, etc… Gradually the patients are followed less closely, though the team always makes sure the routines are respected. This type of intervention can be carried out in other settings, including the therapeutic or rehabilitative community or at home with the assistance of a rehabilitation therapist.

Progressive implementation of the protocol with keeping a diary. During the implementation phase of the programmed routines much information is collected from different sources and with different modalities. The patients themselves, along with their diaries, furnish useful data. Even the lack of keeping a diary is an important indicator of attitude and adherence to treatment.

Other sources of information depend on the setting and include nursing personnel, the rehabilitation therapist, and family members living with the patient.

For behavioural routines that do not seem to be within the actual abilities of the patient, behavioural techniques including self-instructional training with role play and modeling are programmed and implemented.

3. *Self-Observation and Self-Control through Biofeedback*

One important objective, in the short run, is to furnish the patient with new instruments for coping with anxiety. One method I have developed and widely applied with excellent results is electrodermal biofeedback (Scrimali & Grimaldi, 1982). We are also beginning to accumulate encouraging data regarding the possible use of neurofeedback.

Electrodermal biofeedback is used in the earliest phases of the treatment, while neurofeedback is implemented subsequently in order to improve neuropsychological parameters including attention and concentration. By implementing training with electrodermal feedback, patients are taught to diminish arousal and, therefore, develop new emotionally activated strategies of coping they were previously unable to manage.

This newly acquired competence, thanks to biofeedback, contributes not only the improvement of the coping skills of the patient but also to an increase in self-efficacy and self-esteem. If the patient is then provided with a small appliance for electrodermal biofeedback for personal use, a variety of therapeutic goals can be accomplished (Scrimali, 2005a).

The patients will feel gratified because they have been entrusted with an instrument for which they are responsible. The patients know that they control a new instrument for coping that can be used to better manage their symptoms. I would also like to mention how the use of biofeedback in psychotic patients constitutes an excellent example of the negative loop constituted by the scientific preconceptions I have spoken of earlier.

Some authors have judged biofeedback unusable in psychotic patients because these patients, in the presence of electronic instrumentation, would immediately develop delusions of being influenced (Fuller, 1977). The affirmation was judged indisputable and destined not to be disproved because experimentation using this new therapeutic instrument with psychotic patients was strongly discouraged.

Other authors, including members of our group, believed that this new therapeutic tool was worth trying as long as the necessary precautions were adopted. And that is what we did, with notable success. Today we know that biofeedback, combined with solid therapy, can be used successfully in the treatment of schizophrenic patients.

4. Improvement of Behavioural Competences

An important topic in the treatment of schizophrenic patients is related to the improvement of behavioural competences. In the therapeutic program, this constitutes a target of rehabilitation on both the individual and group level. From a psychotherapeutic point of view, it is also necessary that the patient, early on, is able to autonomously carry out a series of procedural activities with relative competence.

The difficulties which many psychotic patients have in this area are tied to interference in the functioning of neuropsychological planning and to deficits in executive functions of the frontal lobe.

Because these deficits are observed on the behavioural level in schizophrenic patients, they are thought to be traceable to neuropsychological and cognitive deficits. In the 1970s, Meichenbaum and Cameron (1980) proposed that actions and procedures are constantly monitored by an internal dialog that uses instructions, present in memory, then repeating them as the executive procedure is gradually implemented.

Since this process is altered in persons with schizophrenia, the two authors proposed teaching patients an actual set of instructions in order to carry out various procedures they want to use. The patients would then be asked to repeat these instructions out loud as they gradually performed the relative behavioural phases.

In this context, Meichenbaum created a specific training program defined *Self Instructional Training* (1977). Patients are trained to focus attention on the procedures to be carried out, repeating the instructions verbally. Initially, this is done in the "open" mode, i.e., taking to oneself quietly, then as this ability increases, through an internal dialog. A preliminary evaluation of the behaviors the patient is not able to carry out correctly, but desires to develop, is necessary. Subsequently, a set of instructions is prepared in detail and placed on a note card. The patients are asked to study and repeat the set of instruction out loud.

When they are able to easily remember all steps of the routine, they are asked to carry out the procedure, step-by-step, as they repeat the instructions out loud. With practice the instructions become internalized and need to be repeated only in the internal dialog; in the end, the processes of monitoring the different behavioural sequences become automatic.

This application recalls cognitive learning theory and emulates the procedures that all individuals use when they must learn new skills. For example, when we acquire a new instrument, we carefully read the instructions and follow the steps suggested. When the information has been memorized, we no longer need the written instructions. We are, however, all obliged in this phase of learning to repeat the instructions to ourselves mentally, occupying computationally controlled processes. Only later does the procedure become automatic, freeing up precious computational capacities for the strategic planning of other complex tasks.

For psychotic patients, it is as if they must relearn what *homo sapiens* normally already know from childhood, and the *Self Instructional Training* methodology is simply the implementation of what is suggested by the cognitive psychology of learning.

5. Management and Treatment of Perceptual Distortion Phenomena

Before entering into the merits of this important topic as it is related to therapeutic strategy, it is my opinion that the treatment of hallucinations must be considered as closely tied to that of delusion and to the dynamics of emotional self-control. The management and resolution of hallucinatory phenomenology should be conducted in terms of cognitive restructuring aimed at the treatment of delusion and with the gradual institution of new competencies of arousal management. The role of the therapeutic relationship is crucial to this strategy.

The hallucinatory experience can be approached and discussed only after a solid therapeutic relationship has been established. Often the patients tend not to speak of the perceptual distortion experience afflicting them for fear of not being believed, or made fun of, or *considered crazy*.

Sometimes concrete clues indicating the presence of hallucinations, e.g., eye or head movements (usually straight ahead and upwards or toward the right) in a direction away from the interlocutor, emerge during a session. In this case, it is opportune to wait until the patient decides to speak about the problem.

In the area of behavioural and cognitive orientation, numerous therapeutic methodologies have been proposed and experimentally tested for working with hallucinations, especially auditory hallucinations.

The earliest forms of intervention were behavioural, based on counter-conditioning with adverse stimuli such as electric and acoustic shocks (Chadwick, Birchwood & Trower, 1996; Fowler, Garety & Kuipers, 1995; Kingdon & Turkington, 1994).

Patients are given a small electronic instrument with which they can administer a cutaneous electric shock to themselves every time a hallucination occurs. The technique has provided moderate results, even if it is based on a controversial rationale.

In my opinion, this technique does not result in counter-conditioning as predicted behaviorist model but should be considered a method able to increase the coping capacity and self-efficacy of the patient. Thanks to the new methodology, patients finally feel able *to do something* about the torment that afflicts them.

In the cognitive field, *attention focusing* and *distraction techniques* have been proposed (Temple 2004). The *distraction* or *counter-stimulation techniques* use different acoustic stimuli including reading, math calculations, and word games. The patient can be advised to engage in specific activities based on the possibilities offered by the patient's life style.

Distraction techniques are based on the attempt to create a flow of information that competes with the hallucinations, removing cerebral computational capacities from them. *Focusing techniques* are based on reducing of the dramatic nature of the event. In this way the patient becomes comfortable with the event and is able to subsequently attribute a new meaning to it, promoting its progressive integration into the dynamics of the self. The second option seems to be the most convincing and is part of the methodology used in the Negative Entropy protocol.

Chadwick, Birchwood and Trower (1996) have proposed a new, cognitively based rationale for the treatment of hallucinations. They consider the voices to be an activating phenomena generated by a cerebral malfunction to which the patient attributes a negative meaning. This, in turn, generates emotional reactions closely tied to that meaning.

According to the three English authors, the crucial aspect of the psychopathological dynamics of hallucinations consists of a biphasic process, including the attribution of negative meaning and the catastrophic emotional reaction this provokes. The therapeutic method suggested appears positive and interesting.

According to this therapeutic model the patient is given a theory in which the hallucination is not considered a phenomena coming from the outside world, and therefore an inexplicable, threatening event not shared by others, but it is presented as a process of the internal world, i.e., of the mind of the patient. Once this hypothesis is suggested, the patient is not asked to accept it passively but to put it to the test, using an experiential dynamic based on collaborative empiricism.

In this approach the attention focusing techniques concentrate on the contents and characteristics of the hallucinations. The data collected tend to furnish elements of proof that the hallucinations can be traced to information, memories, and experiences of the patients and their internal worlds.

Fowler, Garety and Kuipers have formulated, and successfully experimented, a therapeutic protocol that is articulated in three topics (1995):

- change in the convictions of the patient regarding the voices;
- provocation and management of the voices during a session;
- problem-solving and coping to train the patient to identify conditions that can cause hallucinations.

The methodology I have developed and experimented successfully within the *Negative Entropy* protocol appears consistent with a good part of the observations and proposals elaborated by the English authors.

As I have tried to demonstrate earlier in this book, the motor conception of the mind and the adoption of a constructivist epistemology provide an excellent background for the conceptualization of hallucinatory symptomatology. The narrative and hermeneutic perspective also appear to be a perfect corollary for developing an integrated methodology for the treatment of these symptoms.

I will now briefly describe the protocol I have elaborated for the management and treatment of hallucinations. This treatment is a phase of the *Negative Entropy* protocol that is by no means preliminary. It can only be initiated after having overcome the crisis and reestablishing an acceptable reintegration of daily routines. It is indispensable, as already noted, that a positive emotional climate for the patient be established.

In order to accomplish the intervention I am about to describe, it is important that the patient learn self-control skills through biofeedback. The possibility of reducing arousal and using a new instrument for coping constitute a precious resource in the treatment of hallucinations. The phases of the protocol are the following:

- formulation of new explanatory theories;
- conduction of behavioural experiments and of self-observation;
- reflection on data gathered;
- development of new methodologies of coping and problem solving;
- realization of further behavioural experiments that include that use of newly acquired competences;
- acquisition of cognitive confirmation and restructuring;
- creation of meaning for the hallucinations through the analysis of their content;
- insertion of the contents of the hallucinations into a history of the personal life events of the patient and the development of a new narrative regarding the hallucinatory experience.

Now we will look at each of the above-mentioned points.

Formulation of new explanatory theories. When the patient finally decides to talk about the hallucinations, it is important to show an understanding and supportive attitude. One should not act surprised or alarmed; in fact, it is opportune to tell the patient that hearing voices is a very common experience that happens to thousands of persons in very different circumstances. Even in the case of visual hallucinations, the same procedure should be used.

Immediately after, the patient is asked to describe as much information as possible about the hallucinations and will be listened to attentively. It may be the first time the patient has someone who listens with interest to what is being described, without contradicting or criticizing.

Obviously, it is unthinkable that during the classic "visit" of the head physician with a large number of doctors in tow (assistants, interns, residents), together with nurses, therapists and students, the patient will reveal having heard voices. The patient will only confide this terrible secret in a climate with a secure base that can be created only after much work.

There are many occasions in which our patients only decide to talk about the problem after their release from the hospital. It is often the general improvement and the increasing belief in being helped to get better that convince the patient to talk. After listening to the description of the phenomena, it is important to ask the patient the significance of the hallucinations and what consequences they have for the patient's life.

A crucial step in the therapeutic strategy is assume hallucinations are present at least during the brief and middle periods and to concentrate on reducing the negative impact they have on the patient's life.

Once the patient has formulated a conception of the hallucinatory phenomenon, we can suggest that the idea that, for instance, *demons* are responsible for the hallucinations, is legitimate; we also suggest, however, that *there may be other explanations,* including the possibility that the voices or visions do not actually come from the outside world, but are produced by the patient's own mind.

We can compare the hallucination to daydreaming, explaining that in certain circumstances the brain experiences images and sounds actually coming from memory, as if they were coming from an external reality. At this point, one may ask why the patient should accept this new hypothesis, if one had already been formulated and adopted. The rationale for this is that of the negotiation and adoption of a more effective and efficient coping mechanism.

The patient's attribution of meaning to the hallucination, considering it to be a paranormal phenomenon, performs the crucial function of attributing sense to a disquieting experience, permitting the integration of the hallucination into one's own life experiences. This is a coping mechanism that the patient can renounce only if we are able to offer a better one.

Imagine that an adult who does not know how to swim has a great big life preserver in the shape of a turtle. It is a solution, even if ridiculous and embarrassing, that will be hard to renounce if the person is in deep water and risks drowning. Now imagine bringing that person to shallow water and helping him or her learn how to swim. Isn't it possible that the scenario will change?

Returning to hallucinations, we are now offering the patient an attractive option, whose adoption appears more useful and reassuring. In fact, we always stress that after having established the exact nature of the phenomenon, we will be able to furnish the help and methods necessary to reduce and resolve the problem. If, in the end, an agreement is reached that the hallucination is a pathological phenomenon related to the brain, and that the patient will not be stigmatized but will actually be able to resolve the problem, the probability that the new prospective will be accepted is very high. In fact, we tell the patient that now we have two hypotheses:

Hypothesis A (that of the patient): The voices I hear are those of evil spirits controlling me. Or: The monsters I see are hostile extraterrestrials, here to invade the world.

Hypothesis B (the therapist's) the voices that you hear and the images you see are *processes of the mind* that are activated because of a negative condition of the brain, similar to when one takes substances like LSD. In your case, it is your own brain that is producing the substance.

Empirical verification through the use of "behavioural experiments". The rationale for this step, crucial for the hallucinatory treatment protocol, it consists of the so-called "behavioural experiments". This approach has received much attention in cognitive psychotherapy and has been discussed by Bennet-Levy, Butler, Fennel, Hackman, Mueller, and Westbrook (2004). The theoretical foundations of such a therapeutic approach are traceable to the strict coordination among the cognitive, emotional, and procedural processes of the human mind.

On the basis of this premise, it is possible to modify such a conviction by initiating a new procedure which furnishes elements of an innovative judgment and activating different emotions. A final theoretical reference to a similar clinical approach can be identified in learning theory for adults.

The value of behavioural experiments for learning in adults was originally conceptualized and presented by Dewey (1961).

Particularly appropriate for our ends is the work of Kolb (1974). This author had formulated a multilevel model of the adult learning. According to this model there are four steps that can be described:

- planning;
- realization of new experiences;
- observation and accurate gathering of information;
- reflection.

Within the fourth topic, the following processes must be carried out:

- connect new data to previous beliefs and schema;
- put the new elements gathered in relation to new possible meanings;
- formulate new conclusions;
- restructure the previous beliefs.

To this set, referable to the standard cognitive orientation, it is possible to add the implications of the constructivist and motor approach to the mind which constitutes the perspective of this monograph.

In fact, in agreement with the theories of the active construction of the processes of meaning which are developed through action and not only through rationalist thought, it is evident that the patient cannot simply incorporate the point of view of the therapist into his or her system of knowledge, but must be gradually guided to autonomously effect new observations and try to discuss new explanations. Obviously, the planning phase of the behavioural experiments is crucial and the methodology I have developed is as follows.

After having suggested to the patient the possibility that other explanations exist for the phenomena experienced, I propose that no *a priori* hypothesis should prevail over others, but that we do some experiments to verify the validity of the theory proposed by the therapist.

As I have already stressed, it is very important that the experiments are preceded by adequate conceptualization and planning.

In accord with the epistemology of scientific discovery described by Popper, it is evident that scientific experimentation does not create new theories, but simply selects them.

Therefore, it is not the event that will create new meaning, but it is the new meaning, promoted in the psychotherapeutic setting, that can generate new interpretations of the event! The set of actions that I have developed and adopted are the following and include some recent developments in neuroscience that are presented to and discussed with the patient.

- Voices and images that are perceived only by the patient can be hallucinations, i.e., processes of the mind.

- Hallucinations appear when the quantity of information that arrives to the brain from the outside world is not optimal, i.e., too much light or too much noise, or, on the contrary, too much darkness or silence.
- The hallucinations appear when one is agitated, worried, or scared.
- The hallucinations often appear when relational conflicts with others occur.
- Insomnia and poor sleep activity favour the appearance of hallucinations.

Conduction of behavioural experiments and self-observation. The patient is encouraged to record the presence of hallucinations, the condition of sensory input, and the emotional state at the moment of their appearance in a diary.

Reflection on the data gathered. The data gathered tend to demonstrate the validity of the therapist's theory. But it is not a given, at this point, that the patient will abandon his or her theory and old behaviors. We do not, however, insist on this, but we move on to the following phase, considering it as further research and not an absolute panacea.

It is necessary to complete our theoretical position with a new series of behavioural experiments able to corroborate the substance of the new theory. Here we might talk to the patient in clear and simple terms about research methodology in medicine.

One useful idea is to explain how John Snow was able to discover the mechanism for the diffusion of cholera (Commonwealth Fund, 1936). The great English physician had formulated the hypothesis that the disease was transmitted by water contaminated by sewage. This was only a theory and needed to be corroborated with accurate experimental observation. John Snow, in fact, during a cholera epidemic, went through the streets of London checking the distribution of cases of cholera.

It is evident that the gathering of data was the first crucial phase of the research. Through it Snow discovered that there was a street in London in which everyone who lived on the left side became ill, while everyone on the right did not.

Further verification showed that the two sides of the street were provided with water by two different private companies. One collected the water to be distributed near the mouth of a sewer, while the other got its water from a clean mountain source. (See the advantages of entrusting private enterprises that think only of profits, with the management of public services!).

At this point, however, a new experiment was necessary that could definitively confirm the new theory and resolve the problem. In fact, when Snow finally convinced the company that got water from near the sewer to change its source, the cholera epidemic ceased.

If this anecdote is too complicated for the patient, it is possible to adopt the following simpler, more intuitive example. Based on our sensory experience, the earth appears absolutely flat; this has led humans formulate and maintain the wrong belief that our planet was a disk until the 15th century. Even so, small clues have always existed demonstrating that the earth is a sphere.

One of these clues is that when ships appear on the horizon, one sees the flags on the tallest masts first, then the other masts and sails, and then the body of the ship. This fact, in the past, was not sufficient for a new theory. A crucial experiment was needed. If the earth was really round, it would be possible to circumnavigate it, returning to the point of departure by sailing in the same direction.

This was at the base of Christopher Columbus's project, even though Magellan was the first to actually circumnavigate the globe. Only circumnavigating the globe finally undermined the conviction that our planet was flat and opened a new era for humanity.

Using these metaphors and others the reader will surely know how to develop in a clinical setting, can we say that the patients who have already conducted a series of experiments regarding the observation of sensory input and arousal will find themselves in the condition of Snow when he identified the street with the sick people all living on the same side, or the observer who has seen the ship's banners appear on the horizon before the ship itself. Now is the moment to carry out the crucial experiment and find solutions. This is achieved through the subsequent phase of the treatment.

Development of new methodologies of coping and problem-solving. Based on the rationale identified together with the patient in the preceding phase, new effective coping mechanisms can be proposed, including the following:

Act to always maintain a condition of optimal sensory input. Do not frequent crowded, noisy, and excessively bright places. Avoid watching too much television, or better, don't watch it at all (this advice, given the actual state of television, I would extend to all people who want to avoid brain damage!). Use a Walkman with relaxing and pleasant music which can be listened to if the auditory hallucinations occur. Illuminate rooms appropriately in case visual hallucinations appear in the shadows.

One important aspect of the coping strategies is biofeedback, to use with a personal instrument called *PsychoFeedback* which I developed at the Research Laboratory of the Institute for Cognitive Science in Enna (Scrimali, 2005a).

Implementation of further behavioural experiments that include the use of newly acquired competences. The patients are encouraged to implement what was discussed and learned in the therapeutic setting.

Confirmation of cognitive restructuring. When the patients are able to refer to having obtained empirical confirmation of the new theoretical set, we can finally observe the beginning of an active phase of cognitive restructuring. At this point, it is possible to move on to the next phase.

Analysis of the contents of the hallucinations in order to create a new meaning. This can be addressed only when the patients have accepted the new conceptualization of hallucinatory phenomena and have acquired new coping skills. In this phase of the treatment the visual hallucinations usually disappear. The auditory hallucinations might remain longer and, in some cases, indefinitely. In this situation, progress can be made by beginning an analysis of the content of the voices.

Here it is possible to discover that the voices are none other than the materialization of rigid schemas and rules coming from parents. This internal activation is common to all human beings, but in our case it assumes a sensory connotation in which an internal dialog of the patient is perceived as an external voice.

The reconstruction of schemas and their historic dynamic tied to the life cycle of the patient, especially to the kind of parenting the patient received, permits the discovery of how the voices are simply the externalization of cautionary, critical, and censorial behaviour long experienced by the patient.

It is, in fact, the climate of trust, acceptance, non-intrusiveness, respect, and the optimizing of communicative patterns implemented in the therapeutic setting that, over the mid and long-range periods, definitively helps put an end to the phenomenon.

Insertion of the contents of the hallucinations into the personal history of the patient and the development of a new narrative regarding the hallucinatory experience. This constitutes the final phase of the treatment for the hallucinations. The patient now possesses a new theory regarding the hallucinatory experience, and this theory must be integrated into his or her personal story. The patients will now learn to narrate a new story to themselves and to others in which this strange hallucinatory phenomenon assumes sense and meaning. The search for significance, the construction of meaning, the creation of order from disorder, with the lowering of the Entropy of Mind and the promotion of Negative Entropy, now take a step ahead!

6. *Analysis and Treatment of Delusion, Cognitive Distortion, and Dysfunctional Schemas*

As I have already discussed in the first part of the book, Jasper's conception of the non-modifiability of delusional thought has for many years impeded the development of effective therapies for this important psychotic problem. Fortunately, the adoption of the constructivist and narrative perspective and the development of a motor paradigm of the mind have revolutionized this negative situation, opening the doors to the possibility of cognitive restructuring.

Delusion is a dysfunctional coping mechanism that serves to create meaning, even if it does so in a rigid and not easily falsifiable way, thus making it essentially ineffective.

Together with the patient, a relativistic position must be constructed in which a possible preliminary acceptance of delusional thought is proposed without, however, a completely uncritical adhesion to it. Obviously, like the work with hallucination, delusion will not be addressed in the first phase of treatment.

At this stage, as has been amply discussed in the part of the book on crisis intervention, the delusion must be accepted and only protection and care must be furnished. Subsequently, together with the patient, a probabilistic and constructivist perspective will gradually be developed using a personal diary in which the facts, possible interpretations, and the emotional climate of the moment are reported.

During the rereading of the diary, the patient will realize that the greater the emotional discomfort, the more persuasive and absolutist does the interpretive attitude regarding reality become.

Beyond this, the therapist will formulate other possible interpretations of the facts without ever contesting or making the proposals of the patient appear ridiculous.

The patient will gradually learn that every event can be interpreted in different ways.

In this sense, the patient is gradually helped to learn the difference between "I know" and "I think that..."

Substantially, a new attitude must be created in the patient characterized by the basic epistemological conception that the reality of every human individual constitutes the end of a constructivist process and not the simple recording of an evident and axiomatic truth.

For example, the presence of a young man who stops everyday on a street where the patient lives is interpreted as sure proof of an emissary of something negative (mafia, secret services, etc...) The therapist hypothetically accepts this idea, without making fun of it (can we be certain that some patients are not actually under surveillance by someone?), but also formulates another. It may be that in the street where the patient lives, there is a pretty girl with whom the boy is in love. His presence in the neighborhood is, therefore, not necessarily related to the patient.

A training program is initiated in which events are observed and multiple interpretations are formulated, without immediately jumping to a single conclusion.

A complementary aspect to this training is constituted by the improvement of neuropsychological performance. For example, the difficulty in recognizing emotions in the faces of others or even on one's own face can contribute to delusional thought as I have demonstrated in the earlier parts of this monograph.

Imagine being surrounded by persons who appear all the same, without distinctive characteristics or emotions; wouldn't you feel uncomfortable and worried? At this point, wouldn't you try to protect yourself by becoming defensive and suspicious?

The fact that the schizophrenic patient doesn't easily recognize faces can lead to the legitimate conviction that it is *always the same person* outside the house when, in fact, there are many persons in the neighborhood. Last winter, I experience something that helped me understand, first hand, new things about delusion.

Don't worry, I didn't have a psychotic breakdown (at least, I don't think so), I was simply afflicted with a viral keratitis that reduced my vision drastically, making it impossible to recognize people beyond a distance of three meters. I also could not decipher the emotional expressions on the faces of people standing only one and a half meters away from me. As I have already explained, this keratitis permitted me to experience sensory deprivation. I already wrote about what happened to me at the conference in Syracuse. Now I would like to add some further thoughts to the matter.

During this illness, which I describe as a period of "visual sensory deprivation", I experienced what it is like to not know how to behave when one doesn't recognize a person.

Everyday because dozens of individuals arrive at the clinic—patients, students, nurses, colleagues, etc...—I developed a standard coping mechanism that entailed emitting a forced smile offered to anyone, accompanied by the monosyllabic, "Yes?". This same expression, vacuous and stereotypical, I had seen many times on the faces of my psychotic patients. I postponed recognition and, therefore, the appropriate facial expression until I could recognize the person, thanks to the voice. I can assure you that this was a superficial strategy that permitted a certain adaptation but was able to provoke errors, misunderstandings, and even conflict.

Another interesting aspect that I discovered during my illness was the following. While teaching at the Aleteia School, I would normally regulate my exposition and my emotional state based on visual feedback coming from the posture and expressions of the students (like any competent teacher). During the illness, I suddenly found myself in a classroom with 20 persons whose faces were confusing and undecipherable.

I began to feel uncomfortable and imagine that the students were getting bored, that my exposition was not effective, that the lesson was going poorly, etc... What was I to do? If I asked them, "How's it going?" I didn't have reliable elements to know how things were really going; I couldn't perceive their expressions and thought what was being said might be nothing more than a formal reassurance.

In a very short time, this inability to not recognize faces created in me a sense of acute anxiety, low self-efficacy, and a tendency to avoid social relations. Only the full recovery of the ability to recognize my interlocutors and their facial expressions restored my serenity.

Based on all this, I am more convinced than ever that the improvement in attention, concentration, and the recognition of faces and emotions must constitute crucial collateral training for the treatment of delusion. Another important aspect to consider is the emotional climate.

As I have already noted, emotion and cognition are closely correlated. Therefore, a negative emotional situation and, in particular, a climate of emotional hyper-involvement, hostility, and criticism in the family (and also in the therapeutic setting) can contribute to the maintenance of delusional thought.

It is clear how intervention within the family and the network and the creation of a solid therapeutic alliance constitute inviolable aspects of the treatment of delusion. From an operative point of view, the indications to follow are these:

After instituting the therapeutic alliance and normalizing daily routines based on the now positive therapeutic relationship, one can begin to systematically work on delusion which, up to this point, has been opportunely avoided. The first step is the assignment, as homework, of the diary that will be examined and discussed.

From the diary, themes will emerge upon which analysis and discussion (which is always Socratic and probabilistic, and never dogmatic and rationalistic) can be based. The most frequent topics found to be discussed are:

- extreme mistrust of others;
- expectations of being harmed;
- inadequate and arbitrary interpretations of events;
- excessive sensibility to criticism;
- tendency to keep others at a distance;

- episodes in which the patient has been derided, insulted, or tricked;
- excessive suspicion.

Cognitive restructuring, realized through the Socratic method and beginning with more peripheral beliefs to minimize the resistance the system of knowledge to change, should aim to achieve the following objectives, starting with the setting:

- construct a climate of trust;
- demonstrate tranquility and understanding;
- analyze the conviction of vulnerability regarding others and reality, in general;
- analyze the conviction of hostility on the part of others.

Patients usually propose a conceptualization of interpersonal relationships characterized by the logic of *homo homini lupus (man is a wolf to man)*. Such a belief is profoundly rooted and comes from family myths, as the reconstruction of the patient's developmental history almost never fails to demonstrate.

The argument normally used to gradually discredit these beliefs is scientific and ethological. With the patient I discuss that from the ethological, thus scientific, point of view, *homo sapiens* is a very social species, and this means that each individual can live and prosper only by trusting others and collaborating with them.

Obviously, these theories must not remain in the abstract but must be made appropriate to the emotional level of the setting, creating a climate of affection, cooperation, and promotion of development that the patient has probably never experienced. Meanwhile, work with the family is also carried out in order to improve the emotional climate in which the patient lives.

The treatment of specific themes relative to the delusions of the patients is subsequently completed with the systematic analysis of dysfunctional cognitive schemas.

7. Management and Overcoming of Negative Symptoms

The so-called negative symptoms of schizophrenia represent the most significant area of the patient's disability and the most difficult challenge in the treatment of the disorder (Stolar, 2004).

Since psychotherapeutic treatment consists substantially of an exchange of information in the context of a relationship rich in emotional weight, we must take into account that the presence of negative symptoms make the exchange of information and the creation of a secure base particularly difficult.

In fact, the flattening of affect blocks communication at a tacit level and, therefore, the construction of a therapeutic alliance; the difficulty in speech also makes the exchange of digital information difficult. Apathy also makes experience, exploration, and thus the acquisition of new information nearly impossible.

Beyond this, the loss of the ability to perceive positive feedback makes the patient hardly open to a relationship with the therapist and to the gratifications that arise from clinical improvement, while neuropsychological deficits worsen the communicative dysfunctions.

The treatment of negative symptoms is a target of rehabilitative intervention, rather than psychotherapy. It is necessary, however, to point out that the patient with negative symptoms shows enormous difficulty in adhering to the treatment and, therefore, accepting participation in a therapeutic program. It is necessary to prepare the patient for the rehabilitative work, both individually and in a group, through psychotherapy. In order to progressively initiate a therapeutic relationship, it is necessary to focus on the slow rhythms of the patient, reaching him or her in the crystallized universe where time has stopped and everything is without color.

Any impatience on the part of the therapist, any excess of stimulation, provokes an immediate and often catastrophic closure. Progress is slow, and the time lost during the sessions to long and difficult silences must be accepted.

It is surprising to note how after sending some input to a patient, a question, for instance, there is a long, painful informational blackout. This can often be difficult to manage for the therapist. The patient seems lost in a void, but just when we are about to give up, moving on to another argument, the feedback arrives.

Our information was not lost, however, it just got stuck in the dysfunctional processes of the entropic mind before finding an interpretation. It is important to underline the fact that even if the patient seems unreceptive, in a kind of hibernation, in reality, he or she is very sensitive and perceives much more information than their behaviour would suggest.

It often happens that even with experienced psychiatrists, inopportune comments slip out in the presence of relatives or other persons, as if the patient were not there. The patients appear absent but they are not, and in many cases, I have received feedback much later, even after many sessions. This demonstrates to me that the patients, even when they seemed far-off and absent, were vigilant and present during the session.

It should also be remembered that negative symptoms are not simply a type of deficit but can be an active coping mechanism, protecting the mind of the patient from destructive levels of Entropy of Mind. It is unwise to try and eliminate these coping processes when others have not yet been created.

These may include a sense of trust, acceptance, and protection, separate from intrusiveness, that the therapist proposes. It should also be remembered that the closure of the patient is particularly vivid in the face of relatives and people with high expressed emotion. The sessions must be carried out in a relaxed climate and in a setting that excludes the presence of emotional, hostile, and critical persons who can increase the condition of defensive closure.

If the emotional and relational component is, in my opinion, crucial for entering in synchrony with the patients and involving them in the therapeutic and rehabilitative program, it is also necessary to identify the presence of cognitive distortions described by Rector, Beck, and Stolar (2005), in order to analyze and restructure them. This is achieved not only with a simple cognitive intervention, based on the Socratic dialog, but also involving the patient actively in the rehabilitative techniques that can unblock the vicious circles which I discussed in the part of the book dedicated to psychopathology. To exemplify this I will cite the therapeutic and rehabilitative methodologies that can be used to treat the idiosyncratic cognitive aspects identified and described by Rector, Beck, and Stolar.

Conviction of the need for relational distance. Group therapy based on musical and narrative activities.

Negative convictions regarding one's own possible skills. Act to always maintain a condition of optimal sensory input. Improve neuropsychological skills through specific training programs already described in the book (e.g., attention, memory, concentration, strategic planning, faces and emotional facial expression recognition).

Negative convictions activated by positive symptoms. The resolution of these aspects is achieved as a consequence of the treatment of positive symptoms (delusional thought and hallucinations).

Low expectations of gratification. Stimulate gratifying activities, physically helping the patient, e.g., gymnastics in a group together with the staff.

Low expectations for success. The convictions are discredited thanks to gradual success reached in the different training programs. In fact, it is important to document progress in order to show patients when they formulate negative previsions about success not having been achieved.

Pessimistic expectations tied to stigma. The battle against stigma is one of the key topics in the treatment of schizophrenia and is achieved, not only on an individual level, but also in the family and social environment, thanks to the application of specific psycho-educational programs.

Idiosyncratic perception regarding limited resources. This aspect is treated by showing the patients that their cognitive and neuropsychological resources can be implemented successfully through new systems of rehabilitation that are part of the *Negative Entropy* protocol.

8. Enrichment of Meta-Cognitive Functions

As I have pointed out in the second part of this monograph, the schizophrenic condition is characterized by the impairment of meta-cognitive skills involved in the capacity to reflect on one's own mental processes (self-reflexivity), to the comprehension of minds of others, and to the mastery of reality using one's own mind. An important aspect in the psychotherapy of the schizophrenic patient must consist of the analysis and progressive enrichment of meta-cognitive skills.

This topic, like others, can be considered from a psychotherapeutic and a rehabilitative point of view. Thus I would now like to discuss the more general aspects of enriching meta-cognitive functions and the work that can be carried out in the psychotherapeutic setting; afterwards, I will discuss the rehabilitative treatment of these functions.

Adrian Wells has formulated an original conceptual approach call "meta-cognitive psychotherapy" (Wells, 2002). According to his guidelines, psychotic patients must be made to relate to their own cognitive activity differently. The objective is pursued through the following steps:

- establishment and emphasis on the mode of functioning of the meta-cognitive processes of the mind;
- increase in the flexibility of control of attention;
- progressive institution of the ability to abstain from rumination and active worrying;

Adrian Wells maintains that these therapeutic objectives can be realized through a mental condition of "meta-cognitive distancing" from mental activities *in progress*, with the institution of a progressive restructuring of the system of knowledge. From an operative point of view, according to Wells, the patients must be progressively trained to identify dysfunctional mental activity and avoid acting on it. Specifically, Wells proposes to:

- help the patient develop meta-cognitive behaviour;
- activate "controlled" alternative cognitive processes for the dysfunctional automatic ones;
- develop new plans for the regulation of alternative behaviors;
- progressively restructure the belief system.

Wells' therapeutic program has been used primarily with neurosis, but it may furnish useful suggestions for the realization of meta-cognitive psychotherapy for psychotic patients. The ability to formulate theories about one's own mental state or the mental states of others requires the efficient working of diverse functions. One of these is the identification of internal states, constituted by the emotions and cognitive processes of internal representation.

A second aspect is the differentiation among mental processes, including the belief system and regulatory and meta-cognitive schemas and activities, or, in other words, the ability to reflect on and achieve changes in oneself. An important skill of standard cognitive inspiration which one tries to construct in the patients during psychotherapy is that of identifying the so-called "automatic thoughts".

A patient suffering from panic attacks, for example, must progressively become aware of being afflicted by recurrent and automatic mental processes, arising from the fact that any somatic sensation coming from the precordial area, can elicit automatic thoughts relative to an imminent infarction. These automatic thoughts activate somatic and neuro-vegetative reactions, creating and maintaining a loop that brings the patient to a panic attack.

It is not too difficult to institute and develop, in the neurotic patient, the meta-cognitive process of identification and differentiation. The patient, in fact, learns to activate a meta-cognitive process able to supervise and control of the mental events activated by the perception of an anomalous somatic sensation coming from the precordial area. The patient is taught to activate processes controlled by meta-cognition that are able to substitute the dysfunctional automatic ones. As soon as the cognitive and emotional cycle of the panic attack begins, the patient must:

1. identify the dysfunctional mental process;
2. try to block its progress;
3. substitute controlled mental activity for the dysfunctional automatic processes.

These operations, which require a reasonable level of meta-cognitive functioning, are easily realizable in neurotic patients. The situation regarding the psychotic patient is quite different since the ability to identify different mental processes and achieve control through the acquisition of new functions of self-regulation is notably impaired. In fact, it is this skill that must be progressively reconstructed.

For example, during the sessions the psychotic patients must begin to describe their own emotions and current cognitive activity while being helped to realize the difficulty of such a task.

Greenberg and Safran (1987) have pointed out how the psychotherapeutic process must help the patient become aware of their own inhibited emotions and integrate them into a conscious mental set.

An area to work on is the identification of active emotions in the patients and in the therapist, in a given moment, starting from the therapeutic setting. The therapist uses his or her skills in de-codifying their own emotions which are the result of the interaction taking place, carefully observing the tacit signals coming from the patient. Once a certain emotion has been identified, the therapist asks the patient to try and describe what is being felt so that the patient becomes progressively more competent in identifying that specific emotion. The gradual increase in meta-cognitive skills can subsequently be pursued outside the therapeutic setting.

Using homework, the patient will begin to reflect (like the phobic patient) on the existence of a complex process behind the hallucinations, including the presence of an activating event, traceable almost always to problematic interactions with a person with high expressed emotion. This interaction generates intense feelings of anger, frustration, and fear as well as the activation of an internal dialog that assumes the character of an external voice.

One very important aspect in the enrichment of meta-cognitive skills is the work to help the patient develop more adequate theories about the mental state of others. This also begins in the setting by asking the patient to describe what might be the thoughts and emotions of the therapist at that moment. The patient is supplied with useful suggestions to help formulate an appropriate hypothesis.

For example, the patient is told to carefully observe the tacit signals regarding posture, tone of voice, and gaze, in order to formulate an hypothesis about the emotional condition of the therapist. The patient is then asked to describe what might be the thoughts of the therapist regarding the patient. After the patient has written down his or her considerations, feedback is provided and discussed.

It is clear that this kind of work can be carried out in a group, but as I have noted, it is a good idea that individual work with the psychotherapist precedes the group setting in order to create some minimum abilities, leading to sufficient mastery. And mastery, by the way, is the third meta-cognitive skill to be discussed.

The sense of mastery regarding one's own mental processes is the result of the preceding therapeutic steps, with particular reference to learning emotional regulation and developing the capacity to recognize and competently manage one's own emotions and cognitions in a relational context. The strengthening of mastery is correlated to an increase in a sense of personal competence and self-efficacy.

The rehabilitative, meta-cognitive treatment for schizophrenic patients has been tested experimentally in Italy primarily by a group coordinated by Massimo Casacchia (Casacchia, Mazza, Frangou, Giosuè & Roncone, 2005).

Based on studies by Sarvati, Passerieux, and Hardy-Bayle and adopting the method called Instrument Enrichment Programme (IEP of Fuerstein, 1988), Casacchia and his collaborators treated twenty schizophrenic patients for 22 weeks in a controlled pilot study. The treatment consisted of six stages:

1. awareness of one's own deficit;
2. improvement in recognizing the emotions of others;
3. communication training;
4. improvement in neuropsychological processes, including attention, memory, and concentration;
5. development of the ability to know social rules and respect them;
6. group training in the recognition of the thoughts of others.

The treatment was conducted in a group which consisted of 10 patients and 5 therapists, including 1 psychologist, 2 psychiatrists, and 2 rehabilitation therapists.

The pilot study produced positive results with the treated patients exhibiting an evident improvement in behavioural and social skills.

In my own clinical experience with therapeutic and rehabilitative work, the six points of Casacchia's training program emerge as important for achieving and maintaining good relational functioning in the patient and, therefore, constitute an integral part of the *Negative Entropy* protocol.

9. *Promotion of Self-Efficacy and Self-Esteem*

In the second part of the monograph, I pointed out that in psychiatric patients, and especially schizophrenic ones, there is a progressive impairment of the sense of self-efficacy. A study was conducted that objectively documents this assertion whose results have already been discussed.

The perception of low self-efficacy feeds and maintains vicious circles characterized by the fact that patients do not perceive themselves to be competent in controlling psychological processes and relationship transitions. Because of this they avoid all situations in which problematic dynamics could present themselves.

Systematically avoiding these situations, the patients enter into a loop in which the maintenance of low levels of coping and problem-solving and a negative sense of personal efficacy occur. Thus, it is evident that one of the objectives of the psychotherapeutic and rehabilitative treatment must be the promotion of a higher sense of self-efficacy.

This objective is achieved by promoting new skills of emotional self-regulation and coping in the patients when they face specific problems related to hallucinations, problem-solving, and meta-cognition. It would seem, therefore, that the construction and maintenance of self-efficacy constitute secondary processes in the achievement of the therapeutic objectives just cited.

However, the general improvement in the level of functioning of the patient does not constitute the only process able to increase a sense of perceived self-efficacy. In patients, in fact, processes of maintenance of prior cognitive patterns are present that could create resistance to the promotion of a sense of self-efficacy, sustaining dysfunctional mechanisms in human information processes that can negate or minimize the progress and results achieved.

This means that it is not enough for the patient to show tangible improvement in the performance of these skills. This improvement must be clearly and concretely perceived in order to increase self-efficacy. It is, therefore, necessary to objectively document the levels of functioning of the patients, offering to them and their families periodic feedback regarding the positive results reached.

For example, psychophysiological and neuropsychological data and video-monitoring can be used in feedback sessions so that the patients can benefit from this information in a positive context of growth and personal promotion. It is very important that cohabitating family members participate in this process.

These family members often do not perceive the small changes in the patient and continue to be skeptical and critical. The objective data that documents the changes in the patient must be shown to them and commented upon. This makes it possible for family members to finally begin to contribute positive feedback to the patient, substituting a virtuous circle for the previously existing negative loops.

10. Restructuring and Development of Coalitional Processes

The process of integration of mental activity, as mentioned previously, must be carried out in both synchronic and diachronic terms. The therapeutic methodologies I have discussed up to now are primarily aimed at producing a synchronic integration. Mental activity, including perception, ideational thought, behavioural planning, and management of emotions is progressively made more efficient and better integrated according to the methodologies presented.

We must now deal with the problem of how to proceed at promoting the diachronic integration of the mental processes of the patient. How do we reach memories of the past and tie them to the present, and how, above all, do we construct a new and novel projection toward the future in patients who have lived a good part of their lives in a continual "here and now", without strategic anticipation and historic perspective?

To answer these questions means conceptualizing and initiating new treatment methodologies that have been specifically developed in a constructivist and systems-processes context. Nodal themes in this type of treatment are evolutionary reconstruction and narrative rewriting.

10.1. Evolutionary Reconstruction

Evolutionary reconstruction constitutes a crucial step toward recovery.

It was primarily Vittorio Guidano who introduced the methodology of evolutionary reconstruction to cognitive therapy (Guidano,

1992). The main objective of this crucial phase of the constructivist and post-rationalist psychotherapy is to analyze and relive, together with the patient, the origins of tacit information that—from the earliest emotional experiences—have contributed to the construction of patterns of self-coherence.

It is necessary to guide the patient to remembering and recounting the crucial experiences of their lives, not in chronological terms, but in terms of recognizing the emotional dynamics and comparing them to new emotional and cognitive interpretations that can be constructed on the base of the actual condition of the mind.

The patient, progressively reassured by the therapeutic work and by the solid relationship of the secure base created with the therapist, is finally able to revisit his or her own painful history. The methodology of the evolutionary reconstruction was not, however, used by Guidano with schizophrenic patients, but applied only to those with neurotic disorders.

The implementation of this methodology with patients who have exhibited a psychotic decompensation is definitely more problematic. Patients who have experienced *Entropy of Mind* try to systematically avoid reflecting on the past which they perceive as a period tied to failure, suffering, and frustration.

Thus, the emotions coming from a memory of the past are predominately painful and characterized by frustration, sadness, and a continual lowering of self-esteem and personal amiability. The therapist must work with the patient to reconstruct memories of positive experiences in which the patient was competent, adequate, and loved. The therapist will teach the patient to systematically draw on these memories.

The patients will gradually perceive that in reality they are not incompetent, unlovable, or inadequate, but the people who raised them made them live these emotions that were progressively incorporated into dysfunctional internal operative models.

Subsequently, one works to construct the substantial acceptance of the psychotic experience as linked to the deployment of the life cycle of the patient, from conception (biological vulnerability), to developmental history (reciprocity and nurturing), to the life events.

The construction of a new sense of existence can start from historicizing the psychosis and recognizing the recovery, thanks to the results of the therapeutic work. In this way a positive attitude toward the future is constructed. Unrealistic expectations should not be cultivated, but gradually realizable goals must be programmed. The reconquest of evolutionary *indeterminacy*, beyond the determinist destiny of *insanity*, obviously constitutes the final aim of the therapeutic and rehabilitative work.

A central component of evolutionary reconstruction is accomplished by the analysis of the reordering of developmental history. Vittorio Guidano developed a schematic guideline for the reconstruction of personal history that I will propose here, with some variation, based on my experience working with psychotic patients.

10.2. Analysis of Developmental History

Structure of the family and living conditions from the moment of the patient's birth.

Personal profile of the parents and other cohabitating family members.

Critical events identified through key scenes and episodes that can be related to the construction of internal dysfunctional operative models.

- **Infancy and preschool years (0-6)**
  - *Collection of earliest available memories;*
  - *Description of parents and living conditions;*

    Special attention to meaningful areas and experiences including:
    - *Exploration;*
    - *Order-disorder;*
    - *Experience of nurturance and being loved;*
    - *Communication;*
    - *Social relations;*
    - *Perceptive and self-perceptive experiences;*
    - *Sense of cohesion and integration of the self;*
  - *Information about behavioural, emotional, relational, and cognitive patterns at the base of parental narrations.*

- **Childhood (6-11)**
  - School;
  - Rapport with peers;
  - Rapport with teachers;
  - Reciprocity of emotional attachment with others;
  - Construction and development of religious sentiment.

- **Puberty and early adolescence (age 12-15)**
  - Sexual maturity and related experiences;
  - Management and evolution of first sentimental relationships;
  - Relation with same/sex parent regarding the learning of skills related to dating and sexual relationships;
  - Relations with opposite sex parent and his or her role in the validation of the child's self-image and amorous and sexual desirability.

- **Late adolescence and early adulthood (age 16-25)**
  - Reconstruction of the process of progressive autonomy from parents, relative to the construction of a personal adult identity;
  - Construction and development of intimate relationships.

- **Adulthood**
  - Relational style;
  - Affective relationship with partner within the couple;
  - Parenting style.

11. Revision of the Family History and Construction of a Genogram

In order to improve comprehension of the biographical events of the patient, it is useful not to limit the analysis to the reconstruction of the personal history of development, but to extend it to the family history, constructing the so-called genogram; this is a map of the extended family which includes all relatives who have influenced the patient (Lerner, 1983).

The patient is asked to prepare a kind of genealogical tree and include as much information as possible about personality and behavioural aspects of family members. The following is an example of a reconstruction by a patient whom I successfully helped overcome a psychotic decompensation. The patient was asked to identify and describe bizarre behaviors, unusual emotion conditions, and idiosyncratic relational aspects in relatives whom may have had an important role in the patient's development.

1. Bizarre, excessive, extreme, or unusual behaviors.
2. Emotional states.
3. Relational aspects.

- **Dad**
  1. Proven marital infidelity, clamorously denied.
  2. Irascible, pompous, arrogant, easily provoked to excessive and sudden attacks of rage. Hates being criticized and ordered about, selfish, more interested in professional prestige then in actual family situation, inclined to raise tone of voice and interrupt the conversation rudely and then leave without warning.
  3. Taciturn at home, witty and amusing with friends, liar.

- **Mom**
  1. Particularly capable in expressing herself with facial mimicry, interested in unsolved crimes, mysterious disappearances, mysteries, etc…, tends to give incoherent or inconclusive or irritating responses: undisguised repulsion for the opposite sex, with lots of taboos.
  2. Tenacious, apparently sweet, subtly vindictive, answers rudely.
  3. Diffident, closed, timid, inhibited with a sense of inferiority, of inadequacy, very quiet, doubts own intelligence, distracted.

- **Thomas (brother)**
  1. Very impetuous and passionate and with his girlfriend in crowded, public places, inclined to make and keep promises.

2. Very affectionate, sensitive, conceited capable of denying evidence, tends to exaggerate small ailments or health problems, often very egotistical with contradictory character traits.
3. Open, always willing to make new friends, often naive, unable to pick up on nuances.

- **Paternal Grandfather**

1. Son in Greece, before marriage, carries out family business at the beck and call of his wife, often ready to exaggerate and brag about something.
2. Emotional, anxious, generous, patient, devoted to the family and work, apprehensive.
3. Available, cordial, convinced of ability to understand people, fun.

- **Paternal Grandmother**

1. Takes care of her appearance, has ring with a meaningful design, interested in card reading, and is a friend of a woman who reads cards for a living, vain.
2. Conceited, bossy, liar, cutting responses, haughty.
3. Goes out infrequently, does not go unnoticed, humiliates husband in public, hypocritical.

- **Maternal Grandmother**

1. Never sleeps with the door closed and always with the clock nearby, uses favouritism which is always clamorously denied, repulsion for the opposite sex.
2. Stubborn, anxious, obsessive, nosy, affectionate, very generous, inclined to make sacrifices.
3. Suspicious, closed, no other man in her life except a violent, unfaithful gambler.

- **Maternal grandfather**

1. Fanatical gambler, more a happy loser than winner, fanatically unfaithful, illegitimate daughter, loves to eat.

2. Violent, not very affectionate, bossy, close ties to family of origin and considers their needs first, interested in material needs, but not of his children and not in every possible scholastic "sacrifice" his children make.
3. Very generous, will invite anyone to dinner, even a mere acquaintance, loves to eat, friend to everybody, willing to lend money even with repayment unlikely, willing to receive goods instead of money in repayment, affectionate with grandchildren and during the illness, also with other members of the family in recent years.

- **Aunt Nina (mother's sister)**
  1. Theatrical, capable in a subtle and planned way of gaining access to family wealth.
  2. Anxious, emotional, apprehensive, nervous, conceited, bossy in the family and with contradictory character traits.
  3. Gossipy, available, generous for show's sake, very supportive during the illness, careful in observing people, capable of worming information out of people.

- **Uncle Ciccio (mother's brother)**
  1. Loves dancing, goes to the movies, goes out on Sunday with family to dine in restaurants.
  2. Very affectionate, very attached to the family, emotional, anxious when faced with a serious problem.
  3. Very generous, trusting, hopeful, friendly.

- **Uncle Pippo (father's brother)**
  1. Plays cards, attends the cultural club of the town, tends towards exaltation and exaggeration, loves cars which he takes meticulous care of.
  2. Very emotional, apprehensive, sensitive, goes off like a fuse and burns out like a match in the wind.
  3. Greedy, outgoing and fun-loving in company, still living at home, often victimized, more or less without realizing it by his wife.

- **Uncle Gianni (father's brother)**
  1. Uninterrupted hours giving private math lessons with the goal of accumulating money.
  2. Severe, haughty, conceited.

12. Synchronic and Diachronic Therapeutic Approaches

Diachronic integration within the *Negative Entropy* protocol is ideally carried out after synchronic integration since the need to quickly construct new integrative competencies of the self in the "here and now" and a more positive rapport with reality are crucial. This means that, technically, the analysis of the developmental story is initiated many months after the start of psychotherapeutic and rehabilitative treatment.

Guidano (1992) has presented a temporal scale which establishes that developmental reconstruction for neurotic patients should begin many months after initiating psychotherapy. It should be noted, however, that these indications on times and modes of the therapeutic protocols have a relative importance for methodology. In reality, the synchronic and diachronic approaches often intersect.

It can happen that the patient, while occupied with the "here and now" technique, will suddenly want to recount a past episode. Obviously, in this case, the request of the patient should be accommodated, and the diachronic approach adopted.

13. Narrative Rewriting

A crucial passage in the *Negative Entropy* protocol is the reconstruction and progressive development of new and efficient narrative processes.

The first part of the book illustrates the theme of narrative in light of a constructivist approach informed by the logic of complex systems. The second part of the book deals with the compromising of narrative processes as one of the crucial topics of the *Entropy of Mind* model; now I will address narrative within the dynamics of therapy.

The process of narrative reconstruction is the progressive acquisition by the patients of the ability to narrate in terms that are acceptable to them and that can be shared in the relational social context in which they live.

Systematic research carried out with war veterans and victims of catastrophic events demonstrate that those who are not able to effectively integrate the critical episode into the narration of their lives have trouble getting over the negative aspects of the episode and are at a higher risk of developing post-traumatic stress disorder. Some experimental studies by Lysaker and Lysaker (2002) have shown how clinical improvement in schizophrenic patients who have recovered from a psychotic episode corresponds to the return of adequate narrative processes.

The condition of alienation from the self and others in schizophrenic patients originates from the incapacity to narrate a story acceptable to themselves and plausible for others. It is also true that the use of the narration is very low in current practice because of the prevailing reductionist, medical approach.

For biologically oriented psychiatrists, there are no stories to be told or listened to; there is only an organic illness to be addressed. The myth that psychiatrists are available to listen is only found in the glossy booklets of the pharmaceutical companies. The patient doesn't complain! The patient is simply a clinical case to diagnose and cure with a good mix of psychotropic drugs.

It is discouraging to have to point out how people are losing the capacity to narrate painful events in their lives, preferring a diagnostic conceptualization based on easy labeling. How many times during an initial interview have I asked the patient to tell me the story of his or her problem, only to hear the response, "What story? I suffer from panic attacks or OCD or depression". There are no stories to tell but only a nice CAT scan to have done and lots of medicine (the rights ones, please) to swallow or shoot into the veins (it makes more of an impression that way!).

A great deal of work is needed before the patient learns once again to tell or better narrate his or her story. The reactivation of the narrative process must pass through an intense relational experience starting from the patient-therapist dyad in which a rapport of reciprocity and re-parenting is constituted.

The narrative process, however, can and must be implemented in an extended relational dimension which is the group setting.

In working with narrative it is possible to identify some structured passages. At the beginning we must encourage patients to tell their mysterious stories; very gradually we begin to propose possible alternatives. We do not doubt the truth of the stories, but the possibility of sharing them. The metaphor I adopt in therapeutic work may be useful to explain this to the readers. The reference is to film language and gives me the chance once again to recognize Vittorio Guidano (1992) who, with his innovative "cinematic" technique, introduced this language to cognitive psychotherapy.

But let's return to the metaphor. Imagine we are producing a film which requires a huge sum of money that must be recouped. The author, screenwriter, director, and actors have to prepare the story that, no matter how much it is informed by the desires of the writer, director and screenwriter, must be able to attract and satisfy the spectators. Who would go see a boring, repetitive, poorly filmed and horribly acted movie?

So the therapist-producer proposes changes in the screenplay, the direction, the choice of actors, the acting, and the final editing. In the end, if things have gone well, everyone will be happy, from the author, screenwriter, director and actors (the patient), to the producer (the therapist) and the public (the people with whom the patient interacts).

But how does the patient become more competent at narrating stories and, in particular, the story of the self? There are no standard protocols for this. One can proceed stochastically, asking the patient to talk about what happened or write about it in a diary or in letters.

Speaking of diaries, do not confuse the creative instrument with reports or newspaper articles. Our patient is writing a screenplay, not a newspaper article, which demands maximum objectivity, separating facts from emotions.

In narrative, facts are of little interest. We want to know the story and in every story that is worth telling, reality, emotion, and perception intertwine and get mixed up in a constructivist-generative dynamic. A technique structured for the activation of processes of determination of significance in narrative entitled, Self-Confrontation, has been proposed by Hermans and Hermans-Jansen (1995).

The two Dutch authors place the process of evaluation (referring to a theory that considers the Self as a "process of organized evaluation") at the center of their method. The method consists of three phases:

1. proposing personal stories;
2. validating or invalidating the stories proposed through the enactment of new scripts;
3. restructuring and constructing new stories.

The facilitation of the story's narration is activated by the therapist with a series of questions that are gradually proposed to the patient.

- **Set 1: the past**
  - Is there something particularly significant in the past that continues to exert a strong influence on you?
  - Who were the people in the past who have conditioned your life in important ways, and who are the people who still have an influence on you?
- **Set 2: the present**
  - Is there something in your present life that determines it in a notable way?
  - Are there circumstances and persons particularly able to influence your present life?
- **Set 3: the future**
  - Could you indicate anything that seems particularly able to modify the future development of your life? Do you feel that there are people who are particularly important in influencing your future life? Are there goals or projects able to exert an important role in the development of your future life?

The elements furnished by the patients compose the mosaic of their most important *"life themes"*. In fact, the stories they recount are not unrelated but are united more or less coherently by one or two life themes. The procedures for reconstructing the personal stories attempt to develop a more coherent and cohesive sense of self. The search for new meanings and the construction of new identities constitute a subsequent phase of therapy.

A first important step is helping the patient identify basic common themes in the personal narrations. In this way, it gradually becomes clear that in the patient's life cycle there is a certain recursiveness to the events that occur, to the life theme that is being constructed and consolidated, and to the stories that are narrated.

The therapist will help the patient realize that some events are systematically and idiosyncratically read in such a way as to maintain the coherence of the life theme and the stories that emanate from it. For example, if one of the themes is that of always being discredited, harmed, manipulated, attacked, and persecuted by others, one tends to activate processes of reality construction in synchrony with this theme.

Thus a new series of processes needs to be promoted which Hermans and Hermans-Jansen define in the following terms:

Data-gathering phase. The patient must face reality in innovative terms, paying attention to factors normally neglected. In this way new narrative scenarios are possible.

Phase of the creation of new scripts. In this phase the therapist proposes some modifications to the stories narrated and encourages the patient to put the new scripts into play. The realization of the different programs permits the patient to gather new elements that will enrich and render increasingly coherent the new narrations.

Consolidation phase. The therapist encourages the patient to systematically repeat the "performance" of the new scripts. In this way the sense of self is progressively modified. One very useful method for developing new narrations is to write letters. A classic example is the letters from anorexics written to anorexia.

The first is: "Letter to anorexia, my friend".

The next, after therapeutic work, is "Letter to anorexia, my enemy".

The two letters cover and consolidate the progressive evolution of the sense of self that the patient experiences. This method can also be used with psychotic patients during the narrative reconstruction phase by having them write letters to the therapist first, then to significant others later.

Since cognitive and digital competences are often impaired in schizophrenic patients, more analogue narrative techniques using puppets, marionettes, or dramatization can be employed. In this way the story is performed instead of written.

Material produced by one of my schizophrenic patients is an example. After having completed the part of the work focused on the "here and now" in the *Negative Entropy* protocol, we began the *narrative rewriting* work.

The theme I asked the patient to gather information and memories about him as the center of malevolent attention and somehow guilty of every negative event that occurred. The patient was fascinated by the research and gathered much material. He recounted the following episodes that occurred during the summer he was 12 years old.

A neighbor complained to the father that one of her chickens had been killed, explicitly accusing the boy. The father punished the boy severely even though he claimed to be innocent. The boy discovered later that is was his sister who killed the chicken.

On another day, the father noticed that the family's scooter was damaged and again punished the boy, who repeated his claim to innocence. And once again his sister was responsible. The third crucial episode the patient remembered was the following. He began to think that he was at the center of some sort of curse that made him seem responsible for every negative event that occurred in the family.

In the end, he thought he found a solution. A short time before, during catechism, he had sculpted a small wooden statue of Jesus and placed it in his room. He convinced himself that the object and God, more generally, were responsible for the persecutory episodes that had afflicted him recently. So he took the sacred image and destroyed it. This, however, worsened the situation because he felt an acute sense of guilt and disgrace grow inside him. Thus, the belief that he would be punished for his whole life for that iconoclastic gesture took root.

The same patient was able to connect the constant sensation of being at the center of negative events, the fear of being accused and harmed, and his problematic relationship with the *beyond* with the events he recounted. He then said to me, "Want to bet that these feelings began back then?" From that moment on, the work of analysis and narrative rewriting went quickly and profitably.

14. Conclusion of Systematic Therapy and the Initiation of Counseling and Monitoring

An important question which must be answered convincingly is related to the length of the psychotherapeutic treatment of schizophrenia and its articulation through time.

Abdel-Baki and Nicole (2001) have analyzed different factors regarding the behavioural and cognitive treatment of schizophrenia.

They reached the conclusion that one of the most problematic aspects of treatment that must be further studied is the length of treatment.

Rector and Beck (2002), in their review article of seven trials of behavioural and cognitive therapy for schizophrenia, identified from 10 to 20 sessions in the different protocols, lasting from 3 to 9 months.

Based on my experience, I should point out that the patient who receives cognitive therapy must be followed, even if in less systematic terms, for longer periods that those identified by Rector and Beck's study. The structured treatment of the psychotic patient, according to my proposal, lasts on an average of 10 months. In the first two months there are two sessions a week which are subsequently reduced to one. Overall, about 50 sessions are carried out.

After the completion of the systematic phase of the psychotherapeutic and rehabilitative treatment, a period of counseling must be provided that can last for many years. In this case, bimonthly or monthly meetings are planned, furnishing the patient with the possibility of contacting the therapist in case of necessity, or whenever he or she feels the need to discuss any current problems.

As I have repeatedly pointed out in the context of the model described in this book, the therapist must carry out the role of a secure base. Referring to the theory of attachment, the role of the secure base performed by the parents lasts for the entire life cycle, obviously modulating itself and evolving continually.

Every human being whose developmental history was positive knows they can count on their parents in all critical circumstances even if, for example, they only see them infrequently. The same must happen in the case of psychotherapy, especially in the psychotherapy of the schizophrenic patient.

Obviously, the therapeutic process must not create dependence, must be standardized, and must limited over time; after the reaching of the goals of the therapeutic phase, however, it is necessary to make sure that the evolution of the patient's sense of self can continue, even if a certain vulnerability remains that needs to be effectively managed.

For these reasons the therapeutic process for schizophrenia, according to this book's model, is articulated in three phases: *structured treatment*, *systematic counseling*, and *counseling on demand*. The transition from one phase to another occurs naturally and without stress, adopting a flexible attitude. A good psychotherapist will attain a virtuous equilibrium between teleonomy and teleology. To conclude this section on the psychotherapy of the schizophrenic patient, three other topics must be discussed: family intervention, social and occupational reintegration, and suicide prevention.

15. Family Intervention

Therapeutic work with the family must start from consideration of the family situation; this is achieved through the accurate evaluation of expressed emotion and with the use of the *Family Assessment Measure* (Skinner, Steinhauer & Santa-Barbara, 1983).

The patient's electrodermal activity in the presence of family members is recorded according to the procedure described in the *Family Strange Situation* (Scrimali, 2005b). All the data produced by the assessment are shown to the family and the patient during a feedback session.

From my constructivist point of view, it is important that the therapist does not furnish a "diagnosis" of the family, but that the problems, difficulties, and systematic errors emerge from a process of self-evaluation that the family itself carries out. The treatment program, therefore, is negotiated on the basis of data that the family has identified as symptomatic of the problems to be resolved (Roncone & Casacchia, 2005).

Thus, a therapeutic and rehabilitative program, even if characterized by the classic format proposed by Falloon (1985), is adopted: coping, problem solving, information, cognitive restructuring, communication training, and social skills and network promotion are all personalized according to the characteristics of the individual families.

16. Social and Occupational Reintegration

Just as family intervention is crucial, so is social and occupational reintegration. The creation of a positive network is very important in the therapeutic and rehabilitative strategy. This can be achieved with different and complementary modalities. A first step is the activation of direct networking by the staff and the support structure.

To achieve this, the de-medicalization of the setting and the creation of a space for meetings between patients and the staff are necessary. This means spending time together, getting involved in different activities, or creating, in other words, real emotional and affective ties.

The operative model that can respond to this need is the day center where social support activities, rather than rehabilitation and therapy, is carried out. Here the patients can spend their free time and receive support, encouragement, or simply friendship.

This option, however, is only a tactical step in a strategy that must aim to create a real network in the life of the patient. Social support networks can be promoted at the political and administrative levels and through different interlocutors, including the local health services and other social and volunteer organizations, all in order to take advantage of the services available.

The goal of rehabilitative work in this case is to widen the relational and referential horizons of the patient's life, thus permitting access to new experiences that can offer enrichment and gratification.

In these interventions the rehabilitation therapist, in the role of facilitator, motivates the patient to accept new forms of social life through the use of support, information, and education.

This type of patient usually has underdeveloped social and relational skills and little experience with free time and cultural activities. Often the patient is crushed under the weight of simply resolving everyday problems and surviving.

The rehabilitation therapist can intervene to mobilize and stimulate the patient to make better use of the services present in the area, thus promoting more active participation in social group life. Here two forms of intervention are useful: *a*) relational; *b*) opening up and discovering.

In the first technique the patients are encouraged to amplify their relational context based on their needs and skills. This permits a progressive learning to communicate with unfamiliar persons and institutions. The relationship created with the therapist constitutes a first experience of this type and can be used as an occasion to introduce others.

In the first place, relationships with peers can be initiated within small groups organized by the therapist or with already existing groups in the neighborhood. In fact, it is in the context of egalitarian relationships with peers that real affective ties and positive communication can be created.

These techniques will stimulate the patients to look for other opportunities in their social environment that will lead them to discover other persons, groups, or situations that had previously gone undiscovered.

One must investigate to discover the presence of persons, resources, institutions, group, etc... in the social context. The rehabilitation therapist can inform the patients about what is out there, help them make contact, even accompany them to the group activities. The desire to discover and know the environment must be stimulated in the patient.

Another important topic in the rehabilitation of the schizophrenic patient regards work. Many studies have demonstrated that the possibility of holding a job that is not too stressful, but satisfying on an emotional level, helps socialization and is a positive element in the prognosis.

It is necessary to program an intervention aimed at finding a job, or if the patient already has a job, keeping it. Finding a job is particularly difficult given the difficult job market situation in the south of Italy.

There is also a widespread mentality regarding receiving a "pension" that may push the patients and their family members to prefer a disability pension, with the concomitant accentuation of the disability, to rehabilitation therapy.

It is not hard to understand these people who, finding themselves in a very bad economic situation, begin to see that maybe their *crazy* relative, if declared an invalid, can become the primary breadwinner in the family.

It is easy to see that between a sure pension and the very problematic possibility of a job (because of the patient's own problems and the high unemployment rate in the South), why people would choose the first. This presents a huge obstacle in therapeutic and rehabilitative treatment. In my own experience, however, the crowning moment in therapeutic and rehabilitative treatment coincides with the resumption or initiation of a job, or in young patients, the continuation of school or professional training.

17. Suicide Prevention

Regarding the third and last topic of suicide prevention, it should be noted that this is a crucial problem closely tied to psychotherapy of the schizophrenic patient.

The life expectancy of the schizophrenic patient is much shorter than normal subjects (Tsuang, Woolson & Fleming, 1980). The life expectancy of a schizophrenic is on average 15 years less than people with no form of mental illness.

The real cause of this shortened life cycle is not entirely clear, but the elevated probability of suicide contributes considerably to the lowered life expectancy in schizophrenics.

What is worrisome and saddening is that in the last decades the rate of mortality in schizophrenic patients has actually increased (Warner, 1985). This shows that the methods of treatment of schizophrenia have not actually improved in recent years. Many good studies have been carried out analyzing the phenomenon of suicide in schizophrenic patients (Conwell, Cholette & Duberstein, 1998).

These studies, based on large samples, show that this high rate of suicide is even higher among male schizophrenics (Tandon & Jibson, 2003). Moreover, the means schizophrenics use to attempt suicide are almost always very violent and effective.

The life-time prevalence of death by suicide among schizophrenics is between 10% and 13% (Westermeyer, Harrow & Marengo, 1991). Attempted suicide among schizophrenics varies according to the survey and goes from 18% to 55% (Osby, Correia & Brandt, 2000; Bralet, Yon, Loas & Noisette, 2000). In any case, this is a very grave problem for anyone who treats schizophrenic patients.

Thus the prevention of suicide is a fundamental objective in therapeutic and rehabilitative strategies (*primum vivere, deinde filosofare!*). It is, therefore, necessary to initiate systematic procedures for monitoring the warning signs that might indicate an increase in the probability of suicide in a patient.

For this end, it is useful to identify the risk factors and the conditions that make suicide more likely. Particularly important risk factors for suicide in the schizophrenic patient are the following:

- male sex;
- being single;

- no family support;
- social isolation;
- unemployment and negative economic prospects;
- having had good premorbid functioning, with high expectations regarding economic, occupational, and social success;
- the belief that the person with psychotic problems will inevitably suffer from grave stigma;
- the belief of a negative prognosis.

The phases in illness's course and in the therapeutic and rehabilitative process, which are particularly critical for the possibility of suicide, have been identified by numerous studies and can be summarized in the following terms (Goldacre, Seafroatt & Hawton, 1993):

- the phase *immediately after release,* following hospitalization for an acute decompensation;
- the phase of *further improvement in the clinical situation,* when the dysfunctional coping mechanisms are gradually being abandoned (thanks to psychotherapeutic and rehabilitative intervention);
- the phase of increasing stress, especially in relation to events perceived as abandonment on the part of loved ones.

With these three points in mind, it is possible to identify a series of problems and procedures aimed at improving the management of these critical phases.

How to plan the release of schizophrenic patients at high risk for suicide. The suicides of schizophrenic patients are particularly frequent during the first month after release from the hospital (Krupinski, Fisher & Grohmann, 2000). In fact, the risk of suicide in schizophrenics in the first month after release from a psychiatric ward is over 200 times higher than in the general population (Schwartz & Cohen, 2001).

One scientific study has shown that one schizophrenic patient in ten, among those who have attempted suicide, says they were obeying hallucinatory orders. Besides, two thirds of the group studied showed a condition of serious depression before the suicide attempt.

Other indicators have been identified that significantly lower the risk of suicide and can be summarized as follows:

- establish a solid therapeutic alliance and make the patient feel that he or she will be supported after release;
- plan a trip to the patient's home in order to identify, with the patient's consent, risk factors including, for example, the presence of firearms. This trip must be conducted with the full collaboration of the patient. Also it is necessary to eliminate any medicines still around that were used in previous treatment. Alcohol and dangerous substances that can be ingested should also be removed. Besides making the house safe, it is also necessary to actively involve the family and social network of the patient in the therapy. Without creating undue alarm or fear, the elevated risk of suicide must be explained, as well as the fact that the best antidote for suicide is a serene and affectionate climate of support and acceptance.

Suicide risk and cognitive therapy. It may seem paradoxical, but the psychotherapeutic experience can increase the risk of suicide (Zoler, 1999). Today this dynamic is clear and can be explained in the following way; for the patient delusion constitutes a coping mechanism which attributes an acceptable meaning, even if negative, to external reality.

In this same way hallucinations are conceptualized as paranormal phenomena. One of the objectives of cognitive therapy is to work with the patient in order to develop a different conceptualization of the condition. According to this new conceptualization, a hypothesis can be formulated in which the patient's thought processes are afflicted by biases due to negative experiences from the past as well as biological vulnerability.

The hallucinations are proactive motor phenomena of the mind, rather than paranormal manifestations. The patient must, therefore, develop a new theory in which what happens to him or her is perceived as nothing more than an illness. This conceptualization can, however, lead to the problem of stigma and catastrophic previsions.

"Okay", thinks the patient, "I'm not tormented by spirits, I'm not persecuted by secret agents, I have schizophrenia! But if I am schizophrenic, I will lose my family, my job, everything!"

Does this seem to be an exaggeration? I can assure you, it is not. In fact it represents an extremely probable scenario. A while ago, I was treating a patient suffering from paranoid schizophrenia.

He was a professional nurse and had developed a delusional belief that a pediatrician had wrongly provoked a serious and incurable illness in the patient's newborn son that would soon manifest itself and kill the baby.

In his delusional behaviour, the patient often thought about murdering the pediatrician, who was very worried. I began my treatment and slowly helped the patient see that what he believed was the product of his delusional thinking. He then confessed to me that he was hearing voices and experiencing visual hallucinations. He learned to manage these better, but the voices did not abate, even with neuroleptics.

I also began psychoeducational work with the patient's wife, but the result was a failure because the woman decided to leave her husband since she felt she could no longer handle the situation. The patient went to live with his elderly mother and one day threw himself out a second-story window. He survived, though with many fractures.

I went to see him in the Orthopedics ward and asked him why he did it.

"What did I have to lose?" he asked me. "Up until recently, I thought I was being persecuted by others, now I know I am the persecutor, and I can't tolerate this". I told him I would help him find a new dimension to his life in which the psychotic experience could be overcome.

"Okay", he said, "Doctor Scrimali, you are opening my mind; I will try!"

That night, however, he jumped out the window in the hospital, and this time he succeeded in killing himself. This left an enormous void inside me and a terrible sense of regret! Good-bye, Francesco!

Here it is appropriate to say that in these awful circumstances, the patient *died, cured*.

I never tire of repeating (to myself and to my students): the phase of abandoning the delusional dimension of the disorder is a very difficult step for the schizophrenic patient. The risk of depression and suicide is extremely high.

Other factors that are particularly critical in determining suicide are:

- not being able to count on good social support;
- living in a family with high expressed emotion, especially involving criticism and hostility;
- maintaining negative convictions regarding the incurable nature of schizophrenia;
- maintaining negative convictions regarding stigma linked to the disorder.

As we have seen, it is indispensable to enact systematic procedures to identify and monitor the suicide risk in schizophrenic patients. At this point we may ask what are the fundamental aspects of the cognitive approach to the prevention of suicide in schizophrenic patients?

Based on the literature (Conwell, Cholette & Duberstein, 1998) and on personal experience, I have identified the following factors:

- the therapeutic relationship;
- restructuring convictions regarding the impossibility of being cured;
- acceptance of the schizophrenic event as part of life experience, able to enrich us with new positive meanings;
- monitoring of automatic thoughts connected to suicide;
- systematic monitoring of stress factors;
- stress management with biofeedback and problem solving;
- family intervention;
- the construction and development of a support network.

CHAPTER TEN

Rehabilitation

1. The Complex Orientation

For the patient, the schizophrenic condition means not only the weight of a specific clinical symptomatology, but also and above all, a marked diminution of autonomy and independence. In this way a particular condition of disability is created.

The rehabilitative project, however, from the point of view of complexity, must not present itself as a recovery of lost skills, but rather as an initiation, together with the psychotherapist, of a process of change that aims to reach a new psychological condition and a new life. Rehabilitative work that is oriented toward the logic of complex systems, as described in this book, is an evolutionary process.

2. Meta-Cognitive Functions

Rehabilitative procedures aimed at the implementation of diverse meta-cognitive functions have been developed primarily for treatment of autistic children.

Patricia Howlin and Simon Baron-Cohen (1999) have put together a well-structured methodology to teach autistic children how to comprehend their own psychological states and those of others.

The processes considered the target of the therapeutic and rehabilitative intervention are the following:

- poor emotional resonance regarding the feelings of others;
- inability to understand what others should know;
- inability to socialize because of the impossibility to understand the intentions of others;
- difficulty in understanding whether what one is saying is interesting to listeners;
- inability to understand metaphor and irony;
- impossibility to anticipate what others think of what we do;
- difficulty in lying and, above all, in understanding if others are lying.
- inability to understand the motivations at the base of the actions of others;
- poor understanding and observance of formal, non-explicit rules.

Howlin, Baron-Cohen and Hadwin have proposed an integrated program that is articulated in three areas:

- emotions;
- beliefs;
- illusion.

Each area has 5 levels, and each one contains specific exercises and methodologies.

The material and methodologies proposed by the three authors were used with autistic children between the ages of 4 and 13. The authors note, however, that by adapting the material, it should be possible to use the program with adults; this is exactly what we began to do with encouraging results.

From this experience with schizophrenic patients, we were able to observe that meta-cognitive training can be carried out with great success in a group setting because it permits the experimentation of skills regarding interpreting the minds and mental states of others.

The computer is useful for projecting photos and vignettes used in the different exercises and involve all members of the group in the rehabilitative work.

3. *Memory, Attention, and Concentration*

In the context of our study on the evaluation of attention functions through computerized assessment procedures, a new instrument called the "Attention and Concentration Test", developed at the University of Catania by Santo Di Nuovo (2000), was used.

The test consists of a series of trials that are carried out by the patient using a personal computer. Once the base result is obtained, the program permits training to gradually improve performance. The patient's progress is recorded by the computer, providing for subsequent analysis.

The training program involves 42 parameters, divided into 12 types of trials. Carried out in 4 to 6 sessions, it is possible to note significant improvement in patients in the phase of clinical compensation. Over the course of the training sessions, compliance usually improves, often becoming quite positive and helping to mitigate the low self-efficacy and low self-esteem which are always present in psychotic patients.

4. *Visual Analysis and Cognitive Strategies*

The program "Visual Analysis and Cognitive Strategies" (VAACS) by Felix Studer (1998) uses cognitive strategies for the rehabilitation of problem solving skills. The ability to use cognitive or meta-cognitive problem solving strategies is subjective and varies from individual to individual (Borkowki & Kurtz, 1987).

The inadequacy of cognitive strategies in the patient with schizophrenia is not only related to problem solving but also to a reduced skill in learning and to inadequate information processing of emotions. The VAACS program rehabilitates "functional fixity" or the tendency to not be able to identify new, flexible strategies in scenarios that change.

The lack of mental flexibility, associated with a lack of cognitive and metacognitive strategies, means that the subject will have reduced self-esteem and self-efficacy, correlated to low motivation in learning new skills. The patient thus exhibits passive or avoidance behaviors regarding new and difficult situations.

Through the VAACS program, learning new strategies comes about progressively, respecting the individual rhythms of the patients who are undergoing the training. The goal of the "game" is to reproduce increasingly difficult models proposed by the computer. In the reproduction of the model visualized by the computer, it is possible to follow the strategies or procedures based on attempts and errors.

The difficulty of the models that must be reproduced is self-regulating, increasing or decreasing the level depending on the performance of the subject. During the exercise the following statistics are recorded:

- number of models presented;
- number of errors committed;
- number and type of feedback furnished by the computer:
  - encouragement following a period of inactivity by the subject;
  - approval following a correct response;
  - suggestions regarding the solution of models that the patient cannot resolve;
- the arithmetical average for rapidity and strategy indexes.

These last two indexes permit the analysis of the type of strategy used for each model and the way in which the strategies were modified during the exercise. The *rapidity index* is calculated by multiplying the value derived from the time, in seconds, divided by the number of shapes needed to compose the model by 100. The *strategy index* is calculated by multiplying the value derived from the number of shapes moved, divided by the number of shapes necessary to compose the model by 100.

If the patient works rapidly and uses the correct strategy, the values of the two indexes are low. To favour cognitive and meta-cognitive development of strategy learning skills for problem solving, the figure of a supervisor is fundamental.

Based on the degree of deficit present in the subject, the therapist-supervisor must choose the right level of difficulty to begin the trial. He or she must then encourage the patient during difficult moments and give opportune indications in order to identify the best strategies for composing the increasingly complex models.

The test was preliminarily used by the author on healthy young subjects and on patients with "learning strategy and problem solving deficits".

The aim of a study carried out by our group at the Department of Psychiatry at the University of Catania was the evaluation of the validity of this rehabilitation instrument on adult subjects with neurotic or psychotic disorders, who had large deficits in attention skills and in the ability to identify the appropriate problem solving strategies. The results obtained are very encouraging.

Using the VAACS project with paranoid schizophrenic subjects, in whom positive symptoms were in remission, the dysfunctions in the occupational and social contexts were notably reduced, while self-esteem and self-confidence grew.

5. *Relational and Social Skills*

Relational and social skills are an important aspect of the every human being's cognitive complement, indispensable for everyday existence. The impairment of these skills, typical in schizophrenic patients, constitutes a significant source of disability and hardship.

In the context of clinical research carried out at the Department of Psychiatry at the University of Catania, we have identified, in the relational and social skills and in group therapeutic work, a topic of marked importance in the therapeutic and rehabilitative process.

Social skills cannot be considered as a set of isolated competences but must be conceptualized as complex processes closely tied to motor, affective, cognitive, and relational functioning, requiring an appropriate emission and coordination of verbal and non-verbal responses.

Social skills can be considered a coping strategy crucial for survival and successful adaptation, if we consider that our species, from an ethological point of view, is highly social and finds well-being and security only through cooperation with others.

Verbal and non-verbal communication of feelings and the perception of interpersonal contexts mediate the positive outcome of social interaction and, therefore, the achievement of goals, in part, because of the good impression we make on others.

Important aspects of social skills include the accurate perception of the characteristics relevant to interpersonal relationships and awareness of the sentiments and goals of the interlocutor, as well as of one's rights and responsibilities in the exchange in progress. The realization of these skills is closely tied to the ability to recognize the emotions of others and to develop theories about their mental states.

The study of social skills in schizophrenic patients has shown how many of the deficits are actually a negative consequence of neuropsychological deficits in facial and emotional recognition and of meta-cognitive deficiencies.

An important role in the functioning of good relational skills is developed from the belief systems and by the management of emotional reactions. It is evident that the therapeutic and rehabilitative processes of Machiavellian intelligence, even if aimed at the improvement of relational skills, must be multi-dimensional and cover many areas.

It is not possible to improve relational skills if the patients will not reconsider and modify their belief systems and dysfunctional schemas, and if they are not able to positively manage the emotional dynamics of interpersonal interactions.

Besides this, it is very important that the patients feel competent in recognizing the emotions of others and in elaborating theories about the minds of their interlocutors. In the end, it is indispensable that they are able to communicate with others, exhibiting appropriate behaviour, both verbal and non-verbal.

Research in this area has shown that premorbid social adaptation is a valid predictor of the course and outcome of psychiatric disorders, and that the deficit in social skills in psychiatric patients predicts subsequent relapses and hospitalizations.

Numerous studies have documented that inadequate interpersonal behaviour in psychiatric patients can be improved by involving them in sessions aimed at learning, generalizing, and maintaining specific behavioural and cognitive skills (Bellack & Mueser, 1993).

The results of these studies suggest that psychiatric patients can be helped to develop behaviors that improve their social abilities in specific interpersonal situations through a series of therapeutic and rehabilitative methodologies defined as *Social Skill Training* (Bellack, Mueser, Gingerrich & Agresta, 1997).

Training to develop social skills has shown its efficacy in increasing relational competences regarding Machiavellian intelligence in patients with disabilities.

Possessing adequate social skills constitutes a positive prognostic factor for patients afflicted with serious psychiatric disorders since there is a significant correlation between the level of Machiavellian intelligence and the frequency of relapse (Liberman, 1988).

The *Social Skill Training* must be applied to both the patients and their families. The first step in the planning of training is to analyze the problems in the relational and social skills of the patients and their families. Subsequently, with the active collaboration of the patients, objectives are formulated that must be achieved during the *Social Skill Training* sessions.

Once the objectives are defined, the behavioural trials can begin in which the skills to be achieved are practiced in simulated situations that are similar to the real life situation of the patients. These trials can be carried out in groups which include other patients and members of the staff. In this way, the different participants can interpret figures that the patient might encounter during daily life; the scenes related to the objectives are acted out and repeated.

One fundamental part of the program regards the importance of the positive comments and encouragement from the therapist and the group members in evoking interest and motivation, on the part of the patients, in what is being done. This helps them to complete the assigned tasks. The therapist, in this sense, must maintain a directorial role, indicating even the small results that the patient obtains and furnishing suggestions that can help the patient reach the desired behaviour.

A strategy that can be used, especially when the patient presents deficits in elaborating verbal messages and, therefore, encounters difficulty in taking advantage of the suggestions, instructions, and support is modeling. Here the therapist, or other member of the group, acts as a positive model to demonstrate the skills in question in order to favour quicker learning.

The program also uses homework so the patient can practice in his or her natural environment, with all its difficulties. Homework is checked by the rehabilitation therapist who evaluates the results, helping the patient in moments of difficulty.

The *Social Skill Training* program used by our group includes video-tapes in order to offer immediate positive feedback to the patient. This provides complex but easily understood information.

Following Liberman (1994), the patient is usually shown a recording of the simulated scenes. The parts they are particularly good at are pointed out, as are the areas that need improvement.

The efficacy of the *Social Skill Training* in the treatment of schizophrenia has been shown in a study based on 103 patients already undergoing neuroleptic therapy. The patients were divided into groups that were randomly assigned to received the *Social Skill Training* by itself, a form of educational family therapy, a combination of both the family therapy and the social skills training, or treatment with the neuroleptics alone (Hogarty, Anderson & Reiss, 1986).

The objectives of the *Social Skill Training* were to improve the social competence of the patients, making them able to constructively relate to others in the family and in the community, reducing, in this way, the stress and arousal that could cause a relapse. The sessions were carried out during scheduled visits to the out-patient clinic over a period of one year after release from the hospital for an acute psychotic episode.

Both programs, the social skills training and family therapy, showed a percentage of relapse during the year of 20%, compared to 41% for the group using only the neuroleptics. This result was independent of patient compliance with the maintenance therapy.

The protective effect of the two treatment modalities studied was additive, thus none of the patients receiving both of the psychosocial treatments relapsed in the follow-up period. Video-monitoring and video-feedback are two very useful instruments in the rehabilitative work with social skills (Heilveil, 1983).

The use of video-recording in psychotherapy is of great relevance for the psychotic patient in the remission phase because of the direct, detailed feedback the patient receives regarding behavioural and relational patterns.

In 1996, at the Department of Psychiatry at the University of Catania, I began a program which systematically used video for rehabilitation adopting the self-portrait technique, with the collaboration of Roberto Cotroneo. Patients were asked to introduce themselves for 2-3 minutes in front of the camera. To help them feel at ease and show them what to do, members of the staff presented themselves first.

These self-presentations were carried out in a group, recorded, looked at, and briefly commented on by the person who was filmed, and then by the other members of the group. Afterwards, the staff, without the patients, discussed the results in order to better evaluate the clinical condition of the patients and the method being used. This early project permitted the accumulation of data regarding the verbal and non-verbal behaviour of the individual patients.

It was very clear that some patients did not follow the directions, speaking for more than the allotted time and losing themselves in irrelevant details, until they had to be interrupted; others, instead of presenting themselves, talked almost exclusively about their family members or stressful events that, in their opinion, caused the illness, furnishing, in any case, useful information about their way of seeing and relating to things.

Because of the camera frame used, the non-verbal behaviour analyzable was limited to the facial expression and gaze of the patient, elements, in themselves, relatively rich in meaning. The comments of the patients, seeing themselves on the screen, usually related to their physical appearance, which was never satisfactory. Subsequently, we considered using a longer camera perspective in order to shoot the whole body. This meant resolving some technical problems including the use of a microphone.

This type of session was replicated many times, sometimes with the same patients who, because of repeating the experience, or improvement in their condition, or the feedback they received, were able to improve their performance. In the subsequent sessions a new activity was tried: the patients were given a card with an emotion or sentiment written on it that had to be simulated so that the others in the group would recognize it (affect simulation).

Carried out in a group, this exercise became a type of game; it was clear that some patients were unable to modulate facial expressions based on the emotion to be expressed. The experience of self-presentation in a group and the simulation of different emotions produced very positive results identifiable, above all, in the possibility for patients to observe themselves and learn new and effective modalities of tacit and explicit communication. The use of video-monitoring and video-feedback are useful in the restructuring of the self, an important objective in the rehabilitative process of the patient afflicted with *Entropy of Mind*.

CHAPTER ELEVEN

Prevention

1. Introduction

Considering the gravity of the schizophrenic condition and the enormous costs in terms of suffering for the patient, family, and society, it seems clear that primary, secondary, and tertiary prevention are of maximum importance.

Primary prevention reduces the incidence and decreases the emergence of new cases of the illness being considered. The efforts to identify the illness in its earliest presentation in order to intervene and reduce the length of the disorder are part of secondary prevention strategies. This type of action leads to the reduction of the prevalence of the cases, in an area, at a specific moment. In the end, tertiary prevention processes are those able to reduce or avoid complications for a specific ailment.

Primary prevention of schizophrenia consists in the attempt to reduce the incidence of the phenomenon so that psychotic apophany does not manifest itself at all; secondary prevention aims to make the treatment as quick and efficient as possible, thanks to a early diagnosis and the adoption of increasingly valid therapeutic protocols. Tertiary prevention is aimed at bettering the course of the illness, limiting or impeding the reappearance of the disability.

Based on these considerations, it is evident that the operative strategies of primary prevention must eliminate or significantly reduce the etiological pathogenic factors of schizophrenia; secondary prevention aims its efforts at identifying all the procedures and provisions that make an early diagnosis possible and reliable, and treatment timely and efficacious.

Tertiary prevention focuses attention on the identification of methodologies to prevent the consolidation of dysfunctional coping strategies that tend to reduce skills and generate disabilities. Relapse prevention is a crucial issue for tertiary prevention in schizophrenia.

Given current understanding, unequivocal scientific foundations do not exist in the literature for a program of primary prevention aimed at early identification and modification of the factors responsible for the onset of schizophrenia. The prevention strategies can be planned only on the basis of identifying the factors and the etiological pathogenic dynamics of the disorder.

We have seen in the second part of this monograph that a single understanding or consensus does not exist for this crucial topic. It is evident that those who consider schizophrenia a prevalently biological and degenerative disorder look to biology for primary preventive measures.

Tsusng, Stone, Gamma, and Faraone (2003), for example, have reflected on the possibility of identifying the operative and theoretical basis for primary prevention in schizophrenia using a marked reductionistic and biological approach.

They refer to the early studies if Meehl (1962) who focused on the concept of "schizotaxis" as a condition that precedes schizophrenia. This condition is characterized by a defect in the integration of the superior nervous functions and is linked to biological vulnerability.

Subsequently, Tsuang and his collaborators proposed a different concept of schizotaxis based on the presence of neuropsychological deficits and on vague negative symptoms. After formulating this conceptualization, they elaborated a series of reflections that can be summarized as follows:

- schizotaxis is a condition linked to the genetic vulnerability for schizophrenia;

- schizotaxis, being a trait condition, is a permanent attribute of the individual and can be identified in adult subjects;
- if it is possible to obtain an improvement in the condition of schizotaxis in adult subjects, this means that the same type if intervention could have protective and primary prophylactic value during the growth years.

Starting from this conceptual base, the authors conducted research in which six individuals suffering from a condition of schizotaxis were treated with low doses of risperidone, for six weeks. The results of the trial, an improvement in the schizotaxic condition, led the authors to formulate a hypothesis that neuroleptic treatment with risperidone constitutes a primary prophylactic measure in schizophrenia.

These conclusions are, in my opinion, debatable, even if perfectly consistent with the Zeitgeist of the context in which they were formulated, i.e., coming from authors who have always denied the efficacy of psychotherapy and psychosocial therapy in the treatment of schizophrenia.

Given the only therapeutic approach they are able to conceive of is pharmacological, it is not surprising that the only prophylactic measure they propose is the administration of neuroleptics as a preventive measure!

The research of Tsuang, Stone, and Faraone, based on only six patients treated for six weeks, is methodologically and conceptually objectionable. It is a reductionist position, in the most extreme terms. Besides which, a similar orientation to the prevention of schizophrenia fits perfectly with the indiscriminate use of drug therapy in the young, a practice which is spreading, especially in the United States, thanks to the pressure of the powerful, multinational drug companies.

It began with Ritalin, used for attention deficit disorder and hyperactivity, and moved to Prozac, used in the formative years to treat so-called adolescent depression, and now they are talking about precociously treating schizotaxis with risperidone as a prophylactic measure for schizophrenia! It seems that an actual plot exists to extend the indiscriminate use of psychotropic drugs, in general, and neuroleptics, in particular, from therapy to prophylaxis. In fact, as

Colin Ross and John Read (2004) have pointed out, neuroleptics are prescribed with increasing frequency for non-psychotic conditions during the growth years.

The two authors add that some drug companies direct their promotional campaigns to scholastic psychologists and parents in order to help identify the early signs of psychosis and begin preventive neuroleptic treatment. Many children simply had to admit to believing in telepathy and the possibility of foretelling the future to be subjected to treatment with neuroleptics when it is well known that these attitudes in adolescents are not necessarily prodromal symptoms of schizophrenia.

Obviously, my position, in which drug therapy is considered a treatment for symptoms within a complex therapeutic and rehabilitative strategy, has led me to the net refusal of neuroleptic use as a preventive measure in schizophrenia.

2. *The Complex Orientation*

The complex orientation relative to the prevention of schizophrenia described in this book is based on a much more wide-ranging, articulated approach consisting of the following processes:

- biological vulnerability;
- parenting;
- educational and relational factors in the growth years;
- life events;
- social support.

Biological vulnerability given the current state of knowledge can be identified thanks to monitoring psychophysiological and neuropsychological trait markers, as has already been amply discussed. Parenting can be investigated using a number of instruments. For instance, in a large sample of children the parameters relative to biological vulnerability as well as dysfunctional parenting should be monitored and the educational and relational factors analyzed. Once the subjects at risk have been identified, a longitudinal study should be initiated, dividing the subjects into two random subgroups.

One subgroup would simply be monitored periodically over time. The other would be included in a primary prevention program. This program would be prevalently psychoeducational and psychotherapeutic and would attempt to create higher coping, problem solving, neuropsychological, and social intelligence skills. Family members and the social networks would also be involved.

After an appropriate period of time, significant statistical differences should be observed regarding the onset of schizophrenia in the two groups. Unfortunately, the realization of such a program entails a notable series of difficulties.

Among these is the need to follow the subjects for 5-10 years, the elevated costs, the need to guarantee high levels of compliance, and the identification of an adequate sample of subjects in which the vulnerability markers are present. If one considers that the prevalence of schizophrenia is one percent of the population, then 5000 children and their respective families would need to be tested, in order to identify a group of 50 subjects at risk. Such a project obviously entails exceptional and very costly efforts.

There are also numerous ethical problems that must be faced, including false positives and the random selection of the group members. I still think, however, that this type of study can be quite promising, and I plan to carry out just such a project in the next few years.

As always, I do not believe in short-cut solutions (like six patients treated for six weeks with risperidone) to complex problems. In this respect, one very interesting British study, covering the years 1984-1988 and involving 35,000 persons, was coordinated by Ian Falloon (1992).

With the collaboration of general practitioners, a mass screening was conducted which permitted the identification of individuals in a prodromal phase of schizophrenia. These persons then underwent preventive, psycho-educational treatment.

During the four years of the program, only one person out of the 35,000 studied, developed schizophrenia. In this way, the prevalence of schizophrenia in the area of the study was 4 times lower than what was expected, based on past rates for the disorder.

Primary prevention of schizophrenia is a particularly complex topic. It is costly, difficult to plan and carry out successfully, and whose full development requires much study.

Patrick D. McGorry (2002), in an article in World Psychiatry, emphasizes that the need to recognize psychosis promptly is an objective whose usefulness has emerged from many studies. Early recognition has even become a criterion in the restructuring of treatment protocols and the organization of psychiatric services.

According to McGorry, the *early psychosis* construct and the guidelines for its recognition and early treatment in schizophrenia are givens. The guidelines outlined by the Australian author, based on numerous studies, are the following:

- intervention in the pre-psychotic phase;
- early diagnosis of the first psychotic episode;
- integrated treatment of the first psychotic episode;
- the phase of overcoming the first episode;
- the critical period.

Intervention in the pre-psychotic phase. This is still an object of research, rather than a well-defined methodology. The possibility of intervening in this phase ought to constitute an important objective given the many complications and disabilities that begin to take shape in this delicate period.

In order to favour the correct identification of young people at high risk, a series of methodologies to avoid the so-called false positives has been developed.

A controlled study has documented the undoubted success of a combined treatment with low doses of risperidone and cognitive psychotherapy in preventing the transition to true psychosis (Wyatt & Henter, 2001).

From my point of view, these studies are of major interest because they apply the methodologies of cognitive psychotherapy to primary prevention. The times seem ripe for work leading to the early identification of young people at risk. A sense of optimism and hope for the possibility of promoting a non-psychotic direction for brain and personality development must be communicated to these children and their parents.

A topic of major importance in planning strategies of primary prevention consists in identifying effective and efficient screening instruments. To this end the development of assessment methodologies for psychophysiological markers for vulnerability can be extremely important.

Recordings of electrodermal activity and evoked potentials are possible candidates for this role, and our laboratories are currently conducting research in this area.

Early diagnosis of the first psychotic episode. A crucial topic is related to the possibility of quick access to adequate treatment for the schizophrenic patient. Numerous studies have documented that considerable delay frequently occurs before access to treatment and this results in longer, less effective, and more costly treatment (McGorry & Jackson, 1999). The delay is even greater when the syndrome is characterized by negative symptoms since the illness's onset is more insidious and the clinical condition is less evident.

I have had the opportunity to observe young patients with schizophrenia with a prevalence of negative symptoms, treated for depression. This caused the loss of precious time as the neuropsychological disability spread and worsened. Some of these children also received electroshock which, as is well-known, damages memory and the attention span even further.

Preliminary studies carried out on schizophrenic patients have shown that the later the specific therapeutic and rehabilitative treatment, the greater the disabilities exhibited by patients. On the contrary, early intervention seems to reduce the levels of disability that develop, even if uncertainties about the intervention still exist (Larsen, Johannessen & Opjordmoen, 1998).

Beng-Choo Ho and Nancy Andreasen (2001), in their review of the problem of early diagnosis and treatment of schizophrenic psychosis, point out how there are still no unequivocal scientific data able to support the development of screening methodologies that would permit early treatment of schizophrenia.

Nevertheless, it is clear that this is only part of the problem. Also important is the psychoeducation of the population, the information general practitioners and family doctors have, and the development of psychiatric services able to reach patients in difficulty and quickly recognize psychotic symptoms, so appropriate treatment can begin.

Essentially, we are again faced with a very complex problem in which a multi-level and integrated solution must be found. A surprising result of the first systematic studies on the delay in initiating a specific and efficacious treatment is that, paradoxically, despite the gravity of schizophrenic symptoms, the delay in diagnosis is not inferior to that found in other less serious problems, such as anxiety and mood disorders.

This might be due to the fact that the patient who begins to experience psychotic phenomena will try to hide the condition because of the stigma attached to insanity and only with difficulty will turn to psychiatric services for help.

McGorry, Kristev, and Harrigan (2000) conducted a study of 200 psychiatric patients in which they showed that the 61 schizophrenic patients went untreated for psychosis for an average of 508.9 days.

As we can see, this is an incredibly long period in which the terrible Entropy of Mind has time to disorganize the brain, mind, family, and network. But the consequences of a delay in the beginning of treatment are not homogeneous in schizophrenic patients. Other factors, including age at onset, sex, and social class play an important role.

Early onset, during adolescence, may be recognized after an even longer delay, given adolescents are expected to act bizarrely and display psychological entropy. Poverty and conditions of social hardship also influence the delay in treatment.

Well-off persons are usually better informed about schizophrenia and have access to private specialized services. The probability that family members are able to convince the patient to see a well-known specialist in the comfort of a private office, is much higher than the possibility that a patient will go to the public health psychiatric services, where stigma is greater.

The disorder is identified later in males, in part, because they are considered to be more turbulent than females, and their behavioural disorders are easily neglected. They are also less willing to begin a diagnostic, therapeutic, and rehabilitative course of treatment.

The period that is interposed between the psychotic apophany and the beginning of therapy—and all the factors that work to shorten or delay it—constitute a crucial topic for the improvement of prognosis in schizophrenia. This topic falls into the area of secondary prevention, and the critical factors that positively influence it are:

- the possibility of the population to recognize the early syndromes of the schizophrenic condition;
- the skill of the family doctor to quickly recognize the symptoms at the onset of schizophrenia;
- the presence of local, efficient, and effective health services;
- ease in access to these services;
- the ability of these services to promote adherence to the treatment;
- the ability of these services to propose efficient and effective therapeutic and rehabilitative protocols.

On the basis of this conceptualization, the objectives to pursue are clear, some of which have already been discussed in other parts of the monograph. The principal components of the strategy favouring the early treatment of schizophrenia are the following:

- initiate an informational campaign and the psychoeducation of the population and of family physicians, aimed at the early recognition of schizophrenia;
- reduce the stigma connected to the diagnosis, so that once the entropic psychosis is identified, the diagnosis will not cause despair but will lead to the search for help and to adherence to the proposed therapeutic programs;
- improve the functional diagnostic methods of schizophrenia through the increasing diffusion of psychophysiological and neuropsychological techniques of assessment.
- continually institute and update effective and efficient centers for the treatment of schizophrenia, staffed by specialized personnel.

An experimental program, characterized by aspects similar to those described above, has been carried out in Rogaland, Norway by a group of researchers coordinated by Jan Johannessen (Johannessen, Larsen, Horneland, Joa, Kvebecc, Friis, Melle, Opjordsmoen, Simonsen, Vaglum & McGlasham, 2001).

Concomitantly with the restructuring of the psychiatric services in Rogaland at the beginning of the 1980s, the passage from hospitalization in mental asylums to long-term treatment by local health services was instituted. Besides having structured a program of integrated treatment for schizophrenia based on a significant role for psychotherapy, a program was initiated that aimed at reducing the time between the apophany and the patient's access to the health services. A preliminary study revealed that this time period was very long (114 weeks, or more than two years, on average).

The program in Rogaland concentrated on the reducing the time period between the psychotic apophany and reaching the psychiatric services. This was pursued through informational campaigns directed at the population and family doctors and by creating psychiatric services able to quickly identify the pathology and furnish immediate help.

If there could be a reduction in the time between the beginning of schizophrenia and access to treatment, is would then be possible to see if such an abbreviation actually improves the course of the illness.

This aim was pursued by comparing the therapeutic results of the group that was able to reduce the time between the onset of the illness and access to treatment and the group that worked with patients in which no effort was made to form an early diagnosis.

The first positive results of the Norwegian research regarded the significant shortening of the period between the apophany and the beginning of treatment, from 2 years to 17 weeks.

An important consideration stemming from the work of the Norwegian colleagues (whom I had the pleasure to meet and host in Catania) is that the cost of the informational campaign aimed at the population and at the family doctors was less than the cost of treating one schizophrenic patient for one year. Returning to the topics identified by McGorry, we must still discuss the following points:

- the integrated treatment of the first psychotic episode;
- the phase of overcoming the first episode;
- the critical period.

The first two points have been illustrated in the preceding chapters. Only the critical period remains to be discussed here.

Critical period. In my own experience, the treatment phase of the first psychotic episode, as I have already indicated, lasts for about 10 months. This is essentially in agreement with the 12 month period cited in the literature.

After the first year of treatment, once a condition of well-being has been attained, a period of about 5 years begins in which the risk of relapse is very high (Birchwood, Todd & Jackson, 1998). This observation, which my own clinical experience confirms, represents the delicate problem of what to do. Obviously, drug companies are ready to propose studies and experimental proof about the utility of prolonged neuroleptic treatment to avoid relapse. I have already outlined my negative position regarding this option.

The position I am putting forth is that of maintaining a relationship of counseling and of a secure base over time, able to initiate effective and efficient strategies of relapse prevention when necessary. Regarding tertiary prevention in schizophrenia, the topics that appear most cogent in light of the systemic model I am proposing here are: the family's emotional climate and the monitoring of warning signs of relapse.

The first topic which I have already discussed is relevant to expressed emotions and to the family's involvement in the therapeutic strategy.

The monitoring of warning signs of relapse and the development in the patient and family members of specific coping strategies constitutes a crucial aspect in the tertiary prevention of schizophrenia.

Warning signs are the early symptoms able to furnish precious information that a new psychotic crisis is dangerously near. These are traceable to vague deviations from positive base conditions of cognitive activity, of emotions, and of behaviour.

An important aspect discussed in numerous studies is that 70% of the schizophrenic patients studied and 93% of their family members were able, if correctly informed, to identify the warning signs of a relapse (Birchwood, 1999). This theoretical premise has motivated Birchwood to develop a therapeutic program aimed at the early identification of relapse signals.

This program consists of the following steps:

- active involvement of the patient in psychoeducation;
- identification of the constellation of prodromal symptoms of relapse, specific for each individual patient;

- development of coping methods that effectively prevent the relapse;
- monitoring of the work carried out by the patient and family members as well as the use of information obtained for the increasingly effective restructuring of the process of relapse prevention;
- continual monitoring of the attempt to adopt new coping strategies in order to conceptualize and improve them.

An important aspect of the above-cited points is relative to training the patient in the identification of the prodromal condition characterized by warning signs that are personalized based on the experience of the patient.

To help the patient in the identification of symptoms, Birchwood proposes using a deck of cards with the most important psychotic and psychiatric symptoms that may be present in schizophrenia written on each one. These will include symptoms that are not pathognomonic for the disorder, such as insomnia, increased anxiety, and a lowering of mood.

The patients are asked to choose the card the best describes their specific prodromal relapse symptom. The monitoring of the warning signs of relapse is a topic of major relevance for therapeutic success in the treatment of schizophrenia.

Since experimental data show that relapse in psychotic patients is in correlated with a progressive increase in Skin Conductance Levels (Dawson, Nuechterlein & Adams, 1989), I have developed a small, portable instrument, called *PsychoFeedback*, able to measure electrodermal conductance with ease (Scrimali, 2005b).

The instrument is given to the patient who is asked to monitor the conductance values daily and record them in a type of psychophysiological diary. The increase in conductance values and the appearance of subjective warning signs, including emotional tension, restlessness, lowering of mood, insomnia, and feelings of fear and persecution constitute important warning signs. The coping strategies we teach the patients are:

- *Pharmacological coping.* To immediately take benzodiazepine and neuroleptics, according to the instructions and dosage previously described by the staff.

- *Psychophysiological coping.* Diligently practice biofeedback, using the *PsychoFeedback*.
- *Behavioural coping.* Initiate a scrupulous control of behaviour, avoiding stressful situations and regulating times schedules and daily routines with special regard to sleep.
- *Relational coping.* Optimize relational patterns by reducing contacts with bothersome people and increase the time spent with people who make the patient feel good.
- *Therapeutic coping.* The staff must be immediately notified by phone and, if necessary, a meeting can be planned in the shortest time possible, outside of the regularly scheduled sessions. Family members must also be involved in the monitoring of the warning signs and trained to help the patient positively realize the coping strategies. A specific task for family members is to maintain a climate of trust, serenity, and low emotional stimulation. The systematic realization of training for the recognition of the prodromal syndrome has furnished very encouraging results.

In Italy, a program of early identification and treatment at the onset of psychotic disorders has been conducted with particular regard to schizophrenia. This project, called *Programma 2000,* was conducted in Milan by the Department of Mental Health at the Niguarda Ca' Granda Hospital, which serves over 20,000 patients (Cocchi & Meneghelli, 2004).

Programma 2000 is a pilot study, which through a series of complex and differentiated interventions, promoted the psycho-education of the population, the precocious recognition of psychosis, and the prompt treatment of patients through cognitively-inspired protocols.

CHAPTER TWELVE

The Prevention of Stigma

The problem of social and personal stigma, which affects people with mental disorders, especially schizophrenics, is a variable of considerable importance in the treatment of schizophrenia, that is even able to influence its outcome. The term stigma was used in ancient Greece to indicate a mark, consisting of a tattoo, that permitted the identification of a slave, who in ancient times was, more often than not, an enemy captured in battle.

The word, therefore, refers to a sort of label, tied to the particular condition of the one bearing it. It is a negative condition that induces in the person who perceives the stigma in others, emotionally idiosyncratic attitudes, the activation of powerful cognitive schemas, and hostile behaviors towards the stigmatized individual, considered inferior or marked by some negative characteristic.

The processes implicated in the phenomena of stigma are complex and involve the cognitive, emotional, behavioural, and relational spheres. Stigmatization, from the evolutionary point of view, has deep roots linked to biological phylogeny and cultural ontogenesis. Biologically speaking, the process of stigmatization seems connected to survival-based coping strategies. Stigma serves to identify something dangerous that should be avoided or managed with prudence and diffidence. Because of its evolutionary importance tied to survival, stigma is a process able to activate potent emotional dynamics. This explains the difficulty in trying to modify schemas linked to the mechanisms of stigma. But, more specifically, what are these schemas? The most common among those that have been identified are the following:

- *people with schizophrenia are violent and dangerous;*
- *people with schizophrenia can infect others with their madness;*
- *schizophrenics are bizarre and unpredictable;*
- *everything a person with schizophrenia says should not be taken seriously because it makes no sense.*

These are part of the category relative to the dangerousness of the patient. Other schemas regard the dynamics of the illness and include:

- *schizophrenia is incurable;*
- *you never recover from schizophrenia*
- *schizophrenia gets progressively worse;*
- *people who have schizophrenia cannot hold a job;*
- *schizophrenia is due to parents and their dysfunctional educative strategies.*

Each of these affirmations appears today unfounded because of recent scientific discoveries, yet these stereotypes are incredibly widespread and persistent! But let's get back to the ethological aspect of stigma. In many animal species, mechanisms of labeling exist that can signal danger and delimit territory.

Each of us remembers how our parents *marked* safe territory for us, forbidding us to go beyond certain limits and, above all, how certain categories of people were stigmatized as dangerous. I particularly remember my childhood nightmare about being kidnapped by gypsies. My mother would tell me horrible stories of children stolen by gypsies, who were evil, astute, and therefore very, very dangerous.

"Be careful", she would say, "When you play outside, if you see a woman with a long skirt, black hair, and lots of jewelry, run back home immediately!" Gypsy men were even more dangerous!

"How do you recognize them", I asked my mother.

"Easy" she said, "They have gold teeth".

In this way an efficient internal operative model kicked in the moment a danger sign. Unfortunately, things backfired. One day may beloved maternal grandfather had a molar replaced by a gold tooth. As soon as he smiled at me, I almost fainted. He had become a gypsy! I understood early on how the mechanism of stigma, geared to survival, contains hidden perils that make serious errors possible.

Based on this, stigma that is attributed to people with mental disorders, works to *mark* them as *insane* and keep them away from spaces where they might harm our progeny, with their upsetting and potentially aggressive behaviour (obviously according to the false stereotypes).

Stigma is not only linked to mental illness, but applies to those who, rightly or wrongly, are identified, in a given social or historical context, as different and, therefore, able to disturb the prevailing order.

The discussion of historical, cultural, and social processes that have contributed to the construction of stigma attached to people suffering from serious mental disorders like schizophrenia, is beyond the scope of this text. I will, however, discuss the implications of stigma for the treatment and cure of schizophrenic patients. Before beginning, I want to illustrate the distinction between social stigma and personal stigma as regards schizophrenia.

Social stigma, on one hand, refers to an attitude of rejection by members of society regarding a category of persons, in our case, schizophrenics. Personal stigma, on the other hand, is the negative attitude that patients have toward themselves, once they recognize themselves as carriers of the despised label.

In western, so-called advanced societies, the stigma that is attributed to people who show signs of mental illness, is constructed beginning in early infancy. So when the first signs of the disorder emerge, the patient is already endowed with a belief system and internal operative models that are ready to be activated.

Unfortunately, stigma is unexpectedly directed against oneself and mechanisms of protection are activated within the person, with devastating consequences. It is almost like an allergic reaction of the immune system. The defenses are activated, by mistake, against the cells of one's own organism. Patients are now afraid of themselves, of a future colored by *insanity*, of rejection by others. The processes of self-esteem and self-efficacy are compromised. To defend themselves, the patients implement further coping mechanisms that turn out to be inefficient and counterproductive.

One of these is the denial of their pathological condition and the refusal of treatment. Imagine if, one day, a person begins to hear voices, and hearing voices has been codified from childhood as nothing more than a dysfunctional process that occurs in pathological conditions that can happen to anybody and, most importantly, that can be cured successfully. In this admittedly Utopian scenario, the patient would readily seek help, and the problem would be resolved with relative ease.

This is what happened with epilepsy, which was once a highly stigmatized, disabling disorder. The introduction of new, accurate diagnostic methods, including electroencephalograms and effective drugs that perfectly control the symptoms, have gradually reduced the stigma tied to this illness.

Hearing voices, still today, activates an internal operative model relating to the stigma of madness and fear of being personally involved. The patient will do everything to avoid admitting to suffering from a mental disorder and will not seek help from a psychiatrist. If the patient forms the idea that the problem is due to magic, he or she no longer feels *insane*, but only the victim of some magic spell. Going to a psychic or fortune teller means avoiding the stigma of *insanity*, and this precious benefit explains the plethora of magicians, faith healers, and fortune tellers that abound in Italy.

Personal stigma is a serious obstacle from the very beginning of therapy. When we propose new models of conceptualizing the pathological process that lead, not to magic spells, but to mental illness, an alarm goes off: *"So, I'm insane?"* In this way defense mechanisms are activated, sometimes leading to the refusal of treatment. As we have seen, the psychic processes connected to stigma are characterized by heavy emotional baggage, and can be modified only by the construction of new internal operative models.

A crucial instrument in treatment is the therapeutic relationship which can transfer positive emotions of acceptance and reassurance to the patient. It is incredible to note how powerful an instrument this relationship can be in therapy. In institutional contexts, in the psychiatric wards, and in the reductionist and biological approach, there is "stigma in the stigma" consisting of the dysfunctional behaviors of patients defined as "hysterical". When patients receive the label of hysterical (not always merited), they are immediately considered patients who do not respond to medication and are potentially problematic for the staff, putting the biological model of mental illness, adopted by the staff, in crisis. We should not forget that the study of hysteria gave birth to that much maligned (obviously, by exponents of the biological approach) discipline of dynamic psychiatry.

The following episode is a particularly good example. One day, on the psychiatric ward I heard a woman lamenting painfully. I resisted my usual tendency to interfere, since she was not my patient, but in the end I was unable to mind my own business (I did, after all, swear to the Hippocratic oath), and I put on my white coat, entered the room and, since the patient's doctor was absent, I called the interns assigned to her case. They said, with conviction, "There is nothing we can do, she is hysterical and does not respond to therapy".

"OK", I answered, trying not to get mad. "But what therapy has been prescribed for her problem?" "A placebo", they answered. "But the patient", I continued angrily, "is complaining of abdominal pain". "Exactly, hysterical symptoms", they said. I drew near the woman, sat on the edge of her bed and asked how I might help her, trying to reassure her by gently touching her brow. She said she had terrible stomach pains and added despairingly, "I know you don't believe me, but I am sick!" I believed her, or that is I believed her version of reality, so I carefully examined her stomach which I found to be tense and colicky; I prescribed anxiolytic and antispasmodic drugs. The patient accepted, but she had already calmed down!

This episode is illustrative of how unconscious mechanisms of stigma, on the part of the staff in charge of her care, can influence the therapeutic relationship and, therefore, the clinical process. Any other patient would have "merited" a stomach palpitation and a minimum of care, but not the *hysteric*, guilty of challenging the biological model of Psychiatry!

Personal stigma in patients can be addressed starting with this relationship, activating motivational processes of cooperation and nurturing by the staff in order to gradually restructure internal operative models responsible for stigma. It should be evident how important this type of training is for health personnel.

If emotional variables are crucial in the process of stigmatization, obviously relational components play an important role. In the course of a grave illness, such as schizophrenia, the patient tends to gradually modify his or her physical appearance, neglecting personal hygiene, dress, and assuming bizarre and provocative behaviors. This provokes rejection by those who come into contact with the *insane* person, who then tends to become more isolated, losing further relational and social skills and eventually even a reason to care about personal appearance. It is clear that the treatment relative to improvement in behaviour and personal appearance leads to a diminution of social stigma and, consequently, personal stigma.

Another positive instrument in treating personal stigma is the use of a group setting in which patients who have already reached positive results and are in good condition, talk about their own experiences and how overcoming both personal and social stigma helped them to lead a normal life. Here it is important to point out how the adoption of a clinical context that favours the integration of schizophrenic patients with persons suffering from other problems, even medical, plays an important role. This was observed with the closure of the mental institutions and the placement of mental health services within the general hospital structure. The adoption of local day hospitals, community centers, and outpatient care facilities favour the exchange between patient and population, avoiding the segregation that only increases stigmatization.

There is, however, a kind of negative vicious circle that needs to be discussed. To reduce stigma we must get people to understand that patients with psychiatric problems can live perfectly well in a communal environment. Unfortunately, condominiums will deny access to apartments, using the most captious argumentation or even resorting to racist condominium regulations, in order to avoid having the "insane" move in. To reduce the stigma, it is necessary that these "crazies" are brought closer to normal people. The presence of stigma, however, makes this difficult, if not impossible.

The objective to pursue is to convince people that schizophrenia is a disorder whose dynamics are known and can be cured, just like any other illness that affects human beings.

Since the problem of personal stigma is considered fundamental in the treatment of patients, social stigma must also be reduced through the adoption of psycho-educational programs for the population. Different strategies have been identified for the reduction of social stigma toward the mentally ill, especially those suffering from schizophrenia. It is also important to favour the promulgation of legislation that is attentive to the problems of the mentally ill and their social and occupational integration. From this point of view, Italian legislation is on the forefront. Thanks to the Democratic Psychiatry Movement and Franco Basaglia, years ago, legislation was enacted that provided for locally-based mental health services, rehabilitation, and social and occupational integration for psychiatric patients.

With this legislation, obligatory hospitalization is no longer discriminatory, in that it is now tied to public health needs, rather than the specific characteristics of the psychiatric patient. Obligatory hospitalization is used not only for the mentally ill, but for any person affected with a medical condition that, without treatment, could harm the community. Personal freedom may be briefly suspended for any illness, infectious disease, for instance, in which the patient does not voluntarily accept treatment and which constitutes a danger to the collectivity.

With the recognition that obligatory medical treatment is not exclusively the domain of psychiatry, but regards many branches of medicine, a significant advance in overcoming legislative discrimination of psychiatric patients has been reached. The position of those who opposed the laws regarding the integration of psychiatric patients (known in Italy as law no. 180), saying that the law denied the existence of mental illness, is absurd. Nothing is more untrue! No one denies the existence of mental illness, but rather, persons affected by psychiatric disorders are recognized to have the exact same status as those who exhibit other medical problems.

The second crucial aspect involves educational programs for the population. These should be directed at people of all ages, and information about mental illness, their demystification, and the battle against stigma should be part of scholastic programs. These programs should include information and, above all, a chance for students to meet patients who have recovered from psychiatric disorders or who are in a treatment program.

The negative role the media—the cinema, in particular—play in maintaining the stigma regarding schizophrenia, should also be considered. In general, the attitude of the movie industry in the representation of schizophrenia is almost always negative. Inserting the words schizophrenia or schizophrenic in a film data-base will reveal over two hundred films.

Of these, the great majority propose a negative vision of schizophrenia, often associated with perverted criminal actions. One classic example is Hitchcock's Psycho where Norman Bates is portrayed as a schizophrenic, who has resolved the negative relationship with his mother by killing and embalming her and then continuing to resurrect her through himself, only to commit more horrendous crimes.

Besides the undoubted narrative interest of the film, a horror masterpiece (with its legendary and violent shower scene), the negative role attributed to the schizophrenic condition is all too evident. Norman Bates is a lucid assassin and the story ends in the police station with his capture. Presenting persons afflicted with schizophrenia as brutal and perverted murderers is a leitmotiv in the majority of these films. Moreover, the condition of schizophrenia described is almost always unrealistic, with very negative connotations.

This appears counterproductive, since the cinema could exert a psychoeducational role and contribute to the reduction of stigma. Another example of a negative film on schizophrenia is the relatively recent (2000) *The Cell,* directed by Tarsem Singh, with Jennifer Lopez. The film shows a futuristic psychiatric center in which a psychologist mentally connects to patients through complicated machinery, exploring their minds, in order to cure them.

One day a schizophrenic serial killer arrives in coma and our hero, Jennifer, must explore his mind, not only as therapy but to help the police discover where the monster has imprisoned an innocent, young woman, who risks an atrocious death, if not found quickly. The situation becomes an occasion for an intolerable series of nonsense and bad taste. The film moves between images of shockingly violent crimes of the schizophrenic and a demented trip into his poor brain. The audience is treated to stupid conceptualizations of schizophrenia, either considered a biological lesion to repair, or a psychological condition to explain.

This boring, poorly filmed and scripted film, is full of holes and looks like a glitteringly plastic music video, starring the hardly credible (and ridiculous-looking) cyber-shrink, Jennifer Lopez. Perhaps the reader is wondering why I am going on about this? Well, this and other bad films of the same genre, are seen by our patients, including those being treated for schizophrenia. You can imagine the devastating effect viewing this film has on them.

Recently, the young wife of a patient, who had exhibited psychotic decompensation and who was successfully following the *Negative Entropy* protocol, asked me if it was alright to continue living with her husband, and if she and their young son were at risk by staying in the same house with a "schizophrenic". I had to try hard to explain to her that the number of violent actions committed by schizophrenics did not exceed those committed by "normal" persons. My patients inevitably suffer when they see such films, even experiencing attacks of depression and despair!

The cinema also has great positive potential when it proposes a more balanced view of schizophrenia. This is what happened in the film *"A Beautiful Mind"* that narrates, in an appropriate and non-romanticized way, the life of John Nash, an American mathematician, with schizophrenia, who won the Nobel Prize in 1994. This is an interesting film I would like to discuss in order to explain the impact such a work can have on improving the information the public receives on schizophrenia.

> Mathematicians have won the war. Mathematicians have deciphered secret Japanese codes. The declared objective of the Soviets is world communism. Today we entrust the future of American to your able hands.

These lines at the beginning of the film, spoken by a famous professor from Princeton University, follow a close-up of the glassy-eyed John Nash, genius from West Virginia and winner of a prestigious scholarship. The "roommate" soon appears, but we are already entering a delusional world, since the attentive spectator will note that the roommate only interacts with Nash when others are not present. It's a type of alter-ego, and he almost always has something to say about John's behaviour. Nash, meanwhile, begins to think about game theory and hopes to identify new possibilities for zero sum difference. In the scene when he and his colleagues notice a group of girls in a bar, he conceptualizes the need to correct the theory of Adam Smith, whom his colleagues define as the "father of modern Economics".

"Adam Smith needs to be rethought", he says, and proposes, there and then, a theory that would lead to success flirting with the girls. It is a theory based a collaboration that introduces the idea of a game with zero sum difference. Each fellow must follow his own interests, as well as the interests of the whole group. Thus, a simplified version of game theory, defined by Nash as "dominant dynamics", is presented to the public.

"Do you realize that your hypothesis is a slap in the face of 150 years of economic theory?" his professor tells him, while his imaginary roommate is overjoyed by the success. The action moves, unexpectedly, to the Pentagon, some years later. Nash, hallucinating, observes sequences of numbers that compose a code. This is how a break in the narrative occurs, as what now appears to be a spy-story is introduced. This apparent adventure story runs parallel to the story of Nash's brilliant academic career.

Nash is teaching a course and meets the beautiful Alicia. It's love at first sight. In this way the double narrative unravels: the real life of the protagonist and the imagined life which features the mysterious CIA agent. There is a plot by an out-of-control faction of the Red Army to provoke a war. Nash must decipher secret codes in which the enemies of America are plotting its destruction. The love story with Alicia, meanwhile, continues. Alicia gets to Nash by solving a difficult math problem he had assigned to the class. Nash is hesitant, but Alicia invites him to dinner, anyway.

The love story goes on, but Nash is slipping into dissociation. He begins to see signs and hidden meanings in real life, and his spy-story is becoming more and more dramatic. By now a new imaginary figure has appeared, the niece of his roommate. Regardless, Nash and Alicia marry. After the marriage the situation worsens. The spy-story Nash is living takes a turn for the worse with the appearance of violent behaviour and death threats by the "bad guys". Even Alicia sees that something is wrong because her husband is increasingly bewildered and remote. Nash keeps getting worse. He believes he is being controlled and spied upon. The CIA agent is progressively more threatening. In the meantime, Alicia becomes pregnant, and Nash continues to worsen. The hallucinations are more frequent and intrusive, while his behaviour is increasingly disorganized. During a conference at Harvard, he sees himself surrounded by spies and tries to escape. The spies are not spies but collaborators of a psychiatrist. At this point, the *headshrinker* suddenly appears, portrayed by a magnificent Christopher Plummer.

Nash is captured and obliged to accept therapy, which is not exactly subtle: massive doses of thioridazine and physical restraints. Hallucinations and delusions continue until Nash ends up in isolation. The psychiatrist emerges immediately as a negative figure. More alarming even than the agent in the delusions, cold and unfriendly, espousing a rationalist point of view. Alicia asks him to explain Nash's problems. The psychiatrist, faithful to his cold and rational tone, says: "The only way I can help him is to show him the difference between what is real and what is inside his head".

This phrase is the leitmotif of biological psychiatry. The message is clear. Meaning, reality are not our constructions but a gift any psychiatrist can prepackage, with the help of restraints, abuse, and huge doses of neuroleptics. Alicia also begins her parallel journey in the mental illness of her husband. Initially, she believes him, but little by little she discovers the terrible reality. The scene of apophany is beautiful, with Nash in his office, plastered with newspaper clippings. Was this all he was doing, clipping articles from journals? Alicia wants to know and tries to discover the shocking truth. They then meet in the clinic cafeteria. Nash still dissociating, continues to feel victim of a plot, and thinks he's being watched. Alicia can't take it anymore. She provokes a show-down and denies everything her husband says. "It's not real", she says, "Do you understand? You're sick John!" Nash breaks down and the psychiatrist decides to subject him to insulin shock. This scene is magnificent. While Nash is undergoing the treatment, in a setting similar to the execution chamber used for lethal injection in the USA, the psychiatrist finally explains what Nash has to Alicia.

"It's schizophrenia", he says, "and the problem of schizophrenia is that the patient doesn't know what is real". The psychiatrist effectively describes the dramatic nature of the condition. "Imagine that everything you know disappears suddenly, and you are in a completely new situation. What kind of hell would that be?" In the meanwhile, Nash is experiencing the hell of insulin shock, packaged and dispensed by the psychiatrist. The focus of the film then moves to Alicia who is now caring for her child. Alicia must construct a sense of what is happening, and she does this gradually and with suffering. "At times I hate him!" she says to a friend, "but, my god, then I see my husband and I know I must help him".

She cares for Nash lovingly, making sure he takes his medication regularly. The neuroleptic therapy and the illness dull his cognitive abilities, however, and he must interrupt his research. Nash is no longer credible now that he is suffering from mental illness. The sequence in which Nash is mumbling, and Alicia is convinced he is delusional, is wonderful. "No", he justifies himself, "I was talking to the garbage man". "They never come at night", says Alicia. But in that exact moment the camera catches a glimpse of the garbage man outside the window. Alicia notices, too. Nash is not able to make love to his wife and she is in despair. Nash stops taking his pills and another decompensation occurs. The terrible world of spies and the alarming special agent reappears. "You don't exist", says Nash. "Of course I exist", responds the hallucination and the game continues.

The delusion is maintained, finding in itself the subtlest and most convincing justifications. Nash, however, has become clever. Now he uses a double cover on his books. At home he helps out and is silent about his nightmares; when he can, however, he hides out in a small bungalow where he can sink into his delusions. Alicia finds out and understands that a new crisis has arrived. Her world collapses around her, together with her hopes for a cure. She is even afraid that Nash might hurt her or their small son. In fact, at one point Nash actually entrusts his child to a hallucination, risking catastrophe. Alicia has had enough and calls the psychiatrist. Nash's voices now tell him to kill Alicia. All his hallucinations are present, in a climactic moment, telling him to kill her. It is a match between the Entropy of Mind that wants to take over and the attempt of a sound mind to resist an entropic catastrophe. The crisis is avoided by the arrival of the psychiatrist, who asks Nash why he stopped taking his drugs. Nash's response is revealing.

"Because I couldn't do my work, and I couldn't make love to my wife. Do you think this is better than being crazy?" The psychiatrist is not flustered and restates his reductionist logic. "We need to resume the insulin shock treatments", he affirms and then repeats. "Schizophrenia is degenerative. Some days it seems better, but then the crises reappear". Nash refuses the desperate approach of the psychiatrist and says that he can find a solution. The psychiatrist repeats that only medication can help him. The situation with Alicia arrives at a climax and she asks, "Are you going to hurt me?"

"I don't know", answers Nash and Alicia, now defeated, leaves in the most beautiful and poetic scene in the movie, disappearing quickly down a staircase. Some minutes go by and Alicia returns. She's changed her mind. She draws near John and asks him, "Do you want to know what is real?" "This", she says touching his face. "Do you want to know what is real?" and she takes his hand and places it on her breast. "This is real". The decision has now been made, and Alicia decides to stay by her John and help him go on. Finally, a new phase in Nash's life begins. In fact, in the subsequent sequence, we see, for the first time, an attempt at coping with the hallucinations. Nash goes to find his old friend at Princeton and during the meeting he swats the images that are tormenting him with a newspaper, like he would bothersome flies. Then speaking with his friend, he says, "Alicia thinks I should become part of the community of colleagues and that would help me". He asks to be helped and accepted. The friend understands and proposes that he come work with him. Nash continues to suffer and fight his hallucinations and delusions. He even has a psychotic breakdown in the middle of the campus. Arriving home, he tells Alicia of his failure, but finds comfort and understanding. "You know tension makes the hallucinations appear", she reassures him kindly. Nash is discouraged and proposes returning to the hospital. His wife is wonderful and hugs him, saying only "You can try again tomorrow". Nash returns to work and tries hard to battle his psychotic symptoms.

The sequence in which his dearest hallucinations, his roommate and his young niece ask to not be abandoned, is moving. Nash, however, has decided to change and he greets them affectionately, almost sadly. "No", he says, "I have decided, I'm not going to speak to you anymore!" In a touching scene he kisses the crying *niece* on her forehead, and says goodbye to her forever.

This is how his slow recovery begins, even if the delusions and hallucinations try not to be abandoned, and they return punctually, sometimes threateningly, sometimes endearingly. Nash, however, goes ahead, slowly resuming his work and finding a new equilibrium. Young students seek him out and show their affection. In this way, Nash decides he wants to return to teaching. His friend asks him, "Have those hallucinations gone away?"

"No, they are always here, but I have learned to live with them. They are my past, and we all have to deal with our past". His friend is convinced and decides to help him return to teaching. We find Nash again in 1994, at the end of a lesson, surrounded by his students. At that moment, he is contacted by the Swedish Academy that is considering the idea of awarding him the Nobel Prize for his theory on equilibrium dynamics. In honor of winning, he decides to return to the tea room at the University. His colleagues notice him, after years of absence, and they offer an affectionate and traditional homage, the "gesture of the pen", placing all their fountain pens on his table.

In the next scene Nash is in Stockholm, giving his acceptance speech at the award ceremony. "I always believed in numbers", he says, "but today after a life spent with formulas, I ask myself what logic really is. Who decides what reason is? My research has conducted me outside science, toward metaphysics, but then I returned and only then I made the most important discovery of my life. It is only in the mysterious equation of love that one finds every logical reason". Then turning to his wife, in the audience, he says, "I'm here tonight solely thanks to you. You are the only reason I exist. You are all my reasons. Thank you!" The film ends with John Nash turning his back on the hallucinations, and he goes off, a little uncertainly, supported by his dear Alicia, while the credits inform us that John Nash lives and works in Princeton, and that his theories have influenced the development of the disciplines of economics, physics, and biology.

This beautiful film is an excellent instrument for organizing psycho-educational sessions in school. Personally, I have carried out this type of activity in schools in Catania. In the first part of the event, I briefly present the problem of schizophrenia, with particular attention to furnishing realistic and reassuring information about the possibility of a cure. I reserve an important role in my presentation for the identification of symptoms for an early diagnosis. I then show the film and afterwards start a debate that is always interesting for the students. I can affirm that this activity works really well and would suggest its adoption to anyone interested in psycho-education regarding schizophrenia.

To conclude this chapter, I want to briefly discuss a topic that seems to be of extreme interest. Recent research has shown the utility of substituting the term schizophrenia, indissolubly linked to stigma, with other more optimistic, innovative terms. In Japan, for instance, an official effort in this regard was launched. With the goal of reducing stigma linked to the term *schizophrenia*, in 2002 the Japanese Society of Psychiatry and Neurology changed the old term *Seishin Bunretsu Byo* (which means schizophrenia) to *Togo Shitcho Sho* (which means integration disorder). The name change for the disorder was linked to a Kraepelian vision of chronicity and to a more optimistic conception of the illness, based on the vulnerability to stress model (Sato, 2006).

A series of controlled research, carried out after the adoption of the new terminology, has shown very positive results. After only seven months from the official change, the new name was already adopted in 78% of official documents. After dropping the term schizophrenia, encouraging data emerged regarding the fact that the percentage of cases in which the patient was informed of the diagnosis went from 36.7%, in the period during which schizophrenia was still used, to 69.7% three years after the adoption of the term *integration disorder*.

The Japanese experience has proven experimentally what I have thought and experienced in my clinical practice, i.e., that use of the term schizophrenia makes communication and discussion of the diagnosis with the patient difficult, just as the prescription of neuroleptics is rendered more problematic because of the presence of that frightening Bleulerian term on the label. I think it will be useful to consider the adoption of a different term for schizophrenia that is new and at the same time grounded in an innovative conceptual framework, tied to valid therapeutic proposals that are able to kept the hopes of the patient and family alive.

Continual improvement of the integrated treatments that are being developed should find confirmation in the search for a new term for this psychotic condition. In my clinical work I introduced the definition *Phrenentropy*, which is described in this monograph. I can assure you that the use of a new word produces positive results in the clinical setting. The term *Phrenentropy*, which patients and their families want explained, is presented during the informational meetings as a condition that can be managed and overcome. I would, therefore, like to propose the use of the term "*Phrenentropy*" for the disorder Bleuler called schizophrenia.

Scientific, clinical, and didactic experience, accumulated over the years, demonstrates the advantages of using the new conceptualization, *Entropy of Mind,* and the new name, *Phrenentropy.*

The constructivist and narrative paradigm, in these conditions, is confirmed. New words create a new realities!

CHAPTER THIRTEEN

Piero's Story

To conclude this book I would like to describe the clinical experience of one of the many patients I have treated.

Because I detest cold, ascetic clinical reports, based on a normative and rationalist logic, I have decided to recount, in rather anecdotal and narrative form, the story of Piero.

Young Piero

A child who doesn't cry much. Calm, he watches the world go by, taking his time.

Piero, however, arrives late for every appointment in life. He walks later than the others and speaks only a few words in the first two years of his life.

As a child he is strange and unpredictable. He shows interest but then changes his mind. If you speak to him it is unlikely he will answer coherently; he seems to follow his own train of thought which his interlocutor cannot penetrate.

A strange world

That's what appears before Piero's eyes. How many mysteries and how to decode them? Mother and father are of little help.

Mother always worried, father on his own. Who is taking care of me? And then why don't I understand them when they speak to each other and when they speak to me? It's as if they are always thinking the opposite of what they are saying. I never get it right!

We don't have many friends and we are isolated.

Yes, that's because Father says it's better not to trust anybody, because in the end everybody will cheat you.

Could it be true? But I am being careful anyway, also because I can't figure out what goes through their heads and I don't understand their intentions. Father is right: it's better not to trust anyone.

Jeez, Mother is a pain, she never leaves me alone, she wants to know everything, she is always butting in. She says she always understands what I am thinking. Could it be true? Sometimes I have the feeling that she is stealing my thoughts!

Anyway, I made it to high school. The problem is I don't understand much and seem to be understanding less and less.

When the teacher is explaining, I follow with difficulty for a few minutes, then I get distracted while confusing thoughts fill my head.

In school I am isolated. My classmates say I'm "strange" and they leave me alone.

And forget about the girls. I don't even know how to meet them.

But now I'm really worried. Everyday it seems as if the world is changing and I feel different.

Apophany

There is a heavy feeling of mystery in the air. It's not something you can explain, but you "feel" it. At home there are secrets. Around me they are preparing something.

"They" know; the others have been informed and they are whispering about it among themselves; but when I get close, they look at me strangely as if to say, "they are coming, and we know about it!"

Also on TV they talk about it constantly, staring directly at me from the cathode tube and saying: "They are coming!"

But who is coming?

Maybe the voices I have started hearing are involved, first like a whisper and then growing more distinct and threatening. They are saying that I will die soon and that "they" are coming.

Entropy of Mind

What a strange day! The atmosphere is purplish, like the aurora borealis and the voices are stronger and scarier.

I have to do something; "they" are probably really coming!

Oh no! It's starting! They've transformed me!

Who is that monster looking at me from the mirror? They've transformed me! Everything is starting!

Mother, father, help, help!

Oh no! You've been transformed too! Go away, monsters! You've killed my parents! Help!

No, leave me alone! Who are they and what do they want? Let me go!

The capture

The patient is delusional, is hallucinating and does not collaborate. What we need here is a nice, obligatory medical treatment!—decrees a "drug-dispensing" psychiatrist, convinced.

A nice, big syringe full of haloperidol, to start, and then we move on to the atypicals. Go ahead get him and, before long, he's in a locked ward!

Torture-cure

Where am I and how come I'm tied to the bed? What are those bars doing on the windows? Am I in prison?

I should try to escape but I have no strength, I feel like marble. Movement is difficult but the voices are gone.

OK, OK, I'll collaborate! But untie me. Anyway, what could I do in this state? No, please, the anti-Parkinson, no! You say it helps unblock me but it only seems to get rid of what little saliva I have left in my mouth, and my tongue gets stuck to my palate.

Oh look, my parents are back. What did those monsters do to you and what were you hiding from me? I would like to go home.

What? Another psychiatrist? Please, no I've had enough of these doctors who have turned my butt into a pin cushion.

And one you can talk to? And what am I going to say to him? OK, OK, I'll go; just bring me home.

A safe haven

How nice! No sign of syringes!

This psychiatrist listens and I can finally speak!

He seems interested in the stories I tell and maybe he even believes me a little.

He says he wants to help me. We'll see!

OK, I can trust him and maybe there really is something in me that's not working and with his help I might be able to straighten out what's in my head.

Who knows, maybe he can help me solve all these mysteries.

Negative Entropy

I've been in therapy for six months and I feel pretty good.

Once a week I have an appointment with the psychiatrist-psychotherapist, once a week I also participate in group therapy and after I often work on the computer to get the mind going with lots of exercises. My memory is returning and I am able to concentrate.

We also work with the video camera. Awesome! They are teaching me how to meet girls.

Who would have imagined! They also teach me to understand people's expressions and try to figure out what they have in mind. This is called "meta-cognition training".

Hey! It works! Now I am able to relate to others better and I am less afraid.

Narrative reconstruction

A year has gone by and I am well. They helped me with my studies and I have received a diploma: It's called "Training for learning and didactic planning".

A while ago I started a new project with my therapist. First, we talked about my problems, and now that we have, little by little, resolved them, I need to go over my life.

The doctor says that it's not a good idea to forget. I would, however, prefer not to think about everything I went through.

The doctor insists and says that not knowing one's story means not being able to live well.

He says I need to understand what happened to me. OK, we'll work on it.

A New Story

I finally get it!

No mysteries, no plots! It was all in my brain!

Yes, because we invent reality. It's not that it simply happens outside of us. No, we tell it, like writers do with their stories.

The truth of the matter is that I didn't understand much and didn't know how to talk about what happened.

Nobody, when I was little, told me stories; I spent hours by myself, in front of the TV.

And the voices? They came from inside my brain! Like a phantom limb, my doctor explained!

During the First World War soldiers with amputations wanted to scratch a limb that was not actually there. But they felt it and it hurt because it was inside their brains!

I now know that I am a person with a brain that is a little more fragile than others.

It's in my family, like my "whimsical" uncle who never spoke to the others, was always alone, and dressed in a strange way.

Creating sense

It's hard to accept everything that has happened to me. Why me?

The doctor suggested this example.

He has a predisposition for hypertension, like his paternal grandparents, both dead from stroke; so, no alcohol, easy on the food, lots of exercise, and no gaining weight.

I have a predisposition for... what's it called? Oh yes, "Entropy of Mind" like my "whimsical" uncle who talked to himself.

If the doctor overdoes it, his circulatory system suffers. If I don't control myself, my brain suffers. To each his own problem. He says I'm lucky because you don't die from my problem like you do from his. (He often thinks about heart attack and about his friend who died prematurely from a heart attack in Argentina).

I'd still change places, however.

He writes books and has a really cool Alfa, which he drives around Europe and then he goes north from Catania to Norway having a lot of fun and then he heads west reaching Portugal, the place he says is the westernmost point in Europe.

Anyway, everybody needs to take care of their own problems. Now I live my life which is good.

My aim to balance the stress and create a positive environment.

My parents have also been in therapy. Now they talk to me more and I often understand them.

Excuse me, but now I have to go.

If I may, for an instant, I would like to say something the "neuroleptic-dispensing" psychiatrists, those who are always ready to shoot you up or fill you with pills.

Please, every now and then, listen to what we have to say instead of limiting yourselves to shooting haloperidol, atypicals and anti-Parkinsonians.

EPILOGUE

Perennial Possession

If you have been patient enough to read up to here, or if you are sneaky enough to get to this point quickly, you've earned the opportunity to learn the motive and meaning of the epigraph of this book, without the need to go and read (or reread) *The Peloponnesian War*.

The cultural reference for the epigraphs in my other books has been Philosophy. Heraclitus, Socrates, Protagoras. For the epigraph of this book, I wanted to look to History. The motive is linked to the enormous importance the evolutionary vision and the narrative dimension assume in a psychotherapy and therapy, informed by the logic of processes and complex systems, with particular reference to schizophrenia. Each human being, through time, constructs, memorizes, then recounts his or her own story, negotiating it with whoever is nearby and with the events of the day.

Each human being, in every moment of the life cycle, constitutes an end point in a historical, evolutionary, biological, and cultural process that has lasted, phylogenetically, for millions of years, and, ontogenetically, for a lifetime. All humans are narrators of stories and knowing how to narrate means being able to live fully and develop a unique and unrepeatable personal story.

Those who do not adequately know or understand their own stories cannot successfully construct a positive future and a knowing present. In schizophrenia, the historic and narrative dimensions are interrupted and their reconstruction must constitute an important objective for the therapeutic process. This is why I've decided to refer to a historian, in fact, to the first historian if western culture, for the epigraph of this book.

Thucydides has always fascinated my, from back when I was a schoolboy. I was stunned by the incredible modernity and perfect comprehension of the destiny of human beings as cultural and historical animals.

The introduction to *The Peloponnesian War* struck me profoundly, when Thucydides wrote, nearly 2500 years ago:

"I am not writing these words to amaze or entertain the reader, I write them because they are a '*perennial possession*' to share with future generations" (Thucydides, 1996).

From when I was a boy I knew the meaning of my life and probably the meaning of life, *tout court*, must be knowledge as, years later, Vittorio Guidano lucidly conceptualized, when he defined humans as *epistemic animals*. With Thucydides I understood that knowledge does not degrade or get lost but remains a *perennial possession*.

I remember with joy the wonderful hours spent listening to stories my grandparents told, about their adventurous lives at the beginning of the 20th century; I remember with tender nostalgia the time spent with my daughters, still small, narrating my own adventures from the second half of that century.

The first stories were for me a *perennial possession* incorporated into my mind, forever part of my life, while my stories will remain a *perennial possession* for the future, within the minds of Giulia and Susanna.

To them who, in fact, represent the future and the biological and cultural continuity of my being, to them who will see things I can only imagine, and to them who will recount stories I cannot listen to, I want to donate, not only the memories of games, fables, and adventurous discoveries, but also and forever, this book.

For Giulia and Susanna, this will be a gift that has no end, that lasts forever, *κτῆμα ἐς ἀεί*, a *perennial possession*.

REFERENCES

Abdel-Baki, A. A., & Nicole, L. (2001). Schizophrenia and cognitive behavioural psychotherapy. *Can. J. of Psychiatry, 46*: 511–521.

Ainsworth, M. (1989). Attachment beyond infancy. *American Psychologist, 44*: 709–716.

Ainsworth, M. D. S., Blehar, M., Waters, E., & Wall S. (1978). *Patterns of attachment. A Psychological Study of the Strange Situation.* Hillsdale, NJ: Erlbaum.

Aleman, A., Hijman, R., De Haan, E. H., & Kahn, R. S. (1999). Memory impairment in schizophrenia: a meta-analysis. *American Journal Psychiatry, 159*: 1358–1366.

Alford, B. A., & Beck, A. T. (1997). *The Integrative Power of Cognitive Therapy.* New York: The Guiford Press.

American Psychiatric Association (1987). *Diagnostic and Statistic Manual of Mental Disorders.* Washington, DC: APA Press.

American Psychiatric Association (1994). *Diagnostic and Statistical Manual of Mental Disorders* (4th edition). Washington, DC: APA Press.

American Psychiatric Association (1997). *Practice Guideline for the Treatment of Patients with Schizophrenia.* Washington, DC: American Psychiatric Press.

American Psychiatric Association (2000). *Diagnostic and Statistical Manual of Mental Disorders* (4th edition, text revision). Washington, DC: APA Press.

Andreasen, N. C. (1987). *Schizofrenia. Scale per la valutazione dei sintomi positivi e negativi* (Italian edition, M. Moscarelli & C. Maffei Eds.), Milano: Raffaello Cortina Editore.

Andreasen, N. C. (1990). Methods for assessing positive and negative symptoms. In: N. C. Andreasen (Ed.), *Modern Problem of Pharmacopsychiatry: Positive and negative symptoms and syndromes*. Base: Karger.

Arciero, G. (2002). *Studi e dialoghi sull'identità*. Torino: Bollati Boringhieri.

Arieti, S. (1969). The meeting of the inner and the external world in schizophrenia, everyday life and creativity. *American Journal of Psychoanalysis, 39*: 115–130.

Arieti, S. (1969). The psychodynamics of schizophrenia: A reconsideration. *American Journal of Psychotherapy, 22*: 366–381.

Arieti, S. (1974). An overview of schizophrenia from a predominantly psychological approach. *American Journal of Psychiatry, 131*: 241–249.

Arieti, S. (1978). *Interpretazione della schizofrenia*. Milano: Feltrinelli.

Asaad, G., & Shapiro, B. (1986). Hallucinations: Theoretical and clinical overview. *American Journal of Psychiatry, 143* (9): 1088–1097.

Baddeley, A. D. (1986). *Working memory*. Oxford: Oxford University Press.

Baldessarini, R. (1977). *Chemotherapy in Psychiatry*. Cambridge: Harvard University Press.

Bandura, A. (1971). *Social Learning Theory*. Morristow, NJ: General Learning Press.

Bandura, A. (1982). Self-efficacy mechanism in human agency. *American Psychologist, 37*: 122–147.

Bara, B. (Ed.) (2005). *Nuovo manuale di Psicoterapia Cognitiva*. Torino, Bollati Boringhieri.

Baron-Cohen, S., Leslie, A. M., & Frith U. (1985). Does the autistic child have a theory of mind? *Cognitive psychology, 21*: 37–46.

Basaglia, F. (1968). *L'Istituzione negata*. Milano: Baldini Castoldi Dalai.

Bebbington, P. (1993). "Expressed emotion as a predictor of relapse in schizophrenia". Paper presented at the International Symposium on The role of compliance in the treatment of schizophrenia, Copenhagen, (Nov. 12–13).

Bebbington, P. (2002). Early Intervention in Psychosis: Pharmacotherapeutic strategies. In: M. Birchwood, D. Fowler, C. Jackson (2002). *Early Intervention in Psychosis*. New York: John Wiley & Sons, Ltd.

Beck, A. T. (1952). Successful outpatient psychotherapy of a chronic schizophrenic with a delusion based on borrowed guilt. *Psychiatry, 15*: 305–312.

Beck, A. T. (1963). Thinking and Depression: 1. Idiosyncratic contents and cognitive distortion. *Archives of General Psychiatry, 10*: 561–571.

Beck, A. T. (1967). *Depression: Cause and Treatment*. Philadelphia: University of Pennsylvania Press.

Beck, A. T. (1971). Cognition, Affect and Psychotherapy. *Archives of General psychiatry, 24*: 495–500.

Beck, A. T. (1976). *Cognitive Therapy of the Emotional Disorders*. New York: Guilford Press.

Beck, A. T. (1979). *Cognitive Therapy of Depression.* New York: Guilford Press.

Beck, A. T., Freeman, A., et al. (1993). *Cognitive Therapy of Personality Disorder.* New York: Guilford Press.

Beck, A. T., & Rector, N. A. (2000). Cognitive therapy of schizophrenia: a new therapy for the new millennium. *Am. J. Psychotherapy, 54*: 291–300.

Beck, A. T., & Rector, N. A. (2003). A Cognitive Model of Hallucinations, *Cognitive Therapy and Research, 26* (1): 19–52.

Beck, A. T., & Rector, N. A. (Eds.) (2004). Special Issue on Cognitive Theory and Therapy of Schizophrenia. *Journal of Cognitive Psychotherapy, 18* (4).

Beck, J. (2003). *Cognitive Therapy. Basics and beyond.* New York: Guilford Press.

Bellack, A. S., & Mueser, K. T. (1993). Psychological treatment for schizophrenia. *Schizophrenia Bulletin, 19*: 317–336.

Bellack, A. S., Mueser, K. T., Gingerrich, S., & Agresta, J. (1997). *Social Skill Training for Schizophrenia. A Step by Step Guide.* New York: Guilford Press.

Bellantuono, C., Balestrieri, M., & Amaddeo, F. (1993). Gli psicofarmaci nella terapia delle sindromi schizofreniche. In: C. Bellantuono, & M. Tansella (Eds.), *Gli psicofarmaci nella pratica.* Roma: Il Pensiero Scientifico.

Bennet-Levy, J., Butler, G., Fennel, M., Hackmann, A., Mueller, M., & Westbrook, D. (2004). *Oxford Guide to Behavioural Experiments in Cognitive Therapy.* Oxford: Oxford University Press.

Bentall, R. P. (1990). The illusion of reality: A review and integration of psychological research on hallucinations. *Psychological Bulletin, 107* (1): 82–95.

Bentall, R. P. (1994). Cognitive biases and abnormal beliefs: Towards a model of persecutory delusion. In: A. S. David & J. Cutting (Eds.), *The neuropsychology of schizophrenia* (pp. 337–360). London: Lawrence Erlbaum Associates Ltd.

Bentall, R. P. (2003). *Madness Explained.* London: Penguin Books.

Bentall, R. P., & Corcoran, R. (2001). Persecutory Delusions: A Review and Theoretical Integration. *Clinical Psychology Review, 21* (8): 1143–1192.

Bentall, R. P., Corcoran, R., Howard, R., Blackwood, N., Kinderman, & P. (2001). Persecutory Delusions: A review and theoretical integration. *Clinical Psychology Review,* 2: 1143–1192.

Bentall, R. P., & Kaney S. (1989). Content-specific information processing and persecutory delusions: An investigation using the emotional Stroop test. *British Journal of Medical Psychology, 62*: 335–364.

Bentall, R. P., Kinderman, P., & Kaney, S. (1994). The Self, attributional processes and abnormal beliefs: Towards a model of persecutory delusion. *Behaviour Research and Therapy, 32*: 331–341.

Bertalanffy, L. v. (1968). *General System Theory, Foundations, Development, Applications*. New York: George Braziller.
Bettelheim, B. (1984). *Il mondo incantato*. Milano: Feltrinelli.
Birchwood, M. (1999). In: P. D. McGorry & H. J. Jackson (Eds.). *The Recognition and Management of Early Psychosis. A Preventive Approach*. Cambridge: Cambridge University Press.
Birchwood, M., Fowler, D, & Jackson, C. (2002). *Early intervention in Psychosis*. New York: John Wiley & Sons, Ltd.
Birchwood, M., & Spencer, E. (1999). Psychotherapies for schizophrenia: a review. In: M. Maj & N. Sartorius (Eds.), *Schizophrenia*. Chichester: John Wiley & Sons, Ltd.
Birchwood, M., & Tarrier, N. (Eds.) (1992). *Innovation in the Psychological Management of Schizophrenia. Assessment, Treatment and Services*. Chichester: John Wiley & Sons, Ltd.
Birchwood, M., Todd, P., & Jackson, C. (1998). Early intervention in psychosis: the critical period hypothesis. *British Journal of Psychiatry, 172* (Suppl. 33): 53–59.
Blackwood, N. J., Howard, R. J., Bentall, R. P., & Murray, R. M. (2001). Cognitive Neuropsychiatric Models of Persecutory Delusions. *American Journal of Psychiatry, 158*: 527–539.
Bleuler, E. (1950). *Dementia praecox or the group of schizophrenias*. New York: International University Press.
Borkowski, L. G., & Kurtz, B. F. (1987). Metacognition and executive control. In: L. G. Borkowski & I. D. Day (Eds.), *Cognition in Special Children*. Norwwod: Ablex.
Bosc, M., Dubinj, A., & Polin, V. (1997). Development and validation of a social functioning scale, the Social Adaptation Self-evaluation Scale. *European Neuropsychopharmacol., 7* (Suppl. 1): 7–70.
Bouchsein, W. (1992). *Electrodermal activity*. New York: Plenum Press.
Bowlby, J. (1988). *A Secure Base*. London: Routledge.
Bralet, M. C., Yon, V., Loas, G., & Noisette, C. (2000). Cause of mortality in schizophrenic patients; prospective study of years of a cohort of 150 chronic schizophrenic patients. *Encephale, 26*: 32–41.
Breier, A. (1999). Cognitive deficit in schizophrenia and its neurochemical basis. *British Journal of Psychiatry, 174*: 16–18.
Breier, A., & Strauss, J. S. (1983). Self-control in Psychotic Disorders, *Archives of General Psychiatry, 40* (October): 1141–1145.
Brenner, H. D., Bettina, H., Roder, V., & Corrigan, P. (1992). Treatment of Cognitive Dysfunction and Behavioural Deficits in Schizophrenia. *Schizophrenia Bulletin, 18* (1): 21–26.
Broadbent, D. E. (1958). *Perception and Communication*. London: Pergamon.
Brown, G. W., Birley, J. L. T., & Wing, J. K. (1972). Influence of family life on the course of schizophrenic disorders: A replication. *British Journal of Psychiatry, 121*: 241–247.
Bulmer, M. (1970). *The Biology of Twinning in Man*. Oxford: Clarendon Press.

Callaway, E., & Naghdi, G. (1986). An human information processing model for schizophrenia. *Archives of General Psychiatry, 39*: 339–347.

Canova, P. (2003). Le scimmie e noi. *Incontro, 78*: 87–89.

Cantor-Graee, E., McNeill, T. F., Rickler, K. C., Sjöström, K., Rawling, R., & Higgins, E. S. (1994). Are neurological abnormalities in well discordant monozygotic co-twins of schizophrenic subjects the result of perinatal trauma? *Am. J. Psychiatry, 151*: 1194–1199.

Caprara, G. V. (Ed.) (2001). *La valutazione dell'autoefficacia. Interventi e contesti culturali.* Trento: Erickson.

Carcione, A., & Falcone (1999). Il concetto di metacognizione come costrutto clinico fondamentale per la psicoterapia. In: A. Semerari (Ed.), *Psicoterapia cognitiva del paziente grave.* Milano: Raffaello Cortina Editore.

Carcione, A., Falcone, Magnolfi, G., & Manaresi, F. (1997). La funzione metacognitiva in psicoterapia. Scala della Valutazione della Metacognizione (SVaM). *Psicoterapia, 3*: 91–107.

Casacchia, M., Mazza, M., Frangou, I., Giosuè, P., & Roncone, R. (2005). La riabilitazione metacognitiva nella schizofrenia. In: C. Di Berardino (Ed.), *L'approccio multimodale nella riabilitazione psichiatrica.* Milano: McGraw-Hill.

Chadwick, P. D., & Birchwood, M. J. (1994). Challenging the omnipotence of voices: A cognitive approach to auditory hallucinations. *British Journal of Psychiatry, 164*: 190–201.

Chadwick, P., Birchwood, M. J., & Trower, P. (1996). *Cognitive Therapy for Delusions, Voices and Paranoia.* Chichester: John Wiley & Sons, Ltd.

Chadwick, P., Birchwood, M., & Trower, P. (1996). *Cognitive Therapy for delusions, voices and paranoia.* Chichester: John Wiley & Sons, Ltd.

Chaika, E. (1982). *Language, the social mirror.* Rowley, MA: Newbury House Publishers.

Chapman, L. J., & Chapman, J. P. (1988). The genesis of delusion. In: T. F. Oltmanns & B. A. Maher (Eds.), *Delusional beliefs* (pp. 167–183). New York: John Wiley & Sons, Ltd.

Chen, E. Y. H. (1994). Verbal fluency and semantic memory in schizophrenia. *British Journal of Psychiatry, 165*: 704.

Chen, E. Y. H. (1994b). A neural network model of cortical information processing in schizophrenia. Role of hippocampalcortical interaction: A review and a model. *Canadian Journal of Psychiatry, 40*: 21–25.

Chen, E. Y. H., & Berrios, G. E. (1998). The nature of delusions: A Hierarchical neural network approach. In: D. Stein & J. Ludick (Eds.), *Neural Networks and Psychopathology* (pp. 167–188). Cambridge: Cambridge University Press.

Chomsky, N. (1985). *The Logical Structure of Linguistic Theory.* Chicago: University Chicago Press.

Ciompi, L. (1988): *The Psyche and Schizophrenia.* Cambridge, MA: Harvard University Press.

Ciompi, L. (1994). *Logica affettiva.* Milano: Feltrinelli.

Ciompi, L. (2003). Toward a more gentle psychiatry—to patients and understanding illness of affect logic. *Psychiatr. Prax, 30*: 28–36.
Clark, D. A. (1995). Perceived limitations of standard cognitive therapy: A consideration of effort to revised Becks' theory and Therapy. *Journal of Cognitive Psychotherapy: An international Quaterly, 9*: 153–172.
Clark, D., Beck, A. T., & Alford, B. (1999). *Scientific Foundations of Cognitive Therapy of Depression.* New York: John Wiley & Sons, Ltd.
Clausius, R. (1867). *Abhandlungen über die mechanische Wärmetheorie.* Braunschweig.
Cocchi, A., & De Isabella, G. (1996). *Centri diurni nella nuova psichiatria.* Milano: Nova Ars Libraria.
Cocchi A., & Meneghelli, A. (2004). *L'intervento precoce tra pratica e ricerca. Manuale per il trattamento precoce delle psicosi all'esordio.* Torino: Centro Scientifico Editore.
Cohen, J. D., & Servan-Schreiber, D. (1992). A Neural network model of disturbances in the processing of context in schizophrenia. *Psychiatric. Annals, 22*: 131–136.
Commonwealth Fund (1936). *Snow on Colera.* London: Oxford University Press.
Conley, C. C., & Mahmoud, R. A. (2001). A randomize, double blind study of risperidone and olanzapina in the treatment of schizophrenia and schizoaffective disorder. *A. J. of Psychiatry, 158*: 765–774.
Conwell, Y., Cholette, J., Paul, R., & Duberstein, P. R. (1998). Suicide and Schizophrenia: Identifying Risk Factors and Preventive Strategies. *Medscape Psychiatry & Mental Health e Journal, 3* (3).
Cozolino, L. (2002). *The Neuroscience of Psychotherapy.* New York: W. W. Norton & Company, Inc.
Crow, S. (1966). The Middlesx Hospital Questionnaire. *British Journal of Psychiatry, 112*: 917–920.
Crow, T. J. (1980). Positive and negative schizophrenic symptoms and the role of dopamine. *Br. J. Psychiatry, 137*: 383.
Crow, T. J. (1997). Schizophrenia as a failure of hemispheric dominance for language. *Trends in Neuroscience,* 20: 339–343.
Crow, T. J. (2000). Schizophrenia as the price that homo sapiens pays for language: a resolution of the central paradox in the origin of the species. *Brain Research Reviews 31* (March): 118–129 [Issues 2–3].
Csikszentmihalyi, M. (1993). *The evolving self.* New York: Harper & Collins Publishers.
Cutting, J. (1985). *The Psychology of Schizophrenia.* New York: Churchill Livingstone.
Damasio, A. (1999). *The feeling of what happens.* San Diego: Harvest Book Harcourt, Inc.
Darwin, C. (1968). *The origins of species by means of natural selection.* Baltimore: Penguin Book.

Davis, J. M. (1980). Antipsychotic drugs. In: H. Caplan, A. M. Freedman & B. J. Sadock (Eds.). *Comprehensive Textbook of Psychiatry*. Baltimore: Williams & Wilkins.

Davis, R. C. (1929). Factors affecting the galvanic reflex. *Archives of Psychology, 18* (115): 1–64.

Davidson, R. J. (1988). EEG measures of cerebral asymmetry: conceptual and methodological issues. *Int. J. Neurosci., 39* (1–2): 71–89.

Dawson, M. E., Nuechterlein, K. H., & Adams, R. M. (1989). Schizophrenic disorders. In: G. Turpin (Ed.), *Handbook of Clinical Psychophysiology*. Cambridge: Cambridge University Press.

De Benedetti, G. (1976). *Neuropsicologia*. Milano: Feltrinelli.

De Benedetti, G. (1987). *Psychotherapy of schizophrenia*. New York: New York University Press.

Decety, J., Chaminade, T., Grèzes, J., & Meltoff, A. N. (2002). A PET exploration of the neural mechanisms involved in reciprocal imitation. *Neuroimage, 15*: 265–272.

Delay, J., & Deniker, P. (1952). *Trente-huit cas de psychoses traitè par la cure prolongée et continue de 4560 RP*. Proceedings of Congrés des Al et Neur. Paris: Masson.

Demos, N. J. (2005). *Getting Started with Neurofeedback*. New York: W. W. Norton & Company, Inc.

Despert, L. (1938). Schizophrenia in children. *Psychiatr. Q., 12*: 366–371.

Dewey, J. (1961). *Come pensiamo*. Firenze: La Nuova Italia.

Diels-Kranz, C. (1983). *I Presocratici*. Bari: Laterza.

Di Nuovo, S. (2000). *Attenzione e concentrazione*. Trento: Edizioni Centro Studi Erickson.

Doane, J. A. (1978). Family interaction and communication deviance in disturbed and normal families: A review of research. *Fam. Process, 17*: 357–376.

Doane, J. A., & Diamond D. (1995). *Affetti e attaccamento nella famiglia*. Milano: Raffaello Cortina Editore.

Doane, J. A., West, K. L., Goldstein, M. J., Rodnick, E. H., & Jones, J. E. (1981). Parental communication deviance and affective style. *Arch. Gen. Psychiatry, 38*: 679–685.

Docherty, N. M., & Gordinier, S. W. (1999). Immediate memory, attention and communication disturbances in schizophrenia patients and communications disturbances in schizophrenia patients and their relatives. *Psychological Medicine, 29*: 189–197.

Docherty, N. M., Hawkins, K. A., Hoffman, R. E., Quinlan, D. M., Rakfeldt, J., & Sledge, W. H. (1996). Working memory, attention and communication disturbances in schizophrenia. *J. Abnorm. Psychol., 105*: 212–219.

Dohrenwend, B. P., Shrout, P. E., Link, B. G., & Skodol, A. E. (1987). Social and psychological risk factors for episodes of schizophrenia. In: H. Hafner, W. F. Gattaz & W. Janzarik (Eds.), *Search for the Causes of Schizophrenia*. Amsterdam: Elesevier.

Domarus, E. v. (1944). The specific law of logic in schizophrenia. In: Kasanin, J. S. (Ed.). *Language and thought in schizophrenia*. Berkley: University of California Press.

Dominey, P. F., & Georgieff, N. (1997). Schizophrenics learn surface but not abstract structure in a serial reaction time task. *Neuroreport, 8* (13): 2877–2882.

Dozier, M., Stovall, K. C., & Albus Kathleen, E. (1999). Attachment and Psychopathology in Adulthood. In: J. Cassidy & P. R. Shaver (Eds.), *Handbook of attachment*, New York: Guilford Press.

Duffy, F., Hughes, J. R., Miranda, F., Bernad, P., & Cook, P. (1994). Status of quantitative EEG (QEEG) in clinical practice. *Clin. Electroencephalography, 25* (4): VI–XXII.

Duffy, L., & O'Carrol, R. (1994). Memory impairment in schizophrenia comparison with that observed in the alcoholic Korsakoff syndrome. *Psychological Medicine, 24*: 155–165.

Dunbar, R. I. M. (1993). Coevolution of neocortical size, group size and language in human. *Behavioral and Brain Sciences, 16* (4): 681–735.

Duncan, C. C. (1988). Event-Related Brain Potentials: A Window of Information Processing in Schizophrenia. *Schizophrenia Bulletin 14* (2): 199–203.

Edelman, G. M. (1992). *Bright air, brillant fire, on the matter of the mind.* New York: Basic Books.

Einstein, A. (1975). *Come io vedo il mondo.* Roma: Newton Compton.

Ekman, P. (1993). Facial Expression and Emotion. *American Psychologist 48* (4): 384–392.

Ekman, P., & Friesen, W. V. (1969). The repertoire of nonverbal behaviour. *Semiotica, 1*: 49–98.

Ellring, H. (1991). The applicability of Video: Feedback and self-confrontation. In: W. Dowrick (Ed.), *Practical guide to using video in the behavioral science.* New York: John Wiley & Sons, Ltd.

Erickson, R. C., & Binder, L. (1986). Cognitive Deficits among functionally psychotic patients: A rehabilitative perspective. *Journal of Clinical and Experimental Neuropsychology, 8*: 257–274.

Evans, J. R., & Abarbanel, A. (1999). *Quantitative EEG and Neurofeedback.* San Diego: Academic Press.

Falloon, I. R. H. (1985). *Family Management of Schizophrenia.* Baltimore, MD: Johns Hopkins University Press.

Falloon, I. R. H. (1992). Early intervention for first episodes of schizophrenia: a preliminary exploration. *Psychiatry, 55*: 4–15.

Falloon, I.R.H., & Liberman, R. P. (1983). Behavioral family intervention in the management of chronic schizophrenia. In: W. R. McFarlane (Ed.), *Family therapy in schizophrenia.* New York: Guilford Press.

Faris, R. E. L., & Dunham, H. W. (1939). *Mental Disorders in Urban Areas.* Chicago: University Press.

Farmindustria, 2005. *Campagna istituzionale di informazione sui maggiori quotidiani.*

Feinstein, A., Goldberg, T. E., Nowlin, B., & Weinberger, D. R. (1998). Types and characteristics of remote memory impairment in schizophrenia. *Schizophrenia Research, 30*: 155–163.

Fenton, G. W., Fenwick, P. B. C., & Dollimore, J. (1980). EEG spectral analysis in schizophrenia. *Br. J. Psychiatry, 136*: 445.

Festinger, L. (1957). *A Theory of Cognitive Dissonance*. Stanford: Stanford University Press.

Fisher, M. (1971). Psychoses in the offspring of schizophrenic monozygotic twins and their normal co-twins. *British Journal of Psychiatry, 118*: 43–52.

Flack, W. R., Laird, J. D., & Cavallaro, L. A. (1999). Emotional expression and feeling in schizophrenia: Effects of specific expressive behaviors and emotional experiences. *Journal of Clinical Psychology, 55* (1): 1–20.

Flavell, J. H. (1979). Metacognition and cognitive monitoring: a new area of cognitive developmental inquiry. *American Psychologist., 34*: 906–11.

Fodor, J. (1983). *The Modularity of Mind*. Cambridge: Mit Press.

Fonagy, J. (1995). *The influence of attachment on the representational world in the pre-school years*. Relazione tenuta al Convegno su Attaccamento: teoria, ricerca e implicazioni cliniche, Roma.

Fonagy, P., Redfern, S., & Charman, A. (1997). The relationship between belief-desire reasoning and a projective measure of attachment security (Sat). *British Journal of Developmental Psychology, 15*: 51–63.

Fowler, D., Garety, P., & Kuipers, E. (1995). *Cognitive Behaviour Therapy for Psychosis. Theory and Practice*. Chichester: John Wiley & Sons, Ltd.

France, J., & Muir, N. (1997). *Communication and Mentally Ill Patient*. Bristol: Jessica Kingsley Publishers.

Freud, S. (1950). Psychoanalytic notes upon an autobiographical account of a case of paranoia (Dementia Paranoides). *Collected Papers, Vol. III* (pp. 387–466). London: Hogarth Press.

Freud, S. (1978). *Opere*. Torino: Boringhieri.

Friedman, D. (1991). Endogenous scalp-recorded brain potentials in schizophrenia: a methodological review. In: H. A. Nasrallah (Ed.), *Handbook of schizophrenia*. Amsterdam: Elsevier Science Publisher B. V.

Frith, C. D. (1979). Consciousness, information processing and schizophrenia. *British Journal of Psychiatry, 134*: 225–235.

Frith, C. D. (1992). *The cognitive neuropsychology of schizophrenia*. Hove, East Sussex: Lawrence Erlbaum Associates, Ltd., Publisher B. V.

Frith, C. D., & Done, D. J. (1989). Experiences of alien control in schizophrenia reflect a disorder in the central monitoring of action. *Psychological Medicine, 19*: 359–363.

Frith, U., & Frith, C. (2004). Development and neurophysiology of mentalizing. In: C. Frith & D. Wolpert (Eds.), *The Neuroscience of Social Interaction*. Oxford: Oxford University Press.

Fromm-Reichmann, F. (1950). *Principles of Intensive Psychotherapy*. Chicago: University of Chicago Press.

Fuerstein, R. (1988). *Instrumental enrichment.* Baltimora: University Park Press.

Fuller, G. D. (1977). *Biofeedback. Methods and Procedures in Clinical Practice.* San Francisco: Consolidated Printers, Inc.

Fulton, J. F., & Howell, W. H. (1971). *Fisiologia e biofisica.* Roma: Società Editrice Universo.

Gabrieli, J. D. E. (1992). Neurology of memory. *Curr. Opinion. in Neurol. & Neurosurg., 5*: 359–363.

Galeno, C. (1986). *Le opere psicologiche di Galeno.* Atti del Terzo colloquio galenico internazionale, Pavia (September 10–12).

Gallagher, S. (2003). Self-narrative in schizophrenia. In: T. Kircher & A. Davis (Eds.), *The Self in Neuroscience and Psychiatry.* Cambridge: Cambridge University Press.

Garety, F. A. (2003). The future of psychological therapies for psychosis. *World Psychiatry, 2* (3): 147–152.

Garety, P. A., Kuipers, L., Fowler, D., et al. (1994). Cognitive behavioural therapy for drug-resistant psychosis. *British Journal of Medical Psychology, 67*: 259–271.

Gellhorn, E., & Loofbourrow, G. N. (1963). *Emotion and Emotional Disorders.* New York: Harp & Row.

Goldacre, M., Seafroatt, V., & Hawton, K. (1993). Suicide after discharge from psychiatric inpatient care. *Lancet, 342*: 223–286.

Goldapple, K., Segal, Z., Garson, C., Lau, M., Bieling, P., Kennedy, S., & Mayberg, H. (2004). Modulation of Cortical-Limbic Pathway in Major Depression. *Archives of General Psychiatry, 61* (1) (January): 34–41.

Goldberg, T. E. (2001). *The Executive Brain. Frontal Lobe and the Civilized Man.* Oxford: Oxford University Press.

Goldberg, E. M., & Morrison, S. R. (1963). Schizophrenia and social class. *British Journal of Psychiatry, 109*: 785–802.

Goldberg, T. E., Weinberger, D. R., Pliskin, N.H., Berman, K. F., & Podd, M. H. (1989). Recall memory deficit in schizophrenia. A possible manifestation of prefrontal dysfunction. *Schizophrenia Research, 2*: 251–257.

Goldman-Rakic, P. S. (1992). La memoria di lavoro. *Le Scienze, 49* (291): 77–85.

Goncalves, O. F. (1994). Cognitive narrative psychotherapy, the hermeneutic construction of alternative meanings. *Journal of Cognitive Psychotherapy, 8* (2): 105–125.

Gopnic, A., Meltzoff, A., & Kuhl, P. (2001). *How Babies Think: The Science of Childhood.* London: Orion.

Gottesman, I. I. (1991). *Schizophrenia Genesis: The Origins of Madness.* New York: Freeman.

Gottesman, I. I., & Shields, J. (1972). *Schizophrenia and Genetics: A Twin Study Vantage Point.* New York: Academic Press.

Gray, J. A., Feldon, J., Rawlins, J. N. P., Hemsley, D. R., & Smith, A. D. (1991). The neuropsychology of schizophrenia. *Behavioural and Brain Sciences, 14*: 95–107.

Green, M. F. (1996). What are the functional consequences of neurocognitive deficits in schizophrenia. *American Journal of Psychiatry, 153*: 321–330.

Greenberg, L. S., Safran, J. D. (1987). *Emotion in Psychotherapy: Affect, Cognition and the Process of Change*. New York: Guilford Press.

Grimaldi, L., Frasca, G., & Scrimali, T. (1993). Un approccio sistemico-processuale alla riabilitazione: impiego del video-feedback e cambiamento in pazienti cronici. *Complessità & Cambiamento, II* (2): 92–96.

Grimaldi, L., & Scrimali, T. (2001). *Il "Parental Bonding Instrument"* (Italian version). Enna: Istituto Superiore per le Scienze Cognitive Editore.

Grimaldi, L., Scrimali, T., & De Masi, A. (1996). Attaccamento e schizofrenia. *Formazione Psichiatrica, XII* (3): 24–29.

Grimaldi, L., Scrimali, T., & Sciuto, M. (1997). Efesto, un protocollo originale per la valutazione della disabilità psichiatrica. *Complessità & Cambiamento, VI* (2): 50–62.

Grossberg, S. (2000). The imbalanced brain: From normal behavior to schizophrenia. *Biological Psychiatry, 48*: 81-98.

Gruzelier, J. H. (1984). Hemispheric imbalance on schizophrenia. *International Journal of Psychophysiology, 1*: 227–240.

Gruzelier, J. H. (1991). Hemispheric imbalance: Syndromes of schizophrenia, premorbid personality and neurodevelopmental influences. In: H. A. Nasrallah (Ed.), *Handbook of schizophrenia, Vol. 5*. Amsterdam: Elsevier Science Publisher B. V.

Gruzelier, J. H. (2003). Theory, methods and new directions in the psychophysiology of the schizophrenic process and schizotypy. *International Journal of Psychophysiology, 48* (2) (May): 221–245.

Gruzelier, J., Seymour, K., Wilson, L., Jolley, A., & Hirsch, S. (1988). Impairments on neuropsychologic tests of temporohippocampal functions and word fluency in remitting schizophrenia and affective disorders. *Archives of General Psychiatry*: 623–629.

Guidano, V. F. (1988). *La Complessità del Sé*. Torino: Bollati Boringhieri.

Guidano, V. F. (1992). *Il Sé nel suo divenire*. Torino: Bollati Boringhieri.

Guidano, V. F. (1996). Lo sviluppo del Sé. In: B. Bara (Ed.), *Nuovo Manuale di Psicoterapia Cognitiva*. Torino: Bollati Boringhieri.

Guidano, V. F., & Liotti, G. (1983). *Cognitive Processes and Emotional Disorder*. New York: Guilford Press.

GW Elektron (2004). Research tools [Computer hardware/software]. San Donato Milanese: Elemaya (http://www.elemaya.com).

Haack-Dees, B. (2001). Dyadic Affect Regulation in Interaction of Schizophrenic Adolescent and their Parents. *ISPS Newsletter, 8, 5* (1).

Hansen, J. C., & Hillyard, S. A. (1980). Endogenous brain potential associated with selective auditory attention. *Electroenceph. Clin. Neurophysiol., 49*: 277.

Hare, E. H. (1988). Schizophrenia as a recent disease. *British Journal of Psychiatry, 153*: 521–531.

Heilbrun, A. B. (1973). *Aversive Maternal Control. A Theory of Schizophrenia Development*. New York: John Wiley & Sons, Ltd.

Heilveil, I. (1983). *Video in Mental Health Practice*, New York: Springer Publishing Company.

Heinrichs, R. W. & Zakzanis, K. K. (1998). Neurocognitive deficit in schizophrenia: A quantitative review of the evidence. *Neuropsychology, 12*: 426–445.

Heisenberg, W. (1985). *Natura e fisica moderna*. Milano: Garzanti.

Hemsley, D. R. (1977). What have cognitive deficits to do with schizophrenic symptoms. *British Journal of Psychiatry, 130*: 167–173.

Hemsley, D. R. (1994). A cognitive model for schizophrenia and its possible neural basis. *Acta Psychiatrica Scandinavica, 90*: 80–86.

Hemsley, D. R., & Garety, P. A. (1986). The formation and maintenance of delusions: A Bayesian analysis. *British Journal of Psychiatry, 149*: 51–56.

Hermans, H. J. M., & Hermans-Jansen, E. (1995). *Self-narratives: The construction of meaning in psychotherapy*. New York: Guilford Press.

Heston, L. L. (1966). Psychiatric disorders in foster home reared children of schizophrenic mothers. *British Journal of Psychiatry, 112*: 819–825.

Hillyard, S. A., Hink, R. F., Schwent, V. L., & Picton, T. W. (1973). Electrical signs of selective attention in human brain. *Science, 1982*: 177.

Ho, B. C., & Andreasen, N. (2001). Long delays in seeking treatment for schizophrenia. *The Lancet, 357* (March 24): 898–899.

Hoffman, R. E. (1997). Neural network simulations, cortical connectivity, and schizophrenic psychosis. *MD Computing, 14* (3, May–June): 200–208.

Hogarty, G. E., Anderson, C. M., & Reiss, D. J. (1986). Family psychoeducation, social skill training and maintenance chemotherapy in the aftercare treatment of schizophrenia. One year effects of a controlled study on relapse and Expressed Emotions. *Archives of General Psychiatry, 43*: 633–642.

Holzman, P. S., Kringlen, E., & Levy Haberman, S. J. (1980). Deviant eye tracking in twins discordant fro psychosis. A Replication. *Archives of General Psychiatr., 37*: 627–631.

Howlin, P., & Baron-Cohen, S. (1999). *Teaching Children With Autism to Mind-Read: A Practical Guide for Teacher and Parents*. Chichester: John Wiley & Sons, Ltd.

Jablensky, A., Sartorius, N., Ernberg, G., Anker, M., Korten, A., Cooper, J. E., Fay, R., & Bertelsen, A. (1992). Schizophrenia: Manifestation, Incidence, and Course in Different Cultures. *Psychological Medicine Monograph* (Suppl. 20). Cambridge: Cambridge University Press.

Jackson, J. H. (1932). *Selected Writing of John Hughlings Jackson* (edited by J. Taylor). London: Hodder and Stoughton.

Jacobs, L. (1980). A cognitive approach to persistent delusion. *American Journal of Psychotherapy, 34*: 556–563.

James, W. (1997). *The Writings of William James: A Comprehensive Edition*. New York: Phoenix Book.

Jaspers, K. (1982). *Psicopatologia generale*. Roma: Il Pensiero Scientifico Editore.

Jaynes, J. (1976). *The Origin of Consciousness in the Breakdown of the Bicameral Mind*. Boston: Houghton Mifflin.

Jaynes, J. (1996). *Il crollo della mente bicamerale e l'origine della coscienza*. Milano: Adelphi.

Johannessen, J. O., Larsen, T. K., Horneland, M., Joa, I., Kvebecc, R., Friis, S., Melle, I., Opjordamoen, S., Simonsen, E., Vaglum, P., & McGlasham, T. H. (2001). The TIPS project; a systematized program to reduce duration of untreated psychosis in first episode schizophrenia. In: T. Miller (Ed.), *Early Intervention in Psychotic Disorders*. Dordrecht: Kluwer Academic Publisher.

Johns, L. C., Nazroo, J. Y., Bebbington, P., & Kuipers, E. (2002). Occurrence of hallucinatory experiences in a community sample and ethnic variations. *British Journal of Psychiatry, 180*: 174–178.

Johnston, P. J., Katsikitis, M., & Carr, V. J. (2001). A generalised deficit can account for problems in facila emotion recognition in schizophrenia. *Biological Psychology, 58*: 203–227.

Kane, J. M. (1999). Tardive dyskinesia. In: A. B. Joseph & R. R. Young (Eds.). *Movement Disorders in Neurology and Neuropsychiatr.*: 31–35.

Kane, J., Honigfeld, G., Singer, J., & Meltzer, H. (1988). Clozapine for the treatment resistant schizophrenia: A double-blind comparison with chlorpromazine. *Arch. Gen. Psychiatry, 45* (1988): 789–796.

Kaney, S., & Bentall, R. P. (1989). Persecutory delusions and attributional style. *British Journal of Medical Psychology, 62*: 191–198.

Kaney, S., & Bentall, R. P. (1992). Persecutory delusions and the self-serving bias. *Journal of Nervous and Mental Disease, 180*: 773–780.

Kasanin, J., Knight, E., & Sage, P. (1934). The parent-child relationship in schizophrenia. *J. Nerv. Ment. Dis., 79*: 249–263.

Kay, S. R., Fiszbein, A., & Opler, L. A. (1987). The positive and negative syndrome scale (Panss for schizophrenia). *Schizophrenia Bulletin, 13*: 261–276.

Kelly, S., & Allison, M. A. (1999). *The complexity advantage*. New York: McGraw-Hill.

Kendler, K. S., & Gruenberg, A. M. (1982). Genetic Relationship Between Paranoid Personality Disorder and the Schizophrenic Spectrum Disorders. *American Journal of Psychiatry*, 139: 1185–1186.

Kety, S. S., Rosenthal, D., Wender, P. H., Schulsinger, F., & Jacobsen B. (1978). The biological and adoptive families of adopted individuals who become schizophrenic. In: L. C. Wynne, R. L. Cromwel & S. Matthysse (Eds.). *The Nature of Schizophrenia*, New York: John Wiley & Sons, Ltd.

Khalil, N., & Stark, F. M. (1992). Do perceived parental rearing patterns influence social behaviour dimensions and disease severity in schizophrenia? *Acta Psychiatr. Scand., 86*: 146–152.

Kinderman, P., & Bentall, R. P. (1996). The development of a novel measure of causal attributions: The Internal Personal and Situational Attributions Questionnaire. *Personality and Individual Differences, 20*: 261–264.

Kingdon, D. G., & Turkington, D. (1994). *Cognitive-Behavioural Therapy of Schizophrenia*. New York: Guilford Press.

Kircher, T., & Davis, A. (Eds.) (2003). *The Self in Neuroscience and Psychiatry*. Cambridge: Cambridge University Press.

Kircher, T., & Davis, A. (2003). Self Consciousness: an integrative approach from philosophy, psychopathology. In: T. Kircher & A. Davis (Eds.) (2003). *The Self in Neuroscience and Psychiatry*, Cambridge, Cambridge University Press.

Kirkpatrick, B., Buchanan, R. W., Breier, A., & Carpenter, W. T. Jr (1993). Case identification and stability of the deficit syndrome of schizophrenia. *Psychiatry Research, 47*: 47–56.

Kirkpatrick, B., Kopelowicz, A., & Buchanan, Ro. W. (2000). Assessing the efficacy of treatment for the Deficit Syndrome of schizophrenia. *Neuropsychopharmacology, 22* (3): 304–309.

Koh, S. D. (1978). Remembering of verbal materials by schizophrenic young adult. In: S. Schwartz (Ed.). *Language and Cognition in Schizophrenia*. Hillsdale: Lawrence Erlbaum Associates, Ltd.

Kolb, B., & Whishaw, I. Q. (1983). Performance of schizophrenic patients on tests sensitive to left or right frontal, temporal, or parietal function in neurological patients. *Journal of Nervous and Mental Diseases, 171*: 435–443.

Kolb, D. A. (1974). On management and the learning process. In: D. A. Kolb, I. M. Rubin, J. M. McIntire, *Organizational Psychology. A book of readings*. Englewood Cliffs: Prentice-Hall.

Kondel, T. K., Mortimer, A. M., Leeson, V. C., Laws, K. R., & Hirsch, S. R. (2003). Intellectual differences between schizophrenic patients and normal controls across the adult lifespan. *Journal of Clinical Neurospychology, 25* (8, December): 1045–1056.

Kraepelin, E. (1919). *Dementia praecox and paraphrenia*. Edinbourgh: Livingstone.

Kring, A. M. (1999). Emotion in schizophrenia: Old Mystery, New understanding. *Current Directions in Psychological Science, 8*: 160–163.

Krupinski, M., Fisher, A., & Grohmann, R. (2000). Schizophrenic psychoses and suicide in the clinic. Risk factors end psychopharmacologic treatment. *Novernartz, 71*: 906–911.

Kwapil, T. R., Hegley, D. C., Chapman, L. J., & Chapman, J. P. (1990). Facilitation of words recognition by semantic priming in schizophrenia. *Journal of Abnormal Psychology, 99* (3): 215–221.

Lam, D., Jones, S. H., Hayward, P., & Bright, J. A. (1999). *Cognitive Therapy for Bipolar Disorder: A Therapist's Guide to Concept, Method and Practice*. Chichester: John Wiley & Sons, Ltd.

Lanin-Kettering, I., & Harrow, W. M. (1985). The thought behind the words: a view of schizophrenic speech and thinking disorders. *Schizophr Bull., 11* (1): 1–15.

Larsen, T. K., Johannessen, J. O., & Opjordmoen, S. (1998). First episode schizophrenia with long duration of untreated psychosis: pathway to care. *British Journal of Psychiatry, 172* (Suppl. 33): 45–52.

Lazarus, A. A. (1971). *Behavior Therapy and Beyond*. New York: Mc Graw-Hill.

Leask, S. J., Done, D. J., & Crow, T. J. (2002). Adult psychosis, common childhood infections and neurological soft signs in a national birth cohort. *Br J Psychiatry, 181*: 387–392.

Leff, J. P., & Vaughn, C. E. (1981). The role of maintenance therapy and relatives expressed emotions in relapse of schizophrenia: A two years follow up. *British Journal of Psychiatry, 139*: 102–106.

Lerner, S. (1983). *Constructing the multigenerational family genogram exploring a problem in context*. Topeka: Menninger Foundation.

Leslie, A. M. (1987). Pretence and representation: The origins of 'theory of mind'. *Psychological Review, 94*: 412–426.

Levy, D. M. (1931). Maternal overprotection and rejection. *Arch. Neurol. Psychiatry, 25*: 886–889.

Lewis, S. W., Davies, L., Jones, P. B., Barnes, T. R., Murray, R. M., Kerwin, R., Taylor, D., Hayhurst, K. P., Markwick, A., Lloyd, H., & Dunn, G. (2006). Randomised controlled trials of conventional antipsychotic versus new atypical drugs, and new atypical drugs versus clozapine, In people with schizophrenia responding poorly to, or intolerant of, current drug treatment. *Health Technology Assessment 10*: iii–iv, ix–x1, 1–165.

Liberman, R. P. (1988). *Psychiatric Rehabilitation for Chronic Mental Patients*. Washington, DC: American Psychiatric Press.

Liberman, R. P. (1994). Psychosocial treatments for schizophrenia. *Psychiatry, 57*: 104–114.

Liddle, P. F. (1987). The symptoms of chronic schizophrenia: a re-examination of the positive/negative symptom dichotomy. *British Journal of Psychiatry, 151*: 145–151.

Liotti, G. (1993). *Le discontinuità della coscienza: etiologia, diagnosi e psicoterapia dei disturbi dissociativi*. Milano: FrancoAngeli.

Liotti, G. (2001). *Le opere della coscienza*. Milano: Raffaello Cortina Editore.

Llinàs, R. R. (2001). *I of the Vortex*. Cambridge: MIT Press.

Lorenzini, R., & Sassaroli, S. (1995). *Cattivi pensieri*. Roma: La Nuova Italia Scientifica.

Lowing, P. A., Minsky, A. F., & Pereira, R. (1983). The inheritance of schizophrenic spectrum disorders. *American Journal of Psychiatry, 140*: 1167–1171.

Lyddon, W. J. (1987). Emerging views of Healths: A Challenge to Rationalist Doctrines of Medical Thoughts. *Journal of Mind and Behavior, 8*: 365–94.

Lyddon, W., & Schreiner, G. (1998). Post-modernismo e Psicoterapia. *Complessità & Cambiamento, VII* (1): 17–28.

Lysaker, P. H., & Lysaker, J. T. (2002). Schizophrenia and the Dialogical Self. *Theory & Psychology, 12* (2): 207–220.

Magana, A. B., Goldstein, M. J., Falloon, I. R. H., & Doane, J. (1985). A brief method for assessing expressed emotion in relatives of psychiatric patients. *Psychiatric Research, 17*: 203–207.

Maher, B. A. (1988). Anomalous experience and delusional thinking: The logic of explanations. In: T. F. Oltmanns & B. A. Maher (Eds.), *Delusional Beliefs*. New York: John Wiley & Sons, Ltd.

Mahoney, M. J. (1991). *Human Change Processes*. New York: Basic Books.

Main, M. (1991). Metacognitive knowledge, metacognitive monitoring and singular (coherent) vs multiple (incoherent) models of attachment: Findings and directions for future research. In: C. Parkes, C. M. Stevenson-Hinde & P. Marris (Eds.). *Attachment across the life cycle*. London: Tavistock & Routledge.

Mannino, G., & Maxia, G. (2001). Psicopatologia e psicoterapia della schizofrenia: verso un approccio post-razionalista. *Quaderni di Psicoterapia Cognitiva, 4* (1): 44–61.

Mathews, A. M., & Gelder, M. G. (1969). Psychophysiological investigations of brief relaxation training. *Journal of Psychosomatic Research, 13*: 1–12.

Maturana, H. R., & Varela, F. J. (1980). *Autopoiesis and Cognition. The realisation of the living*. Dortrecht: Reidel.

Mazza, M., De Risio, A., Tozzini, C. Roncone, R., & Casacchia, M. (2003). Machiavellism and Theory of Mind in people affected by schizophrenia. *Brain Cogn., 51* (3, April): 262–269.

McEvoy, J. P., Scheifler, P. L., & Frances, A. (1999). The Expert Consensus Guideline Series: Treatment of Schizophrenia. *The Journal of Clinical Psychiatry, 60* (Suppl. 11).

McGhie, A., & Chapman, J. (1961). Disorders of attention and perception in early schizophrenia. *British Journal of Medical Psychology, 34*: 103–116.

McGorry, P. D. (2002). The recognition and optimal management of early psychosis: an evidence-based reform. *World Psychiatry, 1* (2): 76–83.

McGorry, P. D., & Jackson, H. J. (Eds.) (1999). *The Recognition and Management of Early Psychosis. A preventive Approach*. Cambridge: Cambridge University Press.

McGorry, P. D., Kristev, H., & Harrigan, S. (2000). Early detection and treatment delay: Implications for detections and treatment delay: implications for outcome in early psychosis. *Current Opinion in Psychiatry, 13*: 37–43.

McGuire, P. K., Shah, G. M. S., & Murray, R. M. (1993). Increased blood flow in Broca's area during auditory hallucinations in schizophrenia. *Lancet, 342*: 703–706.

McKenna, P. J. (1991). Memory, Knowledge and Delusions. *British Journal of Psychiatry, 159*: 36–41.
McLean, P. D. (1973). *A triune concept of brain and behaviour.* Toronto: University Press of Toronto.
McNeil, T. F., & Kaij, L. (1978). Obstetric factors in the development of schizophrenia: complications in the births of preschizophrenics and in reproduction in schizophrenic parents: In: L. C. Wynne & R. L. Cromwell (Eds.). *The nature of schizophrenia.* New York: John Wiley & Sons, Ltd.
Medscape Psychiatry and Mental Health (2005). *Schizophrenia recovery: An Expert.* Interview With Stephen R. Marder, MD. 10 (1).
Meehl, P. E. (1962). Schizotaxy, schizotypy, schizophrenia. *American Psychologist, 17*: 827–838.
Meichenbaum, D. (1977). *Cognitive Behavior Modification.* New York: Plenum Press.
Meichenbaum, D., & Cameron, R. (1980). Cognitive behavior modification: Current issues. In: C. Franks & G. Wilson (Eds.). *Handbook of behavior therapy.* New York: Guilford Press.
Monod, J. (1970). *Il caso e la necessità.* Milano: Mondadori.
Morosini, P., & Roncone, R. (1994). Presentazione dell'adattamento italiano della Brief Psychiatric Rating Scale, versione 4.0 ampliata (BPRS 4.0). *Rivista diRiabilitazione Psichiatrica e Psicosociale, 3*: 195.
Mosher, L., & Burti, L. (1994). *Community mental health.* New York: W. W. Norton Company.
Musalek, M., Podreka, I., & Walter, H. (1989). Regional brain function in hallucinations: a study of regional cerebral blood flow with 99m-Tc-HMPAO-SPECT in patients with auditory hallucinations, tactile hallucinations, and normal controls. *Compr. Psychiatry, 30*: 99–108.
Nasrallah, H. A. (1982). Laterality and hemispheric dysfunction in schizophrenia. In: F. A. Henn & H. A. Nasrallah (Ed.). *Schizophrenia as a brain disease.* New York: Oxford University Press.
Negroponte, N. (1996). *Being digital.* New York: Vintage Books.
Nesse, M. R. (2002). Evolutionary biology, a basic science for psychiatry. *World Psychiatry, 1*: 7–9.
Norman, D. A., & Shallice, T. (1987). *Attention to action.* New York: Plenum Press.
Nuechterlein, K., & Dawson, M. (1984). A vulnerability stress model of schizophrenic episodes. *Schizophrenia Bulletin, 10*: 300–312.
O'Brien, G., & Opie, J. (2003). The multiplicity of consciousness and the emergence of the self. In: T. Kircher & A. Davis (Eds.). *The Self in Neuroscience and Psychiatry.* Cambridge: Cambridge University Press.
Ohman, A. (1981). Electrodermal Activity and Vulnerability to Schizophrenia: A Review. *Biological Psychology, 12*: 87–145.
Oliver, J. P. J., Huxley, P. J., Priebe, S., & Kaiser, W. (1997). Measuring the quality of life of severely mentally ill people using the Lancashire Quality of Life Profile'. *Social Psychiatry and Psychiatric Epidemiology, 32*: 76–83.

Orhagen, T. (1992). Working with families in schizophrenic disorders. *Linkoping Univ. Medical Dissertations, 363*. Linkoping: Sweden.

Ornstein, R. (1992). *The evolution of consciousness*. New York: Simon & Schuster.

Ornstein, R. (1997). *The right mind*. Orlando: Harcourt Brace & Company.

Osby, U., Correia, N., & Brandt, L. (2000). Mortalità and causes of death in schizophrenia in Stockholm county. *Sweden Schizophrenia Research, 45*: 21–28.

Overall, J. E., & Gorham, D. R. (1962). The Brief Psychiatric Scale. *Psychological Reports, 10*: 799–812.

Panksepp, J. (1998). *Affective neuroscience*. Oxford: Oxford University Press.

Panksepp, J. (2003). The neural nature of the core Self: implications for understanding schizophrenia. In: T. Kircher & A. Davis (Eds.). *The Self in Neuroscience and Psychiatry*. Cambridge: Cambridge University Press.

Pantelis, C., & Maruff, P. (2002). The cognitive neuropsychiatric approach to investigating the neurobiology of schizophrenia and other disorders. *Journal of Psychosomatic Research, 53*: 655–664.

Paquette, V., Lèvesque, J., Mensour, B., Leroux, J. M., Beaudoin, G., Bourgouin, P., & Beauregard, M. (2003). Change the mind and you change the brain: effcts of cognitive-behavioral therapy on the neural correlates of spider phobia. *Neuroimage, 18*: 401–409.

Park, S., Puschel, J., Sauter, B. H., Rentsch, M., & Hell, D. (1999). Spatial working memory deficits and clinical symptoms in schizophrenia: a 4 months follow-up study. *Biol. Psychiatry, 1* (46): 392–400.

Parker, A., Derrington, A., & Blakemore, C. (Eds.) (2003). *The Physiology of Cognitive Processes*. Oxford: Oxford University Press.

Parker, G., Johnston, P., & Hayward, L. (1988). Prediction of Schizophrenic relapse using the parental bonding instrument. *Aust. NZ J. Psychiatyry, 22*: 283–292.

Paul, G. L. (1969). Physiologic effects of relaxation training and hypnotic suggestion. *Journal of Abnormal Psychology, 74*: 425–437.

Paulus, M. P., & Braff, D. L. (2003). Chaos e Schizophrenia: does the method fit madness? *Biological Psychiatry, 53* (1): 3–11.

Perna, P., & Masterpasqua, F. (Eds.). The Psychological Meaning of Chaos: Complexity Theory in Human. *Development and Psychotherapy*, Washington, DC: APA Press.

Perris, C. (1989). *Cognitive Therapy with Schizophrenic Patients*: New York: The Guiford Press.

Perris, C. (1993). *Psicoterapia del paziente difficile*, Lanciano: Metis Editrice.

Perris, C. (1994). Parental rearing and schizophrenic disorders. In: C. Perris, W. A. Arrindell & M. Eisemann (Eds.). *Parenting and Psychopathology*. Chichester: John Wiley & Sons, Ltd.

Perris, C. (1996). Le sindromi psicotiche e dissociative. In: B. Bara (Ed.). *Nuovo manuale di psicoterapia cognitiva*. Torino: Bollati Boringhieri.

Perris, C. (2001). Progress in Cognitive Therapy for Schizophrenic Disorders and a Look at the Future. In: T. Scrimali & L. Grimaldi (Eds.). *Cognitive Psychotherapy Toward a New Millennium.* New York: Kluwer Academic Plenum Publishers.

Perris, C., & McGorry, P. (1998). *Cognitive Psychotherapy of Psychotic and Personal Disorders.* New York: John Wiley & Sons, Ltd.

Philips, D. L. (1966). Public identification and acceptance of the mentally ill. *American Journal of Public Health, 56*: 755–63.

Phillips, J. (2003). Schizophrenia and the narrative self. In: T. Kircher & A. Davis (Eds.). *The Self in Neuroscience and Psychiatry.* Cambridge: Cambridge University Press.

Piaget, J. (1954). *The construction of reality in child.* New York: Basic Book.

Pilling, S., Bebbington, P., Kuipers, E., et al. (2002). Psychological treatments in schizophrenia I: Meta-analysis of family intervention and cognitive behaviour therapy. *Psychol Med, 32*: 763–782.

Pinel, P. (1801). *Traitè medico-philosophique sur l'aliénation mentale ou la manie.* Paris: Richard, Caille & Ranvier.

Pinto, A., La Pia, S., & Mannella, R. (1999). Cognitive behavioural therapy and clozapine for clients with treatment-refractory schizophrenia. *Psychiatratric Services, 50*: 901–904.

Poincarè, H. (1893). *Les méthodes nouvelles de la mecanique celeste.* Paris: Gauthier-Villars.

Popper, K. R. (1972). *Objective Knowledge: An Evolutionary Approach.* Oxford: Clarendon.

Popper, K. R., & Eccles, J. C. (1977). *The Self and its Brain.* Berlin: Heindelberg.

Premack, D., & Woodruff, G. (1978). Does the chimpanzee have a theory of mind? *Beavioural and brain sciences, 1*: 515-526.

Prigogine, I. (1980). *From being to becoming: Time and complexity in the physical sciences.* San Francisco: W. H. Freeman.

Prigogine, I. (1997). *La fine delle certezze. Il tempo, il caos e le leggi della natura.* Torino: Bollati Boringheri.

Pritchard, W. S. (1981). Psychophysiology of P300. *Psychological Bulletin, 3*: 506–540.

Procacci, M. (1999). Una nuova agenda per la psicoterapia cognitiva del paziente grave. In: A. Semerari (Ed.). *Psicoterapia cognitiva del paziente grave. Metacognizione relazione terapeutica.* Milano: Raffaello Cortina Editore.

Prokasy, W. F., & Raskin, D. C. (1973). *Electrodermal Activity in Psychological Research.* New York: Academic Press.

Psychotech (2004). Hardware and software for clinical psychophysiology [Computer hardware/software]. Aci Castello: Psychotech (http://www.psychotech.it).

Raine, A., & Venables, P. H. (1984). Electrodermal non-responding, schizoid tendencies, and antisocial behavior in adolescents. *Psychophysiology, 21*: 424–433.

Rector, N. A., & Beck, A. T. (2002). A clinical review of cognitive therapy for schizophrenia. *Curr. Psychiatry Rep., 4*: 284–292.

Rector, N. A., Beck, A. T., & Stolar, N. (2005). The Negative Symptoms of Schizophrenia: A Cognitive Perspective. *The Canadian Journal of Psychiatry, 50*: 247–257.

Rehacom (2003). Programmi di riabilitazione delle funzioni cognitive computer assistita – Memoria dei volti (Gesi) per Windows [Computer software]. Mödling: Schuhfried GmbH (http://www.schuhfried.co.at). Italian distributor, Bologna: Ems (http://www.emsmedical.net).

Reichard, S., & Tillman, C. (1950). Patterns of parent-child relationships in schizophrenia. *Psychiatry, 13*: 247–257.

Remschmidt, H. (2001). *Schizophrenia in children and adolescents*. Cambridge: Cambridge University Press.

Rezzonico, G., & Meier, C. (1989). Un approccio costruttivista al trattamento della schizophrenia: schizophrenia come ipotesi. *Psicobiettivo, 9* (3): 35–47.

Riva, E. (1998). *I segreti di Esculapio. Genesi del farmaco, dall'empirismo degli antichi alle ricerche dell'era moderna*. Ghezzano: Primula Multimedia.

Rizzolati, G., Fogassi, L., & Gallese, V. (2000). Cortical mechanisms subserving object grasping and action recognition: A new view on the cortical motor functions. In: M. S. Gazzaniga (Ed.), *The New Cognitive Neurosciences* (second edition). Cambridge, MA: MIT Press.

Robertson, R., & Combs, A. (Eds.). *Chaos Theory in Psychology and the Life Sciences*. Mahwah: Lawrence Erlbaum Associates.

Roncone, R., & Casacchia, M. (2005). I trattamenti psicoeducazionali con il coinvolgimento delle famiglie nella schizofrenia. In: C. Di Berardino (Ed.). *L'approccio multimodale nella riabilitazione psichiatrica*. Milano: McGraw-Hill.

Rosemberg, D. R., Benazon, N. R., Gilbert, A., Sullivan, A., & Moore, G. J. (2000). Thalamic volume in pediatric obsessive-compulsive disorder patients before and after cognitive behavioral therapy. *Biological Psychiatry, 48* (4): 294–300.

Rosenhan, D. L. (1984). Essere sani in posti insani. In: P. Watzlawick (Ed.). *La realtà inventata*. Milano: Feltrinelli.

Rosenthal, D., Wender, P. H., Kety, S. S., Schulsinger, F., Welner, J., & Rieder, R. O. (1975). Parent-child relationships and psychopathological disorder in the child. *Arch. Gen., Psychiatry*. New York: Grune & Stratton.

Ross, C. A., & Read, J. (2004). Antypsychotic Medication: Miths and Facts. In: J. Read, L. Mosher & R. Bentall (2004). *Models of Madness*. Andover: Taylor & Francis.

Rossini, R. (1969). *Trattato di Psichiatria*. Firenze: Cappelli.

Rotter, J. B. (1990). Internal versus external control of reinforcement: A case history of a variable. *American Psychologist, 45* (4): 489–493.

Rund, B. R., & Landro, N. I. (1995). Memory in schizophrenia and affective disorders. *Scand. J. Psychol., 36*: 37–46.

Russel, R., & Waldrei, M. (1996). Narrative and the process of psychotherapy: Theoretical foundations and empirical support. In: H. Rosen & K. Kuehlwein (Eds.), *Constructing realities*. San Francisco: Jossey-Bass.

Safran, J. (1998). *Widening the Scope of Cognitive Therapy*. Northvale: Jason Aronsonson, Inc.

Safran, J., & Muran, J. C. (2000). *Negotiating the therapeutic alliance: a relational treatment guide*. New York: Guilford Press.

Safran, J. Z., & Segal, Z. V. (1990). *Interpersonal Process in Cognitive Therapy*. New York: Basic Books.

Salame, P., Danion, J. M., Peretti, S., & Cuervo, C. (1998). The state of functioning of working memory in schizophrenia. *Schizophr. Res., 30* (1): 11–29.

Salokangas, R. K. R. (1983). Prognostic implications of the sex of schizophrenic patients. *British Journal of Psychiatry, 142*: 145–151.

Sartorius, N. (2000). Uno degli ultimi ostacoli ad una migliore cura della salute mentale: lo stigma della malattia mentale. In: F. Asioli & M. della Vita (Eds.), *Lotta allo stigma*. Bologna: Editrice Compositori.

Sato, M. (2006). Renaming schizophrenia: a Japanese perspective. *World Psychiatry, 5* (1): 53–55.

Saykin, A. J., Shatasel, D. L., & Gur, R. E. (1994). Neuropsychological deficits in neuroleptic naive patients with first-episode schizophrenia. *Archives of General Psychiatry, 51*: 124–131.

Scheff, T. J. (1966). *Being Mentally Hill: A Sociological Theory*. Chicago: Aldine.

Schneider, K. (1954). *Psicopatologia clinica*. Firenze: Sansoni Edizioni Scientifiche.

Schwartz, J. M., Stoessel, P. W., & Baxter, L. R. (1996). Systematic changes in cerebral glucose metabolic rate after successful behavior modification treatment of obsessive disorder. *Archives of General Psychiatry, 53*: 109–113.

Schwartz, R. C., & Cohen, B. N. (2001). Psychosocial correlates of suicidal intent among patients with schizophrenia. *Compr. Psychiatry, 42*: 118–123.

Scrimali, T. (1994). *Constructivism and Cognitive Psychotherapy*. Conference held at the Department of Psychiatry of the University of Camden, Camden, NJ.

Scrimali, T. (2000). Constructivist and Complex Approach in Cognitive Psychotherapy. *Psychotherapia*, 2 (113): 5–21.

Scrimali, T. (2001). La Psicoterapia Cognitiva: Dalla Teoria dell'Human Information processing alla Logica dei Sistemi Complessi. *Il Pendolo, I* (2): 42–51.

Scrimali, T. (2003). *Processi della Mente e Disagio Psichico*. Enna: Istituto Superiore per le Scienze Cognitive Editore.

Scrimali, T. (2004a). Negative Entropy. A Cognitive and Complex Approach to Therapy and Rehabilitation of Schizophrenia. *Ceska a Slovenska Psychiatrie, 100*: 82–86.

Scrimali, T. (2004b). *Il Demetra Test: uno strumento per la valutazione del clima emotivo familiare*. Enna: Istituto Superiore per le Scienze Cognitive Editore.

Scrimali, T. (2005). La schizofrenia. In: B. Bara (Ed.). *Nuovo Manuale di Psicoterapia Cognitiva*. Torino: Bollati Boringhieri.

Scrimali, T. (2005a). Il MindLab Set e la Psicofisiologia Clinica. *ISSCo e Aleteia News, IV* (1): 7–8.

Scrimali, T. (2005b). *La Family Strange Situation, una modalità multimodale di valutazione del clima emotivo familiare*. Enna: Istituto Superiore per le Scienze Cognitive Editore.

Scrimali, T. (2005c). L'assessment della disabilità. In: C. Di Berardino (Ed.). *L'approccio multimodale nella riabilitazione psichiatrica*. Milano: McGraw-Hill.

Scrimali, T., & Fisichella, D. (2003). *Riconoscimento dei volti e schizofrenia. Dati teorici ed implicazioni terapeutiche*. Atti del Congresso La Mente tra le Nuvole. Enna: Istituto Superiore per le Scienze Cognitive Editore.

Scrimali, T., & Grimaldi, L. (1982). Il biofeedback dell'attività elettrodermica. Milano: FrancoAngeli.

Scrimali T., & Grimaldi L. (1991). *Sulle tracce della mente*. Milano: FrancoAngeli.

Scrimali T., & Grimaldi L. (1996). Entropia negativa. Terapia cognitiva e riabilitazione della schizofrenia. *Complessità & Cambiamento, V* (1): 14–49.

Scrimali, T., & Grimaldi, L. (1998). Schizophrenia and Cluster A Personality Disorders. From a psychophysiological and ethological approach, towards cognitive therapy. *Journal of Cognitive Psychotherapy, 10* (4): 291–307.

Scrimali, T., Grimaldi, L., Cultrera, G., & Di Stefano, A. (1994). Deviazione dello sguardo e schizofrenia. *Complessità & Cambiamento, III* (1): 53–57.

Scrimali, T., Grimaldi, L., Cultrera, G., & Russo, C. (1998). Parenting e schizofrenia. Una ricerca sperimentale. *Quaderni di psicoterapia cognitiva, 3*.

Scrimali, T., Grimaldi, L., Cultrera, G., & Santagati, M. (1995). L'assessment multidimensionale del clima emotivo familiare nella schizofrenia. *Complessità & Cambiamento, IV* (1): 14–31.

Scrimali, T., Grimaldi, L., Foti, H., & Damigella, F. (2000). Il monitoraggio dei "warning sign" di ricaduta nei pazienti schizofrenici. *Complessità & Cambiamento, IX* (2): 14–26.

Scrimali, T., Grimaldi, L., & Pulvirenti, L. (2004). *Attività elettrodermica fasica evoca e schizofrenia*. Enna: Istituto Superiore per le Scienze Cognitive Editore.

Scrimali, T., Grimaldi, L., & Rapisarda, V. (1988). The passive eliciting of P 300 versus the odd ball+time reaction paradigm in healthy subjects and schizophrenic patients. *Research Communications in Psychology, Psychiatry and Behaviour, 3*: 182–186.

Scrimali, T., Grimaldi, L., Rapisarda, V., & Filippone, L. (1988). Conoscenza, emozione e dissociazione. Un modello cognitivo della schizofrenia e della sua terapia. In: T. Scrimali & L. Grimaldi (Eds.). Conoscenza ed emozione nel processo psicoterapeutico. *Quaderni di formazione psichiatrica, 4.*

Scrimali, T., Grimaldi, L., Salinbene, C., Sambataro, F., & De Leonardis, M. (2002). Memoria e schizofrenia. Aspetti teorici e valutazione clinica. *Complessità & Cambiamento, XI* (1–2): 12–25.

Scrimali, T., Grimaldi, L., Sambataro, F., Petriglieri, G., & Polopoli, K. (2001). Patterns elettroencefalografici di coerenza funzionale emisferica e schizofrenia. *Complessità & Cambiamento, X* (2): 16–28.

Scrimali, T., & Maugeri, S. (2004). *Elettroencefalografia quantitativa e psicoterapia cognitiva.* Enna: Istituto Superiore per le Scienze Cognitive Editore.

Sechehaye, M. (1951). *Autobiography of a Schizophrenic Girl.* New York: Grune & Stratton.

Semerari, A. (Ed.) (1999). *Psicoterapia cognitiva del paziente grave. Metacognizione e relazione terapeutica.* Milano: Raffaello Cortina Editore.

Shiffrin, R. M., & Scheider, W. (1977). Controlled and Automatic human information processing. Perceptual learning automatic attending and a general theory. *Psychological Review, 84*: 127–190.

Siegel, D. J. (1999). *The Developing Mind: How Relationships and the Brain interact to Shape Who We Are.* New York, London: Guilford Press.

Silbersweig, D. A., & Stern, E. (Eds.) (2001). *Neuropsychology and Functional Neuroimaging: Convergence, Advances and New Directions.* Lisse: Swets and Zeitlinger Publishers.

Skinner, H., Steinhauer, P. D., & Santa-Barbara, J. (1983). The Family Assessment Measure. *Canadian Journal of Community Mental Health,* 2: 91–105.

Slade, P. D., & Bentall, R. P. (1988). *Sensory deception: A scientific analysis of allucination.* London: Croom Helm.

Spielberger, C. D., Gorsuch, R. L., & Lushene, R. E. (1970). *Manual for the State and Trait Anxiety Inventory.* Palo Alto: Consulting Psychologist Press.

Spitzer, M. (1997). A cognitive neuroscience view of schizophrenic thought disorder. *Schizophrenia Bulletin, 23*: 29–50.

Spolin, H. E., Theyfors, P. E., & Cancro, R. (1971). The effects of phenothiazine medication on skin conductance and heart rate in schizophrenic patients. *Journal of Mental and Nervous Diseases, 152*: 129–139.

Stanghellini, G. (2002). Verso una psicopatologia sociale della vulnerabilità. *Psichiatria oggi, IV* (3): 1–7.

Stein, D., & Ludik, J. (1998). *Neural Networks and Psychopathology.* Cambridge: Cambridge University Press.

Stein, L. I., Test, M. A. (Eds.) (1985). *Training in the community living model. A decade of experiences.* San Francisco: Jossey-Bass.

Stephens, G. L., & Graham, G. (2000). *When Self-Consciousness Breaks: Alien Voices and Inserted Thoughts*. Cambridge, MA: MIT Press.

Steven, A., & Price, J. (1996). *Evolutionary Psychiatry*. New York: Routledge.

Stip, E., & Lussier, I. (1996). The heterogeneity of memory dysfunction in schizophrenia. *Can J Psychiatry, 41*: 14–20.

Stolar, N. (2004). Cognitive Conceptualization of the negative Symptoms of Schizophrenia. *Journal of Cognitive Psychitherapy, 18* (3): 237–253.

Stroop, J. R. (1935). Studies of interference in serial verbal reactions. *Journal of Experimental Psychology, 18*: 643–662.

Stroup, T. S., McEvoy, J. P., Swartz, M. S., Byerly, M. J., Glick, I. D., Canive, J. M., McGee, M. F., Simpson, G. M., Stevens, M. C., & Lieberman, J. A., (2003) The national institute of mental health clinical antipsychotic trials of intervention effectiveness (CATIE) project: Schizophrenia trial design and protocol. *Schizophrenia Bulletin, 21*: 15–31.

Studer, F. (1998). *Analisi visiva e strategie Cognitive*. Trento: Edizioni Centro Studi Erickson.

Sullivan, R. J., & Allen, J. S. (1999). Social deficits associated with schizophrenia defined in terms of interpersonal Machiavellism. *Acta Psychiatrica Scandinavica, 99* (2, February): 148–54.

Tamlyn, D., McKenna, P. J., Mortimer, A. M., Lund, C. E., Hammond, S., & Baddeley, A. D. (1992). Memory impairment in schizophrenia: its extent, affiliations and neuropsychological character. *Psychological Medicine, 22*: 101–115.

Tandon, R., & Jibson, M. D. (2003). Suicidal Behavior in Schizophrenia: Diagnosis, Neurobiology and Treatment Implications. *Current Opinion in Psychiatry, 16* (2): 193–197.

Tarrier, N. (1992). Psychological treatment of schizophrenic symptoms. In: D. Kavanagh (Ed.). *Schizophrenia: An overview and practical handbook*. London: Chapman & Hall.

Teasdale, J., & Barnard, P. J. (1993). *Affect, Cognition and Change*. Howe: Lawrence Erlbaum Associates.

Temple, S. (2004). Cognitive Therapy for Auditory Hallucinations in Schizophrenia. *Journal of Cognitive Psychotherapy, 18* (3): 223–236.

Thelen, E., & Smith, L. (2000). *A Dynamic Systems Approach to Development of Cognition and Action*. Cambridge: MIT Press.

Thompson, P. M., Vidal, C., & Giedd, J. N. (2001). Mapping Adolescent Brain Change Reveals Dynamic Wave of Accelerated Gray Matter Loss in Very Early-Onset Schizophrenia. *Proceedings of the National Academy of Sciences of the Usa, 98* (20): 11650–11655.

Thucydides (5th century b.C.). *The Peloponnesian War* (translated by Walter Blanco). New York: W. W. Norton & Company, 1998.

Tschacher, W., & Scheier, Ch. (1995). Analyse komplexer psychologischer Systeme II: Verlaufsmodelle und Komplexitaet einer Paartherapie. *System Familie, 8*: 160–171.

Tsuang, M. A., Woolson, R. F., & Fleming, J. A. (1980). Premature deaths in schizophrenia and affective disorders: An analysis of survival curves and variables affecting the shortened survival. *Archives of General Psychiatry, 37*: 979–983.

Tsuang, M. T., & Faraone, S. V. (1997). *Schizophrenia. The facts.* New York: Oxford University Press.

Tsuang, M. T., Stone, W. S., & Faraone, S. V. (1998). Schizophrenia: epidemiology and genetic studies. *I. J. P. Psychiat. Behav. Scie, 2, 98*: 59–71.

Tsuang, M. T., Stone, W. S., Gamma, F., & Faraone, S. V. (2003). Schizotaxia: Current Status and Future Directions. *Current Science, 5*: 128–134.

Turner, R. P., & Wegenfeld, M. O. (1967). Occupational mobility and schizophrenia: An assessment of social causation and social selection hypotheses. *American Sociological Review, 32*: 104–113.

Turocy, T. L., & Stengel, B. v. (2002). Game Theory. In: *Encyclopedia of Information Systems.* New York: Academic Press.

Van Os, J., & Krabbendam, L. (2002). "Cognitive epidemiology as a tool to investigate psychological mechanisms of psychosis". Paper presented at the annual meeting of the European Association for Behavioural and Cognitive Therapies, Maastricht, The Netherlands.

Venables, P. H. (1975). Psychophysiological studies of schizophrenic pathology. In: P. H. Venables & M. G. Christie (Eds.). *Research in Psychophysiology.* London: John Wiley & Sons, Ltd.

Vinogradov, S., Pole, J. H., & Willis-Shore, J. (1998). Produced by either God or Satan: neural network approaches to delusional thinking. In: D. J. Stein & J. Ludik (Eds.). *Neural Network and Psychopathology.* Cambridge: Cambridge University Press.

Vogeley, K. (2003). Schizophrenia as disturbance of self construct. In: T. Kircher & A. Davis (Eds.). *The Self in Neuroscience and Psychiatry.* Cambridge: Cambridge University Press.

Walsh, I. (1997). Conversational Skills and Schizophrenia. In: J. France & N. Muir (Eds.). *Communication and the Mentally Ill patients.* London: Jessica Kingsley Publisher.

Warner, R. (1985). *Recovery from schizophrenia.* London: Routledge.

Watson, J. D. (1968). *The Double Helix: a Personal Account of the Discovery of the Structure of Dna.* New York: Touchstone.

Watzlawick, P., Beavin, J. H., & Jackson, D. D. (1971). *Pragmatica della comunicazione umana.* Roma: Astrolabio.

Weinberger, D. R. (2002). Biological phenotypes and genetic research on schizophrenia. *World Psychiatry, 1* (1, February): 2–4.

Weinberger, D. R., Berman, K. F., & Zec, R. (1986). Psychological dysfunction of dorsolateral prefrontal cortex in schizophrenia. *Schizophrenia Research, 25*: 21–31.

Wells, A. (2002). *Emotional Disorders and Metacognition. Innovative Cognitive Therapy.* New York: John Wiley & Sons, Ltd.

Westermeyer, J. F., Harrow, M., & Marengo, J. T. (1991). Risk suicide in schizophrenia and other psychotic and non psychotic disorders. *Journal of Mental and Nervous Diseases, 179*: 259–266.

Wexler, B. E., Stevens, A. A., Bowers, A. A., Sernyak, M. J., & Goldman-Rakic, P. S. (1998). Word and tone working memory deficits in schizophrenia. *Arch. Gen. Psychiatry, 55*: 1093–1096.

World Health Organization (1979). Schizophrenia. An International Follow-up prognosis and clinical state. *Archives of General Psychiatry, 38*: 260–266.

World Health Organization (1979). *Schizophrenia. An International Follow-up Study.* Chichester: John Wiley & Sons, Ltd.

World Health Organization (1992). *The ICD-10 classification of mental and behavioural disorders: clinical description and diagnostic guidelines.*

Wing, J. K. (1987). Has the outcome of schizophrenia changed? *British Medical Bulletin, 43*: 741–753.

Wirshing, D. A., Marshall, B. D., Green, M. F., Mintz, J., Marder, S. R., & Wirshing, W. C. (1999). Risperidone in Treatment-Refractory Schizophrenia. *American Journal of Psychiatry, 156*: 1374–1379.

Wright, J. (2003). *Psychological treatment of schizophrenia.* Academy of Cognitive Therapy Listserve (http://www.academyofct.org).

Wyatt, R. J., & Henter, I. (2001). Rationale for the study of early intervention. *Schizophrenia Research, 51*: 69–76.

Wykes, T., Parr, A., & Landau, S. (1999). Group treatment of auditory hallucinations. *British Journal Psychiatry, 175*: 180–185.

Wykes, T., Tarrier, N., & Everitt, B. (2004). Cognitive Behaviour therapy (CBT) for schizophrenia: the effect of clinical models and methodological rigour. *Schizophrenia Research, 67*: 2003–2004.

Wynne, L. C, & Cromwell, R. L. (Eds.) (1978). *The nature of schizophrenia.* New York: John Wiley & Sons, Ltd.

Wynne, L. C., & Singer, M. T. (1965). Thought disorder and family relations of schizophrenics. I. Research strategy. *Archives of General Psychiatry, 9*: 191–8.

Young, J. E. (1999). *Cognitive Therapy for Personality Disorder. A Schema-focused approach.* Sarasota: Professional Resources Press.

Young, J. E., Klosko, J. S., & Weishaar, M. E. (2003). *Schema Therapy.* New York: Guilford Press.

Zahn, T. P. (1976). On bimodality of the distribution of electrodermal orienting responses in schizophrenic patients. *Journal of Nervous and Mental Diseases, 162* (3): 195–199.

Zahn, T. P., Carpenter, W. T., & McCloshan, T. M. (1981). Autonomic nervous system activity in acute schizophrenia: II. Relationship to short-term progress and clinical state. *Archives of General Psychiatry, 38*: 260–266.

Zoler, M. L. (1999). Good Function Is Suicide Risk Factor for Schizophrenics. *Clinical Psychiatry News, 27* (4): 32.

Zubin, J., & Spring, B. (1977). Vulnerability: a new view on schizophrenia. *Journal of Abnormal Psychology, 86*: 103–126.